THE ROD OF IRON

ROBERT G. BARBARIA

Enlighten Noah Publishing
3521 Ryder St.
Santa Clara, CA 95051

ISBN 1-929400-45-4

Printed in R.O.C.

First edition 2004

Contents

INTRODUCTION

This BOOK is COMPOSED in such a way that it will SPEAK to ONE'S SPIRIT, rather than simply to ONE'S MIND. Through the BOOK'S entirety certain WORDS will appear in CAPITAL letters, some in *ITALICS,* some in ***BOLD ITALICS***, and some in standard TYPE. Even though YOUR SPIRIT will UNDERSTAND the BOOK'S FORMAT, WE want to point out to you the REASONING for the various changes in TYPE STYLE, for these TYPE STYLE CHANGES have specific meanings to the SPIRIT.

Mindful Comprehension

When ONE READS from a book, the eye INTERPRETS the letters of the words as they are being read and then compiles the letters into words for the brain to process. When the words are put into the brain, the brain does not see them as individual words but rather sees and stores them as complete statements. This is done naturally by the brain so the READER can retain the AUTHOR'S MESSAGE as a statement rather than an assortment of words. Then, when the brain RECALLS the statement, it can dissect the statement, thus putting it back into individual words again. Therefor, because the brain processes and retains its INFORMATION in complete STATEMENTS, rather than by individual words alone, the structure of the sentences creating the statement are KEY to the brain's receiving and processing the statement correctly.

SPIRITUAL UNDERSTANDING

The SPIRIT however does not process WORDS in the same manner as the human mind does, for the SPIRIT sees individual WORDS as complete STATEMENTS. When first writing for THE LORD, I wasn't aware that certain WORDS were being typed with varying type styles, until I went back afterwards and read what was WRITTEN. THE LORD then explained to ME that the SPIRITUAL MESSAGE was contained in specific WORDS rather than in all the tie words making up a particular sentence. ***HE*** also told ME that this is why it is called THE *WORD of* ***GOD,*** and not the WORDS of ***GOD,*** for each and EVERY WORD within a SCRIPTURE, has a SPECIFIC MESSAGE for the SPIRIT and every KEY WORD can stand-alone.

THE LORD said, those BELONGING to ***HIM*** would RECEIVE the MESSAGE in the WORDS having different type styles, whereas those whom ***HE*** has REJECTED, will not, and will be annoyed by them. ***HE*** said, the reason the REJECTED will find the changing of type style annoying, is because the WORDS represent TRUTH and TRUTH is LIGHT; and EVIL does not like to be in the LIGHT, but rather in DARKNESS.

Many times after WRITING something for THE LORD, when I go back and REVIEW what has been WRITTEN, I clearly UNDERSTAND it SPIRITUALLY but I find it very difficult to comprehend mindfully. In many cases I find the STRUCTURING of the sentence to be either fragmented or WORDED oddly so it appears to be grammatically incorrect and very difficult to comprehend. After reviewing what has been WRITTEN MINDFULLY, I often try to rephrase the sentence, however after doing so I find it loses its SPIRITUAL MESSAGE.

THE LORD has told ME, that by MY changing the SENTENCE STRUCTURE to make it easier to READ, I have DILUTED the SPIRITUAL MESSAGE, much like adding water to wine. HOWEVER, it is ***GOD'S*** intent for this BOOK to ENLIGHTEN ONE'S UNDERSTANDING of the HOLY BIBLE Scriptures, and the CHANGES in TYPE STYLE will act as an alternative in DELIVERING ITS SPIRITUAL MESSAGE.

Changes in TYPE STYLE

When the TYPE STYLE changes from lower case to upper case TYPE, either in a WORD or a SENTENCE, this TRIGGERS the SPIRIT that the WORD or the SENTENCE has a STRONG SPIRITUAL MESSAGE in it. Any references being made to ***GOD*** or the ***TRINITY (GODHEAD),*** or *WORDS of* ***GOD,*** will always be in ***UPPER CASE BOLD ITALIC TYPE.*** All Scripture references will be in *ITALIC TYPE,* and when the Scripture make references to ***GOD,*** or *WORDS SPOKEN BY* ***GOD,*** upper case ***BOLD ITALIC TYPE*** will be used.

These changes in TYPE STYLE need not be COMPREHENDED MINDFULLY nor conscious effort made in UNDERSTANDING its meaning, for YOUR SPIRIT will automatically COMPREHEND the MESSAGE on ITS OWN!

NOTES and Footnotes

Throughout the BOOK there are both NOTES and Footnotes. The NOTES will generally explain a Scriptures meaning or offer some additional pertinent INFORMATION relating to the subject of discussion. In explaining a referenced BIBLICAL Scripture, various LAYERS of the Scripture will be used as they pertain to a specific subject. However, it must be remembered that there are THREE LAYERS of DEPTH in OLD TESTAMENT, TWELVE in the GOSPELS and SEVEN in the Book of REVELATION. Therefor the SAME SCRIPTURE may be used more than once in regard to VARIOUS SUBJECTS of discussion, as a particular LAYER of that Scripture applies.

Whenever a Footnote symbol appears in the text, the Footnote should be read prior to starting the next paragraph. Footnotes in some cases may seem to deviate somewhat from the point of discussion, however in the Footnote lies a SPIRITUAL MESSAGE relating to the TOPIC. The BOOK in its MANUSCRIPT FORM has its Footnotes and its NOTES running in a sequential order, so it is important that the Footnote is READ in the proper sequence even though it may be placed at the bottom of the page or on another page.

As explained in OUR previous BOOK, "Revealing the BIBLE'S TRUTH", the HOLY BIBLE is PURPOSELY written to SPEAK to the SPIRIT rather than to the MIND, and this is why it is so DIFFICULT to MINDFULLY COMPREHEND. However in the BIBLE'S SCRIPTURES there are encrypted SPIRITUAL MESSAGES, and even though the READER may feel that he or she hadn't UNDERSTOOD what had been READ, their SPIRIT still RECEIVES the MESSAGE!

This BOOK would have been just as difficult to UNDERSTAND as THE HOLY BIBLE if it were left in its original form. However, THE LORD has ENCRYPTED ***HIS MESSAGE*** into the TEXT of this BOOK by the use of varying TYPE STYLES rather than by specific WORDING, thus making it EASIER to UNDERSTAND.

What is The ROD of IRON?

Revelation 2:26 AND HE THAT OVERCOMETH, AND KEEPETH MY WORKS UNTO THE END, TO HIM WILL I GIVE POWER OVER THE NATIONS:

Revelation 2:27 AND HE SHALL RULE THEM WITH A <u>ROD</u>

> ***OF IRON; AS THE VESSELS OF A POTTER SHALL THEY BE BROKEN TO SHIVERS; EVEN AS I RECEIVED OF MY FATHER.***

The ROD of IRON spoken of throughout the Scriptures of the BIBLE and then ECHOED in the Book of Revelation refers to the *WORD of **GOD.*** Early in the Book of Exodus, once MOSES had been EMPOWERED (ANOINTED) by ***GOD*** to free the Children of ISRAEL from their CAPTIVITY in Egypt, the Scriptures tell how MOSES headed off to Egypt ARMED only with HIS ROD in HIS HAND.

When MOSES CONFRONTED THE LORD after HE had been told by ***HIM*** to return to Egypt and FREE ***GOD'S*** PEOPLE, MOSES was concerned as to whether the Children of ISRAEL would believe that ***GOD*** had sent HIM.

> ***Exodus 4:1*** *And MOSES answered and said, But, behold, they will not believe ME, nor hearken unto MY VOICE: for they will say, THE LORD hath not appeared unto thee.*

> ***Exodus 4:2*** *And THE LORD said unto HIM, WHAT IS THAT IN THINE HAND? And HE said a ROD.*

MOSES was then told to CAST the ROD to the ground, and when HE did, it immediately became a serpent. THE LORD told MOSES to take the serpent by the tail, and when MOSES had done it, it became a ROD again while in HIS hand.

The MESSAGE in the aforementioned Scriptures is; when the *WORD of **GOD*** is cast to the ground, (therefor meaning set aside) it is the same as the releasing of the serpent (the Devil) into your presence, exposing you to his bite. However, once the *WORD of **GOD*** has been taken back into your hand, the serpent (the Devil) is non-existent and cannot cause you any harm! What THE LORD was demonstrating to MOSES was, if he would KEEP the *WORD of **GOD*** (THE ROD) in his hand, it could be used as a METHOD of PROOF HE had been sent to the people by ***GOD***. Furthermore, ***GOD*** was showing MOSES "THE ROD" could also be used to instill the FEAR of ***GOD*** into those who had refused to BELIEVE in ***HIM.***

> ***Exodus 4:20*** *And MOSES took HIS wife and HIS sons, and set them upon an ass, and HE returned unto the land of Egypt: and MOSES took THE ROD of **GOD** in HIS hand.*

The same MESSAGE given by ***GOD*** to MOSES will be given also to ***GOD'S*** CHILDREN in this BOOK; and is the BASIS for the WRITING of IT! The *WORD of* ***GOD*** is MAN'S most POWERFUL tool and it is the INTENT of this BOOK to DEMONSTRATE; that if "THE ROD of IRON" is in YOUR HAND no OBSTACLE in LIFE is insurmountable.

MOSES being only armed with *The WORD of* ***GOD*** went into Egypt and brought both the Pharaoh and ALL of Egypt to their knees. Then after HUMBLING Pharaoh and Egypt by *The WORD of* ***GOD***, MOSES simply walked through open gates, LEADING one and one-half million people (***GOD'S*** PEOPLE) out of Egypt and to their FREEDOM!

It was through the *WORD of* ***GOD*** that MOSES was EMPOWERED (ANOINTED) to perform the MIRACLES in the eyes of Pharaoh, the Egyptians, and the Children of ISRAEL, the likes of which have not been done since. JESUS CHRIST also performed MANY MIRACLES, his GREATEST of which was HIS DEFEATING DEATH! However, what JESUS did was done on an individual basis, thus DEMONSTRATING how each of ***GOD'S*** CHILDREN must establish a RELATIONSHIP with ***GOD*** on an INDIVIDUAL BASIS. Whereas MOSES DEMONSTRATED by the *WORD of* ***GOD, GOD'S*** GREAT WRATH and POWER affecting the multitudes, JESUS CHRIST by the *WORD of* ***GOD*** DEMONSTRATED ***GOD'S*** GREAT LOVE and HEALING POWER on an INDIVIDUAL BASIS. Furthermore, it must be REMEMBERED that in either the case of MOSES or JESUS CHRIST, their EMPOWERMENT came by the way of THE *WORD of* ***GOD (THE ROD of IRON)!***

Foreword

Have you ever heard the expression, "Sticks and stones may break my bones, but names can never hurt me"? Well, if you have, I can tell you that I cannot think of another expression that is further from the TRUTH! A person can physically batter another causing much bodily pain or even death to them, however short of death; the wounds caused by the battering will eventually heal. On the other hand, WORDS aimed at causing pain to another, can not only cause emotional pain, but can traumatize a person's SPIRIT over their entire physical life. The difference between a physical battery and a SPIRITUAL battery, is when a person strikes another physically, the damage caused by it is only temporary. Whereas emotional striking, by use of WORDS, can traumatize one's SPIRIT to the point of their doubting their own SELF-WORTHINESS (self esteem).

A person by touching another can express a feeling of LOVE by a caress or a hug, and by their GENTLE behavior express a POSITIVE feeling towards the other. However striking or choking a person would express a NEGATIVE feeling towards that individual. This phenomenon also holds TRUE with WORDS. Positive WORDS can COMFORT or build another person's confidence, and can even demonstrate COMPASSION or sexually excite the other, while an exchange of NEGATIVE WORDS can cause mutual ANGER, GRIEF, or HATRED towards one another. This is because the SPIRIT reacts to WORDS in the same manner as the physical body reacts to TOUCH.

The 1st Chapter in this BOOK called "The POWER of the ROD", will DEMONSTRATE how GREAT POWER can be dispensed in either a POSITIVE or NEGATIVE form by the use of WORDS. It will do this through the example of MORAL TRUTHS (Parables) and BIBLICAL SCRIPTURES. Many subjects will be covered throughout the BOOK to further your UNDERSTANDING of the *WORD of* ***GOD.*** However, for you to fully comprehend the subject matter you will have had to have READ OUR previous BOOK, "REVEALING The BIBLE'S TRUTH". For those of you who have not READ it, in some circumstances WE will briefly explain what was covered in it, and when WE do, WE will refer to it not by its TITLE but rather as to: the "PREVIOUS BOOK".

The King James 1611 Authorized Version of the HOLY BIBLE will be quoted many times throughout this BOOK, requiring the READER to refer to BIBLICAL SCRIPTURE in it. It is recommended that you obtain the 1611 King James HOLY BIBLE for a reference guide, for no other translation of the HOLY BIBLE will work as a substitute. The reason you will need the King James is because WE are going to breakdown the cited Scriptures in the BIBLE, WORD by WORD, to show you the DEPTH and the POWER in the *WORD of **GOD.*** The wording in the other TRANSLATIONS are different than those in the 1611 King James, and are unsuitable for DISCERNING the SPIRITUAL LAYERS within the SCRIPTURE!

BOOKS in the SERIES

WE have WRITTEN THREE BOOKS in total, inclusive of this BOOK, with the FIRST BOOK being the FINAL BOOK of a THREE BOOK SERIES. I was TOLD originally that the 1st BOOK WRITTEN could not be PUBLISHED, for it was too REVEALING and I did not plan on writing any further BOOKS after the publication of "Revealing the BIBLE'S TRUTH". However, on the morning of November 19th 2002, THE LORD TOLD ME THAT I WAS TO WRITE ANOTHER BOOK, AND THAT ITS TITLE WAS GOING TO BE "**THE ROD of IRON**". ***GOD*** further told me while writing the INTRODUCTION to this BOOK, what the BOOK was going to be about and as with the other two BOOKS, I WRITE IN ACCORDANCE TO THE WORDS GIVEN TO ME BY ***GOD.***

Due to the content of the FIRST BOOK being TOO REVEALING, ***GOD*** will not allow it to be published without EDITING OUT certain things, and I can only tell you at this time that its title is "REVELATION the FOURTH SON". The 2nd BOOK, REVEALING the BIBLE'S TRUTH, currently in publication, explains the COMPOSITION of the HOLY BIBLE and REVEALS many of its SECRETS, all of which is supported by the Scriptures themselves. The SERIES of BOOKS can be thought of like THREE LEVELS of SPIRITUAL UNDERSTANDING, with "REVEALING the BIBLE'S TRUTH being LEVEL ONE, this BOOK being LEVEL TWO, and "REVELATION the FOURTH SON" being the FINAL LEVEL and the LAST in the SERIES. This BOOK is intended to raise one's SPIRITUAL UNDERSTANDING to the next HIGHER LEVEL. Therefor, the FIRST BOOK should be READ prior to this BOOK to RECEIVE the FULL BENEFIT of its MESSAGE.

WORDS

GOD tells us in the Scriptures that ***HE*** is the ALPHA and OMEGA, the FIRST and the LAST, and the BEGINNING and the END. Although there is a GREAT deal of DEPTH to this MESSAGE, the Scripture's PRIMARY MESSAGE is that ***GOD*** is the LETTERS contained in the ENGLISH ALPHABET used to make up WORDS for COMMUNICATION. As explained in the PREVIOUS BOOK, the HOLY BIBLE although originally written in HEBREW, Greek, and Latin, had ALWAYS been intended by ***GOD*** to be TRANSLATED into ENGLISH, and the SPIRITUAL LAYERS of the SCRIPTURES are only DETECTABLE in the ENGLISH LANGUAGE.

The original HEBREW alphabet had 22 characters in it and each character also represented a NUMBER, and the same basis holds TRUE for the ENGLISH ALPHABET. As was explained in the "PREVIOUS BOOK", each letter in the ENGLISH ALPHABET has a corresponding NUMBER assigned to it, by where the letter falls within the 26 letter ALPHABET. For example the letter "A" is the 1st letter and the letter "Z" is the 26th letter and can be expressed as follows:

A=1, B=2, C=3, D=4, E=5, F=6, G=7, H=8, I=9, J=10, K=11, L=12, M=13, N=14, O=15, P=16, Q=17, R=18, S=19, T=20, U=21, V=22, W=23, X=24, Y=25, and Z=26.

This demonstrates that each of the letters in the ENGLISH ALPHABET has a corresponding NUMBER and when the LETTERS make up WORDS, there can be both a definition of the WORD and also a NUMBER assigned to the WORD. The NUMBER can be arrived at when the SUM of the WORDS LETTERS is totaled.

As an example, WE could say the WORD "cat" can be expressed by the NUMBERS 3, 1, and 20, when WE take the corresponding number to each of its LETTERS. WE could also say; if WE were to simply add the total of the three NUMBERS, the NUMBER 24 (3+1+20=24) could also mean the WORD "cat". However, when expressing the WORD "cat" by its sum total alone, WE could be making reference to a variety of WORDS whose letters also total to 24. This same SCENARIO also HOLDS TRUE in regard to the WORDS making up a BIBLICAL Scripture, thus giving EACH WORD in the Scripture a VARIETY of MEANINGS if it were to be used in PARTIALITY.

When looking into the DEPTH of a Scripture there are certain RULES that apply to the SPIRITUAL DISCERNMENT of it. RULE number "1" says; the WORDS making up the Scripture can NEVER be taken out of its ORIGINAL

SEQUENCE within the Scripture, nor can the Scripture be BROKEN to use only a portion of its WORDS. This not only applies to a single verse, but it can carry over to MULTIPLE VERSES when the verse ends with either a semicolon or a colon, or if the following verse starts with an "And". Any of these three SIGNALS indicate that the SPIRITUAL MESSAGE MUST BE CARRIED ON THROUGH TO ITS CONCLUSION, which will be indicated by a PERIOD.

The point being made here can be expressed by us going back to the NUMBER 24 again, and saying that the NUMBER 24 can represent a whole host of words and not just the word "cat"! WE can further say the WORDS or any PARTICULAR WORD making up a Scripture are similar to the NUMERICAL SUM of a WORD, and can also have several MEANINGS. Therefor, it is CRITICAL when applying a Scripture to a SCENARIO, that the SCENARIO fits the Scripture's intended MESSAGE.

For example; If WE were to say, "the dog was chasing the "24"", in this case the probability of the NUMBER 24 meaning the WORD "cat" is high. Whereas if WE were to say, "the dog bit my "24"", this could mean the WORD "cat" or possibly the WORD "leg", which LETTERS also add up to the NUMBER "24". Both the two WORDS and their NUMBERS interrelate, and just as there are RULES associated with NUMBERS in mathematics, so are there RULES applying to WORDS used in a SCRIPTURE. This may be difficult to GRASP at this time, but as WE proceed in the BOOK YOU will RECEIVE the MESSAGE!

In summary: When a Scripture is properly INTERPRETED, the APPLICATION of it will be in CONTEXT with the Scripture's TRUE MESSAGE. However when the Scripture is IMPROPERLY INTERPRETED and taken OUT of context with the Scripture's TRUE MESSAGE, it will be MISLEADING. As explained in the "PREVIOUS BOOK, the HOLY BIBLE is WRITTEN in LAYERS, and it is because of these LAYERS the BIBLE'S SCRIPTURES cannot be UNDERSTOOD or PROPERLY applied without SPIRITUAL GUIDANCE. This SPIRITUAL GUIDANCE can only come to ONE by way of THE ***HOLY SPIRIT of GOD*** and the GUIDANCE is called "ANOINTING". Many of the SAME WORDS used throughout the Scriptures have variable MEANINGS and can easily be MISINTERPRETED; just as WE had demonstrated previously using the NUMBER 24. A WORD used in one Scripture may not have the same meaning when used in another Scripture. Knowing how the WORDS apply to the DEPTH of the SCRIPTURE comes only by ANOINTING, and without that ANOINTING, anyone trying to teach the *WORD of* ***GOD*** in the EYES of ***GOD*** is a "FALSE PROPHET"!

ANOINTING is an EMPOWERMENT by ***GOD*** and is not TRANSFER-

ABLE from one person to another, so therefor one man cannot teach another the SPIRITUAL DEPTH of the Scripture. However, it can be TAUGHT from SPIRIT to SPIRIT, and this is why this BOOK is COMPOSED in this rather ODD manner. The KEY ingredient NEEDED to teach SPIRITUALLY, is the GIFT of SPIRITUAL DISCERNMENT, and without it many that try to teach the *WORD of* ***GOD,*** do so FALSELY. This is because they themselves don't understand the Scriptures and MISINTERPRET them, by their inability to see beyond the 1st LAYER, the LAYER of the PAST. The HOLY BIBLE CANNOT BE READ LIKE A BOOK, FOR IT CONTAINS ENCRYPTED MESSAGES FOR THE SPIRIT. JESUS CHRIST refers to those who try to teach THE *WORD* without ANOINTING as, "the blind leading the blind".

JESUS CHRIST was sent to the earth by ***GOD*** to not only COMPLETE the Scriptures, but to also explain their TRUE MEANING. HE did this by ACCURATELY making references to the Scriptures and by the use of PARABLES. WE will ALSO use the same TECHNIQUE JESUS CHRIST used throughout this BOOK, but the BOOK'S FORMAT is what will further your SPIRITUAL UNDERSTANDING of the *WORD of* ***GOD.*** ANYONE who READS this BOOK in an effort to FURTHER their UNDERSTANDING, will indeed RECEIVE IT SAITH THE LORD, SOME THIRTY, SOME SIXTY, and some ONE HUNDREDFOLD!

> ***Matthew 7:7 ASK, AND IT SHALL BE GIVEN YOU; SEEK, AND YE SHALL FIND; KNOCK, AND IT SHALL BE OPENED UNTO YOU:***

> ***Matthew 7:8 FOR EVERY ONE THAT ASKETH RECEIVETH; AND HE THAT SEEKETH FINDETH; AND TO HIM THAT KNOCKETH IT SHALL BE OPENED.***

WORD Liability

GOD will hold a person LIABLE for the WORDS they either SPEAK or WRITE. ***HE*** does this because your WORDS proceed from your SPIRIT (your HEART), and IMPROPER or EVIL WORDS can cause much damage and pain to another, especially when they are carelessly or maliciously used. ***GOD*** expects you to be responsible for your WORDS as well as your actions, because of the POWER wielded in WORDS.

When the Pharisees came to JESUS and complained about HIS Disciples eating with unclean hands, JESUS told them, how or what a person ate was insignificant, and what went into them through their mouths simply passed through them. However, HE warned them about what came out of a person's mouth, saying, what was said was more important than what was eaten! HE further explained to HIS Disciples what HE had meant by HIM telling the Pharisees this.

> ***Matthew 15:17 DO NOT YE YET UNDERSTAND, THAT WHATSOEVER ENTERETH IN AT THE MOUTH GOETH INTO THE BELLY, AND IS CAST OUT INTO THE DRAUGHT?***
>
> ***Matthew 15:18 BUT THOSE THINGS WHICH PROCEED OUT OF THE MOUTH COME FORTH FROM THE HEART; AND THEY DEFILE THE MAN.***
>
> ***Matthew 15:19 FOR OUT OF THE HEART PROCEED EVIL THOUGHTS, MURDERS, ADULTERIES, FORNICATIONS, THEFTS, FALSE WITNESS, BLASPHEMIES:***
>
> ***Matthew 15:20 THESE ARE THE THINGS WHICH DEFILE A MAN: BUT TO EAT WITH UNWASHEN HANDS DEFILETH NOT A MAN.***

A person must be most cautious as to what they might say or write, for by your own WORDS so shall ye be JUDGED! As you proceed further into this BOOK you will see the POWER of WORDS, and how they can be likened to a loaded gun, or to more correctly say, likened to a "TWO-EDGED SWORD"; one that cuts in either direction. (This refers to an EXCHANGE of WORDS and also to POSITIVE or NEGATIVE WORDS.)

GOD has given man the ability to COMMUNICATE by the use of WORDS, and ***HE*** expects YOU to use those WORDS both RIGHTEOUSLY and WISELY! Many times people will allow their ANGER to drive their WORDS, and if ***GOD*** were to adopt this philosophy, the world would have been DESTROYED long ago. However; ***GOD*** is SLOW TO ANGER, and SLOW to PASS JUDGMENT, however when ***HE*** says something, ***HE MEANS WHAT HE SAYS AND DOES NOT CHANGE HIS MIND ABOUT IT!***

NEGATIVE words bring about NEGATIVE EFFECTS. If you have nothing to say in a POSITIVE manner, SAY NOTHING AT ALL, or keep it to a simple YES or NO!

Matthew 5:37 BUT LET YOUR COMMUNICATION BE, YEA, YEA; NAY, NAY: FOR WHATSOEVER IS MORE THAN THESE COMETH OF EVIL.

Subjects of INTEREST

"THE ROD OF IRON" will span a wide range of TOPICS, for the *WORD of* ***GOD*** encompasses ALL things that are, or shall ever be. Some of the SUBJECTS covered are buried so DEEP in the Scriptures only those with SEVEN GIFTS or MORE can DISCERN them. The *WORD of* ***GOD*** encompasses ALL THINGS, so even though it may appear at times that WE are DEVIATING from the BIBLE, WE are NOT! WE can assure you that ALL SUBJECTS being COVERED in this BOOK bare RECORD of the TRUTH, and do not DEVIATE from the *WORD of* ***GOD.***

The ROD of IRON reveals how certain NUMBERS can be associated with WORDS, and talks about CELESTIAL and PARALLEL DIMENSIONS. It SPEAKS about the DESTINY of ***GOD'S*** CHILDREN and how HEAVEN CONTINUALLY GROWS in POPULATION throughout ETERNITY. There is a chapter dedicated to explaining LIFE elsewhere in the UNIVERSE, and what differences there are between YOU and the other LIFE FORMS. The subject of MUSIC is covered; and how acoustical tones affect the SPIRIT. A description of HEAVEN is given, both BEFORE and AFTER CREATION. The BOOK speaks about the ANGELS and HEAVENLY HIERARCHY and explains what had caused the one time ARK ANGEL, Lucifer, to fall from ***GOD*** and HEAVEN.

READ both this BOOK and the HOLY BIBLE together for the TWO are INSEPARABLE ***SAITH THE LORD;*** and allow "THE ROD of IRON" to bridge the GAP between YOU and ETERNITY! ***A-MEN'***

Chapter 1
The POWER of the ROD

The first time the WORD, "ROD", appears in the HOLY BIBLE (in a singular form) is in Exodus, Chapter 4, in verse 2. There is a very specific reason as to why it appears in the BIBLE at this point in time. The WORD, "ROD", thus meaning both "THE WORD" and "THE WRITTEN *WORD of **GOD***" appears FIRST in The Book, Exodus; during the time ***GOD*** had ANOINTED MOSES to both SPEAK and WRITE for ***HIM.*** Therefor it was MOSES, a DELIVERER, who was the FIRST MAN ***GOD*** ENTRUSTED to WRITE ***HIS*** WORD.

NOAH (being also a DELIVERER) was ENTRUSTED with the WORD up until the time he had released the DOVE from the ARK (thus meaning the releasing of THE ***HOLY SPIRIT***) into the NEW WORLD. Although NOAH RECEIVED the *WORD of **GOD,*** he never RECORDED it, therefor NOAH, had not taken THE ROD into his HAND. However, MOSES did RECORD the *WORD of **GOD,*** making HIM the FIRST PERSON in the NEW WORLD to take THE ROD in HIS HAND, and this is why the WORD, "ROD", appears for the first time in the Book of Exodus.

In the PREVIOUS BOOK, it was explained to you that ***THE DELIVERER,*** the ***182 PERSON*** is the ONE who oversees and MANAGES the *WORD of* ***GOD,*** because ***HE*** is the PERSON of THE ***HOLY SPIRIT.*** It is THE ***HOLY SPIRIT*** who both ANOINTS and DELIVERS ***GOD'S WORD*** to man.

After the RESURRECTION of JESUS CHRIST, any MAN having been BAPTIZED in THE ***HOLY SPIRIT*** (SAVED), RECEIVES one or more of the NINE GIFTS given by THE ***HOLY SPIRIT.*** Each of the GIFTS represents a certain LEVEL of ANOINTING. Any person who has been EMPOWERED to WRITE the *WORD of **GOD*** will have at least SIX of the NINE GIFTS. In the case of MOSES, by HIM being of THE ***HOLY SPIRIT*** (a DELIVERER), HE was GIVEN ALL NINE GIFTS. This EMPOWERMENT GIVEN to MOSES elevated HIS status of ANOINTING to be above even that of the SEVENTH LEVEL ANGEL!

Whereas any person may TESTIFY to the *WORD of **GOD,*** this is to say,

QUOTE SCRIPTURE, anyone claiming to WRITE on the behalf of ***GOD,*** and has NOT the ANOINTING to do so, is BLASPHEMING THE ***HOLY SPIRIT.*** Those in VIOLATION, will RECEIVE ETERNAL DAMNATION for it; for this is an UNFORGIVABLE SIN!

One should also be quite cautious as to what they say or write regarding what ***GOD*** has either said, when ***HE HAD NOT SAID IT,*** or provide DIRECTION from THE LORD to another, when ***HE HAD NOT GIVEN IT!*** Any DIRECTION GIVEN by either Scripture or from ABOVE will always be CONFIRMED by ***GOD.*** YOU MUST BE VERY CAUTIOUS WHEN USING THE LORD'S ***NAME!*** Therefor, if you BELIEVE ***GOD*** has given you a ***MESSAGE*** for you to share with others, WAIT for a CONFIRMATION from ***HIM,*** before you PROCEED with the MESSAGE. For most people, the *WORD of* ***GOD*** will come by way of the Scriptures, but for the VERY ELECT, (people receiving at least SIX GIFTS from THE ***HOLY SPIRIT***), the WORD can come by either SCRIPTURE or by GUIDANCE from the THRONE of ***GOD.***

The GUIDANCE coming from ABOVE can be in the form of a VISION, or a DREAM, by an ANGEL, or DIRECTLY FROM THE ***HOLY SPIRIT*** *of* ***GOD.*** REGARDLESS of how it may be RECEIVED, the TRUTH of the MESSAGE will be UNDENIABLE and will always be CONFIRMED.

HOLY SPIRIT BAPTISM

Although many churches still Baptize with water, the RESULTS of water Baptism is irrelevant and MEANINGLESS. All of JESUS' Disciples were baptized with water prior to HIS Crucifixion. However, after JESUS' RESURRECTION, HE instructed HIS Disciples to REMAIN (tarry) in JERUSALEM until they were EMPOWERED from ABOVE. JESUS so INSTRUCTED HIS Disciples; because they had not yet been BAPTIZED, and EMPOWERED through SPIRITUAL BAPTISM, to PREACH the *WORD of* ***GOD.***

> ***Luke 24:49 AND, BEHOLD, I SEND THE PROMISE OF MY FATHER UPON YOU: BUT TARRY YE IN THE CITY OF JERUSALEM, UNTIL YE BE ENDUED WITH THE POWER FROM ON HIGH.***

JESUS, in the Scripture is explaining to HIS Disciples, that now, (after HE had been RESURRECTED from the dead), HE COULD FULFILL THE PROMISE of HIS ***FATHER,*** THE ***HOLY SPIRIT,*** by way of their BAPTISM in THE SAME SPIRIT. JESUS tells them that they should wait for the EM-

POWERMENT that will come by way of their BAPTISM, prior to their going out to PREACH the GOSPELS and MINISTER to the people.

From the Scriptures it was made very clear to the Disciples; although they had been baptized with water they hadn't yet been ANOINTED or SAVED. This is because SAVING GRACE comes by way of ***HOLY SPIRIT*** BAPTISM and not by water baptism: for once JESUS had been BAPTIZED in THE ***HOLY SPIRIT of GOD,*** water baptism became irrelevant.

BAPTISM is a form of cleansing, and the CLEANSING that was needed for the Disciples had to be a CLEANSING by the BLOOD of THE LAMB (the SACRIFICE), and that came after HIS RESURRECTION. Once the Disciples had RECEIVED their SPIRITUAL CLEANSING, they then became EMPOWERED by the GIFTS of THE ***HOLY SPIRIT*** to go forward and PREACH in THE ***NAME of GOD!***

HOLY SPIRIT BAPTISM is a SPIRITUAL EVENT, and cannot be replaced with a carnal event, such as water baptism. John the Baptist baptized with water, HOWEVER, JESUS CHRIST never baptized anyone with water, but rather in SPIRIT!

> ***John 4:1*** *When therefore THE LORD knew how the Pharisees had heard that JESUS made and baptized more Disciples than John,*
>
> ***John 4:2*** *(Though JESUS HIMSELF Baptized NOT, but HIS Disciples,)*
>
> ***John 4:3*** *HE left Ju-dae'-a, and departed again into Galilee.*

What the Scriptures are saying is; JESUS DID NOT BAPTIZE with water, however HIS Disciples did. The reason JESUS never Baptized with water was because HE KNEW the water baptism did not serve any PURPOSES whatsoever. HE only ALLOWED HIS Disciples to continue with water baptism, so those who were receiving it would BELIEVE they were making a commitment to ***GOD.*** Furthermore, if the Disciples had received SAVING GRACE by way of their water baptism, then Judas Is-car-i-ot could not have BETRAYED JESUS CHRIST, for he would have been reborn in CHRIST and could not have committed that SIN, because he would have been SAVED!

Contrary to what the Churches TEACH, once a person has been REBORN in CHRIST by way of SPIRITUAL BAPTISM, that PERSON becomes BLAMELESS in the *EYES of* ***GOD*** and FREE from any SIN, PERMANENTLY! This is not a temporary STATE for a NEWBORN SOUL, but rather an ETERNAL STATE. Once a person has TRULY RECEIVED SAVING GRACE that PERSON CAN NEVER FALL FROM GRACE. THIS IS A SIMPLE FACT, AND ANYONE CLAIMING IT TO BE OTHERWISE, DOES NOT KNOW THE *WORD of* ***GOD!*** ONCE THE LORD has SAVED a SOUL that SOUL NEVER NEEDS TO BE SAVED AGAIN. IT IS ***FOREVER SAITH THE LORD!***

> ***John 1:32*** *And John bare record, saying, I saw THE* ***SPIRIT*** *descending from HEAVEN like a DOVE, and it abode upon HIM.*

> ***John 1:33*** *And I knew HIM not: but* ***HE*** *that sent me to baptize with water, the SAME said unto me,* ***UPON WHOM THOU SHALT SEE THE SPIRIT DESCENDING, AND REMAINING ON HIM, THE SAME IS HE WHICH BAPTIZETH WITH THE HOLY GHOST.***

> ***John 1:34*** *And I saw, and bare record that this is the SON of* ***GOD.***

NOTE: From the Scriptures it is MADE CLEAR; once a PERSON becomes BAPTIZED in THE ***HOLY SPRIT,*** that PERSON then BECOMES THE SON of ***GOD.***

> ***Revelation 21:7*** *He that overcometh shall inherit ALL THINGS; and* ***I*** *will be HIS* ***GOD,*** *and HE shall be* ***MY SON.***

ANOINTING (EMPOWERMENT)

Once a PERSON becomes BAPTIZED in THE ***HOLY SPIRIT,*** they then RECEIVE their ANOINTING from THE ***HOLY SPRIT.*** This ANOINTING comes in the form of one or more of NINE GIFTS given by THE ***HOLY SPIRIT.*** The following is a list of the NINE GIFTS.

1. The WORD of WISDOM
2. The WORD of KNOWLEDGE
3. FAITH
4. HEALING
5. MIRACLES
6. PROPHECY

7. DISCERNING of Spirits
8. DIVERS TONGUES
9. INTERPRETATION of TONGUES

The ANOINTED will RECEIVE ONE GIFT or more depending on their HEAVENLY STATUS, up to a SIX-GIFT MAXIMUM for a MAN. Only the SEVENTH LEVEL ANGEL, METATRON, or the SERAPHIM can RECEIVE SEVEN or MORE GIFTS. The FIRST GIFT GIVEN is ALWAYS the GIFT of FAITH. After ONE has RECEIVED the GIFT of FAITH, any ONE or more of the remaining EIGHT GIFTS can then be RECEIVED. Some of the GIFTS go hand in hand and are GIVEN in pairs, while some of the GIFTS are rarely GIVEN in pairs to the SAME INDIVIDUAL. For instance, ALL that RECEIVE the GIFT of HEALING also RECEIVE the GIFT of DISCERNING of Spirits. This is because in part, the ability to HEAL relies on the ABILITY to cast out DEMONS. If the HEALER were unable to see DEMONS in POSSESSION of a person, they wouldn't be able to cast them out.

On the other hand, rarely does the same INDIVIDUAL RECEIVE the ABILITY to both SPEAK in TONGUES and INTERPRET them; this subject was covered in the PREVIOUS BOOK. The WORD "TONGUES", as used in the Scriptures, refers to the ancient HEBREWAH LANGUAGE spoken by NOAH, the PROPHETS, and JESUS CHRIST when HE PERFORMED MIRACLES. However, ONE having RECEIVED the GIFT of TONGUES or INTERPRETATION, may also RECEIVE the ability to SPEAK or UNDERSTAND one of the many languages spoken here on earth, without ever being taught the language.

When a person RECEIVES the ABILITY to PERFORM MIRACLES, that person will always have the ABILITY to SPEAK in TONGUES; for the COMMANDS for the MIRACLE must be spoken in the HEBREWAH LANGUAGE. Another PAIR of GIFTS always given together, is the GIFT of KNOWLEDGE and the GIFT of WISDOM. The KNOWLEDGE is the ABILITY to UNDERSTAND SCRIPTURE, and the WISDOM is the ABILITY to PROPERLY APPLY the SCRIPTURE, for BOTH go HAND in HAND to be EFFECTIVE.

The GIFT of PROPHECY, is the ABILITY to see the PROPHETIC MESSAGE contained within the 3rd LAYER of the SCRIPTURE and this GIFT most always is accompanied with the GIFTS of KNOWLEDGE and WISDOM; although at times it is GIVEN on its own without the other two GIFTS. THE ***HOLY SPIRIT*** only GIVES the GIFT of MIRACLES to those who have RECEIVED in total, SIX or MORE GIFTS.

SPIRITUAL GUIDANCE

After a PERSON has RECEIVED their ANOINTING from ***GOD***, THE ***HOLY SPIRIT*** will then let ***HIS PRESENCE*** be known to them. The PERSON with the ANOINTING will be AWARE of THE ***HOLY SPRIT'S PRESENCE*** by an ECSTATIC FEELING coming over them, that at times ***ITS*** INTENSITY is quite overwhelming, but at the same time is also MOST COMFORTING. This is why the Scriptures refer to THE ***HOLY SPIRIT*** as being the COMFORTER. The Disciples experienced this same ECSTATIC FEELING while in the PRESENCE of JESUS CHRIST, because of JESUS' GREAT ANOINTING. This is why JESUS had told HIS Disciples that HE would send to them another COMFORTER after HE had left earth. JESUS also at times in the Scriptures refers to the COMFORTER as HIS PEACE!

> ***John 16:7 NEVERTHELESS I TELL YOU THE TRUTH; IT IS EXPEDIENT FOR YOU THAT I GO AWAY; FOR IF I GO NOT AWAY, THE COMFORTER WILL NOT COME UNTO YOU; BUT IF I DEPART, I WILL SEND HIM UNTO YOU.***

This Scripture explains why JESUS CHRIST had to die and be RESURRECTED before ANYONE could RECEIVE ***HOLY SPIRIT BAPTISM,*** THE PROMISE of ***THE FATHER.*** Although the Scriptures cover this subject throughout the GOSPELS, and are quite clear to THE LORD'S ANOINTED, to those who are not anointed, "THE PROMISE of ***THE FATHER***" may not be so obvious.

When JESUS walked and talked with HIS Disciples, HE explained how HE had to die on the CROSS, for them to be SAVED. HE told them about THE ***HOLY SPIRIT BAPTISM*** they would RECEIVE shortly after HIS RESURRECTION, and how after their BAPTISM they would RECEIVE GIFTS from THE ***HOLY SPIRIT.*** HE also told them how they would have an ETERNAL PLACE with HIM in HEAVEN, once they had COMPLETED THEIR MINISTRIES on earth.

The Disciples at that time, did not UNDERSTAND what JESUS had meant in regard to THE ***HOLY SPIRIT***, and it wasn't until AFTER their BAPTISM in THE ***HOLY SPIRIT*** they could COMPREHEND HIS MESSAGE, and WRITE it into the GOSPELS. The Disciples could not UNDERSTAND at that time, because they had not yet RECEIVED the GIFTS of the WORD of KNOWLEDGE and WISDOM, allowing them to COMPREHEND JESUS' MESSAGE.

John 14:26 BUT THE COMFORTER, WHICH IS THE HOLY GHOST, WHOM THE FATHER WILL SEND IN MY NAME, HE SHALL TEACH YOU ALL THINGS, AND BRING ALL THINGS TO YOUR REMEMBRANCE, WHATSOEVER I HAVE SAID UNTO YOU.

The CHANGE

After ***HOLY SPIRIT BAPTISM*** and ANOINTING, the PERSON RECEIVING it will undergo various types of CHANGE. Being GUIDED by ***GOD*** they will start losing interest in those things that THE LORD wants REMOVED from their LIFE. ***GOD*** will do this in such a way the PERSON will not feel DEPRIVED of anything being taken away. Those things being taken out of ONE'S LIFE will not be the same for each individual and will significantly vary between people. For instance, in one case, THE LORD may remove alcohol from a person's life, and yet allow another to continue to drink. A good example of this is JESUS CHRIST was allowed to drink alcohol, whereas ***GOD*** forbade John the Baptist to drink anything, other than water or milk. John the Baptist was also placed on a strict diet of locust and honey, whereas JESUS ate whatever HE pleased. The Scriptures make mention of this in the Gospel of Matthew.

Matthew 11:18 FOR JOHN CAME NEITHER EATING NOR DRINKING, AND THEY SAY, HE HATH A DEVIL.

Matthew 11:19 THE SON OF MAN CAME EATING AND DRINKING, AND THEY SAY, BEHOLD A MAN GLUTTONOUS, AND A WINEBIBBER, A FRIEND OF PUBLICANS AND SINNERS. BUT WISDOM IS JUSTIFIED OF HER CHILDREN.

GOD does not only REMOVE things from a PERSON'S LIFE ***HE*** may also ADD some things that had not previously been a part of their life! Both the things which are REMOVED, and the things that are ADDED will STRENGTHEN the PERSON'S CHARACTER in ***GOD,*** and make them more suitable for MINISTRY. A PERSON being NEWLY REBORN and in RECEIPT of the GIFTS of THE ***HOLY SPIRIT*** will RECEIVE the necessary CHANGES making them more SUITABLE to WISELY use their GIFTS in the MINISTRY for ***GOD*** and in the TESTIMONY of JESUS CHRIST.

Carnal Empowerment Versus SPIRITUAL EMPOWERMENT

ALL EMPOWERMENT comes from ***GOD,*** whether it is in a carnal or a SPIRITUAL form! This is to say; if a person has been placed in power over people, although they through their OWN IGNORANCE believe its of their OWN DOING, it is not; for they have been empowered by ***GOD.*** When JESUS was brought before Pon'-tius Pilate and refused to speak on HIS own behalf, Pilate boasted of the great power he had over JESUS' life:

> ***John 19:10*** *Then saith Pilate unto HIM, Speakest thou not unto me? Knowest thou not that I have power to crucify thee, and have power to release thee?*

> ***John 19:11*** *JESUS answered,* ***THOU COULDEST HAVE NO POWER AT ALL AGAINST ME, EXCEPT IT WERE GIVEN THEE FROM ABOVE: THEREFORE HE THAT DELIVERED ME UNTO THEE HATH THE GREATER SIN.***

Even the wicked receive their empowerment from ***GOD.*** When King Neb-u-chad-nez'-zar of Babylon was WARNED by ***GOD,*** about his continual boasting of his self established power, and his refusal to GLORIFY ***GOD*** for giving him that power, ***GOD*** took his Kingdom away from him!

> ***Daniel 4:30*** *The King spake, and said, Is not this great Babylon, that I have built for the house of the Kingdom by the might of my power, and for the honour of my majesty?*

> ***Daniel 4:31*** *While the word was in the King's mouth, there fell a VOICE from HEAVEN, saying, O King Neb-u-chad-nez'-zar, to thee it is SPOKEN; The Kingdom is departed from thee.*

> ***Daniel 4:32*** *And they shall drive thee from men, and thy dwelling shall be with the beasts of the field: they shall make thee to eat grass as oxen, and SEVEN times shall pass over thee, until thou know that the MOST HIGH ruleth in the Kingdom of men, and giveth it to whomsoever HE will.*

Therefor with ***GOD*** having the CONTROL over ALL POWER, whether it is of a carnal or a SPIRITUAL form, ALL having RECEIVED that POWER must use it in a WISE and RIGHTEOUS manner, or ***GOD*** will REMOVE them from POWER. Furthermore, with the POWER being in WORDS, ALL men in power will be HELD accountable for their WORDS. Whereas the SPIRITUALLY EMPOWERED RECEIVE their DIRECTION from ***GOD*** by their ANOINTING, the carnally empowered receive their direction from their own minds that are subject to ERROR. Therefor, the ANOINTED need not worry about THEIR WORDS for they come from ABOVE, but the carnally empowered should be quite cautious of their words, for by those same words, they WILL BE JUDGED.

MISUSING THE *WORD*

The greatest misuse of the *WORD of* ***GOD,*** is when one improperly or recklessly quotes SCRIPTURE. This holds TRUE for any misuse of SCRIPTURE, whether it results from IGNORANCE, GREED, VANITY, or PERSONAL GAIN. There are MANY men that are self-ordained or have been ordained by other men, who feel they are qualified to preach the *WORD of* ***GOD.*** These people have either attended schools that proclaim to UNDERSTAND the *WORD of* ***GOD,*** or follow after the doctrine of the Church and are self-ordained by that doctrine believing they are suitable for ministry. These men call themselves Ministers, Pastors, Priests, and Reverends, but THE LORD calls them LIARS and FOOLS.

ALL those falling into this category are most certainly destined for HELL, for they CANNOT be forgiven of their SIN, because they have BLASPHEMED THE ***HOLY SPIRIT*** by their MISUSE of the *WORD of* ***GOD.*** This is a very serious offense, and by their TEACHING and PREACHING the FALSE WORD, they will most certainly LOSE their SOULS (if they have a SOUL). Without ANOINTING by ***HOLY SPIRIT BAPTISM,*** one can neither PREACH nor TEACH the *WORD of* ***GOD.*** THIS HAS ALWAYS BEEN AND SHALL ALWAYS BE ***SAITH THE LORD!***

GOD CHOOSES THEM WHO ARE TO PREACH, TEACH, AND SPEAK FOR ***HIM***. AND, THOSE WHO ***HE*** HAS NOT CHOSEN TO TEACH, PREACH, AND SPEAK FOR ***HIM***, KNOW WHO THEY ARE, ***SAITH THE LORD***. We are now at a time in the LIFE CYCLE of the world when the FALSE TEACHERS of the *WORD*, will be HELD ACCOUNTABLE for it, and will be brought to JUSTICE; for there are <u>MANY!</u>

Jeremiah 29:8 *For thus saith* ***THE LORD of HOSTS****, the* ***GOD*** *of*

ISRAEL; Let not your prophets and diviners, that be in the midst of you, DECEIVE YOU, neither hearken to your dreams which ye cause to be dreamed.

Jeremiah 29:9 *For they prophesy FALSELY unto YOU in MY NAME:* ***I HAVE NOT SENT THEM SAITH THE LORD.***

There are others who MISUSE their WORDS and will be held accountable as well. This pertains to those who use WORDS in a CORRUPTIVE and DESTRUCTIVE way. These are the people who maliciously and purposely use their WORDS to attack and destroy another person's character.

GOD gave man the ability to use WORDS so he could communicate with others in a POSITIVE and CONSTRUCTIVE manner. When a person misuses this gift of communication by deciding to attack another with destructive WORDS, he has VIOLATED the PURPOSE of the gift. We all have at times said things that we were sorry for later and had usually done so out of ANGER. By the use of destructive WORDS we are JUDGED; and OUR SOUL pays the price of JUDGMENT by FEELING GUILT.

ONE must learn first to think of what you are about to say, before saying it, and then relate to how they would FEEL if those same WORDS were being said to them. In a time when YOU feel the need to attack another with WORDS, pause for 30 seconds and think carefully about what is to be said, and then; if you still believe you should say it, proceed. This will give your SOUL enough time to react to what you are about to say, and almost always you will find after pausing for the 30-second period, you will WITHHOLD YOUR WORDS.

Many GOOD PEOPLE have destroyed their relationships with their FAMILIES and FRIENDS and those whom they LOVE, by their MISUSE of WORDS. I would even go so far as to say; if ONE would write down what was to be said, prior to them saying it, and then read it back to themselves, there would be fewer NEGATIVE WORDS SPOKEN! And, what was SPOKEN, would be WORDS of GREATER WISDOM.

WE will close this Chapter with three verses taken from KING SOLOMON'S PROVERBS. Hopefully YOU will SEE how they apply to the MESSAGE in this Chapter, titled: THE POWER of the ROD, for the ROD is the WORD!

Proverbs 17:27 *He that hath KNOWLEDGE spareth his WORDS: and a man of UNDERSTANDING is of an excellent SPIRIT.*

Proverbs 17:28 *Even a FOOL, when he holdeth his peace, is counted WISE: and he that shutteth his lips is esteemed a man of UNDERSTANDING.*

Proverbs 18: 7 *A FOOL'S MOUTH is his DESTRUCTION, and his lips are the snare of his SOUL.*

Chapter 2

GOD, our FIRST LOVE

Revelation 2:4 NEVERTHELESS I HAVE SOMEWHAT AGAINST THEE, BECAUSE THOU HAST LEFT THY <u>FIRST LOVE.</u>

This Scripture cited from the Book of Revelation is the WORDS of JESUS CHRIST given to the Apostle John, WARNING the CHURCH in Eph'-e-sus against their practice of putting JESUS before ***GOD,*** and serving HIM rather than ***GOD!*** If YOU READ Chapter 2, verses 1 through 5 of the Book of Revelation, you will SEE the MESSAGE is CLEAR. JESUS says in the Scriptures; the CHURCH in Eph'-e-sus, appeared to be doing everything right as HE had taught them, **<u>EXCEPT</u>** they were SERVING HIM rather than serving their ***FIRST LOVE, GOD!*** JESUS further WARNS; if they do not REPENT from doing so, HE was going to DISENFRANCHISE them from being HIS CHURCH!

In the PREVIOUS BOOK there was a Chapter dedicated to explaining who is ***GOD***, titled: "WHO is ***GOD?***" In that Chapter WE explained the DESCENDING FORM of ***GOD:*** by what the Apostles called the ***GODHEAD,*** and the more recent CHURCH refers to as ***THE TRINITY.*** It was told to you at that time, although ***GOD*** portrays ***HIMSELF*** as BEING THREE PERSONS; there is only ***ONE GOD.*** The following WORDS spoken by JESUS will CONFIRM THIS:

Mark 12:29 *And JESUS answered him,* ***THE FIRST OF ALL COMMANDMENTS IS, HEAR O ISRAEL; THE LORD OUR GOD IS ONE LORD:***

Mark 12:30 AND THOU SHALT LOVE THE LORD THY GOD WITH ALL THY HEART, AND WITH ALL THY SOUL, AND WITH ALL THY MIND, AND WITH ALL THY STRENGTH: THIS IS THE FIRST COMMANDMENT.

NOTE: JESUS CHRIST is the DESCENDED FORM of ***YESHUA (the 3rd DESCENDANT of GOD)***; whereas THE ***DELIVERER, THE 182 PERSON,*** is the DESCENDED FORM of ***IXOTE,*** THE ***HOLY SPIRIT (the 2nd DESCENDANT of GOD).***

JESUS CHRIST/***YESHUA***, sees HIS ***FATHER/IXOTE,*** who is THE ***HOLY SPIRIT of GOD,*** as being ***GOD;*** whereas THE ***HOLY SPIRIT of GOD*** SEES ***HIS FATHER, THE ALMIGHTY, WHO IS GOD, AS GOD.*** I know this must be a bit confusing to you, however this is the ASCENDING FORM of ***GOD.*** One must look at ***GOD*** as being the SOURCE of ALL LIFE. When ***GOD*** DESCENDS into ***IXOTE*** (THE ***HOLY SPIRIT***) ONE-THIRD of ***HIM*** REMAINS as ***GOD***, thus making ***IXOTE*** BEING TWO-THIRDS that of ***GOD*** and THIS IS THE FIRST DESCENDING FORM of ***GOD.***

When ***GOD*** FURTHER DESCENDS INTO ***YESHUA (The THIRD PERSON of the GODHEAD), HE*** LEAVES ONE-THIRD OF ***HIMSELF*** AS ***IXOTE,*** thus making ***YESHUA*** ONE-THIRD that of ***GOD.*** WHEN ***GOD*** FURTHER DESCENDS THROUGH ***YESHUA, HE*** again SUBDIVIDES ONE-THIRD OF ***HIMSELF*** BY FOUR, AND DESCENDS INTO THE FOUR SERAPHIM, with the SERAPHIM being CALLED "CHRIST" and being one-twelfth that of ***GOD.*** The DIVISION of ***GOD*** outside of the ***GODHEAD (TRINITY)*** however, is not an EQUAL DIVISION, but LINEARLY DIVIDES starting with THE ***DELIVERER.***

NOTE: WE will come back to this TOPIC later and explain this phenomenon in greater detail, further on in this BOOK.

This DIVISION into TWELFTHS explains why there are TWELVE TRIBES making up ISRAEL, for this REPRESENTS CHRIST. The FOUR SERAPHIM are CHRIST, therefor making each of them REPRESENT ONE-TWELFTH THAT OF ***GOD.*** This is also why there were TWELVE Disciples, with each DISCIPLE RECEIVING the ANOINTING of ONE-TWELFTH that of CHRIST. ALL DESCENDANTS of ***GOD*** below the LEVEL of the SERAPHIM ARE A DIVISION of TWELVE.

In HEAVEN, ***THE ALMIGHTY GOD*** only reveals ***HIMSELF*** to ***HIS SON, IXOTE; and IXOTE*** ONLY REVEALS ***HIMSELF*** TO HIS SON, ***YESHUA;*** WHO ONLY REVEALS HIMSELF TO HIS SON, CHRIST; and this is the DESCENDING ORDER of ***GOD.*** The DESCENDING of ***YESHUA*** into CHRIST is only done through ***YESHUA'S THIRD SON,*** the THIRD SERAPHIM, WHOSE NAME IS JESUS; THIS IS THE SERAPHIM HAVING THE FACE OF A MAN.

The aforementioned PROCESS REPRESENTS the DESCENDING FORM of ***GOD.*** This explains why JESUS CHRIST is man's ONLY ACCESS TO

GOD, for only through JESUS can ANYONE ASCEND to ***GOD.*** Even THE ***HOLY SPIRIT*** MUST ASCEND through JESUS CHRIST, the THIRD of the FOUR SONS of ***GOD.***

NOTE: The NUMBERING of the SONS of ***GOD*** REPRESENTS the ORDER in which they HAVE APPEARED on EARTH. The ORDER of their HIERARCHY in HEAVEN is REVERSED, thus making the FOURTH SERAPHIM, the FIRST DESCENDANT OUTSIDE of the ***GODHEAD (TRINITY).*** WE will further expand on this TOPIC later on in the BOOK.

> ***Revelation 4:7*** *And the first beast was like a LION, and the second beast like a CALF, and the THIRD BEAST had a face as a MAN, and the FOURTH BEAST was like a FLYING EAGLE.*

NOTE: The THIRD BEAST is the THIRD SERAPHIM, JESUS CHRIST. The reason HE is DESCRIBED in the Scripture as having the FACE of a MAN, is because it is HE who MAN must ASCEND or DESCEND through.

> ***Ezekiel 44:1*** *Then* ***HE*** *brought me back the way of the GATE of the outward SANCTUARY which looketh toward the EAST; and it was shut.*

> ***Ezekiel 44:2*** *Then said THE LORD unto me; THIS GATE SHALL BE SHUT, IT SHALL NOT BE OPENED, AND NO MAN SHALL ENTER IN BY IT; BECAUSE THE LORD, THE* ***GOD*** *OF ISRAEL, HATH ENTERED IN BY IT, THEREFORE IT SHALL BE SHUT.*

JUST as the sun rises from the EAST and sets in the WEST, so is it with ***GOD.*** One can only ASCEND to ***HIM*** through the EAST GATE, JESUS CHRIST, who is also referred to as the "MORNING STAR". EACH OF THE FOUR SONS of ***GOD*** (the FOUR SERAPHIM) represents a GATE. The 1st SERAPHIM, DAVID; represents the NORTH GATE, the 2nd SERAPHIM, SOLOMON; represents the SOUTH GATE, the 3rd SERAPHIM, JESUS; represents the EAST GATE, and the 4th SERAPHIM, ***THE DELIVERER;*** represents the WEST GATE. Only through the EAST GATE can ONE ENTER IN or EXIT the SANCTUARY of ***GOD*** (HEAVEN).

When ***GOD*** DESCENDS as the SAVIOR (JESUS), ***HE*** DESCENDS only as ***YESHUA*** and into the THIRD SERAPHIM, JESUS CHRIST, and ***GOD*** has already done this. HOWEVER, when ***GOD*** DESCENDS as the ***DELIVERER,*** BOTH ***IXOTE*** and ***YESHUA*** DESCEND THROUGH JESUS CHRIST AND

ENTER INTO THE FOURTH SERAPHIM, WHO IS SYMBOLIZED AS BEING THE FLYING EAGLE AND ALSO AS THE WEST GATE. This EVENT has not happened yet; and this is why only the WEST WALL still STANDS this day in JERUSALEM; for it will remain standing until after the COMING of THE ***DELIVERER.***[1]

> ***John 1:6*** *There was a man sent from* ***GOD,*** *whose name was John.*

> ***John 1:7*** *The same came for a WITNESS, to bear WITNESS of the LIGHT, that all men through HIM might BELIEVE.*

The STAR of DAVID

Although somewhat unrelated to this Chapter's main topic, WE would like to share with you the relationship of the "Star of David" and its DIVINE SYMBOLIC significance to the HEAVENLY REALM:

As explained in the PREVIOUS BOOK, each of the FOUR SERAPHIM represents a KING in HEAVEN, with each KING REIGNING over ONE of the FOUR KINGDOMS (CHRIST) making up the KINGDOM of ***GOD***. The NORTH KINGDOM is that of DAVID'S and the SOUTH KINGDOM that of SOLOMON'S. In HEAVEN, each KINGDOM is in the shape of a PYRAMID, and when the FOUR PYRAMIDS come together at their tips they form a CUBE, called HEAVEN, or NEW JERUSALEM.

The PYRAMID pointing towards the NORTH symbolizes the KINGDOM of the NORTH, whereas the PYRAMID pointing towards the SOUTH symbolizes the KINGDOM of the SOUTH. If one could visualize the KINGDOM of the SOUTH coming through the KINGDOM of the NORTH (because on earth, SOLOMON came through DAVID), they would then pictorially see the "Star of David". To further clarify this, when the PYRAMIDS of the NORTH and SOUTH KINGDOMS are shown pictorially, (as being drawn on paper), the two

---

[1] To help you to UNDERSTAND the DESCENDING FORM of ***GOD,*** WE will express this phenomenon in a visualized form. If you could VISUALIZE ***GOD*** as being a LIGHT SOURCE, such as the sun, and JESUS CHRIST as being the LIGHT emitted from the sun, you can see why JESUS had said HE is the LIGHT of the world. Furthermore, when one RECEIVES the LIGHT coming from the sun, they then feel the HEAT being generated by the LIGHT. This is the RECEIVING of THE ***HOLY SPIRIT*** (the heat) by way of the LIGHT. So in either the case of the LIGHT, or the HEAT from the LIGHT, neither of them could exist without the SOURCE of the LIGHT, ***GOD.*** The WORD "LIGHT" when used in the Scriptures, means; LIFE, TRUTH, and SERENITY (PEACE).

pyramids will appear as two 60 degree equal lateral triangles, with their bases opposite each other and their tips pointing one towards the other. Then by sliding the triangle pointing SOUTH, through the triangle pointing NORTH (because SOLOMON came through DAVID), the two KINGDOMS would then form the "Star of David".

GOD and MAN'S INTIMATE RELATIONSHIP

GOD expects YOUR RELATIONSHIP with ***HIM*** to be an individual ONE. Although we may WORSHIP THE LORD as a GROUP, when the GROUP disburses, ***GOD*** does not remain at the gathering place but rather leaves with each PERSON INDIVIDUALLY. This is why JESUS CHRIST referred to HIS BODY as being the TEMPLE of ***GOD;*** for HE knew ***GOD*** was in HIM. This is a PERSON'S ONENESS with ***GOD*** called, "IMMANUEL".

> ***John 17:22 AND THE GLORY WHICH THOU GAVEST ME I HAVE GIVEN THEM; THAT THEY MAY BE ONE, EVEN AS WE ARE ONE:***
>
> ***John 17:23 I IN THEM, AND THOU IN ME, THAT THEY MAY BE MADE PERFECT IN ONE; AND THAT THE WORLD MAY KNOW THAT THOU HAST SENT ME, AND HAST LOVED THEM, AS THOU HAST LOVED ME.***
>
> ***John 17:24 FATHER, I WILL THAT THEY ALSO, WHOM THOU HAST GIVEN ME, BE WITH ME WHERE I AM; THAT THEY MAY BEHOLD MY GLORY, WHICH THOU HAST GIVEN ME: FOR THOU LOVEST ME BEFORE THE FOUNDATION OF THE WORLD.***
>
> ***John 17:25 O RIGHTEOUS FATHER, THE WORLD HATH NOT KNOWN THEE: BUT I HAVE KNOWN THEE, AND THESE HAVE KNOWN THAT THOU HAST SENT ME.***
>
> ***John 17:26 AND I HAVE DECLARED UNTO THEM THY NAME, AND WILL DECLARE IT: THAT THE LOVE WHEREWITH THOU HAST LOVED ME MAY BE IN THEM, AND I IN THEM.***

The last five Scriptures taken from the GOSPEL of John, represent the CONCLUSION of JESUS CHRIST'S FINAL PRAYER and the FULFILLMENT of HIS MISSION here on earth. The Scripture says, that through HIM, ALL BELIEVING HIM TO BE THE SON of ***GOD***, CAN BE AS ONE WITH ***GOD,*** AS HE IS AS ONE IN ***GOD.*** Let US breakdown the SCRIPTURES for you and REVEAL THE MESSAGE IN THEM.

In the first cited Scripture, John 17:22 (and also the two prior Scriptures 17:20 & 17:21 not cited), JESUS is requesting that ***GOD*** EMPOWER HIS DISCIPLES (by ***HOLY SPIRIT*** BAPTISM) so they might RECEIVE HIS ANOINTING and CARRY FORWARD the *WORD of* ***GOD*** throughout the world. And, they did this by their WRITING the FOUR GOSPELS. The GLORY GIVEN to JESUS (mentioned in the Scripture), represents HIS RECEIPT of ***HOLY SPIRIT*** BAPTISM, WHICH JESUS will continue to PASS ALONG TO ANYONE BELIEVING IN HIM, PROVIDING ***THE FATHER*** HAS DIRECTED THEM to HIM.

NOTE: The CHURCH teaches that anyone at anytime of their own choosing can be SAVED, and this is one of the GREATEST DISCREPANCIES being taught by the CHURCH today. ONLY ***GOD*** can CHOOSE who will be SAVED or who should be DAMNED, for this is ***GOD'S CHOICE AND NOT MAN'S SAITH THE LORD!***

> ***John 6:44 NO MAN CAN COME TO ME, EXCEPT THE FATHER WHICH HATH SENT ME DRAW HIM: AND I WILL RAISE HIM UP AT THE LAST DAY.***

> ***John 6:65*** *And HE said,* ***THEREFORE SAID I UNTO YOU, THAT NO MAN CAN COME UNTO ME, EXCEPT IT WERE GIVEN UNTO HIM OF MY FATHER.***

ONCE those being sent to JESUS by ***GOD*** RECEIVE their ***HOLY SPIRIT*** BAPTISM, they will then be as ONE with ***GOD*** as JESUS CHRIST is as ONE IN ***GOD.*** This represents the INDIVIDUAL RELATIONSHIP ONE WILL HAVE WITH ***GOD (IMMANUEL),*** through ***HOLY SPIRIT*** BAPTISM, GIVEN TO THEM BY JESUS CHRIST, THE SON of ***GOD.*** This is the PROMISE of the ***FATHER,*** a ***FATHER and SON*** RELATIONSHIP with the SAVED.

In John 17:23 and 17:24, JESUS STATES in the Scripture: ALL who RECEIVE SPIRITUAL BAPTISM and REBIRTH in CHRIST, will ENJOY a PERFECT LOVING RELATIONSHIP with ***GOD*** and with HIM, and WILL be with JESUS in HEAVEN and see the LAMB of ***GOD*** RECEIVE HIS GLORIFICATION BY ***GOD.***

> ***Revelation 5:11*** *And I beheld, and heard a voice of many Angels round about THE THRONE and the BEASTS and the Elders: and the number of them was ten thousand times ten thousand, and thousands of thousands.*

> ***Revelation 5:12*** *Saying with a LOUD VOICE, WORTHY IS THE LAMB that was SLAIN to RECEIVE POWER, and RICHES, and WISDOM, and STRENGTH, and HONOUR, and GLORY, and BLESSING.*

JESUS also says in the Scripture (John 17:24), HIS RELATIONSHIP with ***GOD*** was before the CREATION of the world, and JESUS states this because HE PROVIDED the LIGHT for the WORLD to EXIST and the LIGHT for ALL of ***GOD'S CREATION.*** The FIRST WORDS SPOKEN BY ***GOD*** WAS; LET THERE BE LIGHT; and JESUS CHRIST IS THAT LIGHT.

> ***Revelation 3:14 AND UNTO THE ANGEL OF THE CHURCH OF THE LA-OD-I-CE'-ANS WRITE; THESE THINGS SAITH THE A-MEN', THE FAITHFUL AND TRUE WITNESS, THE BEGINNING OF THE CREATION OF GOD;***

The next two Scriptures John 17:25 and 17:26 state, that it wasn't until after JESUS had been crucified and RESURRECTED that those being SAVED by HIS BLOOD could have a PERSONAL RELATIONSHIP with ***GOD,*** for before that time, NO ONE could be SAVED! However, from that point forward in time; ANYONE BELIEVING JESUS CHRIST CAME OUT FROM ***GOD*** (***GOD*** in the DESCENDING FORM), could RECEIVE ***HOLY SPIRIT*** BAPTISM, a LOVING RELATIONSHIP WITH ***GOD,*** and ETERNITY. IF ***GOD*** SO WILLED it to BE.

The underlying MESSAGE in these SCRIPTURES is that the ***HOLY SPIRIT BAPTISM*** that ONE RECEIVES, is GIVEN TO THEM BY JESUS CHRIST; and no one other than HE can OFFER this BAPTISM.

As previously discussed, JESUS CHRIST never performed any water baptism. As a matter of fact, JESUS never performed baptism of any type while on the earth. It wasn't UNTIL AFTER HIS RESURRECTION that HE COULD FULFILL THE PROPHECY GIVEN BY JOHN the BAPTIST, and the PROM-

ISE of ***THE FATHER,*** BAPTIZING WITH THE ***HOLY SPIRIT of GOD.***

> ***John 1:33 And I knew HIM not: but HE that sent me to baptize with water, the SAME said unto me, Upon whom thou shalt see THE SPIRIT DESCENDING, and remaining on HIM, the same is HE which BAPTIZETH with THE HOLY GHOST.***

This brings us now back to the main topic of discussion for this Chapter, called "***GOD, our FIRST LOVE".*** Throughout the GOSPELS, JESUS CHRIST sets the PERFECT EXAMPLE of MAN'S RELATIONSHIP with ***GOD.*** JESUS never says even once in the GOSPELS to WORSHIP HIM, but rather taught ALL FOLLOWING HIM to WORSHIP ONLY ***GOD*** and to BELIEVE HE had come out from ***GOD.***

Although ***GOD HIMSELF*** is not OFFENDED by them choosing to WORSHIP JESUS rather than ***HIM,*** JESUS CHRIST FORBIDS IT! This is why JESUS, in the opening Scripture in this Chapter taken from the Book of Revelation, WARNS the CHURCH against WORSHIPPING HIM rather than ***GOD.***

Through the twisted and false teaching by the Church, many have been taught to WORSHIP JESUS rather than ***GOD,*** however JESUS NEVER TAUGHT THIS! This is why JESUS SAID: HEAR, O ISRAEL; THE LORD **OUR *GOD*** IS ONE LORD: (Mark 12:29). IF JESUS CHRIST HAD PROCLAIMED HIMSELF TO BE GOD, HE WOULD HAVE RATHER SAID, "THE LORD **YOUR *GOD*** IS ONE LORD", rather than saying both HE and YOU WORSHIP the SAME ***GOD.*** JESUS CHRIST is THE SON of ***GOD,*** and you are NOT to WORSHIP the SON, but rather ***THE FATHER.***

JESUS was sent to earth THE FIRST TIME, to be the PERFECT EXAMPLE of MAN, and not to be YOUR GOD. However, as explained in the PREVIOUS BOOK, during the MILLENNIUM, JESUS CHRIST will be YOUR KING, and YOUR GOD, for at that TIME ***GOD*** will REVEAL ***HIMSELF*** THROUGH JESUS CHRIST, and that will be the TIME of JESUS' GLORIFICATION. After JESUS' GLORIFICATION, YOU CAN THEN REFER TO HIM AS GOD and NOT BEFORE, ***SAITH THE LORD.***

JESUS CHRIST IS THE SON of ***GOD*** and not ***GOD.*** When the Pharisees proclaimed CHRIST to be the son of DAVID, rather than the SON of ***GOD,*** JESUS made reference to the 110th Psalm. HE TOLD those who believed DAVID to be the father of CHRIST, that DAVID in the Scripture refers to CHRIST as being his Lord, and if DAVID were the FATHER of CHRIST, he surely would not refer to HIM as Lord.

> ***Psalm 110:1*** *THE LORD said unto my Lord, Sit thou at MY RIGHT HAND, until I make thine enemies thy footstool.*

The Psalm also indicates at what time JESUS takes possession of THE THRONE (HIS GLORIFICATION). The Scripture says it occurs after HIS enemies have been brought before HIM to KNEEL in HIS PRESENCE (thus making them HIS footstool), and that OCCURS at the BEGINNING of the MILLENNIUM. JESUS also SAID, YOU could not SERVE TWO MASTERS, because while you were SERVING the ONE, you would HATE the OTHER, and if you were serving HIM now, you could not SERVE both HE and ***GOD.***

> ***Matthew 6:24 NO MAN CAN SERVE TWO MASTERS: FOR EITHER HE WILL HATE THE ONE, AND LOVE THE OTHER; OR ELSE HE WILL HOLD TO THE ONE, AND DESPISE THE OTHER. YE CANNOT SERVE GOD AND MAMMON.***

The MAMMON referred to in the Scriptures is CARNAL LIFE, however it also applies to SERVING more than ONE ***GOD***. During the period when HEAVEN comes to earth (the MILLENNIUM), ***GOD*** will come in the FORM of a MAN. That MAN will be JESUS CHRIST, and HE WILL REIGN ON EARTH FOR ONE THOUSAND YEARS, and DURING THAT PERIOD OF TIME, JESUS WILL BE GOD on EARTH. ***HOWEVER, IN HEAVEN, JESUS CHRIST IS ONE OF FOUR REIGNING KINGS; AND THERE IT IS THE HOLY SPIRIT WHO WILL BE SERVED AND BE YOUR GOD, FOR ONLY HE CAN BE CALLED GOD IN HEAVEN!***

> ***Revelation 20:4*** *And I saw Thrones, and they sat upon them, and JUDGMENT was given unto THEM: and I saw the SOULS of them that were beheaded for the witness of JESUS, and for the WORD of* ***GOD,*** *and which had not worshipped the beast, neither his image, neither had received his Mark upon their foreheads, or in their hands; and they lived and REIGNED with CHRIST a THOUSAND YEARS.*

Throughout time man has been insistent on SERVING another man rather than ***GOD.*** This is why ***GOD*** DESCENDS down in a SINGULAR FORM into the THIRD SERAPHIM, JESUS CHRIST while on EARTH. During the time when there is HEAVEN on EARTH in the MILLENNIUM, CHRIST WILL BE

GOD, however, in HEAVEN, THE ***HOLY SPIRIT WILL BE GOD FOR ONLY THE HOLY SPIRIT CAN SERVE GOD! A'-MEN.***

Man's RELATIONSHIP with ***GOD*** can only come by way of THE ***HOLY SPIRIT,*** and ONE can only RECEIVE THE ***HOLY SPIRIT*** by JESUS CHRIST BAPTIZING them in THE ***HOLY SPIRIT.*** HOWEVER, JESUS CHRIST will only PERFORM BAPTISMS on THEM WHO WORSHIP ONLY ***GOD, FOR GOD IS YOUR FIRST LOVE!***[2]

[2] THE LORD has asked ME to clear up some CONFUSION in regard to the differences between LOVE and WORSHIP. Although LOVE is the STRONGEST form of WORSHIP, there is a difference between the TWO. YOU can most certainly LOVE, CHERISH, and ADORE another such as JESUS CHRIST, a SPOUSE, BROTHER or SISTER, and FRIENDS, without WORSHIPPING them. While LOVE is a METHOD of WORSHIP, it in itself is not WORSHIP. WORSHIP in the BIBLICAL SENSE is the GLORIFICATION of ***GOD*** without DIVISION in it, which is different than LOVE, which can be SHARED with others. This is to say; a PERSON can LOVE many OTHERS while THEY still WORSHIP ONLY ***GOD***. One can WORSHIP ***GOD*** out of LOVE, or ONE can WORSHIP ***GOD*** out of FEAR, whereas ONE **cannot** be made to LOVE out of FEAR. This is the difference between LOVE and WORSHIP, for ***GOD*** can make YOU WORSHIP ***HIM*** whether YOU LOVE ***HIM*** or NOT, but ***HE*** will not make YOU LOVE ***HIM!***

Chapter 3
RECEIVING the WORD (JESUS CHRIST)

John 1:1 *In the BEGINNING was the WORD, and the WORD was with* ***GOD,*** *and the WORD was* ***GOD.***

Genesis 1:3 *And* ***GOD*** *SAID,* ***LET THERE BE LIGHT:*** *and there was LIGHT.*

John 1:14 *And the WORD was made FLESH, and dwelt among us, (and we beheld HIS GLORY, the GLORY as of the only begotten of* ***THE FATHER,****) full of GRACE and TRUTH.*

The opening three Scriptures go HAND in HAND for all three REPRESENT the COMING of the Lord JESUS CHRIST to the earth, for HE is the LIGHT of the WORLD, and the *WORD of* ***GOD.*** The first Scripture, John 1:1, tells you the *WORD of* ***GOD*** in the BEGINNING was with ***GOD,*** and then ONCE ***HE*** had SPOKEN the WORD, "LIGHT", the LIGHT became the BEGINNING of CREATION; for ALL THINGS came from that LIGHT! The LAST cited Scripture, John 1:14, tells YOU the FIRST WORD, "LIGHT" was then made into FLESH, and the FLESH was GIVEN a NAME, JESUS CHRIST being the only begotten of ***THE FATHER.***

GOD did not say "LET THERE BE LIGHTS" as in a plural sense, but ***HE*** RATHER SAID, ***"LET THERE BE LIGHT"*** in the SINGULAR FORM, thus making THAT LIGHT the ONLY BEGOTTEN of ***THE FATHER.*** The LIGHT spoken of in the SCRIPTURES refers to the *WORD of* ***GOD,*** for from the LIGHT came forth ALL TRUTH and ALL LIFE.

On several occasions I have been asked, "WHAT IS THE BEST WAY TO START A RELATIONSHIP WITH ***GOD***"? After CONFRONTING THE LORD on the matter, I was TOLD; THE RELATIONSHIP BEGINS WITH THE *WORD of* ***GOD.*** What this means, is before ONE can HAVE an INTIMATE

RELATIONSHIP with ANYONE THEY MUST FIRST COME TO KNOW THE PERSON whom they seek to have the RELATIONSHIP. Furthermore, if THAT PERSON is ***GOD,*** they can only come to KNOW ***HIM*** THROUGH ***HIS*** *WORD*, JESUS CHRIST (THE LIGHT) and the HOLY BIBLE, for to know ***HIM*** is to LOVE ***HIM***.

As explained in the PREVIOUS BOOK, the HOLY BIBLE CONSISTS of the 39 Books in the OLD TESTAMENT, the 4 GOSPELS of JESUS CHRIST, and the Book of the REVELATION of JESUS CHRIST and THIS IS THE ENTIRE HOLY BIBLE ***SAITH THE LORD!*** The 22 Epistles added to the HOLY BIBLE by the Church, are NOT the *WORD of* ***GOD*** but rather the words of men. The Epistles being CONFUSING and CONTRADICTORY has caused a division in the Church (Denominations), and has put Lucifer at the HELM of the SHIP that has no sail.

The various Denominations in the CHRISTIAN CHURCH are a DIRECT result of the Church's TAMPERING with the *WORD of* ***GOD,*** by them believing they could add to it! The Epistles written by the Apostles are letters, not BOOKS, and were directed to specific Churches within the Christian Faith, and not to the WORLD as a whole. Whereas the HOLY BIBLE is DIRECTED to ALL ***GOD'S CHILDREN,*** the Epistles were directed to only a small group of people, and the Apostles never intended for them to be added to the HOLY SCRIPTURES. Unlike the HOLY BIBLE that was ALWAYS INTENDED to be TRANSLATED into the ENGLISH LANGUAGE, the Epistles when translated into English are MISLEADING, CONFUSING, CONTRADICTORY, and REEK of RELIGION.

WHEN the Church added the Epistles to the Canon containing the HOLY BIBLE AND CALLED IT "The Holy Bible", they BLASPHEMED BOTH THE ***HOLY SPIRIT of GOD*** and JESUS CHRIST. JESUS CHRIST is the *WORD of* ***GOD*** and only HIS GOSPELS and REVELATION make up the NEW TESTAMENT: FOR THEY REPRESENT THE WORDS SPOKEN BY JESUS. JESUS in the following Scripture PORTRAYS what was to HAPPEN to the *WORD of* ***GOD.*** When JESUS had asked for WATER to drink, they gave HIM VINEGAR instead of WATER. This represents the CORRUPTION of the *WORD of* ***GOD*** by the Church.

> ***John 19:30*** *When JESUS therefore had received the vinegar, HE SAID,* ***IT IS FINISHED:*** *and HE bowed HIS head, and gave up the GHOST.*

JESUS, being the NEW TESTAMENT, stated prior to HIS DEATH that HE

HAD COMPLETED the *WORD of **GOD*** (by saying, "IT IS FINISHED"). Therefor, anything added to the HOLY BIBLE aside from HIS FOUR GOSPELS and HIS Book of Revelation, CONFLICTS with HIS FINAL WORDS, "IT IS FINISHED"! By the Church's adding the Epistles to the Canon and calling it the Holy Bible, they are saying JESUS is a LIAR, the WORD of ***GOD*** is not finished!

FURTHERMORE, BECAUSE THE ***HOLY SPIRIT*** MANDATES the *WORD of **GOD,*** anyone INVOLVED with the inclusion of the Epistles to the HOLY BIBLE had BLASPHEMED THE ***HOLY SPIRIT.*** ANYONE who either TAMPERS WITH, ALTERS, CHANGES, ADDS TO or SUBTRACTS FROM the *WORD of **GOD*** is DESTINED for ETERNAL DAMNATION ***SAITH THE LORD!***

The Apostles who wrote the Epistles committed no SIN, for their intentions were GOOD and they meant only to help the Churches where the Epistles were directed. However, those who to took it upon themselves to make the Epistles part of the HOLY BIBLE, committed the UNFORGIVABLE SIN. This is not to say that ***GOD*** never intended for the Epistles to be included into the Canon, for if that were so, they would have never been added. ***GOD*** allows STUMBLING BLOCKS to occur throughout LIFE, and the Epistles are certainly STUMBLING BLOCKS! ***HE*** SAYS; YOU MUST DILIGENTLY SEARCH OUT THE TRUTH, and the TRUTH comes only by way of ***HOLY SPIRIT*** BAPTISM, and those LACKING in BAPTISM will see the Epistles as truth.

Man continues to TAMPER with the *WORD of **GOD,*** even as I write; believing in his WICKED HEART that he can improve on it! ***GOD*** ANOINTED only King James to TRANSLATE the *WORD of **GOD*** into the ENGLISH LANGUAGE. However the Church continues to try to RE-TRANSLATE the BIBLE over and over again. It was ***GOD*** by way of THE ***HOLY SPIRIT,*** who DIRECTED King James in the HEBREW, GREEK, and LATIN MANUSCRIPTS TRANSLATION, as it appears in the 1611 VERSION of the HOLY BIBLE. This was not the work of the Church ***SAITH THE LORD***, but the WORK of ***MY HOLY SPRIT.*** Therefor I ask; WHO has given the Church the AUTHORITY to CHANGE the *WORD of **GOD?***

> ***Amos 8:11*** *Behold, the days come, saith THE LORD **GOD,** that I will send a famine in the land, not a famine of bread, nor a thirst of water, but of the hearing of the WORDS of THE LORD:*

> ***Amos 8:12*** *And they shall wander from sea to sea, and from the north even to the east, they shall run to and fro to SEEK the*

WORD of THE LORD, and shall not find it.

These Scriptures given by the Prophet Amos WARN of the changing of the *WORD of **GOD*** to the point where it no longer EXISTS. Lucifer's influence on the Church continues to grow by him driving its members to continually change the *WORD of **GOD*** to the POINT OF EXTINCTION. With man's only connection to ***GOD*** being the HOLY BIBLE, THESE NEWER BIBLE TRANSLATIONS and the TAMPERING with the *WORD of **GOD*** HAVE BECOME MAN'S GATEWAY TO HELL, RATHER THAN MAN'S LADDER TO HEAVEN.

NOTE: I STRONGLY RECOMMEND to those of you owning a BIBLE TRANSLATION other than the King James 1611 VERSION, to THROW IT OUT, and get a REAL BIBLE to READ, for the new translations are the work of the Devil!

SPIRITUAL NOURISHMENT

The *WORD of **GOD*** is FOOD to the SOUL and NOURISHMENT for the SPIRIT. This is the MANNA (BREAD) from HEAVEN spoken about by JESUS.

> ***John 6:45 IT IS WRITTEN IN THE PROPHETS, "AND THEY SHALL BE ALL TAUGHT OF GOD". EVERY MAN THEREFORE THAT HATH HEARD, AND HATH LEARNED OF THE FATHER, COMETH UNTO ME.***

In this Scripture JESUS states that every PERSON MUST learn about ***GOD,*** and because JESUS CHRIST is the *WORD of **GOD*** (the HOLY BIBLE), ALL MUST COME TO HIM for the LEARNING.

> ***John 6:46 NOT THAT ANY MAN HATH SEEN THE FATHER, SAVE HE WHICH IS OF GOD, HE HATH SEEN THE FATHER.***

This verifies that which YOU have been told PREVIOUSLY, ONLY ***YESHUA*** can SEE the FACE of ***IXOTE*** (THE ***HOLY SPIRIT),*** and only ***IXOTE*** can look upon THE ***FACE of GOD,*** because ***YESHUA*** and THE ***HOLY SPIRIT*** are of ***GOD.*** FURTHERMORE, ***YESHUA*** can only be SEEN through the EYES of CHRIST, and ONLY THROUGH CHRIST CAN ***GOD*** be AC-

CESSED. Therefor only CHRIST can ACCESS ***GOD,*** and CHRIST is the FOUR SERAPHIM, the BRIDE, and them of the SEVENTH LEVEL or of the HIGHER ORDER in HEAVEN (refer to the PREVIOUS BOOK for further details).

> ***John 6:47 VERILY, VERILY, I SAY UNTO YOU, HE THAT BELIEVETH ON ME HATH EVERLASTING LIFE.***

JESUS is referring to HIMSELF as being the *WORD of* ***GOD*** and is saying, ALL who BELIEVE in the *WORD of* ***GOD*** will never perish and will RECEIVE ETERNITY.

> ***John 6:48 I AM THE BREAD OF LIFE.***

JESUS AGAIN CONFIRMS THAT HE IS THE *WORD of* ***GOD,*** for the *WORD of* ***GOD*** is the BREAD of LIFE.

> ***John 6:49 YOUR FATHERS DID EAT MAN'-NA IN THE WILDERNESS, AND ARE DEAD.***

The MANNA given to the Children of ISRAEL while they wandered in the wilderness, is not the SAME MANNA JESUS is talking about, the MANNA they ate only provided food for their physical bodies.

> ***John 6:50 THIS IS THE BREAD WHICH COMETH DOWN FROM HEAVEN, THAT A MAN MAY EAT THEREOF, AND NOT DIE.***

JESUS is saying, the BREAD HE is speaking about (THE *WORD of* ***GOD***) has come down from HEAVEN for man to EAT, and this BREAD FEEDS the SPIRIT so it may LIVE throughout ETERNITY.

> ***John 6:51 I AM THE LIVING BREAD WHICH CAME DOWN FROM HEAVEN: IF ANY MAN EAT OF THIS BREAD, HE SHALL LIVE FOREVER: AND THE BREAD THAT I WILL GIVE IS MY FLESH, WHICH I WILL GIVE FOR THE LIFE OF THE WORLD.***

JESUS states in this last Scripture that HE is the *WORD of* ***GOD,*** that has come down from HEAVEN and was made into FLESH. ***John 1:14*** *And the WORD was made FLESH, and dwelt among us, (and we beheld HIS GLORY, the GLORY as of the only begotten of* ***THE FATHER,****) full of GRACE and TRUTH.*

HE also is speaking about HIS PENDING CRUCIFIXION and how HE MUST GIVE HIS LIFE (in the FLESH) for the WORLD, and by HIM GIVING HIS LIFE by the GRACE of ***GOD,*** the WORLD may be SAVED![1]

> ***Isaiah 53:5*** *But HE was wounded for our transgressions, HE was bruised for our iniquities: the chastisement of our peace was upon HIM; and with HIS stripes we are HEALED.*
>
> ***Isaiah 53:6*** *All we like sheep have gone astray; we have turned every one to his own way; and THE LORD hath laid on HIM the iniquity of us all.*
>
> ***Isaiah 53:7*** *HE was oppressed, and HE was afflicted, yet HE opened not HIS mouth: HE is brought as a* ***LAMB*** *to the slaughter, and as a sheep before her shearers is dumb, so HE openeth not HIS mouth.*
>
> ***Isaiah 53:8*** *HE was taken from prison and from judgment: and who shall declare HIS generation? For HE was cut off out of the land of the living: for the transgression of my people was HE stricken.*
>
> ***Isaiah 53:9*** *And HE made HIS grave with the wicked, and with the rich in HIS DEATH; because HE had done no violence, neither was any deceit in HIS mouth.*
>
> ***Isaiah 53:10*** *Yet it pleased THE LORD to bruise HIM;* ***HE*** *hath*

---

[1] By JESUS' dying on the CROSS in the most horrible manner (crucifixion), the IMPACT it had on them who had WITNESSED IT were so INSPIRED, they carried forth HIS MESSAGE from ***GOD*** to the WORLD. JESUS gave the MESSAGE in HIS WORDS to them who had FOLLOWED HIM, and those WORDS were WRITTEN into the GOSPELS some SEVENTY YEARS after his RESURRECTION. If JESUS would have lived out HIS YEARS on earth continuing to PREACH, rather than dying on the CROSS, ***GOD'S*** MESSAGE would have been LOST! JESUS CHRIST fulfilled the PROPHECY given by the PROPHETS about HIM, and GAVE THE ***MESSAGE GOD HAD GIVEN TO HIM FOR THE WORLD.***

*put HIM to grief: when thou shalt make HIS SOUL an OFFERING for SIN, **HE** shall see HIS seed, **HE** shall prolong HIS DAYS, and the pleasure of THE LORD shall prosper in HIS HAND.*

***Isaiah 53:11 HE** shall SEE of the travail of **HIS SOUL,** and shall be satisfied: by HIS KNOWLEDGE shall **MY** RIGHTEOUS SERVANT justify many; for HE shall bear their iniquities.*

***Isaiah 53:12** Therefore will **I** divide HIM a portion with the **GREAT,** and HE shall divide the spoil with the STRONG; because HE hath poured out HIS SOUL unto DEATH: and HE was numbered with the transgressors; and HE bare the SIN of MANY, and made INTERCESSION for the transgressors.*

The *WORD of **GOD*** was sent to the earth in the FORM of a MAN, and still remains on earth in the FORM of a BOOK, and the BOOK is called the HOLY BIBLE. ***A-MEN'.***

Being in COVENANT

The last Scriptures cited, taken from the Book of Isaiah, foretells of ***GOD'S DIVINE PLAN*** for the world. ***GOD*** made a COVENANT with the Children of ISRAEL and the COVENANT required the people to live in accordance with ***GOD'S LAWS. GOD*** GAVE the LAWS to MOSES (THE DELIVERER), and MOSES put them on parchments in WRITING for the PEOPLE to READ and follow, but the people refused to obey ***GOD'S LAWS.*** So ***GOD*** BROKE ***HIS OLD COVENANT*** and MADE a ***NEW COVENANT,*** a COVENANT being GOVERNED by ***FAITH*** rather than by LAW, and ***HIS NEW COVENANT*** applies to ALL people and not only the Children of ISRAEL.

The FAITH NEEDED for the ***NEW COVENANT*** would come NOW by way of a SAVIOR, and not by the HAND of the DELIVERER as the LAW had come. HOWEVER, it would still be the ***DELIVERER*** who would bring the FAITH NEEDED to FULFILL the ***NEW COVENANT,*** but the ***DELIVERER*** could only go to them ***HE*** had been DIRECTED to by the SAVIOR.

Although at times ***GOD*** may repent ***HIMSELF*** for what ***HE*** has done, ***HE*** NEVER CHANGES ***HIS*** MIND about what ***HE*** has done. This is because ***GOD*** is "ALL KNOWING" and CANNOT make mistakes. Although ***GOD*** BROKE the OLD COVENANT, the LAW GIVEN in it still REMAINS, for the LAW GIVEN was ETERNAL LAW. Therefor the NEW COVENANT could not VIOLATE the LAW of the OLD COVENANT and had to be established within the FRAMEWORK of the LAWS given to MOSES.

The OLD COVENANT required a BLOOD SACRIFICE for the FORGIVENESS of SIN, so the NEW COVENANT HAS TO also ABIDE BY THE LAW of the BLOOD SACRIFICE. The NEW COVENANT allows a DIRECT access to ***GOD*** whereas only the PRIESTS had access to ***HIM*** in the OLD COVENANT. Therefor PARTAKERS in the NEW COVENANT MUST ABIDE by the SAME RULES given to the PRIESTS regarding their cleanliness in the PRESENCE of ***THE LORD.***

However, the OLD COVENANT was a CARNAL COVENANT whereas the NEW COVENANT is a SPIRITUAL COVENANT, thus making the CLEANLINESS REQUIREMENT apply to the SPIRIT rather than to the FLESH. Therefor, ALL in the NEW COVENANT MUST undergo a SPIRITUAL CLEANSING prior them coming behind THE VEIL and being in the PRESENCE of ***GOD.***

NOTE: You will SEE as WE go forward in this Chapter how the LAWS still apply, however they now apply to the SPIRITUAL MAN rather than to the carnal man as they did in the OLD COVENANT.

There are THREE SET CONDITIONS that MUST be met for ONE to be a PARTAKER in the NEW COVENANT without VIOLATING ***GOD'S LAWS*** of the OLD COVENANT.

- 1st CONDITION: There must be the REMISSION of SIN by REPENTANCE, for ***GOD*** will not look upon SIN.

- 2nd CONDITION: There must be a BLOOD SACRIFICE made for the FORGIVENESS of the REMITTED SIN, and due to the FORGIVENESS being an ETERNAL FORGIVENESS, the SACRIFICE has to be an ETERNAL SACRIFICE.

- FINAL CONDITION: There must be an ETERNAL CLEANSING by way of SPIRITUAL BAPTISM, for them REQUIRING ACCESS to ***GOD.***

Once these three CONDITIONS have been met, REBIRTH of the SPIRIT will take place and with the REBIRTH comes ***FAITH.*** ALL THREE of these CONDITIONS interrelate to JESUS CHRIST, for neither FORGIVENESS nor BAPTISM can be RECEIVED without the ETERNAL SACRIFICE, the BLOOD of the LAMB, JESUS CHRIST.

In summary: Once a person has REPENTED of their SINS to ***GOD,*** and ***GOD*** ACCEPTS their REPENTANCE, ***HE*** will then SEND JESUS CHRIST to that PERSON to BE their ETERNAL BLOOD SACRIFICE. Furthermore, because the SACRIFICE is an ETERNAL SACRIFICE it has been already ACCEPTED by ***GOD,*** so SPIRITUAL CLEANSING (BAPTISM) WILL IMMEDIATELY TAKE PLACE. NOW, BEING IN COVENANT with ***GOD*** through JESUS CHRIST, THE ***HOLY SPIRIT*** will COME TO THAT INDIVIDUAL, AND GIVE THEM THEIR NEEDED FAITH AND GUIDANCE ENSURING THEY REMAIN IN COVENANT.

This by no means implies that just because a PERSON REPENTS their SINS to ***GOD*** they will be FORGIVEN, because FORGIVENESS only comes after the SACRIFICE is GIVEN to that PERSON. By JESUS CHRIST BEING THE SACRIFICE, AND GIVEN TO ONLY THOSE OF ***GOD'S*** CHOOSING, HE COMES ONLY BY THE GRACE OF ***GOD.*** Unlike what is taught by MOST of the CHURCHES; SAVING COMES ONLY BY GRACE and NOT BY WORKS, and ***GOD*** does not have an OPEN DOOR POLICY ACCEPTING ALL COMING to ***HIM. HOWEVER, IF ONE IS PERSISTENT IN THEIR EFFORTS TO RECEIVE GRACE, THEY WILL NOT BE DENIED SAITH THE LORD!***

> ***John 6:65*** *And HE said,* ***THEREFORE SAID I UNTO YOU, THAT NO MAN CAN COME UNTO ME, EXCEPT IT WERE GIVEN UNTO HIM OF MY FATHER.***

Chapter 4

Ruling with the ROD of IRON

In Chapter 1 WE talked about "The Power of the ROD", and in Chapter 3, "Receiving of the WORD (JESUS CHRIST)". Both of these chapters refer to the *WORD of* ***GOD (THE ROD of IRON)***, with the FIRST referring to the POWER of the WORD, and the latter telling how to RECEIVE the WORD. In this Chapter WE shall discuss how ONE may RULE with the WORD after they have been EMPOWERED with IT. Ruling with the ROD of IRON is spoken about several times in the Scriptures, and it is KEY to your UNDERSTANDING that YOU know what this MEANS.

One cannot RECEIVE the WORD until they have been BAPTIZED in the SPIRIT, for they must RECEIVE it before they can be EMPOWERED with it. After a PERSON RECEIVES the *WORD of* ***GOD*** (THE ROD), they will also RECEIVE the ANOINTING (EMPOWERMENT) that comes with it, enabling them in some way to MINISTER for THE LORD. This doesn't necessarily mean everybody RECEIVING the WORD will publicly PREACH it, for the ANOINTING coming with it will be in varying LEVELS. However, even those RECEIVING only the GIFT of ***FAITH*** for their ANOINTING will in some way, SERVE a PURPOSE in ***GOD.***

GOD ANOINTS with a PURPOSE, and that PURPOSE will be SERVED. In some cases it may be simply getting another to READ the BIBLE, whereas in others it may include PUBLIC MINISTRY. This doesn't mean that a PERSON intended for PUBLIC MINISTRY should go off and attend some school to learn how to MINISTER, for the COUNSELING of MINISTRY will come by way of THE ***HOLY SPIRIT*** and not by way of another person or school.

JESUS was sent to earth to be YOUR PERFECT EXAMPLE, and if you are to PREACH HIS GOSPELS, you MUST LEARN how to PREACH in the SAME WAY HE LEARNED, and that is by way of THE ***HOLY SPIRIT.*** The idea of one man ordaining another to preach is NONSENSE ***SAITH THE LORD***; for anyone PREACHING THE LORD'S MESSAGE MUST RECEIVE the MESSAGE from ABOVE, and not from a school or person.

For example, if a NEWBORN PERSON in ***GOD*** RECEIVES the GIFT of

FAITH, THE WORD of KNOWLEDGE, and the WORD of WISDOM as part of their ANOINTING, they would then be QUALIFIED to PREACH the *WORD of **GOD***. There is a MANDATE for PREACHING the GOSPELS, and that MANDATE says; ONE MUST HAVE AT LEAST THREE of the NINE GIFTS GIVEN by THE ***HOLY SPIRIT*** prior to them MINISTERING in the ***NAME of THE LORD.***

One of the many problems existing in the Church today is the Church's belief that they can teach one another the *WORD of **GOD,*** like one may be taught how to read and write or mathematics. This is why there isn't any depth to the MESSAGE being given by the Church, for they haven't any ANOINTING to either TEACH or PREACH the *WORD of **GOD.***

I have seen many tricky and clever sermons given by the Church, where the Preacher tries to roll in the *WORD of **GOD*** at the sermon's conclusion and in some way slip in a Scripture or two. However, even though the audience is in awe by the cleverness of the sermon, the people leave WITHOUT a SPIRITUAL MESSAGE, for the sermon was VOID of one. I also have seen some Ministers who stand up and tell long stories, believing the stories they tell (generally about themselves) contain some sort of Spiritual Message. But in MOST of the sermons, the cited Scriptures used to support their story are generally taken well OUT of CONTEXT and lack DEPTH, nor do they give any SPIRITUAL MESSAGE whatsoever.

The Church services these days are somewhat like Soap Opera's ***SAITH THE LORD***, where its members could miss any number of sessions without feeling they had missed out on any message given in the sermons. This is because the SPIRIT IDENTIFIES that NO MESSAGE had been given in the SERMON and does not feel DEPRIVED by missing it. Also, due to the Minister's lacking in ANOINTING and GUIDANCE by THE ***HOLY SPIRIT*** to PREACH, the members only show up thinking they are serving ***GOD*** by their coming to Church, and leave no different than they were when they came in.

THE LORD has TOLD ME that only ONE out of every SEVEN that PREACH the *WORD of **GOD*** has the ANOINTING to do so! This is to say that only ONE out of every SEVEN Churches serves a PURPOSE in ***GOD,*** while the other SIX are merely money making INSTITUTIONS hiding behind the CROSS. ***GOD*** calls these types of Churches the FALSE PROPHETESS and the WHORE, for they KNOW NOT the *WORD of **GOD,*** and what they do, they do for money!

> ***Revelation 2:20 NOTWITHSTANDING I HAVE A FEW THINGS AGAINST THEE, BECAUSE THOU SUFFEREST***

THAT WOMAN JEZ'-E-BEL, WHICH CALLETH HERSELF A PROPHETESS, TO TEACH AND SEDUCE MY SERVANTS TO COMMIT FORNICATION, AND TO EAT THINGS SACRIFICED UNTO IDOLS.

Revelation 2:21 AND I GAVE HER SPACE TO REPENT OF HER FORNICATION; AND SHE REPENTED NOT.

Revelation 2:22 BEHOLD, I WILL CAST HER INTO A BED, AND THEM THAT COMMIT ADULTERY WITH HER INTO GREAT TRIBULATION, EXCEPT THEY REPENT OF THEIR DEEDS.

The SAD part about these Churches that are lacking in ANOINTING, is that ALL who attend them believe they are going to RECEIVE SAVING GRACE by their attendance, however, THEY WILL NOT ***SAITH THE LORD!*** Church is meant to be a PLACE of WORSHIP and LEARNING, and without the PRESENCE of THE ***HOLY SPIRIT,*** ONE can neither WORSHIP ***GOD***, nor can they LEARN ***HIS*** *WORD*.

WRITING for THE LORD

Some RECEIVING SPIRITUAL BAPTISM will RECEIVE SIX of the GIFTS GIVEN by THE ***HOLY SPIRIT*** at the time of their ANOINTING, and this group is qualified to WRITE for THE LORD. Their WRITINGS will not add to the *WORD of* ***GOD,*** but will rather DECLARE IT, EXPLAIN IT, and UPHOLD IT ***SAITH THE LORD***.

> ***Isaiah 44:5*** *One shall say, I am THE LORD'S; and another shall call himself by the name of JACOB; and another shall SUBSCRIBE with his HAND, and surname himself by the name of ISRAEL.*

This Scripture speaks of ANOINTED who will fulfill various types of MINISTRIES for THE LORD. Those referred to in the Scripture as SUBSCRIBING with the HAND, are those RECEIVING the SIX GIFTS that will WRITE for ***GOD.***

GOD by way of THE ***HOLY SPIRIT*** will TEACH each of ***GOD'S*** WRITERS as to what is to be WRITTEN for ***HIM***. THE ***HOLY SPIRIT*** TEACHES by utilizing several different forms of KNOWLEDGE TRANSFER. The most common METHOD used for the TRANSFER takes place while the WRITER is asleep. However this isn't done in the form of a DREAM. The WRITER will experience an exceptionally DEEP SLEEP and when they AWAKEN a very clear MESSAGE of what is to be WRITTEN will have been IMPLANTED into the WRITERS MIND. The ROOT MESSAGE will be the first thought the WRITER has once they've AWAKENED. Then as the WRITER looks deeper into the MESSAGE, all of the pertinent DETAILS of the MESSAGE will be brought forward and into their conscious MIND.

Another METHOD of TRANSFER used, is the method of INSPIRED THOUGHT. This will generally come into the WRITERS MIND over and over again and may continue to pop in and out of the mind over the course of several hours, or even several days. Then once THE ***HOLY SPIRIT*** gets the WRITER'S ATTENTION, MEDITATION on the ROOT MESSAGE will take place and a VIVID EXPLANATION will be given to the WRITER on the SUBJECT MATTER.

REGARDLESS of the methods of KNOWLEDGE TRANSFER, a CONFIRMATION will always be GIVEN to the WRITER, and the CONFIRMATION can come in several different forms. It most often comes by way of SCRIPTURE taken from the BIBLE, which so UNIQUELY FITS the SUBJECT MATTER of the MESSAGE RECEIVED that the POINT of the WRITER'S MESSAGE will be an UNDENIABLE TRUTH. Another common METHOD of CONFIRMATION will come by way of another PERSON'S WORDS. These will be KEY WORDS that DIRECTLY relate to the MESSAGE, and usually come from a total stranger who is using the WORDS in an unrelated way to the MESSAGE itself.

I have seen at times when I had finally RECEIVED MY FINAL CONFIRMATION, that SEVERAL other people had spoken the same WORDS in MY MESSAGE to ME, even though I was not aware of it at the time they were being said. This is called, "REMEMBRANCE", and JESUS talks about this in the GOSPELS. Many of the things WRITTEN into the GOSPELS about JESUS, the Disciples weren't aware of at the time they had happened, but they were brought back into their MEMORY at the TIME of their WRITING them.

> ***John 14:26 BUT THE COMFORTER, WHICH IS THE HOLY GHOST, WHOM THE FATHER WILL SEND IN MY NAME, HE SHALL TEACH YOU ALL THINGS, AND BRING ALL THINGS TO YOUR REMEMBRANCE, WHATSOEVER I HAVE SAID UNTO YOU.***

There are yet other forms of CONFIRMATION ONE may RECEIVE. These forms are not generally used unless the WRITER is not RECEIVING the CONFIRMATION given in the more common ways. When a WRITER has not RECEIVED a CONFORMATION regarding an IMPORTANT MESSAGE, an ANGEL will be sent to that person to CONFIRM that the MESSAGE RECEIVED has indeed come from ***GOD.*** The ANGELIC VISIT will be in the form of a VISION, in the form of a DREAM, or it can even be in the form of a DIVINE appearance of the ANGEL. In the latter form it is MOST SPECTACULAR, however this rarely happens.

Wielding the ROD

For those who have RECEIVED THREE or more GIFTS of THE ***HOLY SPIRIT, GOD*** expects you to PREACH in one way or another for ***HIM***. This is to say, ***HE*** has EMPOWERED YOU to MINISTER for ***HIM*** in an open and public manner, and ***HE*** will PROVIDE ALL THAT IS NEEDED for YOU to do it.

When JESUS CHRIST sent out HIS Disciples to PREACH the GOSPELS, HE TOLD THEM not to bring any money or extra clothing with them, HE said ***GOD*** would PROVIDE THEM with all they NEEDED for their journey. JESUS did this for a very SPECIFIC REASON, because HE KNEW once the Disciples saw how everything seemed to just fall into place during their travels, their FAITH and TRUST in ***GOD*** would grow.

Matthew 6:31 THEREFORE TAKE NO THOUGHT, SAYING, WHAT SHALL WE EAT? OR, WHAT SHALL WE DRINK? OR, WHEREWITHAL SHALL WE BE CLOTHED?

Matthew 6:32 (FOR AFTER ALL THESE THINGS DO THE GENTILES SEEK:) FOR YOUR HEAVENLY FATHER KNOWETH THAT YOU HAVE NEED OF ALL THESE THINGS.

Matthew 6:33 BUT SEEK YE FIRST THE KINGDOM OF GOD, AND HIS RIGHTEOUSNESS; AND ALL THESE THINGS SHALL BE ADDED UNTO YOU.

Knowing YOUR GIFTS

Once a PERSON has been BAPTIZED and REBORN in CHRIST, significant changes will take place in that INDIVIDUAL. These changes will not only be obvious to the PERSON undergoing them, but they will also be quite obvious to the people who had come to know that PERSON before their BAPTISM. The changes will most certainly be DIFFERENT for each and every PERSON RECEIVING BAPTISM, however they will ALL SHOW a COMMON INTEREST in the *WORD of* ***GOD.***

After BAPTISM and ANOINTING, each INDIVIDUAL will know WHICH GIFTS have been RECEIVED, for ALL GIFTS come at the same time. EACH PERSON'S ENTITLEMENT to GIFTS will vary. Some will RECEIVE only the GIFT of FAITH, while others may RECEIVE up to SIX of the GIFTS. No PERSON can RECEIVE more than any SIX of the GIFTS GIVEN except for a PERSON of the ANGEL, they can RECEIVE up to SEVEN GIFTS.

These GIFTS will appear to the PERSON somewhat like a newly found SKILL, and within a very short period of time, (as with the development of any SKILL), the GIFTED PERSON will become proficient in their USE.

Shortly after ONE'S ANOINTING, ***GOD*** will set up circumstances in the GIFTED PERSON'S LIFE requiring them to use their GIFTS, so it isn't necessary for anyone to go off trying to apply their GIFTS on their own. The GIFTS RECEIVED are an EMPOWERMENT by ***GOD,*** and should only be USED in the SERVICE of ***GOD.***

However, ONE needn't worry about the possible misuse of their GIFTS, for ***GOD WILL NOT ALLOW IT! HE WILL ENSURE HIS*** ANOINTED APPLY THEIR GIFTS RIGHTEOUSLY and WISELY, for they have BEEN EMPOWERED by ***GOD*** to RULE with THE ROD of IRON!

Chapter 5
The Significance of NUMBERS

In the PREVIOUS BOOK WE explained how NUMBERS and WORDS relate to one another. We again mentioned this phenomena in this BOOK'S Foreword to show how each letter in the English ALPHABET has a corresponding NUMBER, based on where the letter falls within the English ALPHABET. The following list identifies the NUMBERS associated with the LETTERS and as WE discuss NUMBERS relating to WORDS and NAMES you may want to refer to this list.

A=1, B=2, C=3, D=4, E=5, F=6, G=7, H=8, I=9, J=10, K=11, L=12, M=13, N=14, O=15, P=16, Q=17, R=18, S=19, T=20, U=21, V=22, W=23, X=24, Y=25, and Z=26.

As WE identify WORDS and NAMES with their NUMBERS, you will SEE how certain NUMBERS routinely appear, both in Scripture and in this BOOK. This is not by COINCIDENCE that there is significance to WORD/LETTER relationships, but it is rather intentional, for ***GOD*** uses NUMBERS to AUTHENTICATE ***GOD'S WORD.***

Let us review some of the things associated with KEY NUMBERS that were discussed in the PREVIOUS BOOK. If you will recall, WE at that time showed how the NUMBER of ***GOD*** was equal to the NUMBER ***26.*** This was arrived at by taking each of the LETTERS making up the WORD, "***GOD***", and converting them to NUMBERS and SUM TOTALING those NUMBERS. **Example:** With the letter "G" being equal to number "7", "O" being equal to "15" and "D" equaling "4", WE can say that the WORD, ***"GOD",*** has a sum total of ***26*** (7+15+4 = ***26***).

This isn't coincidental that the NUMBER of ***GOD*** and the NUMBER of letters contained in the ENGLISH ALPHABET both equal ***26;*** for they were ALWAYS intended to be the SAME. This is because ***GOD*** had always intended the HOLY BIBLE be TRANSLATED into the ENGLISH LANGUAGE. The LAYERS of the HOLY BIBLE and the NUMBERS associated with ***GOD*** and the HEAVENLY REALM are only DISCERNIBLE in the ENGLISH LANGUAGE.

GOD says, ***HE*** is the ALPHA and the OMEGA, the FIRST and the LAST, the BEGINNING and the END. And, although this Scriptural reference has a multitude of meanings, it also means; ***HE IS THE FOUNDATION FOR ALL WORDS, MOST SPECIFICALLY THOSE OF THE ENGLISH LANGUAGE.*** The LANGUAGE SPOKEN in HEAVEN is ENGLISH, except for the HEBREWAH LANGUAGE which is SPOKEN at the THRONE.

Also explained in the PREVIOUS BOOK, the NUMBER of the PERSON of THE ***HOLY SPIRIT*** (referred to as the ***DELIVERER***) is the NUMBER ***182.*** This was arrived at from the ***SEVEN SPIRITS of GOD*** that PROCEED from THE THRONE of ***GOD*** or ***7 x 26 = 182.*** In the PREVIOUS BOOK WE verified the NUMBER ***182*** in several different ways, with one of the more obvious being the SUM TOTAL of the NAMES of the THREE DELIVERERS spoken of in the OLD TESTAMENT. The FIRST DELIVERER had the NAME of NOAH, and when the letters making up the NAME "NOAH" are converted to NUMBERS and SUM TOTALED, they equal to the number 38. When doing the same for the SECOND DELIVERER, whose NAME was JOSEPH, we arrive at the NUMBER 73 and by doing so again for the THIRD DELIVERER, whose NAME was MOSES WE arrive at the NUMBER 71. If WE then add the TOTAL of the THREE NAMES of the THREE ***DELIVERERS*** we get 38 + 73 + 71 = ***182.***

Expressing the THRONE ROOM by NUMBERS

If WE were to VIEW the THRONE ROOM you would SEE by NUMBERS how the ***SEVEN SPIRITS of GOD*** REPRESENT the DESCENDING FORM of ***GOD,*** as was discussed in the 3rd Chapter of this BOOK, titled "***GOD our FIRST LOVE".*** In the THRONE ROOM, you would see on THE THRONE, the ***TRINITY,*** consisting of ***YAHWEH, IXOTE, and YESHUA.*** You would also see the FOUR SONS of ***GOD*** who are the FOUR SERAPHIM, and their FOUR SOULMATES who are the FOUR COVENANT ANGELS. The THREE PERSONS of ***GOD (TRINITY)*** are EACH REPRESENTED by the NUMBER of ***GOD,*** which is the NUMBER ***26*** and as was explained in the PREVIOUS BOOK, the FOUR SONS of ***GOD*** are each REPRESENTED by the NUMBER 13. The FOUR COVENANT ANGELS, BEING SONS of ***GOD*** by MARRIAGE are also REPRESENTED by the NUMBER 13. With this in MIND let US VIEW the THRONE ROOM NUMBERS.

YAHWEH (26)
IXOTE (26)

YESHUA (26)

1st SERAPHIM (13) 2nd SERAPHIM (13) 3rd SERAPHIM (13) 4th SERAPHIM (13)

1st COVENANT (13) 2nd COVENANT (13) 3rd COVENANT (13) 4th COVENANT (13)

OR

26
26
26

13 +13 +13 +13 = 52
13 +13 +13 +13 = 52

You can further CONCLUDE that when the FOUR SERAPHIM and the FOUR COVENANT ANGELS become UNIFIED in MARRIAGE, they then become the NUMBER ***26*** as well, and the THRONE ROOM can be expressed as follows:

26
26
26
26 + 26 + 26 + 26

OR

7 x 26 = 182

The FOUR SERAPHIM and the FOUR COVENANT ANGELS can be further expressed in the DESCENDING FORM of ***GOD,*** and can also be VERIFIED by using NUMBERS.

THE TRINITY

YAHWEH = 70
IXOTE = 73
YESHUA = 79

OR

THEIR SUM TOTAL = 222

OR

DESCENDING FORM of GOD

SERAPHIM = 89
COVENANT = 94 ANGEL = 39

OR

89 + 94 + 39 = 222

What WE have just shown you was the NUMERIC EXPRESSION of the ***SEVEN SPIRITS of GOD,*** in both the ASCENDED and DESCENDED FORM. Let US also CONFIRM this with NUMBERS.

SEVEN = 65
SPIRITS = 110
OF = 21
GOD = 26

OR

65 + 110 + 21 + 26 = 222

Also explained in the 3rd Chapter of this BOOK was how ***GOD*** DESCENDS in the FORM of THE ***DELIVERER (182 PERSON).*** When this is done, both ***IXOTE*** and ***YESHUA*** DESCEND through CHRIST and into the 4th SERAPHIM who is DESCRIBED in the Book of Revelation (Revelation 4:7) as the "FLYING EAGLE" and in the Book of Zechariah (Zechariah 6:12) as "THE BRANCH". This can also be EXPRESSED in NUMBERS.[1]

FLYING (73) EAGLE (30)
THE (33) BRANCH (46)

OR

73 + 30 + 33 + 46 = 182

NUMERIC MESSAGES

NOTE: GOD is continually giving ME NUMERIC MESSAGES. In my house I have several digital clocks and also have digital readouts in my car; such as the clock, the outside temperature monitor, and the odometer. On occasion I will glance at one of these digital readouts and see a familiar NUMBER such as 1:11 or 2:22, or 3:33 and being keyed by these NUMBERS will look about for other HEAVENLY signs. In nearly all of the cases where a NUMBER has caught MY attention, an EVENT takes place shortly thereafter.

For example; if I were to glance at the clock in my car and see that the time was 2:22, the other digital readouts would be displaying numbers such as 77 degrees for the outside temperature while the last 3 digits on my odometer would read some other TRIPLICATE NUMBER. As I become more familiar with WORD and NUMBER associations, the more obvious it has become to me that the phenomena I experience is not coincidental, but rather SIGNS from ABOVE.

Many times when I experience a WORD and NUMBER EVENT, it is just THE LORD'S way of letting me know ***HE*** is with me, and has everything UNDER ***HIS*** CONTROL, even the NUMBERS on my instruments. People have a tendency to UNDERESTIMATE the POWER of the ***ALMIGHTY GOD,*** and they do not UNDERSTAND ***HIS*** INVOLVEMENT in everything taking place in this world and elsewhere. As was explained in the PREVIOUS BOOK, NOTHING can HAPPEN outside of the ***WILL of GOD,*** and I mean ABSOLUTELY NOTHING. ***GOD*** is INVOLVED in EVERYTHING that takes place!

In the PREVIOUS BOOK there was an explanation of how life in this world can be compared to one maneuvering through an OBSTACLE COURSE, and

---

[1] The BRANCH is referred to twice in the Book of Zechariah and if you review your King James 1611 BIBLE, you will SEE that THE BRANCH spoken of in Chapter 3, verse 8 refers to JESUS CHRIST. Whereas THE BRANCH spoken of in Chapter 6, verse 12 refers to ***THE DELIVERER.*** There is a subtlety in the Scriptures pointing out the differences in the TWO BRANCHES! The first reference to THE BRANCH in Chapter 4 uses a small "t" in the WORD "the" whereas as in the 6th Chapter the "T" is CAPITALIZED ("the BRANCH" versus "The BRANCH"). Also in the 13th verse of the 6th Chapter it TELLS YOU of the TWO BRANCHES, THE ***HOLY SPIRIT*** and JESUS CHRIST and how they BOTH will RULE! ***REFERENCE: Zechariah 6:13*** *Even* ***HE*** *shall build the TEMPLE of* ***THE LORD;*** *and* ***HE*** *shall bear the GLORY, and shall SIT and RULE upon* ***HIS THRONE;*** *and HE shall be a PRIEST UPON* ***HIS THRONE:*** *and the COUNSEL of PEACE shall be between them BOTH.*

how each and every person has a predetermined time (life-span) in which they must complete the course. When thinking about this one day, THE LORD reminded me of the Screenplay and MOVIE titled "The Wizard of OZ".

If you recall the MOVIE, there was a young girl by the name of Dorothy who had been knocked unconscious and while in that state she had a DREAM. In this DREAM she had been whisked away to a place called OZ and was determined to FIND her way back HOME. During Dorothy's journey through OZ while trying to find her way HOME, she meets THREE other CHARACTERS. There is a Scarecrow who wants a BRAIN, a Lion who wants COURAGE, and a Tin Man who is seeking a HEART, and both her and the CHARACTERS believe if they can get to the Wizard of OZ their wishes would be fulfilled.

While on their journey in OZ and looking for a place called Emerald City, they meet up with both GOOD and evil types of CHARACTERS along the way. The GOOD CHARACTERS continually tell them to have ***FAITH*** and **FOLLOW THE YELLOW BRICK ROAD** to Emerald City, while the evil characters continually try to prevent them from getting to their DESTINATION.

Although I am certain the person who had WRITTEN the SCRIPT was not AWARE of the DEPTH in its MESSAGE, I am just as CERTAIN it was ***GOD*** who had INSPIRED the WRITER'S MESSAGE. LET ***US*** SHOW YOU HOW NUMBERS CAN VERIFY THIS:

FAITH (44)
FOLLOW (83) THE (33) YELLOW (92) BRICK (43) ROAD (38)

OR

44 + 83 + 33 + 92 + 43 + 38 = 333

As it was with Dorothy and her friends needing help along the way to Emerald City, so it with YOU on YOUR journey through this WORLD, a WORLD being very much like OZ, having both GOOD and evil in it. However, the HELP YOU NEED comes by way of a ***SAVIOR*** and a ***DELIVERER*** and not by a GOOD WITCH and the WIZARD of OZ. If we now look at the TWO WORDS, ***"SAVIOR (84)"*** and ***"DELIVERER (98)",*** WE arrive back at the NUMBER ***182,*** for this is the SUM of their NUMBERS (***84 + 98 = 182***).

With this in MIND, let US review how the DESCENDING FORM of ***GOD*** DESCENDS into the ***DELIVERER.*** AS EXPLAINED earlier in this BOOK, when the SAVIOR had come to earth, it was ***YESHUA*** alone who DESCENDED into the 3rd SERAPHIM, JESUS CHRIST. Whereas you were told when the ***DELIVERER*** comes to earth, both ***IXOTE and YESHUA*** DESCEND THROUGH CHRIST and into the 4th SERAPHIM, the ***182 PERSON.*** If WE now look at the NUMBER association with the NAMES as they DESCEND to FORM the ***DELIVERER,*** WE can arrive at the following:

IXOTE (73)
YESHUA (79)
MAN (28) 3rd SERAPHIM
EAGLE (30) 4th SERAPHIM

OR

73 + ***79*** + 28 + 30 = ***210***

You are probably thinking at this time as to what SIGNIFICANCE the NUMBER ***210*** has? One thing the NUMBER ***210*** represents, is the DESCENDING NATURE of ***GOD,*** and it also REPRESENTS the IDENTITIES of the 4th SERAPHIM and the 4th COVENANT ANGEL. As you were told in the PREVIOUS BOOK, the 4th SERAPHIM is IDENTIFIED by the NUMBER of ***182*** and ***HIS*** SOUL MATE is the COVENANT ANGEL, ***JAEL.*** If you take the NAME ***JAEL (28)*** and add it to the NUMBER ***182,*** then the SUM TOTAL of the two IDENTITIES equals the NUMBER ***210.***

You may also note, when ***GOD*** DESCENDS within the ***TRINITY,*** it is referred to as the DESCENDING FORM of ***GOD,*** and when ***HE*** DESCENDS beyond the ***TRINITY,*** it's referred to as the DESCENDING NATURE of ***GOD.*** This is because while DESCENDING BEYOND the ***TRINITY GOD TAKES ON THE NATURE of A FLESHEN MAN, AND HE DOES SO IN THE FORM OF THE 182 PERSON, THE PERSON OF THE HOLY SPIRIT.***

> ***Genesis 6:3*** *And THE LORD said,* ***MY SPIRIT*** *shall not always strive with MAN, for that* ***HE*** *also is FLESH: yet HIS days shall be an HUNDRED and TWENTY YEARS.*

DESCENDING (84)
NATURE (79)
Of (21)
GOD (26)

OR

84 + 79 + 21 + ***26* = *210***

NOTE: I would like to point out to YOU that the WORD "DESCENDING" bears the same NUMBER as the WORD "SAVIOR", and the WORD "NATURE bears the SAME NUMBER as the NAME ***"YESHUA".*** This relates to what you had been PREVIOUSLY SHOWN, think about it!

Man's Numbers

THE LORD has told ME that the NUMBERS used by Man have a basic FLAW in them, and it is because of this FLAW that Man has not reached his ULTIMATE LEVEL of UNDERSTANDING NATURE (Physics). As it was previously EXPLAINED in this BOOK, when ***GOD*** DESCENDS OUTSIDE of the ***TRINITY, HE*** SUBDIVIDES into TWELFTHS.

This in ITSELF should be an indicator as to what the BASIS of NUMBERS should be in NATURE. THE LORD has told ME that Man has based his numbering system on a TEN'S SYSTEM rather than on a TWELVE'S SYSTEM and by his doing this, he has caused many NUMBERS to be INFINITE NUMBERS, when they need not be. In the TEN'S SYSTEM, the NUMBER 10 is only equally divisible by the NUMBERS, 1, 2, 5, and 10, whereas in the TWELVE'S SYSTEM the NUMBER TWELVE is equally divisible by 1, 2, 3, 4, 6, and 12. Therefor by using the TEN'S SYSTEM, many more INFINITE NUMBERS exist because of them running on infinitely without equally rounding off. Furthermore, the ratio of the diameter of a circle to its circumference in the TEN'S SYSTEM, called Pi, becomes an INFINITE NUMBER. Whereas; the same RATIO within the TWELVE'S SYSTEM will round off equally when it is taken out to the TWELFTH PLACE.

152, WORD and NUMBERS ASSOCIATION

Both our WORDS and our NUMBERS come to us through the ***TRINITY.*** The WORD comes by way of ***YESHUA*** and this is why JESUS CHRIST is referred to as the *WORD of* ***GOD.*** However both our WORD and NUMBERS come by way of ***GOD,*** so both THE *WORD and* ***NUMBERS*** are initiated by ***IXOTE,*** THE ***HOLY SPIRIT of GOD.*** The ***NUMBER of 152*** is REPRESENTATIVE of the WORD and NUMBERS association BETWEEN the ***TWO.***

IXOTE (73)
YESHUA (79)

OR

73 + 79 = 152

OR

NUMBERS (92)
WORD (60)

OR

92 + 60 = 152

MIRACLES, the NUMBER 153

> ***John 2:6*** *And there were set there SIX waterpots of stone, after the manner of the purifying of the Jews, containing TWO or THREE firkins apiece.*

> ***John 2:7*** *JESUS saith unto them,* ***FILL THE WATERPOTS WITH WATER.*** *And they filled them up to the brim.*

> ***John 2:8*** *And HE saith unto them,* ***DRAW OUT NOW, AND BEAR UNTO THE GOVERNOR OF THE FEAST.*** *And they bare it.*

This was the FIRST MIRACLE performed by JESUS CHRIST, the making of WINE out of water. As WE LOOK into the LAYER of the Scriptures there are certain NUMERIC MESSAGES within them. The SIX waterpots REPRESENT MAN, for as you were shown in the PREVIOUS BOOK, MAN, is REPRESENTED by the NUMBER 6. This is ***GOD'S SIXTH DAY CREATION,*** the MAN without a SOUL (the GENTILE). The filling of the waterpots with WATER REPRESENTS the ***LIVING WATERS,*** the *WORD of* ***GOD*** that the MAN RECEIVES from JESUS CHRIST, and this causes the MAN to CHANGE once he has been filled to the BRIM with the *WORD of* ***GOD***. The CONVERSION of the WATER into WINE REPRESENTS the CHANGE of the MAN after his RECEIVING the *WORD of* ***GOD*** and being BAPTIZED in THE ***HOLY SPIRIT.*** So the MIRACLE refers to SPIRITUAL CONVERSION and REBIRTH (water being converted into wine).

If WE look even DEEPER into the NUMBERS CONTAINED in the Scriptures, WE can SEE that there were SIX waterpots containing TWO or THREE firkins apiece. OR, WE CAN SAY THAT THREE of the WATERPOTS contained 2 firkins of water and THREE of the WATERPOTS contained 3 firkins of water, thus making a TOTAL of 15 firkins of water that was MADE into WINE. NOW, if WE CONVERT the measurement of firkins to GALLONS, WE find that ONE FIRKIN equals 10.2 GALLONS. IF WE further multiply the NUMBER of GALLONS by the NUMBER of FIRKINS WE GET: 10.2 GALLONS x 15 FIRKINS = ***153 GALLONS of WINE. THIS WAS JESUS' FIRST MIRACLE, MAKING 153 GALLONS of WINE OUT of 15 FIRKINS of WATER.***

Let US now look at JESUS' FINAL MIRACLE that HE had PERFORMED shortly after HIS RESURRECTION.

After JESUS' RESURRECTION, HE stood on the shore, and PETER and JOHN were about one hundred yards out, in their fishing boat, and JESUS CALLED OUT TO THEM and asked if they had any fish? They told HIM that they hadn't caught any fish even though they had been fishing all night.

NOTE: After HIS RESURRECTION, JESUS appeared on several occasions not looking like HIMSELF. At the time the Disciples were fishing, they were unaware that it was JESUS CALLING OUT TO THEM, for they had not RECOGNIZED HIM.

JESUS then told them, to cast their nets on the RIGHT side of the ship, and when HE had said this they knew it was JESUS, because HE had told them to do the EXACT same thing when they had first met HIM. As soon as they had cast their nets to the RIGHT side of the ship as JESUS had so instructed, the net IMMEDIATELY filled up with fish.

PETER, now knowing it was JESUS who was CALLING from the shore, then jumped into the water and swam ashore.

> ***John 21:8*** *And the other Disciples came in a little ship; (for they were not far from the land, but as it were two hundred cubits,) dragging the net with fishes.*

> ***John 21:9*** *As soon as they were come to the land, they saw a fire of coals there, and fish laid thereon, and bread.*

> ***John 21:10*** *JESUS saith unto them,* ***BRING OF THE FISH WHICH YE HAVE NOW CAUGHT.***

***John 21:11** Simon PETER went up, and drew the net to the land full of great fishes, an **HUNDRED and FIFTY and THREE:** and for all there were so many, yet was not the net broken.*

NOTE: WE could spend hours in the LAYER of these last few Scriptures for CONTAINED in them is a VERY DEEP and IMPORTANT MESSAGE. However WE shall move forward for now into more NUMBERS and come back to this subject later on in the BOOK.

NUMBERS at a GLANCE

In the PREVIOUS BOOK WE listed several NUMBERS of IMPORTANCE, and before WE go any further into NUMBERS WE want to reiterate those NUMBERS along with some others. With NUMBERS being SIGNIFICANT in ONE'S ability to SEE into the LAYER of the SCRIPTURES and also to CONFIRM its meaning, familiarity of certain NUMBERS are KEY to SCRIPTURE DEPTH. We will first start out with TRIPLICATE NUMBERS and then DESCEND into individual NUMBERS.

111 = THE MOST HIGH and THE THRONE of GOD, also (SHILOH (71) and BANDS (40)). THESE ARE THE NAMES IDENTIFYING THE PERSON of THE HOLY SPIRIT and THE PLACE WHERE GOD HAS PUT HIS NAME (HIS HOLY TEMPLE).

222 or 443 = THE TRINITY (YAHWEH (70), IXOTE (73), YESHUA (79)) and the SEVEN SPIRITS of GOD, or the DESCENDING FORM of GOD. The NUMBER 182 (which are the SEVEN SPIRITS of GOD (222) OUTSIDE of the TRINITY) can also REPRESENT the TRINITY.

333 = (HOLY (60) SPIRIT (91) as 182 PERSON), and (JESUS (74) CHRIST (77) and 182 PERSON), and (LORD (49) of (21) HOSTS (81) as 182 PERSON).

*444 = SONS of **GOD,** FOUR SERAPHIM, THE FOUR LIVING BEASTS (LION, OX/CALF, MAN, and FLYING EAGLE).*

555 = BODY of CHRIST, BRIDE, or CHURCH of CHRIST.

*666 or 669 or 696 = All meaning: CONDEMNATION, MARK of the BEAST (loss of IDENTITY in **GOD**), and can also mean BURDEN or TAXATION.*

777 = GOD'S FINALITY, WRATH of GOD, (BREAKING of the SEVEN SEALS, the SOUNDING of the SEVEN TRUMPETS, and the POURING OUT of the SEVEN VIALS).

182 = ***THE SEVEN SPIRITS of GOD, or THE DELIVERER, or THE HOLY SPIRIT of GOD in FLESH. (SYMBOLIZED as the FLYING EAGLE).***

151 = ***HOLY SPIRIT (151), LORD of HOSTS (151),*** and JESUS CHRIST (151).

152 = ***IXOTE (73) and YESHUA (79),*** *NUMBERS (92) and WORD (60) of* ***GOD, and THE DELIVERER'S 1st NAME*** and the NAME JESUS.

153 = *MIRACLES (and, the FIRST and the LAST).*

123 = *BASIC UNDERSTANDING or BEGINNING.*

11 = *SECOND COMING of CHRIST.*

12 = ***GOD'S*** *PEOPLE, ISRAEL.*

13 = *SONS of* ***GOD*** *(SERAPHIM and COVENANT ANGEL) and LIGHT BEING.*

26 = ***GOD, INFINITY, ETERNITY,*** *and the ENGLISH ALPHABET.*

49 = ***LORD (49) in a COMPLETE FORM, or LORD of Lords (SEVEN SQUARED).***

44 = ***GODHEAD, FAITH, ABRAHAM,*** *JUDAH and* ***THE HOLY BIBLE.***

64 = *ISRAEL (64) as* ***GOD'S*** *PEOPLE or* ***ZION (64) as GOD'S PLACE.***

66 = *WOMAN (66) (the NUMBER 69 can also represent a WOMAN giving BIRTH).*

74 = *JESUS (74) or MESSIAH (74).*

77 = ***CHRIST (77),*** *POWER (77), and GLORY (77).*

84 = ***SAVIOR (84) or DESCENDING (84).***

88 = *IMMANUEL (88), ONENESS and UNITY with* ***GOD.***

98 = ***IXOTE, (MEANING THE NUMBER 98 in HEBREWAH) or DELIVERER (98) and DELIVERANCE (98).***

99 = *RAPTURE (99) can also mean WOMAN in a POSITIVE FORM.*

1 = *LIGHT (56) and LIGHT can also be represented by the number 56.*

2 = *HEAVENS (UNIVERSE).*

3 = *EARTH, SEA, and FOOD.*

4 = *SUN, MOON, and STARS.*

5 = *THE LIVING, A NATION, body of people or CHURCH (also called the sea).*

6 = *MAN of the SIXTH DAY CREATION, the GENTILE (also the NON-BELIEVER in* ***GOD****).*

7 = ***GOD'S NUMBER of COMPLETENESS and DESIGNATES BELONGING TO GOD (GOD'S SABBATH).***

8 = *UNITY or ONENESS.*

9 = ***FIRST NUMBER of the HOLY SPIRIT, LEVELS in HEAVEN, and GIFTS of THE HOLY SPIRIT.***

10 = *NUMBER GIVEN TO LUCIFER, the DEVIL, also meaning "THE FALLEN".*

The Number 666, many meanings; ALL COUNTERFEIT

In the INTRODUCTION of this BOOK you were shown how the WORD "cat" can be represented by the NUMBERS 3,1, and 20. This is because the letters making up the WORD "cat" fall within three NUMERIC positions of the English Alphabet, with "c" being the 3rd letter, "a" being the 1st letter, and "t" being the 20th letter of the Alphabet. You were also TOLD that the SUM total of the three NUMBERS could also represent the WORD "cat" (3 + 1 + 20) or the NUMBER "24".

However, it was concluded that when using the NUMBER 24 alone to identify the word "cat" it can be misleading, because there are several other WORDS whose letters also total the NUMBER 24. The MISUSE of NUMBERS and being DECEIVED by them, is the BASIS for this TOPIC'S discussion, because the DEVIL can manipulate both WORDS and NUMBERS to DECEIVE YOU.

The NUMBER "666" has several meanings and one of those meanings refers to Lucifer being a "COUNTERFEIT GOD". The NUMBER 666 itself is arrived at by the DEVIL'S mimicking the ***TRINITY.*** The NUMBERS ***111, 222, and 333*** ALL REPRESENT the ***TRINITY*** and when they are SUM TOTALED they add to the NUMBER 666, making the three persons of the DEVIL a FALSE REPRESENTATION of ***GOD.***

The NUMBER 666 also represents THREE PERSONS, (all being men indicated by the NUMBER 6), the DEVIL, the 2nd BEAST, and the FALSE PROPHET as referred to in the Book of Revelation. The DEVIL further mimics CHRIST and the BRIDE and arrives again at the NUMBER 666 by adding the NUMBER ***222*** (the ***TRINITY***) and the NUMBER *444 (SON'S of **GOD** and the BRIDE).* The DEVIL portrays himself as being GOD, the 2nd Beast portrays himself as being Christ (being the Antichrist) and the FALSE PROPHET portrays himself as being the Bride or the Church.

In the Introduction to this BOOK you were told there are RULES governing the use of SCRIPTURE. These RULES apply to the INTERPRETATION of both the WORDS and the NUMBERS contained within the SCRIPTURE. Lucifer continually tries to use Scripture to CONFUSE or BETRAY YOU by way of the FALSE PROPHET, making NUMBER "666" represent the MISUSE of

Scripture and the MANIPULATION of NUMBERS. JESUS says in the GOSPEL of John (John 10:35) that "the SCRIPTURE CANNOT BE BROKEN", and in the 1st LAYER of the GOSPEL this means the SCRIPTURE must be fulfilled. However, in that same SCRIPTURE'S 4th LAYER, the WISDOM LAYER, it means the SCRIPTURE must be kept in its proper SEQUENCE.

An example of this can be visualized by looking at a simple sentence and then rearranging its WORDS to change its original meaning. For instance, if I were to say, **"Did I not say that?"** by simply moving the WORD "I" to a different location in the structure of the sentence, I can make the same sentence say, **"I did not say that!"** which is exactly the opposite of what was originally said. This manipulation with WORDS is exactly what Lucifer does with SCRIPTURE, to DECEIVE, CONFUSE and TWIST the TRUTH for his own benefit!

In the PREVIOUS BOOK you were shown by taking the WORDS used to list the GIFTS given to the LAMB of ***GOD*** (Revelation 5:12) that the NUMBERS ***111, 222, 333,*** *444, 555, and* ***777*** could be arrived at. You were also TOLD that the NUMBER 666 could be arrived at ONLY if the WORDS listed to make up the GIFTS were MOVED out of their ORIGINAL SEQUENCE. Or, in other WORDS, the RULES governing the INTERPRETATION of a SCRIPTURE were to be BROKEN, thus VIOLATING what JESUS had said cannot be done!

Furthermore, you were just previously told, the NUMBER 666 represents three men, and in how the NUMBER 666 was applied to that statement, was CORRECT. However; the NUMBER 666 can also mean Man and Woman of ***GOD'S*** SIXTH DAY CREATION, with the first 6 representing man, and the following 66 representing woman. What is being said here is this, only ***GOD'S ANOINTED*** CAN INTERPRET SCRIPTURE, WHETHER IT BE IN THE FORM OF WORD, or in NUMBERS. THIS IS TRUE BECAUSE THE RULES GOVERNING INTERPRETATION ARE QUITE COMPLEX, AND ONE MUST BE CAPABLE OF VIEWING ALL THE LAYERS IN THE SCRIPTURE SIMULTANEOUSLY TO ENSURE THE SCRIPTURE IS NOT BEING BROKEN OR VIOLATED IN ANY WAY.

CHAPTERS NUMBERS

There are 929 chapters in the OLD TESTAMENT and 111 chapters in the NEW TESTAMENT if YOU consider each of the 150 Psalms to be chapters. This makes the HOLY BIBLE have a total of 1040 chapters in ALL, excluding the 149 chapters of the Epistles that have been added to make the Canon.

Throughout this BOOK and the PREVIOUS BOOK WE have told you that the HOLY BIBLE consists of 44 BOOKS in total, and in the PREVIOUS BOOK justified that NUMBER by the WORDS ***GODHEAD,*** ABRAHAM, JUDAH, and FAITH. The NUMBER ***44*** represent all FOUR of these WORDS*;* for that is the SUM TOTAL of the LETTERS making up each of the WORDS.

The *WORD of* ***GOD*** came to EARTH by way of the ***GODHEAD,*** and was passed down through ABRAHAM to JUDAH, and then BECAME the NEW COVENANT of FAITH, by JESUS CHRIST'S crucifixion and RESURRECTION unto ETERNAL LIFE and this is the BIBLE STORY.

However THE LORD has told ME that the HOLY BIBLE in its CURRENT FORM is not COMPILED correctly. ***GOD*** said, ***HE*** considers the NEW TESTAMENT to be a SINGLE BOOK consisting of ***111*** Chapters, having FOUR CO-AUTHORS and not FIVE BOOKS as it is so compiled. When I was told this, I asked THE LORD, if the NEW TESTAMENT is only ONE BOOK and not FIVE, how then could the NUMBER ***44*** REPRESENT the HOLY BIBLE'S CONTENT?

HE replied and SAID, ***WHEREAS THE BOOK OF PSALMS IS FIVE BOOKS AND NOT A SINGLE BOOK AS IT IS SO COMPILED, THE NUMBER 44 STILL APPLIES TO THE BIBLE'S NUMERIC STRUCTURE! THUS MAKING THE OLD TESTAMENT CONSIST OF 43 BOOKS AND NOT 39, AND THE NEW TESTAMENT HAVE ONLY ONE BOOK AND NOT 5 AS IT IS SO COMPILED, AND THIS CAN BE CONFIRMED BY NUMBERS.***

I then asked THE LORD how might I CONFIRM the NUMBER 40 represents the HOLY BIBLE in its current FORM and not the NUMBER ***44***; and ***HE*** told ME to take the NUMBER of CHAPTERS in the HOLY BIBLE and DIVIDE that NUMBER by the NUMBER of the WORD ***"GOD".***

So I counted and recounted several times and found the total NUMBER of CHAPTERS in the HOLY BIBLE to be ***1040.*** I then DIVIDED the NUMBER of CHAPTERS by the NUMBER ***26, GOD*** and ARRIVED at the NUMBER 40, and visa versa if I DIVIDE the NUMBER of CHAPTERS by the NUMBER 40, I get NUMBER ***26, THE WORD, GOD!***

I also did further RESEARCH into the MATTER and found the BOOK of PSALMS to be FIVE BOOKS of PSALMS and not a single BOOK, just as THE LORD had said. BOOK ONE of the PSALMS consists of the 1st Psalm through the 41st Psalm. BOOK TWO of the PSALMS consists of the 42nd Psalm through the 72nd Psalm, BOOK THREE consists of the 73rd Psalm through the 89th Psalm, BOOK FOUR, the 90th Psalm through the 106th Psalm, and BOOK FIVE, from the 107th Psalm through the 150th Psalm. I also found the MIDDLE of the HOLY BIBLE to be residing in the 42nd Psalm at the 8th verse.

Psalm 42:8 *Yet THE LORD will COMMAND* ***HIS*** *LOVINGKINDNESS in the daytime, and in the night* ***HIS SONG*** *shall be with me, and my PRAYER unto the* ***GOD*** *of MY LIFE.*

Chapter 6

More about JESUS

YESHUA, the ***THIRD PERSON of GOD, THE SAVIOR,*** while in FLESH is JESUS CHRIST. JESUS, the DESCENDED NATURE of ***YESHUA*** is the THIRD SERAPHIM (the THIRD LIVING BEAST) and is described in the Scriptures as HAVING a FACE of a MAN. ALL FOUR of the SERAPHIM (the FOUR LIVING BEASTS) REPRESENT CHRIST in HIS ENTIRETY, the SON'S of ***GOD***. This is why in the SCRIPTURES taken from the Book of Revelation it says, the LAMB of ***GOD*** is of the FOUR BEASTS (the FOUR SERAPHIM), thus meaning the FOUR BEASTS make up CHRIST.

> ***Revelation 5:6*** *And I beheld, and, lo, in the midst of THE THRONE and of the FOUR BEASTS, and in the midst of the Elders, stood a LAMB as it been slain, having SEVEN HORNS and SEVEN EYES, which are the SEVEN SPIRITS of* ***GOD*** *sent forth into all the earth.*

John says in the Scripture he saw an EVENT happen while in HEAVEN, and was shocked at what he had seen. So what was it that John saw? In his VISION John saw the LAMB of ***GOD*** ASCEND out of the FOUR LIVING BEASTS and was AMAZED by the EVENT.

The appearance of the LAMB SYMBOLICALLY REPRESENTS the RISING of CHRIST in SPIRIT out of the FOUR SERAPHIM (the FOUR SONS) and the FOUR COVENANT ANGELS (the BRIDE) into ***THE TRINITY.*** As it was explained in the LAST CHAPTER, the SEVEN SPIRITS of ***GOD*** represent ***GOD*** in ***HIS ENTIRETY, THE TRINITY,*** and the FOUR SERAPHIM and the FOUR COVENANT ANGELS, REPRESENT the FAMILY of CHRIST. The NAME CHRIST can be seen as a FAMILY NAME or a LAST NAME GIVEN by ***GOD*** to ***HIS*** SONS and their BRIDES.

Many will say that JESUS CHRIST is ***GOD,*** however I will tell YOU that this is an INCORRECT UNDERSTANDING. ONLY when ALL FOUR of the SERAPHIM and THEIR BRIDES are in UNITY, is CHRIST COMPLETE.

This COMPLETENESS requires ALL MEMBERS OF THE BODY OF CHRIST (the CHURCH included) be intact and only then can CHRIST ASCEND INTO ***GOD.*** The EYES encompassing the FOUR SERAPHIM SYMBOLICALLY (as described in Revelation 4:8) represent the CHURCH.

Furthermore, because ***GOD*** DESCENDS into the FOUR SERAPHIM through JESUS CHRIST (the EAST GATE), CHRIST in HIS ENTIRETY can only ASCEND back into ***GOD*** through JESUS, thus making HIM the DOOR of the SHEEP. JESUS' being a SERAPHIM, can be CONFIRMED by the WORDS of JESUS CHRIST HIMSELF.

When Mary, the mother of James and John went with her two sons to JESUS to ask HIM if they (James and John) might sit one on HIS left side and one on HIS right side in HEAVEN, JESUS TOLD them this:

> ***Matthew 20:22*** *But JESUS answered and said,* ***YE KNOW NOT WHAT YE ASK. ARE YE ABLE TO DRINK OF THE CUP THAT I SHALL DRINK OF, AND BE BAPTIZED WITH THE BAPTISM THAT I AM BAPTIZED WITH?*** *They say unto HIM, We are able.*

> ***Matthew 20:23*** *And HE saith unto them,* ***YE SHALL DRINK INDEED OF MY CUP, AND BE BAPTIZED WITH THE BAPTISM THAT I AM BAPTIZED WITH: BUT TO SIT ON MY RIGHT HAND, AND ON MY LEFT, IS NOT MINE TO GIVE, BUT IT SHALL BE GIVEN TO THEM FOR WHOM IT IS PREPARED OF MY FATHER.***

What JESUS is saying in the Scriptures, when HE says to John and James they SHALL DRINK of HIS CUP, is that they too will die by the hand of men, just as HE would. JESUS also tells them that they will be BAPTIZED in THE ***HOLY SPIRIT,*** just as HE WAS BAPTIZED. HOWEVER, JESUS also tells them that HE DOES NOT HAVE THE AUTHORITY to determine where they shall sit in HEAVEN. This is because in HEAVEN, ***GOD*** has DETERMINED whom sits to the RIGHT and LEFT sides of JESUS. At JESUS' immediate RIGHT, sits KING SOLOMON, and at HIS FAR RIGHT sits KING DAVID, and at HIS LEFT SIDE SITS HIS FATHER, ***THE DELIVERER.*** These are the established FOUR THRONES of the SERAPHIM and JESUS did not have the AUTHORITY to give those SEATS to James and John.

JESUS being the HEAD of CHRIST (which is why HE is symbolized as having the FACE of a MAN) is the only ACCESS to the THRONE of ***GOD***!

JESUS is the DESCENDING NATURE of ***YESHUA,*** and NO ONE can ENTER into ***GOD*** except through ***YESHUA*** and ***YESHUA*** can only ASCEND TO ***THE ALMIGHTY GOD,*** by way of THE ***HOLY SPIRIT, IXOTE. THIS IS THE HIERARCHY of the THRONE.***

THE DOOR of the SHEEP

All through the GOSPELS JESUS refers to HIMSELF as being the SON of MAN, rather than referring to HIMSELF as being the SON of ***GOD,*** and HE does this for a very SPECIFIC reason. As just explained, CHRIST can only ASCEND through the SERAPHIM, JESUS, who REPRESENTS the MAN. The same scenario applies for those of CHRIST to DESCEND to EARTH, as this is ALSO done through the MAN, the THIRD SERAPHIM.

Of the FOUR SERAPHIM, only the THIRD (JESUS) and the FOURTH (THE ***DELIVERER***) have OMNI PRESENCE and the SONS of ***GOD*** or those of CHRIST can only DESCEND to EARTH through one of them. HOWEVER, unlike the THIRD SERAPHIM, the FOURTH SERAPHIM, ***THE DELIVERER, HE*** DESCENDS WITH both ***YESHUA*** and THE ***HOLY SPIRIT*** with HIM, and no ONE ELSE can do this; other than ***THE ALMIGHTY GOD HIMSELF,*** although ***GOD*** too DESCENDS to EARTH by way of the THIRD SERAPHIM.

I know this may be a bit CONFUSING and difficult to UNDERSTAND, so WE will try to explain it looking at it from a different PERSPECTIVE. LET US VIEW the THIRD SERAPHIM as a CORRIDOR in the shape of "T" having THREE DOORS, with ONE DOOR at each end of it and ONE DOOR situated in the MIDDLE at its BASE. The DOOR at the FAR END on the RIGHT is the DOOR allowing ACCESS to the THRONE of ***GOD,*** and the DOOR at the FAR END on the LEFT is the DOOR allowing ACCESS to HEAVEN. LET US CALL BOTH OF THESE DOORS, DOORS of ASCENSION, for ONE CAN ONLY ASCEND THROUGH THEM.

Let US now look at the THIRD DOOR, the DOOR at the BASE of the "T" and VIEW IT as both an EXIT to EARTH and AN ENTRANCE to the DOORS leading to ***GOD*** and HEAVEN. This CORRIDOR having the THREE DOORS is the THIRD SERAPHIM, HE who has THE FACE of a MAN, JESUS. Therefor, the only way one can either ENTER or EXIT HEAVEN is by way of the MAN, JESUS! When JESUS CAME in FLESH to earth from HEAVEN, HE CAME BY WAY OF THE THIRD SERAPHIM, THE MAN. This can be EXPRESSED as HIS being BORN of the MAN that is the THIRD SERAPHIM, therefor making HIM *THE SON of MAN.* This is also why JESUS had to possess OMNI-PRESENCE, for if HE did not REMAIN in HEAVEN while on EARTH, there wouldn't be any ACCESS back to HEAVEN, for HE is the DOOR. The following two Scriptures taken from the GOSPEL of John explain what WE are talking about, for JESUS in these Scriptures explains this phenomena to Nic-o-de'-mus, who wanted to learn about HEAVENLY things.

> ***John 3:12 IF I HAVE TOLD YOU OF EARTHLY THINGS, AND YE BELIEVE NOT, HOW SHALL YE BELIEVE, IF I TELL YOU OF HEAVENLY THINGS.***

> ***John 3:13 AND NO MAN HATH ASCENDED UP TO HEAVEN, EVEN THE SON OF MAN WHICH IS IN HEAVEN.***

As was explained in the PREVIOUS BOOK, unlike the others who had COME DOWN from HEAVEN, JESUS RETAINED MOST of HIS MEMORY and COULD RECALL HIS COMING TO EARTH by way of the MAN, and this is why HE referred to HIMSELF as being *THE SON of MAN.*

The only other PERSON that had come to EARTH recalling this EVENT of ENTRY to EARTH, was the Prophet Ezekiel, who also referred to himself as the Son of Man. This is how Ezekiel in the 44th Chapter of his Book could explain how both the ENTRANCE to HEAVEN and the EXIT from HEAVEN had to come by way of the EAST GATE, the MAN. The EAST GATE is the THIRD SERAPHIM and referred to in the Scripture as the PRINCE, meaning the PRINCE of PEACE, JESUS CHRIST.

> ***Ezekiel 44:1*** *THEN HE brought me back the way of the GATE of the OUTWARD SANCTUARY which looketh toward the EAST; and it was shut.*

> ***Ezekiel 44:2*** *Then said THE LORD unto me; THIS GATE SHALL BE SHUT, IT SHALL NOT BE OPENED, AND NO MAN SHALL ENTER IN BY IT; BECAUSE THE LORD, THE* ***GOD*** *OF ISRAEL, HATH ENTERED IN BY IT, THEREFORE IT SHALL BE SHUT.*

> ***Ezekiel 44:3*** *IT IS FOR THE PRINCE; THE PRINCE, HE SHALL SIT IN IT TO EAT BREAD BEFORE THE LORD; HE SHALL ENTER BY THE WAY OF THE PORCH OF THAT GATE, AND SHALL GO OUT THE WAY OF THE SAME.*

NOTE: The PORCH referred to in the Scripture refers to the CORRIDOR, the "T" or the CROSS. You may want to also note that the LAST SCRIPTURE bears the NUMBER ***443,*** and in the last Chapter of this BOOK it was told to you that the NUMBERS ***222 or 443*** REPRESENT the ***TRINITY*** and the DESCENDING FORM of ***GOD.***

THE ROOT and the OFFSPRING of DAVID

> ***Revelation 22:16 I JESUS HAVE SENT MINE ANGEL TO TESTIFY UNTO YOU THESE THINGS IN THE CHURCHES, I AM THE ROOT AND THE OFFSPRING OF DAVID, AND THE BRIGHT AND MORNING STAR.***

Although this Scripture has SEVEN LAYERS of UNDERSTANDING to it, at this time WE want to just address what JESUS had meant by referring to HIMSELF as being both the ROOT and the OFFSPRING of DAVID. In order for US to do this, WE must go back to the 2nd Chapter, and the 7th verse of the Book of Genesis.

> ***Genesis 2:7*** *And THE LORD* ***GOD*** *formed MAN of the DUST of the ground, and BREATHED into HIS nostrils the BREATH of LIFE; and MAN became a LIVING SOUL.*

In the PREVIOUS BOOK it was SHOWN to YOU that the OLD TESTAMENT consisted of THREE LAYERS of UNDERSTANDING. However you were not TOLD at that time that ALL THREE LAYERS of the FIRST SIX CHAPTERS of the Book of Genesis has already been FULFILLED. This is to say, the LAYER of the PAST, the LAYER of the PRESENT, and the LAYER of the FUTURE all have become LAYERS of the PAST for the FIRST SIX CHAPTERS of the Book of Genesis, for they have been FULFILLED.

Keeping this in MIND, WE can say ADAM, who was CREATED by ***GOD*** to be a LIVING SOUL had been CREATED THREE TIMES, ONE TIME FOR THE PAST, ONE TIME FOR THE PRESENT, AND ONE TIME FOR THE FUTURE. ALL THREE CREATIONS were FULFILLED prior to the START of the SEVENTH CHAPTER of Genesis.

The FIRST story of ADAM took place in HEAVEN, the SECOND story of ADAM took place on the planet we call MARS, and the THIRD story of ADAM took place here on EARTH. In all three CASES, the MAN ***CALLED ADAM*** is the BEGINNING of CHRIST, ***GOD'S*** MAN with a SOUL.

In the PREVIOUS BOOK you were TOLD that CHRIST is the KEEPER of ALL SOULS, so therefor ALL SOULS had to have COME from CHRIST. WITH CHRIST BEING THE ***SOUL of GOD*** that was given to the MAN ADAM, it FIRST had to come out from ***GOD.*** To help clarify this MATTER, WE must explain the difference between the SPIRIT and the SOUL, for they are not the same. The SPIRIT is ONE'S IDENTITY whereas the SOUL is ONE'S PURPOSE. A person can have a Spirit and not have SOUL however one cannot have a SOUL without a SPIRIT.

The SOUL enables the ONE RECEIVING it to be able to KNOW the difference between GOOD and EVIL, whereas the Spirit by itself cannot JUDGE. The Spirit merely provides one with their IDENTITY, and there are two TYPES of Spirits a PERSON can HAVE. The 1st is the EARTH given Spirit and all animals bearing a heart and lungs receive this Spirit, however it only provides one with their INDIVIDUALITY. This is the Spirit of the EARTH that was given to ***GOD'S*** SIXTH DAY CREATION, who was merely an animal having a gender and a higher order of INTELLIGENCE. The 2nd type of SPIRIT is a ***GOD GIVEN SPIRIT,*** and with this SPIRIT COMES a SOUL, enabling the ***GOD GIVEN SPIRIT*** to KNOW the DIFFERENCE between GOOD and EVIL.

Those RECEIVING a ***GOD*** GIVEN SPIRIT have a JOURNAL ENTRY of their NAME WRITTEN into the LAMB'S BOOK of LIFE, whereas those with an EARTH given Spirit are not entered into the BOOK. Therefor ONE'S IDENTITY in ***GOD*** is the JOURNAL ENTRY of their NAME in the LAMB'S BOOK of LIFE.

Anyone having an ENTRY of their NAME in the BOOK of LIFE has been GIVEN a SOUL and they MUST keep their SOUL FREE FROM SIN! Due to the SINFUL NATURE of MAN the CLEANSING of the SOUL and freeing it from SIN becomes a NECESSITY, as ***GOD WILL NOT RECEIVE BACK A SOUL THAT HAS SIN UPON IT!*** THIS CLEANSING COMES ONLY BY WAY OF SPIRITUAL BAPTISM, and this BAPTISM comes only by WAY of JESUS CHRIST.

JESUS CHRIST was ***GOD'S*** FIRST CREATION of ADAM and HE was cast out of the GARDEN (HEAVEN) because HE had SINNED. THEREFOR being the FIRST with a SOUL, HE had to RETURN to THIS WORLD and LIVE in it WITHOUT SIN and be SACRIFICED for the SIN of the WORLD in order to FREE MAN from the SIN HE had BROUGHT UPON IT.

Therefor by ADAM being the BEGINNING of the SOUL BEARING MAN, ANY and ALL coming into this WORLD must ENTER in by HIM and INTO HIS SIN, and ALL RETURNING must do as HE HAD DONE TO RETURN, be SINLESS. However, JESUS having OMNI-PRESENCE remained in

HEAVEN while on EARTH, thus giving HIM a DIVINE RIGHT to HEAVEN and this is HOW JESUS could DEFEAT DEATH! Whereas a MAN with SIN must be CLEAN and free from SIN before he can EXIT the CORRIDOR in either DIRECTION, JESUS could DIE with SIN upon HIM and still be RECEIVED back into HEAVEN by DIVINE RIGHT.

The ONLY WAY a PERSON can be RECEIVED into HEAVEN after living a carnal life in SIN is if the MIDDLE DOOR of the CORRIDOR is OPENED to them, allowing ACCESS to HEAVEN or to THE THRONE. Then, while in the CORRIDOR they MUST be CLEANSED allowing them to leave their SIN behind before EXITING into the HOLY DOMAIN. Furthermore, with JESUS CHRIST being the CORRIDOR and the PLACE to LEAVE your SIN, only BY HIS BAPTISM can YOU be CLEANSED and FREED from YOUR SIN.

DEATH is SIN, and JESUS DEFEATED DEATH, and ANY RECEIVING JESUS as their SAVIOR WILL DEFEAT DEATH ALSO, LEAVING THEIR SIN BEHIND in the CORRIDOR! ***HOWEVER, ONLY GOD CAN OPEN THE MIDDLE DOOR OF THE CORRIDOR TO YOU.***

NOTE: BY JESUS BEING ADAM, HE CAN BE BOTH THE ROOT AND THE OFFSPRING OF DAVID, and the BRIGHT and the MORNING STAR; for HE IS THE BEGINNING OF THE SOUL BEARING MAN and LIFE and THE LIGHT OF THE WORLD. HE was the ROOT of DAVID by BEING ADAM, and the OFFSPRING of DAVID by BEING JESUS CHRIST who came to EARTH in FLESH through the lineage of DAVID.

The FIVE BOOKS of the NEW TESTAMENT

In this BOOK and in the PREVIOUS BOOK YOU have been TOLD there are ONLY FIVE BOOKS making up the NEW TESTAMENT. These FIVE BOOKS are the FOUR GOSPELS and the BOOK of REVELATION. This is not an OPINION of MINE but rather THE TRUTH of ***GOD.*** THE LORD has shown ME how the Epistles have CORRUPTED the Church with their RELIGIOUS content and have taught the members of the Church to JUDGE one another. This JUDGMENT is ENDORSED by the Epistles and is ROUTINELY practiced by the Church Leaders and its Members. THE WORDS of JESUS CHRIST will CONFIRM how the JUDGMENT that the Church now EMBRACES will be to its own DESTRUCTION.

> ***Matthew 7:1 JUDGE NOT, THAT YOU BE NOT JUDGED. FOR WITH WHAT JUDGMENT YE JUDGE, YE SHALL BE JUDGED: AND WITH WHAT MEASURE YE METE, IT***

SHALL BE MEASURED TO YOU AGAIN.

NOTE: WHAT PART OF THIS SCRIPTURE DOES THE CHURCH <u>NOT UNDERSTAND</u> SAITH THE LORD?

The Church is intended to be a place for those of CHRIST to GATHER and WORSHIP, to REMIT SIN and REPENT of their deeds to ***GOD.*** If SINNERS are not allowed to ATTEND, then WHAT PURPOSE does the CHURCH SERVE, and who is he that enters into the CHURCH that hasn't any SIN? For ALL are SINNERS ***SAITH THE LORD!***

The DOCTRINE of JUDGMENT ENDORSED and taught by the Epistles are an ABOMINATION to ***GOD*** and any Church following after this DOCTRINE WILL BE HELD ACCOUNTABLE for it by ***GOD***. No Pastor, Priest or Minister has the AUTHORITY to PASS JUDGMENT on another, and those who have JUDGED will be JUDGED BY THAT SAME JUDGMENT ***SAITH THE LORD of HOSTS!***

In the previous Chapter you were TOLD that the NUMBER ***111*** REPRESENTS the PERSON or PLACE of THE ***MOST HIGH,*** WHERE ***GOD*** HAS PUT ***HIS NAME. THIS IS GOD'S PERSONAL ENDORSEMENT. THE GOSPEL OF MATTHEW CONTAINS 28 CHAPTERS, THE GOSPEL OF MARK CONTAINS 16 CHAPTERS, THE GOSPEL OF LUKE CONTAINS 24 CHAPTERS, THE GOSPEL OF JOHN CONTAINS 21 CHAPTERS AND THE BOOK OF REVELATION CONTAINS 22 CHAPTERS, THUS TOTALING 111 CHAPTERS. THE NEW TESTAMENT CONTAINS 111 CHAPTERS FROM FIVE BOOKS AND FOUR AUTHORS AND THE ENDORSEMENT of GOD AND HIS WORD IS IN THEIR NUMBERS!***

By HIS *WORD*

I have seen many renderings of JESUS and none have accurately portrayed HIS EARTHLY APPEARANCE. In the renderings HE is always shown to be a very attractive young man, wearing colorful robes and having a very noble appearance. However JESUS CHRIST'S appearance here on earth fit the description given of HIM in the SCRIPTURES.

> ***Isaiah 53:2*** *For HE shall grow before* ***HIM*** *as a tender plant, and as a ROOT out of a dry ground: HE hath no FORM nor COMELINESS; and when we shall see HIM, there is NO BEAUTY that we should desire HIM.*

While on earth, JESUS had the form of a rather normal and very plain looking man, without any distinguishing features whatsoever, neither in body or in facial appearance. JESUS was not sent to EARTH to be remembered by how HE looked, but rather was meant to be remembered by HIS *WORD;* and JESUS took on SEVERAL DIFFERENT PHYSICAL APPEARANCES after HIS RESURRECTION.

Awhile back in this BOOK WE discussed the NUMBER 153, and its association with MIRACLES. During that effort some Scripture was cited taken from the GOSPEL of John, and at that time WE made mention of the DEPTH in those SCRIPTURES and this will be the TOPIC of DISCUSSION for the heading, **"By HIS *WORD*".**

After JESUS' RESURRECTION HE appeared to HIS Disciples on several occasions and more so than not, HE appeared different than HE had looked when HE had walked among them. When JESUS FIRST appeared to Mary Magdalene at the sepulchre (tomb) after HIS RESURRECTION, she had thought HE was the Gardener and it wasn't until after HE had SPOKEN to her she realized it was JESUS (John 20:15).

On another occasion after HIS RESURRECTION, JESUS met with two of HIS Disciples and appeared to them to be a total stranger (Luke 24:16), and it wasn't until after they had talked with HIM awhile that they had come to REALIZE the STRANGER was JESUS.

In the Scriptures previously cited (John 21:4 through 21:12) regarding the NUMBER 153 and MIRACLES, the Disciples again did not recognize JESUS by HIS appearance, and it wasn't until after HE had SPOKEN to them that they KNEW it was JESUS. So why didn't JESUS APPEAR TO THEM AS HE HAD LOOKED BEFORE?

JESUS PURPOSELY DISGUISED HIS APPEARANCE BECAUSE HE WANTED HIS DISCIPLES TO REMEMBER HIM ONLY BY HIS ***WORD*** and not BY HIS APPEARANCE, and this MESSAGE is SHOUTED OUT in the LAYER of the GOSPELS. JESUS CAME TO BE REMEMBERED BY HIS ***WORD*** and this is HOW ALL THOSE WHO HAD COME TO KNOW HIM COULD RECOGNIZE HIM after HIS RESURRECTION.

It was only when HE came amidst them at their GATHERING PLACE to PRAY that HE APPEARED TWICE as HE had looked before, and that was only done so Thomas would BELIEVE that who he was seeing, was JESUS CHRIST, who had been RESURRECTED from the dead.

NOTE: One night in a DREAM I met with JESUS and although in HIS EARTHLY FORM HIS APPEARANCE was nothing special, in HIS SPIRITUAL FORM HE is MAGNIFICENT. I was not allowed to retain OUR CON-

VERSATION that EVENING, however as I DEPARTED from HIM and returned to EARTH, I remember BEHOLDING HIS GLORY for but a brief moment and it was AWESOME! It was as though ALL the ENERGY in the entire UNIVERSE was UNLEASHED when I TOUCHED HIM, and as I awoke, I was SCREAMING OUT, "I LOVE YOU JESUS"!

Chapter 7

CHRIST the CORRIDOR

In the last Chapter WE spoke briefly about the CORRIDOR to HEAVEN and the ***THRONE of GOD***. The CORRIDOR has THREE DOORS and they are called the DOOR of the SHEEP, the DOOR of the THRONE, and the DOOR to ETERNITY. The THIRD SERAPHIM, who has the FACE of a MAN and called JESUS, OVERSEES the CORRIDOR and any access to it. So one can only ENTER or EXIT through HIM. It is IMPORTANT to UNDERSTAND what significance the CORRIDOR has in REGARD to MAN, for the SOUL BEARING MAN originated from it, and can only be RECEIVED BACK into HEAVEN through it. In this Chapter WE will DISCUSS the PRINCIPLES in which ***GOD*** ESTABLISHED a METHOD for the SOUL BEARING MAN to RETURN or GAIN ACCESS to HEAVEN.

Before the CREATION of LIGHT and MAN, only ***YAHWEH, IXOTE,*** and the ANGELS EXISTED in HEAVEN. The POPULATION in HEAVEN at that TIME was held constant and there were NEITHER new ANGELS nor other LIGHT BEINGS CREATED to increase the NUMBERS. ***GOD,*** being the SOURCE of ALL that EXISTS DETERMINED to EXPAND ***HIS KINGDOM, and LIGHT (YESHUA) was CREATED*** for the EXPANSION by ***GOD'S SON, IXOTE.***

Before the CREATION of LIGHT for the WORLD, CHOIRS of ANGELS holding varying POSTS of ASCENSION established the HIERARCHY in HEAVEN, and other than ***GOD (YAHWEH and IXOTE)*** the ANGELS of the HIGHER ORDER POSTS controlled the KINGDOM of HEAVEN. During this time there were neither SERAPHIM nor METATRON and no ANGEL above the SEVENTH LEVEL ORDER. There was only FOUR of the SEVENTH LEVEL and they were all PRINCES, and their NAMES ARE, MICHAEL, GABRIEL, LUCIFER, and RAPHAEL. ALL FOUR PRINCES reported only to ***IXOTE, THE LORD of HOSTS,*** CALLED, THE ***HOLY SPIRIT.***

When ***GOD*** CREATED LIGHT, that LIGHT WAS BORN OF THE ***LORD of HOSTS (IXOTE)*** and WAS NAMED ***YESHUA, MEANING: BORN of THE SPIRIT of GOD,*** and the ***TRINITY*** was then FORMED by the ***THREE,***

YAHWEH, IXOTE, and YESHUA. ***YESHUA*** also MADE for HIMSELF a SON of LIGHT whom ***HE NAMED:*** THE ***DELIVERER 182 and THE SEVEN SPIRITS OF GOD.*** Then FROM THE ***DELIVERER*** CAME FORTH THREE SONS' and ***HE*** NAMED them, JESUS, SOLOMON and DAVID, and this was the BEGINNING of the SOUL BEARING MAN.

The FOUR SONS of ***GOD*** were CREATED of a HIGHER ORDER of HOLINESS than that of the ANGEL, because unlike the ANGEL, they were the DIRECT DESCENDANTS of ***GOD***, rather than a CREATION of ***GOD. GOD*** intended for the FOUR SERAPHIM to TAKE PART in ***HIS CREATION*** and the EXPANSION of HEAVEN, and they were to come to the EARTH in the FORM of FOUR MEN. Their APPEARANCE on EARTH would be in the REVERSE ORDER from that of THEIR EXISTENCE (after the CREATION of ADAM), with the FIRST (THE ***DELIVERER***) COMING LAST and the LAST (DAVID) COMING FIRST. Their APPEARANCES on EARTH would repeat every SEVEN THOUSAND YEARS and would CONTINUE in that FORMAT throughout all of ETERNITY.

ALL FOUR of the SONS, (being BORN out of ***YESHUA (LIGHT)*** and ***THE DELIVERER***), INHERITED FROM ***IXOTE*** THE ***FATHER of CREATION,*** ALL NINE of the GIFTS that ***YESHUA*** HAD RECEIVED. However, THE ***DELIVERER*** RECEIVED also both OMNI-PRESENCE and OMNIPOTENCE, for ***HE*** was the FIRSTBORN outside of the ***TRINITY and HEIR to the THRONE. HE*** then past down to ***HIS*** FIRSTBORN, JESUS, the POWER of OMNI-PRESENCE for JESUS INHERITED THE RESEMBLANCE of ***GOD*** FROM HIS ***FATHER,*** THE ***DELIVERER 182.***

The FOUR SONS being different than the ANGEL and of a HIGHER ORDER, CREATED for THEMSELVES FOUR METATRON, who were ALSO ABOVE the ANGEL and a DIRECT DESCENDANT of ***GOD,*** and this caused LUCIFER to become JEALOUS for THREE LEVELS of HIERARCHY were placed above HIM.

LUCIFER, having one third of the ANGELS in HEAVEN under HIS control REBELLED against the changes in HIERARCHY, and refused to REPORT to anyone other than ***IXOTE.*** To accommodate LUCIFER'S DEMANDS, ***IXOTE*** created a NEW POST for LUCIFER and the POST was called, ANGEL of THE ***HOLY SPIRIT***. Whereas the other THREE PRINCES, MICHAEL, GABRIEL, and RAPHAEL reported to the FOUR SERAPHIM, LUCIFER reported to ***IXOTE, THE LORD of HOSTS,*** and this placed LUCIFER above the other THREE PRINCES. ***IXOTE*** also had the FOUR METATRON report to ***HIM*** FIRST and ***YESHUA*** SECOND, and only one of EACH of the FOUR METATRON was placed under the CONTROL of each of the FOUR SERA-

PHIM, whereas ***IXOTE and YESHUA*** had control of ALL FOUR METATRON.

The Conditions

With LUCIFER reporting DIRECTLY to ***IXOTE, IXOTE*** SET A CONDITION in HEAVEN for the NEW POST of the ANGEL of THE ***HOLY SPIRIT. IXOTE*** SAID, any ANGEL holding the NEW POST had to be RECREATED in a form having GENDER, thus being different from the other THREE PRINCES. SO ***IXOTE*** REMOVED from LUCIFER ALL FEMININE QUALITIES THUS MAKING HIM A MALE AND THE FIRST IN HEAVEN HAVING GENDER.

IXOTE ALSO GAVE LUCIFER ACCESS TO THE EARTH FOR HE WAS THE ANGEL OF THE ***HOLY SPIRIT (IXOTE)*** who OVERSAW EARTH. LUCIFER WAS ALSO GIVEN the RESPONSIBILITY to oversee ALL forms of MUSIC in HEAVEN, thus making HIM the HIGHEST ORDER of the ANGEL and overseer of the CHOIRS. There was also one other CONDITION required of LUCIFER before HE could assume HIS NEW POST. LUCIFER had to SWEAR an OATH to ***GOD*** to remain CELIBATE, for HIS access to earth would put HIM among the women of the earth, and the ANGEL was FORBIDDEN to MATE with either the WOMAN or with another ANGEL, should they also be sent to EARTH and GIVEN GENDER.

THE COVENANT ANGEL

With ALL FOUR SERAPHIM DESTINED for EARTH, they ALSO had to have GENDER like LUCIFER, to be on EARTH. SO ***IXOTE*** REMOVED the FEMALE GENDER from the FOUR SERAPHIM, but UNLIKE that which ***HE*** had done with LUCIFER when ***HE*** had made HIM a MALE, ***IXOTE*** did not remove the FEMININE part of the SERAPHIM from EXISTENCE; but rather made them into SEVENTH LEVEL ANGELS. ***IXOTE*** then CALLED the FOUR NEW ANGELS of the FEMALE GENDER, COVENANT ANGELS, for they were the other HALF of the SERAPHIM, and were to be MATES to the SERAPHIM throughout ETERNITY. Thus was the FIRST CONTRACT of MARRIAGE MADE, BETWEEN the FOUR SERAPHIM and the FOUR COVENANT ANGELS, and ***IXOTE CALLED THE COVENANT, MARRIAGE,*** and gave the MARRIAGE the NAME, ***CHRIST!***

THOSE of CHRIST

BY CHRIST BEING BORN OUT OF THE ***TRINITY*** by ***YESHUA, YESHUA*** BECAME THE FINAL MEMBER of CHRIST. THE ***DELIVERER 182*** DESTINED to be the LAST to come to the EARTH in the FLESH, and BEING the FIRST DESCENDANT of the ***TRINITY,*** WAS MADE TO BE THE ONLY CONNECTION BETWEEN CHRIST and THE ***HOLY SPIRIT,*** OUTSIDE of the ***TRINITY.*** Therefor there NEEDED to BE a CONNECTION BETWEEN the MAN and THE ***DELIVERER 182,*** and that RESPONSIBILITY was GIVEN to THE ***DELIVERER'S*** FIRSTBORN, whose NAME is JESUS.

YOU were previously TOLD about the "T" shaped CORRIDOR and that the CORRIDOR was CONTROLLED by the THIRD SERAPHIM HAVING a FACE of A MAN. You were also TOLD that THE MAN, JESUS, was the only ENTRANCE and EXIT between HEAVEN and EARTH. Therefor by JESUS being the FIRST DESCENDANT of CHRIST, HE is both the ENTRY and EXIT from HEAVEN, and ONLY THROUGH CHRIST can any MAN ENTER INTO HEAVEN, thus making JESUS the MEANS to HEAVEN. Now that YOU KNOW of the MEANS, WE SHALL speak of the "WAY" to the CORRIDOR.

THE *DELIVERER*

Once ACCESS is ALLOWED to an INDIVIDUAL by the DOOR of the CORRIDOR at the BASE of the "T" being OPENED, ONE must DELIVER the INDIVIDUAL to the DOOR. ***HE*** who DELIVERS to the DOOR is CALLED THE ***DELIVERER,*** and THE DOOR BEING OPENED TO YOU IS CALLED ***SAVING GRACE.*** THE TRANSPORTATION GETTING TO THE DOOR IS CALLED ***DELIVERANCE,*** and the WAY is by ***RAPTURE.*** SAVING GRACE, DELIVERANCE and RAPTURE COME ONLY BY THE ***WILL*** (PERMISSION) OF ***YAHWEH, THE ALMIGHTY GOD,*** AND BY ***WAY of DELIVERANCE*** FROM ***IXOTE,*** THE ***HOLY SPIRIT of GOD,*** and this is CALLED BAPTISM in CHRIST.

In summary, THE ***DELIVERER*** (THE FOURTH SERAPHIM) gets YOU to the DOOR, the THIRD SERAPHIM CALLED JESUS is the DOOR; THE ***HOLY SPIRIT*** OPENS the DOOR, and it is ***YAHWEH, THE ALMIGHTY GOD WHO ALLOWS THE ACCESS THROUGH THE DOOR TO HEAVEN.*** THE SAME APPLIES TO THE ACCESS TO THE THRONE of ***GOD,*** EXCEPT IT IS ***YESHUA*** who ALLOWS that ACCESS, FOR HE IS

CHRIST WITHIN THE ***TRINITY.*** In brief, CHRIST is the ACCESS TO HEAVEN and ***CHRIST*** is the ACCESS to ***GOD.***

Chapter 8
The FALL of LUCIFER

The FOUR MATES to the SERAPHIM, called COVENANT ANGELS, are the MOST POWERFUL ANGELS in ALL of HEAVEN. Being ONE-HALF of the SERAPHIM, they are even GREATER than LUCIFER for they were of CHRIST whereas LUCIFER was not of CHRIST. This created a DIVISION between the ANGELS under LUCIFER'S control and those under the CONTROL of the THREE other PRINCES. The HIERARCHY of those outside of the ***TRINITY*** prior to the CREATION of ADAM was as follows:

SERAPHIM of the HIGHEST ORDER: THE ***DELIVERER 182***
SERAPHIM of the SECOND ORDER: 1st BORN, JESUS CHRIST
SERAPHIM of the THIRD ORDER: DAVID and SOLOMON

METATRON: ANAFI-EL, SAN-DAL'-PHON, ME'-SO-LOT and OR'-THA-BEL

COVENANT of the HIGHEST ORDER: JAEL
COVENANT of the 2nd ORDER: URIEL
COVENANTS of the 3rd ORDER: ZARALL and CHAMUEL

ANGEL of THE ***HOLY SPIRIT:*** LUCIFER

PRINCES of the SEVENTH LEVEL: MICHAEL, GABRIEL and RAPHAEL

6th CHOIR ANGELS
5th CHOIR ANGELS
4th CHOIR ANGELS
3rd CHOIR ANGELS
2nd CHOIR ANGELS
1st CHOIR ANGELS

ADAM, the MAN with a SOUL

SEVENTY THOUSAND YEARS after ***GOD'S*** SIX days of CREATION, the MAN BEARING a SOUL was to be BORN of FLESH and put upon the EARTH in a GARDEN ***GOD*** called EDEN. This was a place that was MADE specifically for the MAN BEARING a SOUL coming from CHRIST and he was to be the FIRST of MANY GENERATIONS to be BORN OUT of CHRIST. This MAN was to be ISOLATED from ***GOD'S*** SIXTH DAY CREATION for he did not have a GENDER, whereas the SIXTH DAY CREATION was both the MALE and the FEMALE GENDERS. Also ***GOD*** had made this MAN for ***HIMSELF*** so ***HE*** could have FELLOWSHIP with the MAN having the SOUL without INTERRUPTION by the others CREATED like the animal, without SOULS.

In order for the MAN who ***GOD*** had made from the DUST of the EARTH to RECEIVE a SOUL, that SOUL MUST FIRST come down from HEAVEN to reside with the MAN. By THE ***DELIVERER*** being the FIRST DESCENDANT of the ***TRINITY,*** HIS FIRSTBORN SON, was the only other ONE outside of the ***TRINITY*** with OMNIPRESENCE. This would allow the SOUL to come down from HEAVEN to reside with the MAN while YET STILL BEING in HEAVEN. So the SOUL from the THIRD SERAPHIM, having the FACE of a MAN, was SENT to the EARTH and put INTO ADAM!

> ***John 3:13 AND NO MAN HATH ASCENDED UP TO HEAVEN, BUT HE THAT CAME DOWN FROM HEAVEN, EVEN THE SON OF MAN WHICH IS IN HEAVEN.***

NOTE: THIS IS JESUS CHRIST VERIFYING THAT HE WAS ON EARTH, WHILE STILL IN HEAVEN!

So ***GOD*** TOOK the SOUL from THE THIRD SERAPHIM and put it into the MAN that ***HE*** had made from the DUST of the EARTH, and the MAN BECAME A LIVING SOUL, and ***GOD CALLED THE MAN, ADAM.***

After nearly one hundred years had past since the CREATION of ADAM, and ADAM having named all the animals, ***GOD*** saw that ADAM was LONELY and in need of a MATE. With ADAM having the SOUL of CHRIST the only MATE suitable for ADAM was from the ONE sharing in that SAME SOUL. SO as ***IXOTE*** had done in HEAVEN with the SERAPHIM, ***HE*** did so again with the MAN and SEPARATED the MASCULINE and FEMININE GENDERS in ADAM, and made from the FEMININE GENDER a WOMAN of

FLESH sharing in the SAME SOUL of CHRIST. So with ADAM being the SPIRIT of JESUS, the WOMAN had to RECEIVE the SPIRIT of URIEL who was the SOUL MATE of JESUS CHRIST. ADAM then NAMED the WOMAN EVE, for SHE was the EVE of ALL GENERATIONS to FOLLOW HAVING a SOUL GIVEN BY CHRIST, MAKING ADAM and EVE to be the FIRST UPON THE EARTH to be HUSBAND and WIFE. Therefore MARRIAGE as it was in HEAVEN was now on EARTH, bringing the COVENANT of MARRIAGE to EARTH.

LUCIFER'S REVOLT

LUCIFER, having ACCESS to earth and being PRESENT with ***IXOTE*** in the GARDEN, SAW ***IXOTE'S*** COMPASSION for the MAN, ADAM, and became JEALOUS of him and wanted to prove the MAN to be unworthy of ***GOD'S AFFECTION.*** However, ADAM being made like the ANGEL COULD NOT BE MADE TO SIN AGAINST ***GOD.*** So prior to the CREATION of EVE, LUCIFER confronted ***IXOTE*** and DEMANDED that the MAN with the SOUL be GIVEN a COMMANDMENT. He further said that if he were GIVEN a COMMANDMENT, the MAN would VIOLATE that COMMANDMENT and SIN against ***GOD.*** So ***IXOTE*** again ACCOMMODATED LUCIFER and gave the MAN a COMMANDMENT.

> ***Genesis 2:16*** *And THE LORD* ***GOD*** *COMMANDED the MAN, saying, OF EVERY TREE OF THE GARDEN THOU MAYEST FREELY EAT:*
>
> ***Genesis 2:17*** *BUT OF THE TREE OF THE KNOWLEDGE OF GOOD AND EVIL, THOU SHALT NOT EAT OF IT: FOR IN THE DAY THAT THOU EATEST THEREOF THOU SHALT SURELY DIE.*

So LUCIFER waited until ADAM was given a GENDER and no longer had the CREDENTIALS of the ANGEL, to CAUSE him to SIN. Once EVE was taken out of ADAM, LUCIFER then MADE HIS APPEARANCE to EVE and CONVINCED her to VIOLATE ***GOD'S COMMANDMENT***, and she in turn caused her husband ADAM to SIN as she had done.

Once ***GOD*** had seen that the MAN and the WOMAN had VIOLATED ***HIS COMMANDMENT and SINNED, HE CAST THEM OUT OF THE GARDEN and OUT OF HIS PRESENCE.*** AT the same TIME, Lucifer was relieved of his POST as ANGEL of THE ***HOLY SPIRIT*** and CAST OUT of HEAVEN and on to the earth, and those who upheld him, were cast out with him. An ETERNAL CURSE was then put upon Lucifer; that he should remain on the earth and be lower than the animal, and only be allowed access to THE THRONE for COUNSEL. Lucifer's access was to be by the way of the METATRON (the Abyss) and could no longer ACCESS THE THRONE through the CORRIDOR.

> ***Genesis 3:14*** *And THE LORD* ***GOD*** *said unto the serpent, BECAUSE THOU HAST DONE THIS, THOU ART CURSED ABOVE ALL CATTLE, AND ABOVE EVERY BEAST OF THE FIELD; UPON THY BELLY SHALT THOU GO, AND DUST SHALT THOU EAT ALL THE DAYS OF THY LIFE:*

> ***Genesis 3:15*** *AND I WILL PUT ENMITY BETWEEN THEE AND THE WOMAN, AND BETWEEN THY SEED AND HER SEED; IT SHALL BRUISE THY HEAD, AND THOU SHALT BRUISE HIS HEEL.*

DEMOTION of URIEL

With the SPIRIT of URIEL making the DECISIONS for the Woman Eve, ***IXOTE*** held URIEL responsible for the Woman's actions. SHE was then removed from being a COVENANT ANGEL and put below the THREE PRINCES, MICHAEL GABRIEL and RAPHAEL. Then, because SHE was now SEPARATED from HER SOUL MATE, SHE must remain as a FEMALE throughout ETERNITY, being an INCOMPLETE Angel, although she was allowed to remain in the SEVENTH LEVEL ORDER of ANGELS.

To REPLACE Uriel, the ANGEL ASAPH of the SIXTH CHOIR (The Chief Musician), was GIVEN the FEMALE GENDER and BECAME the SOUL MATE to JESUS CHRIST, the THIRD SERAPHIM.

PROMOTION of RAPHAEL

RAPHAEL, being ONE of THREE PRINCES, and a LOYAL SERVANT to ***GOD,*** was then PROMOTED to the FORMER POSITION of Lucifer, and made the ANGEL of THE ***HOLY SPIRIT*** and a DIRECT REPORT to ***IXOTE.*** HE was also GIVEN OMNIPRESENCE and RESUMED THE RESPONSIBILITIES as the OVERSEER of ALL the CHOIRS of ANGELS. RAPHAEL was also made the ANGEL over FIRE and WATER, and the CHIEF WITNESS of ALL SPIRITUAL BAPTISM that was soon to take place on EARTH.

GABRIEL was also PROMOTED for both HE and MICHAEL FOUGHT as well with RAPHAEL against Lucifer and his following, so they might EVICT Lucifer from HEAVEN, for he did not leave without a fight. But MICHAEL and HIS ANGELS PREVAILED and Lucifer was cast out. GABRIEL was then MADE the ANGEL and the OVERSEER of ALL of CHRIST, and MICHAEL was MADE the ANGEL of THE THRONE of ***GOD.***

> ***Revelation 12:7*** *And there was a WAR in HEAVEN: Mi'-cha-el and his ANGELS fought against the DRAGON; and the DRAGON fought and his angels,*

> ***Revelation 12:8*** *And prevailed not; neither was their place found any more in HEAVEN.*

> ***Revelation 12:9*** *And the GREAT DRAGON was cast out, that OLD SERPENT, called the DEVIL, and SATAN, which deceiveth the whole world: he was cast out into the earth, and his angels were cast out with him.*

> ***Revelation 12:10*** *And I heard a LOUD VOICE saying in HEAVEN, NOW IS COME SALVATION, AND STRENGTH, AND THE KINGDOM OF OUR* **GOD**, *AND THE POWER OF* ***HIS*** *CHRIST: FOR THE ACCUSER OF OUR BRETHREN IS CAST DOWN, WHICH ACCUSED THEM BEFORE OUR* **GOD** *DAY AND NIGHT.*

After the WAR, ***IXOTE*** allowed MICHAEL to APPOINT SEVENTY ANGELS of the lower ORDER to the SEVENTH LEVEL, and MICHAEL called these ANGELS "THRONES"; with Uriel assuming a temporary POST as one of the THRONES. This CHANGE now brought the TOTAL NUMBER of the SEVENTH LEVEL ANGEL up to SEVENTY-SEVEN, where it had been PREVIOUSLY FOUR. The SEVENTY-SEVEN consisted of FOUR COVENANT ANGELS and THREE PRINCES who ARE TO BE LATER CALLED ARK ANGELS (and not Archangels as the Church incorrectly calls them) and the SEVENTY THRONES.

Chapter 9
DIMENSIONS

There are THIRTEEN DIMENSIONS existing within the UNIVERSE, FOUR being Physical, and NINE being VERTICAL DIMENSIONS. These DIMENSIONS can be expressed as SPHERES CONTAINED within larger SPHERES, with the largest SPHERE being the UNIVERSE itself. Within the UNIVERSE there are EIGHT smaller SPHERES that exist, with the smallest of its SPHERES containing the FOUR Physical DIMENSIONS. Each SPHERE declines in size with the SMALLEST SPHERE being situated at its ABSOLUTE CENTER, and is called the "EARTH PLANE", and the FOUR Physical DIMENSIONS are contained within the EARTH PLANE.

The FOUR Physical DIMENSIONS within the EARTH PLANE are called; LENGTH, WIDTH, HEIGHT, and TIME and are ALL RELATIVE DIMENSIONS. RELATIVE DIMENSIONS are NOT ABSOLUTE (CONSTANTS) and any MEASUREMENT made utilizing the FOUR EARTH PLANE DIMENSIONS can only be expressed in terms of RELATIVE MEASUREMENTS. The FOUR DIMENSIONS within the EARTH PLANE relate to one another and are therefor DEPENDENT on EACH OTHER'S quantitative value.

This is to say; if any one DIMENSION were to be held CONSTANT, then all FOUR of the other DIMENSIONS must also remain CONSTANT. Therefor, with TIME continually changing (for it cannot be held CONSTANT), the other THREE DIMENSIONS are also continually changing. This makes any MEASUREMENT within this CONTINUUM of TIME a RELATIVE MEASUREMENT.

In the EARTH PLANE all objects have LENGTH, WIDTH, HEIGHT, and TIME governing their existence. The first three of these DIMENSIONS are quite obvious to us for WE can see them PHYSICALLY. However the presence of TIME and its EFFECT on objects only reveals itself after a period of TIME has elapsed, because its EFFECTS on OBJECTS are only detectable over the DURATION of TIME. The longer the elapsed TIME, the more evident are the EFFECTS of TIME on the other THREE DIMENSIONS.

The altering or CHANGE of an OBJECT as a function of TIME will vary depending on its MATERIAL COMPOSITION and its relative ENVIRONMENT. For instance; if you were to take a slice of bread and leave it out on a table top for several days, you would see a noticeable CHANGE in its appearance. This CHANGE would occur over a very short period of time, whereas the same slice of bread would change at a slower rate if kept in cold storage. This analogy would demonstrate the INFLUENCE of ENVIRONMENT on an OBJECT as a function of TIME.

By the same token, if you were to perform the same test substituting the slice of bread with a sheet of aluminum foil, it could be seen that it would take a significantly longer duration of time for any change to occur in the object. This 2nd test would demonstrate how the MATERIAL COMPOSITION effects the rate of CHANGE of an OBJECT, as a function of TIME. However, in either case, both the slice of bread and the sheet of aluminum foil will change as a FUNCTION of TIME, with the TIME for CHANGE being a VARIABLE for different MATERIAL COMPOSITIONS and various ENVIRONMENTS.

Therefor it can be said ALL OBJECTS within a TIME CONTINUUM are RELATIVE and are SUBJECT to CHANGE as a FUNCTION of TIME. It can also be said, because MAN lives in a TIME CONTINUUM, ALL methods of MEASUREMENT within that CONTINUUM are RELATIVE, and will VARY as a FUNCTION of TIME. This causes MAN GREAT DIFFICULTY when dealing with ABSOLUTE and INFINITE VALUES, because they are CONSTANT VALUES and are not DEPENDENT on TIME DURATION. Therefor, any MEASUREMENT using TIME as a STANDARD, is an inaccurate measurement because TIME CONTINUALLY CHANGES!

ABSOLUTE DIMENSIONS

WE have talked about the FOUR EARTH PLANE DIMENSIONS, which are variable dimensions, and now WE will discuss the DIMENSIONS above the EARTH PLANE, all of which are ABSOLUTE DIMENSIONS. The FIFTH DIMENSION, which is the SECOND SPHERE above the EARTH PLANE, is called the "GAP" or the "GAP DIMENSION". The GAP DIMENSION is what SEPARATES the EARTH PLANE DIMENSIONS from the CELESTIAL DIMENSIONS, or the VARIABLE DIMENSIONS from the ABSOLUTE DIMENSIONS. This is referred to in the Scriptures as the SEPARATION of the WATERS that are ABOVE the FIRMAMENT from the WATERS that are below the FIRMAMENT.

Genesis 1:6 *And **GOD** said, LET THERE BE A FIRMAMENT in* *the midst of the WATERS, and let it DIVIDE the waters from the WATERS.*

Genesis 1:7 *And* ***GOD*** *made the FIRMAMENT, and DIVIDED the waters which were UNDER the FIRMAMENT from the WATERS which were ABOVE the FIRMAMENT: and it was so.*

This was ***GOD'S*** separation of the EARTH PLANE DIMENSIONS from the upper CELESTIAL DIMENSIONS. Whereas the EARTH PLANE DIMENSIONS are ALL RELATIVE DIMENSIONS, the upper CELESTIAL DIMENSIONS ARE ALL ABSOLUTE (CONSTANT) DIMENSIONS and are not DEPENDENT on other DIMENSIONS or subject to CHANGE due any external influences. The FIFTH DIMENSION and ABOVE are ALL CONTAINED within another PLANE outside of the EARTH PLANE and that PLANE is CALLED the "CONSCIENCE PLANE". There are FIVE DIMENSIONS within the CONSCIENCE PLANE and they are as follows:

The CONSCIENCE PLANE

1. The FIFTH DIMENSION is the "GAP DIMENSION"
2. The SIXTH DIMENSION is the "SPIRITUAL DIMENSION"
3. The SEVENTH DIMENSION is the "SOUL DIMENSION"
4. The EIGHTH DIMENSION is the "CATALYTIC DIMENSION"
5. The NINTH DIMENSION is the "CONTAINMENT DIMENSION"

The GAP DIMENSION which is the FIRST of the CONSCIENCE PLANE DIMENSIONS is VOID of any type of EXISTENCE, and merely SERVES as a DIVIDING line between the EARTH PLANE DIMENSIONS and the CELESTIAL DIMENSIONS. The 6th, 7th, 8th and 9th DIMENSIONS are ALL EMOTIONAL DIMENSIONS, and can ONLY be experienced in a SPIRITUAL STATE, and this is why the ***SIXTH DIMENSION*** is called the SPIRITUAL DIMENSION, for it is the 1st SPIRITUAL STATE. Once in the SIXTH DIMENSION, the SPIRIT transforms into a COSMOS STATE and becomes INFINITE in MEASUREMENT of VOLUME.

The ***SEVENTH DIMENSION***, the SOUL DIMENSION, GOVERNS by JUDGMENT, the CONSCIOUS ACTIONS of the SPIRIT. In this SPIRITUAL STATE the SPIRIT is SELF-JUDGED in an uninfluenced and unbiased manner as to its PERSONAL BEHAVIOR relating to ALL ***GOD'S LAWS.***

The ***EIGHTH DIMENSION***, the CATALYTIC DIMENSION, is a CON-

SCIENCE STATE where SPIRITUAL CONSCIOUSNESS becomes significantly INCREASED causing an overwhelming AWARENESS of SPIRITUAL EXISTENCE. While in this STATE, WISDOM and INDIVIDUALITY (IDENTITY) become UNIFIED and are INSEPARABLE, thus no longer allowing ONE'S PERSONALITY to effect ONE'S SPIRITUAL JUDGMENT, for it is now BASED SOLELY on WISDOM.

The ***NINTH DIMENSION***, the CONTAINMENT DIMENSION, is the MAINTENANCE of INDIVIDUALITY (IDENTITY) while yet being in a COSMOS STATE having an INFINITE SPIRITUAL MASS. This allows the SPIRIT the ability to RETAIN ITS IDENTITY while EXPANDING and occupying an INFINITE AREA of SPACE, without having to commingle with other SPIRITUAL ENTITIES occupying the SAME SPACE.

The CHANGE PLANE

The TENTH, ELEVENTH, and TWELFTH DIMENSIONS are ALL in what is called the "CHANGE PLANE". These DIMENSIONS cause CHANGES to take place within the SPIRITUAL MATTER, thus transfiguring the SPIRIT into another LIFE FORM.

The ***TENTH DIMENSION,*** the "INERTIA DIMENSION", is where the SPIRIT overcomes its natural EQUILIBRIUM; that of which maintains its state of either rest or movement. This is the POINT in which the SPIRIT no longer OPPOSES CHANGE in DIRECTION and can FREELY move about the COSMOS without RESISTANCE or INFLUENCE by other external forces. This is called the "FREEDOM STATE", and is somewhat similar to OMNI-PRESENCE, however this STATE only pertains to FREEDOM to move about within the UNIVERSE while being in INFINITE MASS.

The ***ELEVENTH DIMENSION,*** the "ACCELERATION DIMENSION", is where the SPIRIT ACCELERATES to the SPEED of LIGHT, thus causing SPIRITUAL MATTER to begin to RESONATE and TRANSFIGURE into another FORM.

The ***TWELFTH DIMENSION*** is the "RESONANCE DIMENSION", and is also called ***"RAPTURE".*** ONCE the SPIRIT has reached its TERMINAL VELOCITY (LIGHT SPEED) caused by the "ACCELERATION DIMENSION", RESONANCE occurs, causing the SPIRIT to be TRANSFIGURED from SPIRITUAL MATTER into PHOTO KINETIC ENERGY.

THE THIRTEENTH DIMENSION

After RAPTURE, the SPIRIT takes on a NEW LIGHT LIFE FORM that consists of only PHOTON KINETIC ENERGY with its substance being NEUTRINO BASED LIGHT rather than SPIRITUAL based MATTER. At this point of ASCENSION, CELESTIAL FINALITY has been reached for the SPIRIT, and ABSOLUTE CONSCIOUSNESS is ACHIEVED. This CONSCIOUSNESS has both IDENTITY and PERSONALITY and the FREEDOM of CELESTIAL MOVEMENT. The SPIRIT in this STATE also has the ABILITY to COMMUNICATE with others within the LIGHT FORM and ALSO with them who are not yet in a LIGHT FORM and are outside of the EARTH PLANE. This is the ETERNAL LIGHT STATE for the CELESTIAL BOUND SPIRIT. However, the SPIRIT is NOT YET in its HEAVENLY FORM of LIGHT, and cannot EXIT the UNIVERSE, for there is yet another "GAP" between the UNIVERSE and HEAVEN.

PARALLEL DIMENSIONS

Each VERTICAL DIMENSION has both THREE POSITIVE PARALLELS and THREE NEGATIVE PARALLEL DIMENSIONS, with ALL SEVEN DIMENSIONS per VERTICAL DIMENSION being called "BANDS". The SIX PARALLEL DIMENSIONS are called PERSONALITY DIMENSIONS. The POSITIVE PARALLELS are situated to the RIGHT of the CELESTIAL VERTICAL DIMENSIONS and the NEGATIVE PARALLELS are situated to the LEFT of the CELESTIAL VERTICALS, thus making a total of 39 POSITIVE and 39 NEGATIVE PARALLELS. This brings the NUMBER of CELESTIAL DIMENSIONS up to 91 in total, consisting of 13 VERTICALS (four of which are Physical Dimensions), 39 POSITIVE PARALLELS, and 39 NEGATIVE PARALLELS.

Each column of PARALLELS (called PERSONALITY DIMENSIONS) has a NAME assigned to it. The 1st POSITIVE PARALLEL is called, "FAITH", while the 1st NEGATIVE PARALLEL is called, "DOUBT". The 2nd POSITIVE PARALLEL is called "WISDOM", and the 2nd NEGATIVE PARALLEL is called "MISCHIEF". The 3rd POSITIVE PARALLEL is called, "LOVE", and the 3rd NEGATIVE PARALLEL is called "HATRED". The THREE POSITIVE PARALLELS as a group are CALLED "GOOD", or OPTIMISTIC PARALLELS, and the THREE NEGATIVE PARALLELS are CALLED, "EVIL" or PESSIMISTIC PARALLELS.

PARALLELS within the EARTH PLANE

The PARALLELS that exist within the EARTH PLANE INFLUENCE one's HUMAN BEHAVIOR and STYLE of thinking. When a PERSON is pulled to the RIGHT SIDE PARALLELS (the GOOD) they have a tendency to SEE the cup as being HALF FULL whereas those being pulled towards the LEFT SIDE PARALLELS (the EVIL) SEE the cup as being HALF EMPTY. Lucifer, the Devil, rules the PARALLELS to the LEFT whereas JESUS CHRIST RULES the PARALLELS on the RIGHT.

A CHILD of ***GOD*** is intended to SPIRITUALLY ASCEND in a PERFECTLY VERTICAL PATTERN, however the influences of the LEFT and RIGHT PARALLELS can cause the PATTERN to DEVIATE from its INTENDED VERTICAL PATH. The POSITIVE PARALLELS on the RIGHT will NEVER PULL ONE PASSED the center of VERTICAL, but will only OPPOSE MOVEMENT to the LEFT. However the NEGATIVE PARALLELS on the LEFT will continually try to PULL the Spirit off COURSE and to the LEFT. This is the BALANCE between GOOD and EVIL within the EARTH PLANE, where EVIL has a 2:1 advantage (TWO-THIRDS to ONE-THIRD).

For the Spirit to leave the EARTH PLANE it must be in the MIDDLE of its VERTICAL ASCENDING PATH prior to the Spirit reaching its TERM LIMIT of Physical Life, which is governed by the FOURTH DIMENSION, TIME. This is to say, the Spirit must be leaning towards the RIGHT to overcome the forces being applied from the LEFT, keeping it in a VERTICAL FLIGHT PATH (ASCENSION) PRIOR TO ITS PHYSICAL TERMINATION of LIFE.

PARALLELS outside of the EARTH PLANE

The INFLUENCES of the PARALLELS outside of the EARTH PLANE DECREASE in INTENSITY as ASCENSION INCREASES. Also, the BALANCE between the POSITIVE and NEGATIVE PARALLELS from the GAP DIMENSION and UPWARD, are EQUAL and OPPOSITE and can no longer INFLUENCE ONE'S VERTICAL FLIGHT PATTERN.

The HOLY BIBLE refers to the EARTH as being a WOMAN in TRAVAIL (hard labor) and the WOMB carrying the UNBORN CHILD (the spirit that has not ASCENDED). When ONE VERTICALLY ASCENDS from the WOMB (the EARTH PLANE) BIRTH of the CHILD then BEGINS, and this is called "DELIVERANCE". This in part is what JESUS was speaking about when HE SAID, that one could not ENTER into HEAVEN unless they had been RE-

BORN in the SPIRIT, thus referring to the Spirit ASCENDING beyond the EARTH PLANE!

> ***John 3:3*** *JESUS answered and said unto him,* ***VERILY, VERILY, I SAY UNTO THEE, EXCEPT A MAN BE BORN AGAIN, HE CANNOT SEE THE KINGDOM OF GOD.***

> ***John 3:4*** *Nic-o-de'-mus saith unto HIM, How can a man be born when he is old? Can he enter the second time into his mother's womb, and be born?*

> ***John 3:5*** *JESUS answered,* ***VERILY, VERILY, I SAY UNTO THEE, EXCEPT A MAN BE BORN OF WATER AND OF THE SPIRIT, HE CANNOT ENTER INTO THE KINGDOM OF GOD.***

The WATER spoken of in the Scripture refers to the LIVING WATERS, the *WORD of* ***GOD***, and also the WATERS ABOVE the FIRMAMENT (the GAP). The SPIRIT SPOKEN about, is SPIRITUAL BAPTISM and the ***SIXTH DIMENSION,*** the SPIRITUAL DIMENSION. The SPIRITUAL DIMENSION (the WATERS ABOVE the FIRMAMENT) lies just BEYOND the GAP DIMENSION (which is the DIVIDING LINE between the EARTH PLANE and the upper CELESTIAL DIMENSIONS) and the point where the BALANCE between GOOD and EVIL becomes EQUAL.

With GOOD and EVIL now being EQUAL and OPPOSITE to one another in the SPIRITUAL DIMENSION, EVIL can no longer AFFECT ONE'S VERTICAL FLIGHT (ASCENSION). This is the point at which SPIRITUAL EQUILIBRIUM is achieved and EVIL can no longer INFLUENCE the SPIRIT (CALLED SAVING GRACE). This is the TIME of SPIRITUAL BAPTISM and the REBIRTH of the SPIRIT, thus making the ONE RECEIVING it REBORN in LIGHT (CHRIST the LIGHT of the WORLD).

HEAVENLY DIMENSIONS

As WE gave you Scriptures describing ***GOD'S*** SEPARATION between the EARTH PLANE and the upper CELESTIAL DIMENSIONS, WE will use the SAME SCRIPTURES again, and apply the SECOND LAYER of the SCRIPTURES to the SEPARATION of CELESTIAL DIMENSIONS (the UNIVERSE) from HEAVENLY DIMENSIONS.

> ***Genesis 1:6*** *And* ***GOD*** *said, LET THERE BE A FIRMAMENT in the midst of the WATERS, and let it DIVIDE the waters from the WATERS.*

> ***Genesis 1:7*** *And* ***GOD*** *made the FIRMAMENT, and DIVIDED the waters which were UNDER the FIRMAMENT from the WATERS which were ABOVE the FIRMAMENT: and it was so.*

In HEAVEN there are 56 DIMENSIONS consisting of 8 BANDS of VERTICAL ASCENDING LEVELS. EACH BAND also consists of SEVEN PARALLEL DIMENSIONS, however unlike the CELESTIAL DIMENSIONS, ALL SEVEN are POSITIVE VERTICAL DIMENSIONS. The SEVEN DIMENSIONS in each set of BANDS REPRESENT the ***SEVEN SPIRITS of GOD.*** The EIGHT VERTICAL LEVELS REPRESENT the EIGHT HEAVENLY LEVELS described in the PREVIOUS BOOK, that ASCEND up to the LEVEL OF THE SERAPHIM.

THRONE DIMENSIONS

The SAME SCRIPTURES of Genesis 1:6 and 1:7 apply again, however they now DESCRIBE the DIVISION of the THRONE of ***GOD*** from the 56 HEAVENLY VERTICAL DIMENSIONS. This is the THIRD LAYER of the SCRIPTURES that DESCRIBE the SEPARATION of the ***TRINITY*** from the HEAVENLY BODY. Whereas the GAP was the DIVIDING line of the EARTH PLANE from the upper CELESTIAL DIMENSIONS, and the 2nd GAP the dividing line of the UNIVERSE and HEAVEN, so is the FOUR SERAPHIM the GAP and DIVIDING LINE of the HEAVENLY BODY from the THRONE of ***GOD.***

The ***THRONE DIMENSIONS*** also consist of BANDS of SEVEN, however there are only 5 VERTICAL LEVELS within the ***TRINITY,*** making the TOTAL number of DIMENSIONS of the ***TRINITY 35.*** The FIRST TWO LEVELS consisting of ***14*** DIMENSIONS are the ***DIMENSIONS of YESHUA. THE REMAINING THREE DIMENSION LEVELS ARE THAT of IXOTE, THE HOLY SPIRIT of GOD. THIS BRINGS THE TOTAL ASCENDING LEVELS TO 26 LEVELS and THE TOTAL NUMBER of DIMENSIONS to 182,*** FROM EARTH to ***GOD.*** RESIDING ABOVE ALL 26 LEVELS of ASCENSION is ***YAHWEH, THE ALMIGHTY GOD!***

Chapter 10
CONSCIOUSNESS

Consciousness is AWARENESS and AWARENESS is LIFE! If you were to look at life on earth in the FLESHEN FORM as compared to LIFE in a COSMIC FORM (SPIRITUAL LIFE) it would be similar to the comparison of the human being to the ameba. Consciousness in the FLESH is at the bottom end of the life scale; likening to a number one, whereas COSMIC LIFE within the CELESTIAL DIMENSIONS are equal to the number 1 raised to the 91st POWER. The topic of this Chapter is to bring to your UNDERSTANDING the POWER of ***GOD*** GIVEN SPIRITUAL EXISTENCE.

The MIND has two basic states of CONSCIOUSNESS: the CONSCIOUS and the SUBCONSCIOUS. The CONSCIOUS STATE makes all the secondary and low priority decisions for the body of flesh, whereas the SUBCONSCIOUS makes the PRIMARY and HIGH PRIORITY DECISIONS for the body of flesh. The conscious mind makes decisions such as; where should I go and what should I eat and what should I wear? WHEREAS the SUBCONSCIOUS MIND determines how many heart beats will be needed to fulfill the oxygen required for the muscles to get you where you have decided to go. And, how much food the body will require for its nourishment, and how much clothing will be needed to ensure a pleasant environment for the body of flesh. All of these priorities are COMMUNICATED from the SUBCONSCIOUS to the CONSCIOUS MIND providing the CONSCIOUS MIND with FEEDBACK on how the body of flesh has responded to the decisions made by the CONSCIOUS MIND.

ALL lower level animals have this capability of SUBCONSCIOUS to CONSCIOUS FEEDBACK. This is a BIOLOGICAL FEATURE and merely acts as a GOVERNOR to ENSURE proper BODILY FUNCTIONS. The upper level INTELLIGENCE animals have in addition to this BIOLOGICAL MIND FEED BACK SYSTEM, an earth given Spirit that also provides to its HOST the ability to IDENTIFY its own INDIVIDUALITY. This enables the HOST of the Spirit to recognize its own uniqueness as compared to other BIOLOGICAL ENTITIES.

With MAN being of the highest intellectual order on earth, he through his own genetic makeup retains the traits of his ancestry and can also further his knowledge bank by his ability to understand. This is why MAN today can do far more things through knowledge and technology than his forefathers could have done.

Before WE get further into the subject of CONSCIOUSNESS, let us review the DEFINITIONS of some of the KEY WORDS that will be used to EXPRESS this issue. There are THREE KEY WORDS of importance: UNDERSTANDING, KNOWLEDGE and WISDOM. The WORD "UNDERSTANDING" means the ability of ONE to LEARN. The WORD "KNOWLEDGE" means ONE'S ability to RETAIN what ONE has learned. And, the WORD "WISDOM" means ONE'S ability to APPLY that which has been LEARNED and RETAINED. These three abilities are called "MIND-SETS" and only MAN has these three skills. This is why the animal today does much of the same things in the same way its ancestry had done. The animal can only learn simple things and what it has learned CANNOT be passed down through its offspring. Therefor an animal's genetic makeup can only change through evolution. It cannot retain what it has learned and pass that information down through it generations as the Man can do.

All of mankind having the earth given Spirit possesses these higher level intellectual skills. However, those who RECEIVE a ***GOD*** GIVEN SPIRIT go FAR BEYOND that which the MAN of the earth can accomplish, by RECEIVING in addition to the ***GOD*** GIVEN SPIRIT, also a SOUL. Although the Spirit of the earth born Man can experience EMOTION, it is of a much LOWER ORDER than the EMOTION experienced by ONE having a SOUL. Whereas the Man born of the earth both LIVES and DIES on the earth, the MAN with a SOUL merely begins LIFE on earth, and then transcends through the VERTICAL DIMENSIONS covered in the previous Chapter to an ETERNAL LIFE, a LIFE WITHOUT END!

These Scriptures in Ecclesiastes refer to the Man born of the earth as the "BEAST", whereas they refer to the ***GOD*** GIVEN SPIRIT as the SPIRIT of MAN THAT ASCENDS,

> ***Ecclesiastes 3:19*** *For that which befalleth the sons of men befalleth beasts; even one thing befalleth them: as one dieth, so dieth the other; yea, they have all one breath; so that a man have no preeminence above a beast: for all is vanity.*

NOTE: This Scripture is stating that the earth born man isn't any different than the animal on earth. They both live and they both die on earth even though the man is of a higher order of intelligence, and in regard to death, the earth born man hasn't any preeminence over the animal.

> ***Ecclesiastes 3:20*** *ALL go unto one place, ALL are of DUST, and ALL turn to DUST again.*

> ***Ecclesiastes 3:21*** *Who knoweth the SPIRIT of MAN that go UPWARD, and the Spirit of the BEAST that goeth downward to the earth?*

NOTE: What SOLOMON is saying in these last two Scriptures, is that the earth born Spirit of man comes from the earth ("are of DUST") and returns to the earth. SOLOMON further states that those who have a ***GOD*** GIVEN SPIRIT that ASCEND, cannot be told apart from those having an earth born Spirit that goes back into the earth.

The SOUL BEARING MAN with the ***GOD*** GIVEN SPIRIT looks IDENTICAL in the FLESH as the earth born Man with the earth born Spirit. This is why ***GOD*** told Samuel that ***HE*** LOOKS AT THE INSIDE of a PERSON rather than at the PERSON'S EXTERIOR, and ***ONLY GOD*** can tell the earth born Spirit from the ***GOD GIVEN SPIRIT*** in a PERSON. ***NOTE:*** Whenever the Scriptures refer to the HEART of a PERSON, they are referring to ONE'S SPIRIT, for the HEART of MAN is his SPIRIT.

> ***1 Samuel 16:7*** *But THE LORD said unto Samuel, LOOK NOT ON HIS COUNTENANCE, OR ON THE HEIGHT OF HIS STATURE; BECAUSE **I** HAVE REFUSED HIM: FOR THE LORD SEETH NOT AS MAN SEETH; FOR MAN LOOKETH ON THE OUTWARD APPEARANCE, BUT THE LORD LOOKETH ON THE HEART.*

The BALANCE of GOOD and Evil

In the previous Chapter WE spoke of PARALLEL DIMENSIONS that exist on either side of the VERTICAL DIMENSIONS. Those to the RIGHT of the VERTICAL DIMENSIONS are called the GOOD and those on the LEFT are called the EVIL. The MAN with a SOUL can differentiate between the two FORCES whereas the Man without a SOUL (the earth born man) cannot! The reason that the earth born Man cannot feel these FORCES is due to his lack of EMOTION.

This type of Man can only JUDGE HIMSELF based on MAN'S LAWS, by using his MIND-SETS. If he breaks the LAW, he then realizes he has done wrong, and can further avoid doing wrong by following the LAWS of MAN.

The Devil cannot differentiate between the MAN with a SOUL and the Man without one. So Lucifer ATTACKS both the SOULLESS and those with SOULS and then sees how they react to his influence. If he meets with little or no resistance, he then knows that the one he is attacking is SOULLESS and in the future leaves them alone for they are not of any value to him. This is why it seems to many as though the wicked can get away with murder, while the INNOCENT appear to always be PUNISHED for the lesser crimes.

The Devil RULES the PARALLELS on the LEFT and can literally pull one into the furthermost PARALLEL, called HATRED. This PARALLEL causes the one within it to have HATRED towards any form of life, even, his own, and is capable of committing the most heinous of crimes against life without any remorse whatsoever. However, even though JESUS CHRIST RULES the GOOD PARALLELS, HE cannot pull ONE BEYOND CENTER of VERTICAL. HOWEVER, this does not mean that a PERSON in the VERTICAL POSITION cannot on their own, EMBRACE FAITH, WISDOM, and LOVE, they can, but JESUS cannot do that for them! Therefor it might be said that while in the EARTH PLANE, the Devil has a distinct advantage. This is why he is referred to in the Scriptures as the Prince of the Earth.

This is also why it is so very IMPORTANT that the SOUL BEARING MAN should always be leaning towards the RIGHT and EMBRACING FAITH, for only by FAITH can one overcome the GRASP of the DEVIL.

ONCE a SOUL BEARING PERSON has RECEIVED SPIRITUAL BAPTISM, with that BAPTISM comes the GIFT of FAITH, thus PULLING that PARALLEL of FAITH into VERTICAL CENTER. ONCE FAITH has been brought into the VERTICAL DIMENSION, that INDIVIDUAL becomes a CHILD of ***GOD,*** and can no longer be PULLED off CENTER!

UNDERSTANDING, KNOWLEDGE, and WISDOM

The MIND-SETS WE spoke of earlier, UNDERSTANDING, KNOWLEDGE, and WISDOM, are significantly GREATER for the SOUL BEARING MAN than those same MIND-SETS are for the earth born Man. HOWEVER, these GREATER MIND-SETS can only be DEVELOPED by READING the *WORD of* ***GOD,*** for they are ***GOD*** GIVEN. By the SOUL BEARING MAN having a ***GOD*** GIVEN SPIRIT, he has the ABILITY to SPIRITUALLY INTERPRET the *WORD of* ***GOD.*** This enables that SPIRIT to PROCESS the *WORD of* ***GOD*** for

ITS UNDERSTANDING, KNOWLEDGE, and WISDOM, which is needed to DEVELOP the HIGHER ORDER MIND-SETS. This can be EXPRESSED as the FUEL NEEDED for the SPIRIT to ASCEND ABOVE the EARTH PLANE, and WITHOUT THIS FUEL, ASCENSION CANNOT BE ACHIEVED!

This is what was meant when JESUS SAID, "HE HAD OVERCOME THIS WORLD", and those of YOU with SOULS, can OVERCOME IT ALSO!

> ***John 16:33 THESE THINGS I HAVE SPOKEN UNTO YOU, THAT IN ME YE MIGHT HAVE PEACE. IN THE WORLD YE SHALL HAVE TRIBULATION: BUT BE OF GOOD CHEER; I HAVE OVERCOME THE WORLD.***

NOTE: THE KEY WORDS IN THIS SCRIPTURE ARE THE WORDS "IN ME". JESUS CHRIST IS THE *WORD of **GOD,*** the HOLY BIBLE, and if ONE GOES INTO THE HOLY BIBLE, THEY ARE GOING INTO JESUS! If you are a CHILD of ***GOD,*** YOU have been sent down from HEAVEN and put into a BODY of FLESH, and at that time YOUR SPIRITUAL MEMORY was erased. The ONLY way that YOUR MEMORY can be RESTORED is through the *WORD of **GOD!***

For ONE to RECEIVE ABSOLUTE CONSCIOUSNESS, they MUST ASCEND BEYOND THE EARTH PLANE, FOR ABSOLUTE CONSCIOUSNESS IS ABSOLUTE AWARENESS, AND ABSOLUTE AWARENESS, IS ETERNAL LIFE!

The POWER of Emotion

As previously explained, all Spiritual Beings experience some form of EMOTION and even the animal can express their FEELINGS through EMOTION. However, the SOUL BEARING MAN has EMOTION well beyond the Soulless Man and the animal. The POWER of EMOTION can be EXPRESSED in many, many, ways, and if PROPERLY CHANNELED, EMOTION can OVERPOWER any physical trait, and can be certainly felt physically.

Just prior to the Pharisees taking JESUS captive; HE asked them who they were looking for? When they had told HIM that they were looking for JESUS of Nazareth and HE answered them and said "I AM HE", they all fell backwards and were knocked to the ground.

> ***John 18:4*** *JESUS therefore, KNOWING ALL things that should come upon HIM, went forth, and said unto them,* ***WHOM SEEK***

YE?

John 18:5 *They answered HIM, JESUS of Nazareth, JESUS saith unto them,* ***I AM HE.*** *And Judas also, which betrayed HIM, stood with them.*

John 18:6 *As soon as HE had said unto them,* ***I AM HE,*** *they went backward, and fell to the ground.*

These Scriptures indicate that JESUS was so ANGERED of HIS BETRAYAL by Judas, that when the POWER of HIS EMOTION was UNLEASHED, it was so overwhelming, it knocked all of them to the ground. This was a DEMONSTRATION of HIS CHANNELED EMOTION, to let HIS Captors know that it was HE, WHO WAS IN CHARGE, and not them!

Although there are many EMOTIONS, there are SEVEN basic POSITIVE EMOTIONS and SEVEN basic NEGATIVE EMOTIONS. The POSITIVE EMOTIONS are LOVE, APPRECIATION, COMPASSION, JOY, PLEASURE, PEACE, and RELIANCE. The NEGATIVE EMOTIONS are HATRED, JEALOUSY, ANGER, SORROW, DISGUST, CONFUSION, and DISTRUST.

JESUS DEMONSTRATED that even in an earthly form, HIS EMOTION had enough POWER in it to knock several people to the ground when it was CHANNELED at them. Just imagine the POWER that could be released from ONE'S EMOTION if it was RAISED to the 91st POWER, as it can be, through CELESTIAL ASCENSION, or RAISED to the ***182nd POWER*** in HEAVENLY ASCENSION. These NUMBERS spoken of here are of an INFINITE NATURE! THE LORD has TOLD ME that when ***HE*** puts the SPIRIT of a CHILD of ***GOD*** into a BODY of FLESH, it can be likened to POURING an OCEAN into a THIMBLE!

Chapter 11
Life Elsewhere

GOD has TOLD ME that there are certainly LIFE FORMS ELSEWHERE in this GALAXY and in the other GALAXIES as well. However it is ONLY in the EARTH PLANE that there EXISTS a MAN BEARING A SOUL. This is because it is only on earth where EVIL may exist, and that is why the Devil is held CAPTIVE to the earth.

It is ***GOD'S WILL*** that ALL of ***HIS CHILDREN*** EXHIBIT the NATURE of ***GOD,*** knowing the difference between GOOD and EVIL! ***GOD*** IS THE ***CREATOR*** of BOTH GOOD and EVIL and ***HE*** maintains them BOTH in ABSOLUTE and PERFECT BALANCES. In the EARTH PLANE the BALANCE of GOOD and EVIL is TILTED towards EVIL, whereas outside of the EARTH PLANE, once beyond the GAP, EQUILIBRIUM is again REACHED between the two.

All other LIFE FORMS within the UNIVERSE have Spirits much like the earth borne Man, however; evil is not part of the other LIFE FORM'S makeup. ALL other BEINGS live a PRODUCTIVE LIFE and then return to the DUST of their HOST PLANET. They neither ASCEND, nor, do they DESCEND, and simply live and die like the animals on earth. Whereas Man, causes his own DESTRUCTION every SEVEN THOUSAND YEARS, it is not so with the other Beings; making them by far, more advanced. The Man of the earth is well below the INTELLECTUAL SCALE of the OTHER LIFE FORMS existing elsewhere in the UNIVERSE.

By the other LIFE FORMS being Spiritual hosted BIOLOGICAL UNITS, they come in various shapes and sizes, and some are similar looking to man, where others can be quite different looking. With the Spiritual Beings having MIND-SETS similar to the Man born of the earth, they forever grow more intelligent through their GENERATIONS, with many of them quite capable of inner galaxy travel, however none have matured to the point of INTERGALACTIC TRAVEL.

All LIFE FORMS within the GALAXY called the "MILKY WAY" are aware of the planet Earth, and see it as an INFERIOR form of life, thus steering them clear from ever intentionally making contact with Man. Although they observe earth and its life forms, and have even on occasion taken specimens from the earth, they haven't any desire to communicate with its INHABITANTS out of FEAR of them. It is well DOCUMENTED by the other LIFE FORMS, that every SEVEN THOUSAND YEARS, the INHABITANTS of Earth, DESTROY IT and they see Man as a HOSTILE ENTITY. They are also AWARE that the CHILD of ***GOD*** begins in the FORM of a MAN and are INTELLIGENT enough to not TAMPER with ***THE LORD'S*** MELTING POT!

With all of the other LIFE FORMS being outside of the EARTH PLANE, EVIL does not exist for them. They all have various forms of government, however there isn't any need for LAW, although they do have RULES governing their behavior that are NEVER VIOLATED.

Each of the HOST PLANETS bearing LIFE, have self supporting LIFE SYSTEMS that provide a SUITABLE ENVIRONMENT supportive of that LIFE. ALL forms of LIFE require WATER and LIGHT for their existence, however the BIOLOGICAL nourishment varies between the LIFE FORMS. .

EMOTION also does not exist outside of the EARTH PLANE, and with this being a NECESSARY INGREDIENT for the CHILD of ***GOD,*** this is but another reason why only the Earth can HOST a CHILD of ***GOD.*** This is also why there is a CONTAINMENT DIMENSION that the CHILD BEARING THE SOUL must go through during ASCENSION, thus not allowing EMOTION to COMMINGLE with other SPIRITUAL ENTITIES.

ALL other LIFE FORMS are aware of the EXISTENCE of ***GOD, HIS ANGELS*** and ***HIS CHILDREN,*** and are ROUTINELY VISITED by THEM! They have been TAUGHT about CREATION and USE what they have been TAUGHT in a PRODUCTIVE and POSITIVE manner! UNLIKE Man, the other LIFE FORMS LIVE PEACEABLY WITH EACH OTHER, NEVER HAVING WARS OR UNREST BETWEEN THE VARIOUS LIFE FORMS. INTERPLANETARY TRAVEL IS DONE ROUTINELY THROUGHOUT THE UNIVERSE IN ANY PARTICULAR GALAXY, WITH SOCIETIES COMMINGLING WITHOUT SOCIAL DISPUTE OR ADVERSITY BETWEEN THE VARIOUS FACTIONS OF LIFE.

GOD LOVES ALL FORMS OF LIFE, AND EXPECTS THOSE WHO HAVE RECEIVED THE GIFT of LIFE, TO HONOR AND RESPECT BOTH THEIR LIVES AND THE LIVES OF OTHERS.

It is not IMPORTANT for Man to know anything about the other LIFE FORMS other than there are other LIFE FORMS in existence. For Man has enough difficulty dealing with his own Life form. This is why this is the shortest Chapter in the ENTIRE BOOK!

The Solar System

At this point in time, only the Earth supports Life. In prior times, the planet we call Mars was the HOST planet to Man, however ***GOD*** DESTROYED life on Mars (the FIRST EARTH) with a GREAT FLOOD. Mars at one time sat in the ORBIT the Earth now sits in and ***GOD*** reversed the TWO planet's orbits when ***HE*** TRANSPORTED NOAH to the NEW WORLD. This is why the Earth WOBBLES in its ORBIT producing the SEASONS, whereas on the FIRST EARTH (Mars) there wasn't any rain or any SEASONS. This is also why the GOPHER WOOD that NOAH made the ARK from cannot be found on this Planet, as it is a WOOD that was only present on Mars.

There was also once a TENTH PLANET in this Solar System, called RA'-HAB, that ***GOD*** DESTROYED, and is now the ASTEROID belt that orbits outside of the Planet Mars. The Scriptures speak of this EVENT, and how ***GOD*** DESTROYED the Planet RA'-HAB; for the FIRST PEOPLE of the Earth (Mars) worshipped the Planet RA'-HAB by direction of the Devil, who had CORRUPTED all but NOAH and his family.

> ***Psalm 89:10*** *Thou hast BROKEN RA'-HAB in pieces, as one that is slain; thou hast scattered thine enemies with thy STRONG ARM.*

> ***Isaiah 51:9*** *Awake, awake, put on strength, O ARM of THE LORD; awake, as in the ANCIENT DAYS, in the GENERATIONS of OLD. Art thou not IT that hath cut RA'-HAB, and WOUNDED the DRAGON?*

Life Spans

The LIFE SPANS of the other LIFE FORMS vary, and although they are also in a TIME CONTINUUM, their TIME does not relate to TIME in the EARTH PLANE. However, in earth years, the other LIFE FORMS may live for as few as TWO HUNDRED YEARS or as many as ONE THOUSAND YEARS, with no LIFE FORM exceeding the ONE THOUSAND EARTH-YEAR equivalency. The longer the LIFE SPAN of any particular LIFE FORM, the lower the BIRTHRATE is for that LIFE FORM to ensure that over population cannot endanger the SPECIES.

Disease does not exist outside of the EARTH PLANE, and ALL SPECIES live out their intended LIFE SPAN, with the variation within a particular SPE-

CIES LIFE EXPECTANCY not exceeding 5%. Neither does any form of PAIN exist outside of the EARTH PLANE, so that neither drugs or anesthesia is required for biological surgery.[1]

---

[1] Throughout the HOLY BIBLE, ***GOD*** refers to THE EARTH as being a place where there is DRY LAND and is suitable to SUPPORT Humanoid Life. ***HE*** calls it "THE EARTH" rather than the Planet "Earth", because the GENERATIONS of Man have come from many different PLANETS; other than just the one you call "Earth".

Chapter 12
DIFFERENCES

Thus far WE have discussed both PHYSICAL matters and SPIRITUAL matters, with the two being COMMINGLED in OUR discussions. It is now TIME for US to DIFFERENTIATE between the TWO so you may see the DIFFERENCES between SPIRITUAL LIFE and Physical (Biological) Life.

The DIMENSIONS spoken about earlier in this BOOK RELATE to both SPIRITUAL DIMENSIONS and Physical ones, with the Physical Dimensions only being existent within the EARTH PLANE. For instance; if one were to build a spaceship and travel across the GALAXY in the PHYSICAL FORM of LIFE, the spaceship would be required to provide an EARTH PLANE like ENVIRONMENT for the occupants to survive the trip. However, with TIME being one of the ENVIRONMENTAL ingredients, even if the spaceship were to travel at LIGHT SPEED, it would take the occupants four years and four months to reach the first star outside of this Solar System.

Furthermore, one could say; that in an EARTH PLANE FORM of LIFE that is governed by TIME, travel through space is really quite limited. The reason that this limitation in travel exists is because the travel would have to be in the form of PHYSICAL TRAVEL, that of which is governed by TIME and rate of SPEED. With SPEED reaching TERMINAL VELOCITY at LIGHT SPEED, and MASS becoming ENERGY at LIGHT SPEED, Man's CONQUEST to travel to the stars can only be accomplished if HE were in a LIGHT FORM and TIME were made to be IRRELEVANT.

In this Chapter WE will discuss the DIFFERENCES between the various FORMS of LIFE. WE will review the LIMITATIONS of PHYSICAL (BIOLOGICAL) LIFE versus SPIRITUAL LIFE, and will also cover the subject of the SOUL, which PROVIDES the ESSENCE for LIFE ITSELF.

Physical Vision versus SPIRITUAL VISION

The physical eye functions by detecting light and processing the IMAGE produced by the light in an INVERTED perspective. This means that when the eye

DETECTS the variation in LIGHT, it sees the IMAGE from the LIGHT, 180 degrees out of phase from REALITY, thus making the IMAGE upside down and backwards from its true perspective. The BRAIN, once it receives the signal from the OPTIC NERVES, then INVERTS the IMAGE (shifts phase again by 180 degrees) thus putting the IMAGE back into its PROPER PERSPECTIVE. The point to be made here is what is actually seen by the eye is upside down and backwards from reality, and it is the BRAIN that tells you it is RIGHT SIDE UP! So one might say, that the EYE has DECEIVED YOU by the DATA it provides, however the BRAIN sees the ERROR in the DATA and makes a CORRECTION to it based on KNOWLEDGE and LOGIC with both being CONSCIOUS efforts.

As you can see, there is a basic flaw in PHYSICAL VISION, and only when the BRAIN analyzes the DATA being sent from the EYE and makes its CORRECTION to it, is the DATA viable. Other than this flaw in LIGHT DETECTION, there are other flaws that exist as well.

The response time for the BRAIN to analyze the VISUAL DATA being sent to it by the EYE is rather slow for the CONSCIOUS MIND, whereas the SUBCONSCIOUS MIND is much quicker in analyzing the same data. Therefor with the CONSCIOUS MIND being in control over the analysis of what the EYE DETECTS, the visual data being RECEIVED by the SUBCONSCIOUS MIND does not take part in the CONSCIOUS MINDS analysis of it. Therefor the DECISIONS of what to do and how to REACT to the DATA received from the EYE is a CONSCIOUS EFFORT and could be based on erroneous DATA.

When the EYE detects rapid MOVEMENT, the lag produced by the BRAIN function of that RAPID movement, is only detected by the SUBCONSCIOUS MIND, and is undetected by the CONSCIOUS MIND. Therefor no CONSCIOUS DECISION is made in response to the RAPID MOVEMENT DATA. This is how a MAGICIAN can fool its observers and DECEIVE them into thinking something is REAL when it is NOT!

There is yet another flaw in PHYSICAL VISION; this is the inability for the CONSCIOUS MIND to SEE, camouflaged IMAGES. This occurs when the IMAGES are disguised as part of a larger IMAGE and go undetected by the CONSCIOUS MIND but are seen by the SUBCONSCIOUS MIND.

Both the RAPID MOVEMENT IMAGE and the CAMOUFLAGED IMAGE are what is referred to as SUBLIMINAL IMAGES (MESSAGES). These can be either POSITIVE or NEGATIVELY implanted MESSAGES into the SUBCONSCIOUS MIND without the CONSCIOUS MIND'S AWARENESS of them!

On the other hand, SPIRITUAL VISION is INSTANTANEOUS and there isn't any TIME LAG whatsoever! This is because the SPIRITUAL EYE does not INVERT the IMAGE but SEES it as it is. Neither does the SPIRIT need to PROCESS DATA whereas the MIND DOES, and even though the SUBCONSCIOUS can detect much quicker than the CONSCIOUS MIND, there is still a LAG in TIME that takes place to both DETECT and PROCESS the DATA.

You may further CONCLUDE that within the EARTH PLANE and in a PHYSICAL CONSCIOUSNESS that nothing happens in REAL-TIME; for all EVENTS must be DETECTED and PROCESSED before the EVENT can be REALIZED. This phenomenon applies to ALL BIOLOGICAL SENSES, and not just to VISION alone. While in a PHYSICAL FORM of LIFE, ALL events are experienced after they have occurred rather than while they are occurring.

Awareness while in a SPIRITUAL FORM of LIFE is INSTANTANEOUS, and while in a PHYSICAL FORM of LIFE is REACTIONARY. Therefor ABSOLUTE CONSCIOUSNESS can only be ACHIEVED while in a SPIRITUAL FORM of LIFE.

The Spiritual Being

As has been previously discussed, the Physical Body is merely a VEHICLE of FLESH governed by TIME and physical state. The Earth given Spirit to Man is bound to the SAME LAWS as the VEHICLE of FLESH is, and the Spirit merely provides the Person of Flesh with an IDENTITY and INDIVIDUALITY in the FLESH. Also, the Earth given Spirit may not leave the Earth unless it has been GIVEN a SOUL.

The ***GOD*** GIVEN SPIRIT is significantly different from that of the Earth given Spirit, for it has DESCENDED from HEAVEN and is not a product of the EARTH. Although the ***GOD*** GIVEN SPIRIT also provides ONE with an IDENTITY and INDIVIDUALITY, as does the Earth given Spirit, ITS IDENTITY is an IDENTITY in ***GOD,*** for it is a DESCENDANT of ***GOD.*** While in FLESH, the ***GOD*** GIVEN SPIRIT lives identically to that of the Earth given Spirit up until the TIME that SPIRITUAL CONVERSION takes place.

At the TIME of CONVERSION, the SPIRIT then SEPARATES from the EARTH PLANE, while it still maintains ITS IDENTITY in the EARTH PLANE. Now we're back to where WE can RELATE to what JESUS had said, when HE SAID, "I HAVE OVERCOME THE WORLD". This relates to the SPIRITUAL SEPARATION of the ***GOD*** GIVEN SPIRIT from the EARTH PLANE. Although the SPIRIT remains within the EARTH PLANE, it isn't any longer a PRODUCT of the EARTH PLANE, because the Physical Spirit is now SEPARATED from the ***GOD*** GIVEN SPIRIT, while both still live in the SAME

BODY of FLESH. THIS IS SPIRITUAL REBIRTH, ALSO REFERRED TO IN THE SCRIPTURES AS THE BRINGING FORTH OF THE "MAN CHILD". The "MAN CHILD" does not mean a male child, but it rather relates to the ADULT SPIRITUAL CHILD that has come forth from the BODY of FLESH, which is a product of the Earth.

> ***Revelation 12:5*** *And SHE brought forth a MAN CHILD, who was to RULE all nations with a ROD OF IRON: and HER CHILD was caught up unto **GOD,** and to **HIS** THRONE.*

As has been discussed throughout this BOOK, the ROD of IRON relates to the *WORD of **GOD.*** So therefor, the BRINGING FORTH of the "MAN CHILD", has a DIRECT RELATIONSHIP with the *WORD of **GOD.*** This is because the ***GOD*** GIVEN SPIRIT is in an INFANTILE state while in the EARTH PLANE, and that SPIRIT CANNOT be brought FORTH until it has reached MATURITY and becomes the "MAN CHILD or the ADULT SPIRIT. This MATURING of the SPIRIT requires a CERTAIN amount of SPIRITUAL NOURISHMENT and that NOURISHMENT can only come to IT by way of the *WORD of **GOD!*** The "MAN CHILD" who is to RULE all nations with the ROD of IRON must therefor be ARMED with the ROD (the *WORD)* before HE may do so.

In the PREVIOUS BOOK it was told to you that over the course of the SEVEN-THOUSAND YEAR LIFE CYCLE of the EARTH, TWENTY-ONE BILLION people would have been born of the EARTH. Of those TWENTY-ONE BILLION there are SEVEN BILLION from each of the THREE categories of PEOPLE on EARTH. SEVEN BILLION of them are ***GOD'S*** SIXTH DAY CREATION (Called the Beast or the GENTILE), there are SEVEN BILLION of the seed of the Devil (Called the Damned or the CANAANITE), and there are SEVEN BILLION of the SEED of ADAM (Called the BLESSED or ISRAEL). Of the TWENTY-ONE BILLION, ONE BILLION are of the ANGEL, thus having a DIVINE RIGHT to HEAVEN, and FOUR BILLION ASCEND to HEAVEN by CHRIST, with ONE HUNDRED and FOUR MILLION of them BEING THE BRIDE of CHRIST. This NUMBER indicates that TWO BILLION of them who are of ISRAEL will LOSE THEIR SOULS, and that a grand total of SIXTEEN BILLION will have either gone back to the DUST of the EARTH, or to HELL! The following list will show the NUMBERS of the DIFFERENT categories of PEOPLE and their DESTINIES.

1. 1,000,000,000 Angels (ASCEND to HEAVEN by DIVINE RIGHT)

2. 4,000,000,000 People (ASCEND to HEAVEN through CHRIST)
3. 10,000,000,000 People (Are CAST into HELL)
4. 2,000,000,000 People (Go into the MILLENNIUM by being martyrs, and will RECEIVE a SECOND chance at Life on EARTH to be CONVERTED)
5. 4,000,000,000 People (Return to the DUST of the EARTH and will be no more)

NOTE: As you can see from this LIST, HELL grows at twice the rate of HEAVEN! It can also be noted that the 4,000,000,000 people that go back to the DUST of the EARTH, are those of the BEAST (the GENTILE) who don't have a SOUL. The remaining 3,000,000,000 of them without SOULS are added to the list of them that are cast into HELL. The 2,000,000,000 Martyrs ALL lose their SOULS when they return to the DUST of the EARTH, but they will RECEIVE a SOUL again in their NEXT LIFE. Of the 14,000,000,000 having SOULS, of those who are either cast into HELL or given back to the EARTH, their SOULS RETURN to CHRIST without a Spirit, for HE IS THE KEEPER OF SOULS!

SOULS

Let US explain to you the DIFFERENCE between the SPIRIT and the SOUL. If WE look at this in the DIVINE CATEGORY it can be said that THE ***HOLY SPIRIT*** IS ***GOD'S IDENTITY*** and CHRIST is ***GOD'S SOUL,*** or ***HIS PURPOSE.*** It can also be said that THE ***HOLY SPIRIT*** is the ***FATHER*** of the ***SOUL (YESHUA)*** and ***YESHUA (the SOUL)*** is the FATHER of CHRIST, for CHRIST, (the FOUR SERAPHIM), came out of ***GOD*** through ***YESHUA.***

It can also be said that this SAME PRINCIPLE applies in the DESCENDING of ***GOD*** down to ***HIS CHILDREN.*** ALL, who have been GIVEN a SPIRIT by ***GOD,*** also RECEIVE A SOUL from CHRIST. The SPIRIT provides ONE with their IDENTITY in ***GOD,*** and the SOUL provides ONE'S PURPOSE in ***GOD.***

The SOUL is GIVEN to the ***GOD GIVEN SPIRIT*** to provide the SPIRIT with the ABILITY to DIFFERENTIATE between GOOD and EVIL. This is the INTERNAL JUDGE within the SPIRIT that REACTS to both the RIGHTEOUS and the UN-RIGHTEOUS ACTS of the SPIRIT. When the SPIRIT listens to the SOUL, the SPIRIT BECOMES BLESSED BY ***GOD,*** and when the SPIRIT REFUSES TO LISTEN TO THE SOUL, it becomes DAMNED. This SCENARIO plays out in BOTH directions until the SPIRIT RECEIVES BAP-

TISM. Once BAPTISM has taken place and the SPIRIT is then REBORN in CHRIST, the SPIRIT and the SOUL UNITE (MARRIAGE), and any CONFLICT between the TWO can no longer EXIST. This is CALLED the FIRST MARRIAGE.

This MARRIAGE happens to both the BRIDE of CHRIST and to the GUESTS of the WEDDING SUPPER. The SECOND MARRIAGE, is when the SPIRIT and the SOUL UNITE in CHRIST, and this MARRIAGE only takes place with the BRIDE of CHRIST. The THIRD and FINAL MARRIAGE, is when CHRIST UNITES WITH ***GOD,*** THEREFOR SERVING HIS PURPOSE IN ***GOD,*** HAVING ASCENDED BACK TO ***GOD AND BEING AS ONE WITH HIM.***

This does not mean that ONE LOSES their IDENTITY in ***GOD***, and this is why it is CALLED A MARRIAGE, for a MARRIAGE requires TWO. The BRIDE simply takes on the NAME of the GROOM (CHRIST), and assumes the RESPONSIBILITIES of the SPOUSE, still being TWO, but INSEPARABLE.

Chapter 13
PURPOSE (SOUL)

Each and every SOUL GIVEN has a PURPOSE to serve both on EARTH and in HEAVEN. When the SOUL is taken back into CHRIST, no longer having a SPIRIT with it, that PURPOSE of the SOUL had not been fulfilled. ***GOD'S*** PURPOSE for that SOUL WILL BE SERVED, and even though the previous Spirit of the SOUL misused the ***GOD*** GIVEN SOUL, that SAME SOUL will be given to a NEW SPIRIT to FULFILL its PURPOSE in ***GOD.***

Purpose on Earth

Every SOUL has a different PURPOSE to SERVE both on EARTH and in HEAVEN. On Earth it may include a variety of things or simply one single thing to do during LIFE, and this is why a person cannot tell another what they should be doing to PROPERLY SERVE THE LORD. That DIRECTION can only come AFTER BAPTISM from ABOVE, so therefor any SOUL who had a GOOD PURPOSE to serve, and had not RECEIVED BAPTISM, could not have FULFILLED their PURPOSE on Earth. However, not all SOULS are BLESSED as some people having SOULS are of the SEED of the Devil.

A good example of this, was Judas Iscariot; whose PURPOSE was to BETRAY JESUS CHRIST. Therefor it can be said, that those SOULS sent to the Earth to FULFILL an EVIL PURPOSE, will NEVER RECEIVE BAPTISM and are TAKEN from those individuals at the time of their 1st DEATH (Death of the FLESH). They too are RETURNED to CHRIST, THE KEEPER OF SOULS! These are the SOULS of the DAMNED, all being of the SEED of Lucifer, the Devil. These SOULS do not have a PURPOSE to SERVE in HEAVEN, and will return to the Earth during the NEXT SEVEN THOUSAND-YEAR CYCLE to do as they had DONE BEFORE. Like the Father of their SOUL, the Devil, they TOO ARE BOUND to the Earth throughout ETERNITY and only serve a purpose while on the Earth.

John 17:12 WHILE I WAS WITH THEM IN THE WORLD, I

KEPT THEM IN THY NAME: THOSE THAT THOU GAVEST ME I HAVE KEPT, AND NONE OF THEM IS LOST, BUT THE SON OF PERDITION; THAT THE SCRIPTURE MIGHT BE FULFILLED.

The "Son of Perdition" referred to in the Scripture refers to Judas Iscariot, and the Scripture that needed to be fulfilled was Zechariah 13:6.

Zechariah 13:6 *And one shall say unto HIM, What are these WOUNDS in thine HANDS? Then HE shall answer,* ***THOSE WITH WHICH I WAS WOUNDED IN THE HOUSE OF MY FRIENDS.***

The SOUL'S FUNCTION

Whereas the SPIRIT portrays the PERSONALITY of the LIFE FORM, the SOUL EVALUATES the QUALITY of the SPIRIT'S PERSONALITY. The SPIRIT determines all CONSCIOUS ACTIONS taken, while each of those actions is EVALUATED by the SOUL to determine the RIGHTEOUSNESS of the ACTIONS.

The SOUL also DETERMINES what the PERSON (the SPIRIT) of the SOUL should like or dislike. This is TRUE for any of the FEELINGS that result from an ENCOUNTER or actions experienced by the SPIRIT. ALL FEELINGS are an EXPRESSION of the SOUL, whether the FEELINGS are GOOD ones or BAD ones. These FEELINGS being expressed by EMOTION can be in a SINGULAR form of EMOTION or in MULTIPLE forms of EMOTIONS resulting from the same experience. For example, if ONE were to experience a DIVORCE, the FEELING towards the other partner could take on MULTIPLE FORMS of EMOTION being initiated by the SINGLE EXPERIENCE. It might start first with a feeling of REJECTION, thus causing SORROW, and then evolve into a more serious form of JEALOUSY influenced by ANGER and then into HATRED.

Unlike the exchange between the SUBCONSCIOUS and the CONSCIOUS MINDS, the feedback from the SOUL to the SPIRIT, is INSTANTANEOUS, and a REAL-TIME EVENT. This type of EVENT can be REALIZED when one personality says something NEGATIVE in regard to another PERSONALITY'S behavior. The FEELING of DISAPPROVAL sent forth from the SOUL of the RECIPIENT is IMMEDIATE, and does not require any CONSCIOUS THOUGHT whatsoever to FEEL REJECTED. As the WORDS are being spoken, the FEELINGS caused by the WORDS will be INSTANTANEOUS requiring no thought.

In a world having both GOOD and EVIL, EMOTION can be misconstrued as being a hindrance, however the REALITY of EMOTION is also the NECESSARY INGREDIENT for the LIFE FORM to ASCEND above the EARTH PLANE and achieve ABSOLUTE CONSCIOUSNESS. This is why the SOUL is CONSIDERED to be the ESSENCE of LIFE, because without it, ETERNAL LIFE cannot be EXPERIENCED!

The SOULLESS can only experience PHYSICAL LIFE and not SPIRITUAL AFTERLIFE, and their BLESSING is to return to the DUST of the EARTH. HOWEVER, the SOULLESS can experience ETERNAL DAMNATION when the PHYSICAL LIFE EXHIBITS an UNACCEPTABLE BEHAVIOR! So therefor it can be said, that with the GIFT of LIFE GIVEN by ***GOD*** in any FORM, that LIFE FORM WILL be held responsible for its ACTIONS, ***SAITH THE LORD!***

PURPOSE in HEAVEN

The MAN with a SOUL has both a "PURPOSE" to serve in a CARNAL life and ONE to SERVE in a SPIRITUAL LIFE. After ASCENSION of the SPIRIT bearing the SOUL comes to pass and ABSOLUTE CONSCIOUSNESS is achieved, that PERSON then has a PREDETERMINED RESPONSIBILITY for their SERVICE to ***GOD*** throughout ETERNITY. As it is in the CARNAL life, these responsibilities vary amongst the SPIRITUAL LIFE FORMS. ***GOD*** has GIVEN each SPIRITUAL PERSON a very SPECIFIC SKILL to be UTILIZED in HEAVEN. The SPECIFIC DUTY given to the SPIRITUAL PERSON will be for that PERSON, the PERFECT JOB; and they WILL EMULATE that JOB to EXCELLENCE in their PERFORMANCE of it!

Some will be MASTER CRAFTSMEN and some will be MUSICIANS, some will be SINGERS and some DANCERS; some will aid in CREATION; some will be SPOKESPERSONS, and some will be GARDENERS and CARETAKERS. Some will be SCULPTORS, ARTISTS, AUTHORS, POETS, CHEFS and COOKS; BOATSMEN, ENTERTAINERS, FARMERS, VINTNERS, and some will be OVERSEERS of ANIMAL LIFE. Every ACCEPTABLE job function performed here on Earth will be PERFORMED in HEAVEN, along with many other JOB FUNCTIONS that are above a carnal UNDERSTANDING.

Earth is the similitude to what HEAVEN was like prior to the FALL of Lucifer, having both GOOD and EVIL in it. But after the REVOLT by Lucifer in

HEAVEN, HEAVEN then took on many CHANGES for the BETTER of IT, and many of the previous things in HEAVEN that were found to be GOOD by ***GOD,*** STILL REMAIN!

EGO, the STUMBLING BLOCK

The English Dictionary defines EGO: as the division of the psyche in psychoanalytic theory that serves as the MEDIATOR between the PERSON and REALITY. However, what the EGO really provides for; is the CREATION of a BARRIER between TRUTH and ACCEPTABILITY! An EGO acts much like a SHIELD against those things the person of the EGO refuses to believe in, whether or not those things bear the TRUTH.

What this means; is EGO blocks the COMMUNICATION between the SOUL and the SPIRIT, when the SPIRIT wants to believe something other than the TRUTH. EGO starts at birth and continually grows as the CHILD develops and has further CONTACT outside of themselves; thus seeking the TRUTH from others. EGO will eventually cause the person of the EGO to believe by DECEPTION, that they are in control of all matters concerning themselves, and that EMOTION is not necessary to evaluate themselves.

However this BELIEF is a FALSITY, because the COMMUNICATION between the SPIRIT and the SOUL has been CUT OFF and ALL EMOTIONS produced by the SOUL are then HIDDEN within the person. This lack of EMOTION causes a BARRIER to form ISOLATING the REAL PERSON from their own REALITY, by their believing they are PRESERVING their own INDIVIDUALITY with their EGO.

For the SOULLESS person this WORLDLY belief may satisfy their needs for existence, because they are GOVERNED by TIME in the EARTH PLANE, and Partial TRUTH or RELATIVE TRUTH can move them through their TEMPORARY LIFE. However, for them having ***GOD*** GIVEN SOULS, this is a STUMBLING BLOCK produced by the Devil, for ABSOLUTE TRUTH is necessary to ACHIEVE ABSOLUTE CONSCIOUSNESS.

PRIDE is a PRODUCT of EGO, and PRIDE is VANITY! The Book of Ecclesiastes speaks to the MATTER of EGO and WARNS against it through its ENTIRETY. And, also in the Book of Job, the Devil (Lucifer) is referred to as the King over the children of PRIDE, and this is how the Devil Rules, by using one's PRIDE to BLOCK the TRUTH.

> ***Job 41:33*** *Upon Earth there is not his like, who is made without FEAR.*

> ***Job 41:34*** *He beholdeth all things: he is King over all the children of PRIDE.*

The entire 41st Chapter of Job speaks of the great power given to the Devil, and how only by the HELP of ***GOD,*** can the Devil be defeated. If one has an EGO, they look to themselves (their conscious minds) for the ANSWERS, rather than to their ***GOD*** GIVEN SOULS for the TRUTH.

The CLEANSING of the SPIRIT by BAPTISM, is the ONLY way an EGO can be removed! Once the EGO has been removed, the BAPTIZED SPIRIT will start to see this world for what it is, a DECEPTION and a VEXATION of the SPIRIT; for it is ALL VANITY.

> ***Ecclesiastes 2:17*** *Therefore I hated LIFE; because the work that is wrought under the sun is grievous unto me: for ALL IS VANITY and VEXATION of SPIRIT.*

SOLOMON was the richest and wisest man on Earth, and once HE had come to realize that this world was only a TEMPORARY PLACE for HIM, HE then began to HATE it. SOLOMON also knew by his WISDOM that someone else would take possession of the riches HE had worked so hard for during HIS life; and this further TROUBLED HIM.

> ***John 12:25 HE THAT LOVETH HIS LIFE SHALL LOSE IT; AND HE THAT HATETH HIS LIFE IN THIS WORLD SHALL KEEP IT UNTO LIFE ETERNAL.***

ONE must learn to ACCEPT EMOTION from the SOUL as an INDICATOR of TRUTH, and REALIZE that ***GOD*** is in CONTROL of ALL THINGS in this LIFE and in the AFTERLIFE! At times the TRUTH is hard to bear, SO BE IT; IT STILL REMAINS THE TRUTH.

Chapter 14
Carnal Life, the GLIMPSE

In this Chapter WE will discuss the reasons why ***GOD*** has GIVEN YOU a CARNAL LIFE, and to what purpose it serves. In the PREVIOUS BOOK WE covered the THREE TYPES of PEOPLE on Earth, the BEAST, the DAMNED, and the BLESSED. The BEAST was referred to as the GENTILE, the DAMNED was referred to as the CANAANITE, and the BLESSED was referred to as ISRAEL, or those of ZION. In this Chapter, WE will re-categorize these same groups of PEOPLE and will give them yet another set of NAMES. The GENTILE, WE will call the BIOLOGICAL LIFE, the CANAANITE, WE will call the FALLEN LIFE, and ISRAEL WE will call ***GOD'S*** PEOPLE (HEAVENLY LIFE).

As briefly mentioned earlier in this BOOK, ***GOD*** has MODELED the EARTH to be in the likeness of HEAVEN as it was before the FALL of Lucifer. This was a TIME in HEAVEN when there was both GOOD and EVIL in it, and those of HEAVEN had the opportunity to make a CHOICE between GOOD or EVIL. However, after the FALL of Lucifer from HEAVEN, ALL EVIL WAS CAST OUT OF IT! So therefor it can be said, that ***GOD*** wants ALL who are to DWELL in HEAVEN, to have an OPPORTUNITY to make the SAME CHOICES that were available at the TIME of Lucifer's FALL.

At the TIME of the FALL, ALL that were in HEAVEN were ANGELS, and one-third of them decided to follow Lucifer, rather than ***IXOTE,*** who was their KING, and proclaimed that Lucifer was their new King. This caused a REVOLT to occur in HEAVEN, and ***GOD WILL NO LONGER ALLOW THAT TO HAPPEN.*** With ***IXOTE*** being THE ***HOLY SPIRIT of GOD, GOD PROCLAIMED FROM THAT POINT FORWARD, THAT ANY SIN, WHATSOEVER, AGAINST IXOTE; WOULD BE AN UNFORGIVABLE SIN!***

So the Earth was MODELED to be in the similitude of HEAVEN, so that the MAN who had been GIVEN a SOUL could make his choices on EARTH rather than in HEAVEN, where ALL EVIL had been CAST OUT. This SCENARIO depicts the STORY of ADAM and EVE, whereas they were given the CHOICE between SPIRITUAL LIFE or CARNAL LIFE and they CHOSE to have a

CARNAL LIFE. Once this choice had been made, ***GOD*** had no other CHOICE than to eject THEM from the GARDEN, which represented HEAVEN on EARTH, for in the GARDEN, EVIL WAS NOT ALLOWED TO EXIST, and; it was EVE who had BROUGHT EVIL into the GARDEN.

What is being CONVEYED here; is that EVE had already made her decision to take on a Carnal Life, prior to Lucifer's appearance in the GARDEN. Then, as the GENERATIONS progressed down from ADAM and EVE to NOAH, only NOAH was found worthy of SAVING from the DESTRUCTION that ***GOD*** had PRONOUNCED on the Earth. After the FIRST Earth (Mars) was DESTROYED with a GREAT FLOOD, ***GOD*** saw that there NEEDED to be a more EQUAL BALANCE between the FORCES of GOOD and EVIL. So ***GOD,*** in the NEW WORLD, ALLOWED THE ***HOLY SPIRIT, IXOTE,*** to have CONTROL over the ONE-THIRD of the Earth that ***HE CALLED ISRAEL.*** This was JUSTIFIABLE in THE EYES of THE LORD, TO REPLACE THE ONE-THIRD of POWER that Lucifer had taken from ***IXOTE*** in HEAVEN!

Due to the UNBALANCE on Earth (one-third versus two-thirds) between GOOD and EVIL, it takes the POWER of EVIL SEVEN THOUSAND YEARS to REGAIN ITS CONTROL OVER THE EARTH; and this is why there is a full CYCLE of the Earth, every SEVEN THOUSAND YEARS.

Biological Life

The biological life form on Earth represents ***GOD'S*** SIXTH DAY CREATION of Man and Woman. This Person has not a SOUL, although intellectually, the biological Person is equivalent in all other regards to the other two types of PEOPLE on Earth. The Earth gives this Person a Spirit (Identity) and even though they are soulless, they can either lean towards the RIGHT (GOOD) or they can lean towards the LEFT (EVIL) based on MORAL LAWS.

This Spiritual Form of an INDIVIDUAL can NEVER leave the Earth, because it is a PRODUCT of the Earth. The Spirit can either return to the DUST of the Earth, or go into its BOWELS (HELL), but it can NEVER leave the EARTH PLANE! Through intermarriage, some of ***GOD'S*** SIXTH DAY CREATION has RECEIVED a SOUL, and those with a SOUL can ENTER into the MILLENNIUM through their own Blood by being a Martyr. However, this scenario only applies to them who had DIED as a MARTYR in the NAME of JESUS CHRIST, or those who DIE refusing to DENOUNCE ***GOD*** and take on the "Mark of the Beast". They then can LIVE for the ONE THOUSAND-YEAR period of the MILLENNIUM when there will be HEAVEN on EARTH.

Fallen Life

The Fallen Life form is a PRODUCT of the DEVIL, for he fathered them starting with EVE'S son, Cain. The seed then continued through NOAH'S son, Ham and then down through the generations of the Canaanite. The Fallen also has been given a SOUL that they inherited from EVE, for she shared in ADAM'S SOUL. As previously explained, this type of SOUL serves only an EVIL PURPOSE and is BOUND to the EARTH as is for the Biological Life form. However, these Spirits ALL receive ETERNITY in HELL!

These are the Hitler types and the Terrorists of the World that KILL, and claim they are doing so in the NAME of ***GOD.*** These are also the people who misuse and falsely teach the *WORD of* ***GOD,*** and DECEIVE MANY causing them to LOSE THEIR SOULS as a result of their DECEPTION. These are the people who will smile at you with their mouths, while they RIP YOU apart with their EYES, and will have no REMORSE towards them whom they HURT, for they rejoice in it!

The Fallen Life forms are habitual LIARS, for their father is, "the father of LIES". Unlike those who may lie with a SOUL, these people always have a motive behind their LIES, and try to catch you in their SNARE, and drag you down to the PIT that is RESERVED for them. They always have one foot in HELL, and cling to it for their nourishment, and their every intention is to abound in EVIL. This is the Devil in an ascended FORM.

At the TIME of the END, ALL of the Fallen Life forms WILL have their SOULS RIPPED FROM THEM, ***SAITH THE LORD,*** and will be cast into the PIT whose FLAME cannot be QUENCHED!

> ***Zechariah 14:21*** *Yea, every POT in JERUSALEM and in JUDAH shall be HOLINESS unto THE* ***LORD of HOSTS:*** *and ALL they that SACRIFICE shall come and take of them, and SEETHE therein: and in that DAY there shall be NO MORE the Ca'-naanite in the HOUSE of THE* ***LORD of HOSTS.***

ISRAEL, *GOD'S* PEOPLE

Carnal LIFE for ***GOD'S PEOPLE,*** is meant to be a HISTORY LESSON, and for those WHO LEARN, a GLIMPSE into ETERNITY. In a previous Chapter we listed the TWENTY-ONE BILLION who had walked on the EARTH at the TIME of the END, and, of those TWENTY-ONE BILLION there are SEVEN

BILLION of the BLESSED SEED. You were shown that ONE BILLION of the BLESSED SEED are of the ANGEL, and that FOUR BILLION of the BLESSED SEED will ASCEND UNTO HEAVEN.

When the ANGEL is SEPARATED from the BLESSED SEED GROUP leaving only the MAN, the TALLY of the BLESSED SEED IS THEN SIX BILLION. With FOUR BILLION ASCENDING to HEAVEN, it becomes QUITE clear that the NUMBER FALLING FROM HEAVEN is TWO BILLION SOULS, or ONE THIRD, just as it was in HEAVEN, when Lucifer fell and took one-third with him. This scenario REPEATS itself every SEVEN THOUSAND YEARS and the outcome is ALWAYS the SAME, with ONE-THIRD FALLING FROM THE GRACE of ***GOD!***

OVERVIEW

Hopefully YOU can SEE from the aforementioned that ***GOD*** has GIVEN LIFE to MAN in THREE FORMS. In the Biological form, the Spirit receives the GIFT of LIFE and it, at its BEST, is in a temporary form. The Fallen on the other hand receives the GIFT of LIFE and also an ETERNITY, for this form of life receives a SOUL. However, the ETERNITY for the Fallen, is an ETERNITY in HELL.

ISRAEL, ***GOD'S PEOPLE,*** RECEIVE the GIFT of LIFE and an ETERNITY of their CHOOSING, whether it be HEAVEN or HELL. Even though the BILLET of the NUMBER of PEOPLE making up the POPULATION of ISRAEL is FIXED, the MIX of whom may receive that BILLET is open to INTERPRETATION. This may be related to some NUMBER of PEOPLE showing up at a football game to buy tickets, where there are more people than available seats. Some will be ADMITTED, and some will be TURNED AWAY. The ONE'S who arrive first will have a better chance of getting in than those who wait to the LAST MINUTE to come, and then get TURNED AWAY. This same SCENARIO HOLDS TRUE FOR THOSE WHO ARE REQUESTING BILLET in the LOT DESTINED FOR HEAVEN.

This same analogy is given in the "Parable of the TEN VIRGINS", WRITTEN in the GOSPEL of Matthew, 25:1 through 25:13. ***READ IT!***

Chapter 15

THE *TRINITY of LIGHT*

There are THREE PRIMARY colors of LIGHT: RED, GREEN, and BLUE; and from these PRIMARY colors of LIGHT, all visible colors can be made. When EQUAL amounts of the colors RED, GREEN, and BLUE are MIXED, the COLOR of the ***LIGHT*** is then, WHITE. The THRONE of ***GOD*** can be VIEWED as WHITE ***LIGHT,*** thus containing the THREE PRIMARY COLORS of LIGHT, in an EQUAL MIXTURE.

The COLOR RED indicates the APPEARANCE of THE ***ALMIGHTY GOD, YAHWEH,*** and the COLOR GREEN indicates THE ***HOLY SPIRIT of GOD, IXOTE,*** whereas the COLOR BLUE indicates THE ***SON of GOD, YESHUA.*** Whenever LIGHT EMANATES from THE THRONE of ***GOD,*** it can be EMITTED in a RED, GREEN, BLUE or WHITE COLOR, with the COLOR of LIGHT indicating the PREEMINENCE of the DOMINANT VOICE of ***GOD.***

When THE ***SON of GOD*** SPEAKS, the COLOR BLUE will EMANATE so INDICATING whom is SPEAKING from THE THRONE. The same is TRUE for GREEN LIGHT indicating ***IXOTE*** or RED LIGHT so INDICATING THE ***VOICE of YAHWEH.*** SCRIPTURE can VERIFY this and will be the TOPIC of discussion for this Chapter, titled, The ***TRINITY of LIGHT.***

> ***Exodus 19:17*** *And MOSES brought forth the people out of the camp to meet with* ***GOD;*** *and they stood at the nether part of the mount.*

> ***Exodus 19:18*** *And mount Si'-nai was altogether on a smoke, because THE LORD DESCENDED upon it in FIRE: and the smoke thereof ascended as the smoke of a furnace, and the whole mount QUAKED GREATLY.*

> ***Exodus 19:19*** *And when the VOICE of the TRUMPET sounded long, and waxed LOUDER and LOUDER, MOSES spake, and*

> ***GOD*** *answered HIM by a* ***VOICE.***

This was MOSES' second VISIBLE MEETING with THE LORD, and in both circumstances, ***GOD*** APPEARED as a FLAME of FIRE, thus INDICATING the COLOR of RED LIGHT, for it WAS ***YAHWEH*** who was SPEAKING to MOSES. Although King James INTERPRETED the NAME ***YAHWEH,*** when TRANSLATED as meaning, "JE-HO'-VAH"; THIS NAME CANNOT BE TRANSLATED into any other LANGUAGE other than HEBREWAH, nor can the NAMES ***IXOTE or YESHUA*** be TRANSLATED.

> ***Exodus 6:2*** *And* ***GOD*** *SPAKE unto MOSES, and said unto HIM,* ***I AM THE LORD:***

> ***Exodus 6:3*** *And* ***I*** *appeared unto ABRAHAM, unto ISAAC, and unto JACOB, by the NAME OF* ***GOD ALMIGHTY,*** *but by my NAME* ***(YAHWEH)*** *JE-HO'-VAH was* ***I*** *not known to them.*

You can LOOK at each member of THE ***TRINITY*** as having a DISTINCT FUNCTION of ***GOD.*** ALL COMMANDMENTS come by way of ***YAHWEH,*** for it is ***YAHWEH*** who ESTABLISHES and SETS the LAW. This is why MOSES saw the THRONE of ***GOD*** as EMITTING the COLOR RED (a FLAME of FIRE), for MOSES was being GIVEN the LAW.

HOWEVER, in ALL matters CONCERNING the WORSHIPPING of ***GOD,*** as a CONGREGATION, this is the RESPONSIBILITY of ***YESHUA,*** WHOM is REPRESENTED by the COLOR of BLUE LIGHT.

When the Prophet Ezekiel was taken in a VISION to the THRONE of ***GOD*** to be SHOWN the ABOMINATIONS that were taking place in ***GOD'S TEMPLE*** (PLACE OF WORSHIP), it was ***YESHUA*** who had SPOKEN to the Prophet Ezekiel.

> ***Ezekiel 10:1*** *THEN I looked, and BEHOLD, in the FIRMAMENT that was ABOVE the HEAD of the CHER'-U-BIMS there APPEARED over them as it were a* ***SAPPHIRE*** *stone, as the APPEARANCE of the likeness of a THRONE.*

As you can see from the previous Scripture, the THRONE of ***GOD*** APPEARED to Ezekiel as EMITTING a ***BLUE*** COLOR of LIGHT, described in the Scripture as a ***SAPPHIRE*** STONE. This is because what Ezekiel was being SHOWN in his VISION by ***YESHUA,*** was in REGARDS to the INAPPROPRI-

ATE PRACTICES that were taking place in the TEMPLE of ***GOD.***

IXOTE, PERFORMS the FUNCTION of JUDGMENT, and when JUDGMENT PROCEEDS from THE THRONE of ***GOD,*** the COLOR of LIGHT being EMITTED from THE THRONE will ALWAYS be GREEN, and this can also be VERIFIED by Scripture.

> ***Revelation 4:2*** *And immediately I was in the SPIRIT: and, BEHOLD, a THRONE was set in HEAVEN, and* ***ONE*** *sat on THE THRONE.*

> ***Revelation 4:3*** *And* ***HE*** *that sat was to look upon like a jasper and a sardine stone: and there was a RAINBOW round about THE THRONE, in SIGHT like unto an EMERALD.*

What the Apostle John saw in his REVELATION VISION was the PRESENCE of ALL THREE COLORS of LIGHT (the RAINBOW), however the LIGHT was PREDOMINANTLY GREEN like an EMERALD. This so INDICATES that JUDGMENT was EMANATING from THE THRONE of ***GOD,*** and it was ***IXOTE*** whom John had seen sitting on THE THRONE.

A SPIRIT of LIGHT

In previous Chapters of this BOOK WE have spoken about the SPIRITUAL PERSON who ASCENDS to BECOME a BODY of LIGHT. Throughout the Scriptures in the Book of Revelation, those whom are RECEIVED into HEAVEN are ALL given WHITE ROBES to wear.

> ***Revelation 3:5 HE THAT OVERCOMETH, THE SAME SHALL BE CLOTHED IN WHITE RAIMENT; AND I WILL NOT BLOT OUT HIS NAME OUT OF THE BOOK OF LIFE, BUT I WILL CONFESS HIS NAME BEFORE MY FATHER, AND BEFORE HIS ANGELS.***

The WHITE RAIMENT spoken about in the Scripture refers to a BODY of LIGHT, that those who are RECEIVED into HEAVEN will EMIT. The WHITE LIGHT REPRESENTS the BLESSING and the ACCEPTANCE of ALL THREE PRIMARY LIGHT SOURCES of the ***TRINITY.*** This BODY of WHITE LIGHT will take on the FORM of a MAN or a WOMAN of the HEAVENLY DOMAIN.

When the BEHEADED SOULS asked ***GOD*** how long it would be before ***HE*** would AVENGE THEIR DEATHS and JUDGE them on the earth who had killed them; THE LORD said, they must wait awhile until the others who were to be MARTYRED had been killed as they were. The BEHEADED SOULS were looking to RECEIVE a NEW body of FLESH for them to LIVE in during the MILLENNIUM. But because it was not yet TIME for the MILLENNIUM to begin, (for only the FIFTH SEAL had been BROKEN), THE LORD gave them **TEMPORARY** BODIES OF LIGHT for mobility rather than FLESHEN BODIES. For they could not RECEIVE PERMANENT BODIES of LIGHT because these PEOPLE cannot RECEIVE ETERNITY, for one cannot enter into ETERNITY by way of their own blood.

> ***Revelation 6:9*** *And when HE had opened the FIFTH SEAL, I saw under the ALTAR the SOULS of them that were slain for the WORD of* ***GOD,*** *and for the TESTIMONY which they held:*

> ***Revelation 6:10*** *And they cried with a loud voice, saying, How long, O LORD, HOLY and TRUE, dost thou not JUDGE and AVENGE our blood on them that dwell on earth?*

> ***Revelation 6:11*** *And WHITE ROBES were given unto every one of them; and it was said unto them, that they should rest yet for a little season, until their fellowservants also and their brethren, that should be killed as they were, should be fulfilled.*

CHILDREN of LIGHT

LIGHT is LIFE and LIGHT is TRUTH, and the CHILDREN of ***GOD*** are CHILDREN of LIGHT. JESUS spoke most frequently about LIGHT being the KEY to ETERNITY, and how HE was the LIGHT of the WORLD. HE meant this most LITERALLY, for it was not meant to be a figure of SPEECH. THE ***HOLY SPIRIT*** is referred to in the Scriptures as the SPIRIT of TRUTH, so if LIGHT is LIFE and TRUTH, both must come by way of JESUS CHRIST, for HE IS THE LIGHT of the WORLD.

> ***John 3:19 AND THIS IS THE CONDEMNATION, THAT LIGHT IS COME INTO THE WORLD, AND MEN LOVED DARKNESS RATHER THAN LIGHT, BECAUSE THEIR DEEDS WERE EVIL.***

John 3:20 FOR EVERY ONE THAT DOETH EVIL HATETH THE LIGHT, NEITHER COMETH TO THE LIGHT, LEST HIS DEEDS SHOULD BE REPROVED.

John 3:21 BUT HE THAT DOETH TRUTH COMETH TO THE LIGHT, THAT HIS DEEDS MAY BE MADE MANIFEST, THAT THEY ARE WROUGHT IN GOD.

As physical vision comes by the way of light, so is it with SPIRITUAL VISION; only the LIGHT NEEDED FOR THE SPIRITUAL VISION, IS THE BODY OF LIGHT THAT COMES ONLY TO A CHILD OF ***GOD.***[1]

---

[1] THE LORD has asked ME to clarify something that was said earlier in this Chapter. It was said that the NAMES ***YAHWEH, IXOTE and YESHUA*** couldn't be TRANSLATED into any other LANGUAGE other than in the HEBREWAH form. THE LORD has told me that the Clergy when reading this will say that the NAME JESUS is the TRANSLATION of the NAME ***YESHUA,*** so what had been said earlier in this Chapter cannot be TRUE. However, ***THE LORD SAITH:*** JESUS CHRIST is called the *WORD of **GOD,*** and you have been told that the *WORD of **GOD*** was ALWAYS INTENDED to be TRANSLATED into the ENGLISH LANGUAGE, and that the BIBLE'S LAYERS are only visible in the KING JAMES ENGLISH. THE WORD CHRIST is an ENGLISH WORD, and the NAME JESUS is an ENGLISH NAME THAT HAS BEEN GIVEN TO THE SON of ***GOD,*** by the TRANSLATION of KING JAMES. The ONLY error in the KING JAMES 1611 version of the HOLY BIBLE is in regard to the NAMES of ***GOD, NOT IN THE NAMES OF THE SONS OF GOD,*** and the **only error** is by KING JAMES TRANSLATING the NAME ***YAHWEH*** into JE-HO'-VAH.

Chapter 16
MUSICAL EXPRESSIONS

MUSIC can be defined as the ORGANIZED MOVEMENT of SOUND through a TIME CONTINUUM. The SOUND produced in a MUSICAL SCALE consists of ***SEVEN*** FULL TONES and FIVE INTERMEDIATE TONES (or half tones) giving the FULL SCALE of MUSIC, **TWELVE TONES** in total. There are SEVEN musical TONES that are called NOTES in ONE MUSICAL SCALE, and each of the NOTES have been given a LETTER from the ENGLISH ALPHABET; from the letter "A" through the LETTER "G" to distinguish them apart. However the FIRST NOTE is the LETTER "C" NOTE rather than the LETTER "A" NOTE, thus having the BEGINNING of the MUSICAL SCALE starting with the "C" NOTE TONE, or the 1st TONE in the SCALE. The INTERMEDIATE TONES or HALF NOTES can either RAISE or LOWER the FULL NOTE TONES by ONE HALF of that NOTE'S TONE. When it raises the TONE by ONE-HALF it is called a SHARP, and when it LOWERS a NOTE'S TONE it is called a FLAT.

When the FULL TONE of any of the SEVEN FULL TONE NOTES is DOUBLED in PITCH, that TONE has then been RAISED by EIGHT FULL TONES and this is called an OCTAVE. For example, if the "C" NOTE is raised by ONE OCTAVE, it will have been raised to the next higher "C" NOTE thus starting the NEXT HIGHER SCALE.

Music is achieved when the CHANGE in TONES over a specific amount of time produces a PLEASING SOUND. This TIMING between the TONE CHANGES is called RHYTHM. When several complimentary TONES are made at one time, creating a HARMONIOUS COMBINATION of TONES, the combination is called a CHORD. MUSIC consists of TONE CHANGES, TONE COMBINATIONS, and the RHYTHM at which the CHANGES are made.

In this Chapter WE will explain the EFFECTS of MUSICAL EXPRESSIONS on the SPIRITUAL PERSON, and SHOW how MUSIC can be COMPARED to the STRUCTURE of the HEAVENLY REALM. WE will also discuss how the EMOTION sent forth by MUSIC INFLUENCES the SPIRIT, in either a POSITIVE or a NEGATIVE MANNER.

TONE Progression

With the "C" NOTE being the BEGINNING of the MUSICAL SCALE, all TONES in a DESCENDING SEQUENCE from the middle "C" NOTE are called BASS NOTES, whereas all TONES ASCENDING from the "C" NOTE are called TREBLE NOTES. Therefor the "C" NOTE in between the BASS NOTES and the TREBLE NOTES has been given the NAME of "MIDDLE C".

Although there are HIGHER and LOWER PROGRESSIONS of MUSICAL TONES within the general audible range, MOST MUSIC is played in plus or minus FOUR OCTAVES from the MIDDLE "C" NOTE. This makes the complete MUSICAL SCALE consist of EIGHT OCTAVES, or SIXTY-FOUR FULL TONE NOTES, with thirty-two below MIDDLE "C" and thirty-two above MIDDLE "C". This would be consistent with a piano keyboard having TWELVE KEYS per OCTAVE that consist of SEVEN FULL TONE KEYS and FIVE HALF TONES KEYS.

TONE and RHYTHM BALANCE

When the BASS NOTES below MIDDLE "C" are played, a certain ABRUPTNESS is felt in the SPIRIT creating a feeling for wanting CHANGE, whereas the TREBLE NOTES have a tendency to SOOTHE the SPIRIT causing it to want to RELAX. This is why the MELODY of a song is always carried by the TREBLE NOTES while the RHYTHM is carried on the BASS NOTES. When the BASS NOTES and the TREBLE NOTES are in EQUAL BALANCE and in a complimentary RHYTHM, and a HARMONY of the TONES is achieved, the SPIRIT can CONSCIOUSLY FEEL the EMOTION produced by the MUSIC.

This EMOTION can be TILTED from a POSITIVE to a NEGATIVE direction, when either the EMPHASIS on the BASS side or on the TREBLE side of the NOTE SPECTRUM is at an EXTREME LEVEL. The TIMING between TONE CHANGES (RHYTHM) can also have varying effects on the SPIRIT, and cause the MOOD of the SPIRIT to CHANGE (SWING) as a function of RHYTHM SEQUENCE. Quicker RHYTHMS have a tendency to LIFT the SPIRIT while SLOWER RHYTHMS have a tendency to LOWER the SPIRIT (slow it down), and this can also be in a POSITIVE or NEGATIVE form for either of the two MOOD SWINGS.

Both the Earth given Spirit and the ***GOD*** GIVEN SPIRIT react in a similar MANNER to MUSIC. There are ONLY small differences between how the two SPIRITS react when MUSIC is heard; the Earth given Spirit has a tendency to react more so to RHYTHM SEQUENCE while the ***GOD*** GIVEN SPIRIT reacts more so to the TONE HARMONY of the MUSIC.

SEVEN NOTES and SEVEN CHOIRS

Just as there are SEVEN FULL NOTES making up the MUSICAL SCALE, there are also SEVEN CHOIRS of ANGELS making up the SEVEN LEVELS of HEAVEN. Each of the HEAVENLY LEVELS can be VIEWED as being SEVEN FULL NOTE changes just as it is in the MUSICAL SCALE.

As you have been previously told, the FOUR SERAPHIM (THE SONS of ***GOD***) reside at the EIGHTH LEVEL or ONE might say ONE OCTAVE ABOVE the FIRST LEVEL of HEAVEN. You were also told about the DESCENDING form of ***GOD*** within THE ***TRINITY*** and the DESCENDING NATURE of ***GOD*** outside of THE ***TRINITY***, and how each of the FOUR SERAPHIM REPRESENTED ONE TWELFTH that of ***GOD.*** WE have also discussed that there are ***SEVEN SPIRITS of GOD*** that PROCEED from the THRONE of ***GOD.*** I hope you are starting to see the CONNECTION between HEAVEN and the MUSICAL SCALE.

By the FOUR SERAPHIM, being ONE TWELFTH that of ***GOD,*** this can be RELATED to the TWELVE MUSICAL KEYS WITHIN AN OCTAVE, and the ***SEVEN SPIRITS of GOD*** can be RELATED to THE SEVEN FULL TONES WITHIN AN OCTAVE. You can also RELATE the FIRST LEVEL of HEAVEN to being ONE OCTAVE LOWER than the EIGHTH LEVEL of HEAVEN, therefor making the FIRST HEAVENLY LEVEL the same as the MIDDLE "C" is in the MUSICAL SCALE.

This can also be applied to the TWELVE DIMENSIONS WE had spoken about earlier in this BOOK, with the THIRTEENTH DIMENSION in the UNIVERSE being the LIGHT DIMENSION. While the piano keyboard has twelve ASCENDING KEYS before it repeats, so are there TWELVE ASCENDING DIMENSIONS before they REPEAT. Whereas the THIRTEENTH KEY of ASCENDING NOTES on a piano is the SAME as the FIRST KEY of the NEXT HIGHER ORDER of NOTES, so is it with the DIMENSIONS. Whereas the LIGHT DIMENSION is the THIRTEENTH DIMENSION in the UNIVERSE so is the THIRTEENTH DIMENSION in HEAVEN the next HIGHER LEVEL of that LIGHT.

This should also explain why the SON'S of ***GOD*** are REPRESENTED by the NUMBER 13, while they are yet ONE-TWELFTH that of ***GOD.*** This SAME scenario also applies to THE ***TRINITY of GOD.*** The THRONE of ***GOD*** is the NINTH LEVEL, ***YESHUA is the TENTH LEVEL, IXOTE is the ELEV-***

ENTH LEVEL, YAHWEH is the TWELFTH LEVEL and GOD is the THIRTEENTH LEVEL or the 26th DIMENSION ABOVE THE EARTH PLANE!

The EMOTION EXPRESSED by MUSIC

Every form of EMOTION that can be EXPERIENCED by the SPIRIT can be either EXPRESSED or INFLUENCED by MUSIC. Only the CREATOR of the MUSIC can EXPRESS the EMOTION by its composition and pass that EMOTION along to those listening to it. Then those who have been INFLUENCED by the MUSICAL composition RECEIVE its MESSAGE, and will feel the NEED to further express that same EMOTION along to others. As it is with ALL EMOTIONAL EXPERIENCES, this is a REAL TIME EVENT, and it does not require any CONSCIOUS THOUGHT whatsoever to react to the MUSIC'S MESSAGE! One should be quite CAUTIOUS as to what type of MUSIC they LISTEN to, for the INFLUENCES of the MUSICAL MESSAGE can be quite overwhelming at times, causing its LISTENERS to react in some instances inappropriately. MUSIC can be as POWERFUL as WORDS and even INSTRUMENTALS can pass along a MESSAGE to the Spirit, for the BETTER or for the WORSE. For those PEOPLE having a ***GOD*** given SOUL, even though they may not have yet RECEIVED SPIRITUAL BAPTISM, they will find any MUSIC bearing a NEGATIVE or EVIL MESSAGE to be OFFENSIVE to them.

One must remember that Lucifer at one time, was the Chief Musician in HEAVEN, and he knows how to use MUSIC to his benefit. Some MUSIC can be disguised to appear to be of an INNOCENT NATURE, while it yet bears an EVIL MESSAGE. If you find any discomfort whatsoever in listening to certain types of MUSIC, do not TOLERATE it, but rather DISCARD IT IMMEDIATELY! ALSO, BE CAUTIOUS OF ANY FORM OF CHANTING, FOR CHANTING IS ALSO A FORM OF MUSIC, and a CLEVER way of IMPLANTING EVIL MESSAGES into both the Spirit and the MIND.

As with ALL ***GOD*** GIVEN SKILLS and TALENTS, they can be exercised in either a POSITIVE or NEGATIVE MANNER. One way to reveal the MESSAGE of the MUSIC, is to look at the MUSIC'S INTENT. If it SPEAKS to LOVE, UNDERSTANDING, HARDSHIP in LIFE, FELLOWSHIP, FAITH, or SERVICE TO ***GOD,*** then the MESSAGE should be an acceptable one.

However, if the MUSIC SPEAKS of VIOLENCE, HATRED, LUSTS, or IMMORAL ACTS, then the MESSAGE is an UNACCEPTABLE ONE, and this is TRUE even if it appears to be presented in an INNOCENT FORM!

The Effects of MUSIC on the Physical Body

WE have talked about how the SPIRIT reacts to various types of MUSIC, but WE have not yet discussed how MUSIC affects the Physical Person as well. MUSIC can be physically felt in the abdomen and lower bowel area when the BASS volume exceeds the 60-decibel level and also in the upper chest and head when the TREBLE exceeds 75 decibels. But even below these levels the CENTRAL NERVOUS SYSTEM reacts to SOUND both in its duration and repetition (rhythm) and in its frequency (pitch) similarly to how the SPIRIT REACTS, and this can have either a POSITIVE or an ADVERSE effect on the NERVOUS SYSTEM.

The heart rate and blood pressure of the body can also be either raised or lowered as a result of MUSICAL EXPRESSION. Rapid paced MUSIC with a heavy BASS content will have a tendency to increase both the heart rate and blood pressure of the body, whereas the slower paced MUSIC with balanced tones, will have the opposite effect. This is because the Earth given Spirit of man is so intertwined with the physical body it makes both inseparable from the other, and they will react in much the same manner to external influences of sound. Brain waves can also be affected by MUSIC and cause them to rapidly change as a result of it.

These changes that take place in one's physical metabolism, as a result of the MUSIC, can alter attitudes and behavior rather quickly, and these can be either POSITIVE or NEGATIVE changes. Behavior of an individual can be severely compromised if the MUSIC is received in a NEGATIVE way, and can cause one's mental state to change from a PEACEFUL MODE into a state of RAGE. MUSIC however, can also do the opposite and have a CALMING EFFECT, if the MUSIC'S MESSAGE is PERCEIVED as being a POSITIVE one.

There is a delicate balance between one's current state of mind and the MUSICAL COMPOSITION. MUSIC has a tendency to COMPLIMENT the MOOD, more so than to CHANGE it. For example, if one were dealing with a TIME of ANGER, MUSIC with a POSITIVE MESSAGE would slowly reduce that level of ANGER. However, if in a TIME of ANGER the MUSICAL MESSAGE were a NEGATIVE one, the ANGER could then be elevated to a VIOLENT behavior in a very short span of time.

If properly applied, MUSIC can be used in various types of medical treatments. When the proper MUSICAL MESSAGE is used in the form of therapy, both the PHYSICAL and MENTAL condition of the PATIENT can be improved more expediently. For instance, if a PATIENT had just recently endured some form of traumatic surgery, a MUSICAL COMPOSITION giving a MESSAGE of CALMING, would speed up the time of RECOVERY, and there is a very specific reason for this improvement of recovery time to occur.

The human body is self-healing, and when all conscious effort of the body is put into the healing effort, the time for the healing is quickened. When MUSIC is induced as a CALMING AGENT, the energy required to sustain one's bodily functions is reduced, and that unused energy can then be applied naturally by the body to the healing process.

THE LORD has told ME that if more EMPHASIS were put on EMOTIONAL HEALING, as opposed to SURGICAL or MEDICINAL HEALING, many more people would have survived their illnesses. MUSIC is only ONE of many such ways of EMOTIONAL HEALING!

Chapter 17
John's GOSPEL

In the PREVIOUS BOOK you were shown that there were FOUR GOSPELS WRITTEN, to LOOK at JESUS CHRIST from four different perspectives, and WE called those PERSPECTIVES the FOUR DIRECTIONS. It was said at that time, the GOSPEL of MATTHEW looked at JESUS CHRIST as being the *PERSON of* ***GOD.*** The GOSPEL of MARK looked at JESUS CHRIST as being the *MIRACLES of* ***GOD,*** the GOSPEL of LUKE looked at JESUS CHRIST as being the *MAN of* ***GOD*** and the GOSPEL of John LOOKED at JESUS CHRIST as BEING the *SPIRIT of* ***GOD.***

When reviewing the first three GOSPELS (Matthew, Mark, and Luke) you can SEE that they are nearly all COMPOSED in the SAME MANNER. There is only a minor difference in the GOSPEL of Mark by it beginning at the TIME of JESUS' BAPTISM, rather than at the TIME of HIS BIRTH. WE had also explained, because JESUS never had spoken about HIS CHILDHOOD to HIS Disciples, much of that which is WRITTEN in Matthew and Luke's versions of the GOSPELS was SPECULATIVE, and based more on RUMOR, than on FACT.

WE also pointed out some DISCREPANCIES in the first three GOSPELS (however minor in nature), and said that ONLY the GOSPEL of John was ERROR FREE, except for some SPELLING errors in it due to DIALECT changes in the Hebrew Language. But when reviewing ALL FOUR GOSPELS, YOU should also NOTICE that the GOSPEL of John is COMPOSED entirely DIFFERENT than the other THREE GOSPELS, and this will be OUR POINT of DISCUSSION in this Chapter.

Obvious DIFFERENCES

Even though Mary, the Mother of JESUS lived with John for the remaining years of her life after JESUS' death and RESURRECTION, John mentions nothing about JESUS' CHILDHOOD in his entire GOSPEL. In the PREVIOUS BOOK it was explained that one of the reasons John omitted JESUS' CHILD-

HOOD from his GOSPEL, was because it didn't bear any SIGNIFICANCE to JESUS' STORY, other than the mentioning of HIS IMMACULATE BIRTH. Also, JESUS considered HIS SPIRITUAL BIRTH, rather than his PHYSICAL birth, to BE HIS TIME of BIRTH, so John PURPOSELY left that part of the STORY OUT. John wanted to PORTRAY JESUS CHRIST as the SPIRITUAL PERSON of ***GOD,*** and that portion of JESUS' LIFE came after HIS ***HOLY SPIRIT*** BAPTISM.

When reviewing the GOSPELS it may also be NOTED that only in the GOSPEL of John is there no mentioning of the "END of the AGE" PROPHECY given to the Disciples by JESUS. John also purposely OMITTED this from his GOSPEL, for John KNEW SPIRITUALLY he would later author the BOOK of REVELATION, which would more ACCURATELY DESCRIBE the "END of the AGE" PROPHECY given to him by JESUS CHRIST.

John was also the ONLY ONE who referred to JESUS CHRIST as ***BEING*** the *WORD of* ***GOD,*** and he does so both in his GOSPEL and in the BOOK of REVELATION. John saw JESUS as BEING the *WORD of* ***GOD*** that had COME DOWN from HEAVEN and was made into the FORM of a MAN.

> ***John 1:1*** *In the BEGINNING was the WORD, and the WORD was with* ***GOD,*** *and the WORD was* ***GOD.***

> ***John 1:2*** *The SAME was in the BEGINNING with* ***GOD.***

NOTE: The FIRST recorded WORDS that were SPOKEN by ***GOD*** were, ***"LET THERE BE LIGHT".*** So, in the BEGINNING the WORD was "LIGHT"!

> ***John 1:3*** *ALL things were made by* ***HIM;*** *and without* ***HIM*** *was not any thing MADE that was MADE.*

NOTE: This refers to JESUS CHRIST as BEING the FIRST LIGHT that ALL of ***GOD'S*** CREATION had come from (REMEMBER LIGHT is LIFE and TRUTH!).

> ***John 1:4*** *In HIM was LIFE; and the LIFE was the LIGHT of men.*

NOTE: You were told in an earlier Chapter of this BOOK; that LIGHT and WATER are the TWO necessary ingredients for LIFE! Let US now jump down to the 14th verse of this 1st Chapter of John's GOSPEL and SEE what becomes of the FIRST WORD, "LIGHT", that was spoken by ***GOD.***

> ***John 1:14*** *And the WORD was made FLESH, and dwelt among us, (and we beheld HIS GLORY, the GLORY as of the only begotten of the* ***FATHER,****) full of GRACE and TRUTH.*

YOU can SEE from the Scriptures how John saw JESUS CHRIST as being both the *WORD of* ***GOD,*** and also as BEING the ***LIGHT*** that ALL of ***GOD'S*** CREATION had come from. As explained earlier to you, a CHILD of ***GOD*** MUST VERTICALLY ASCEND to ABSOLUTE AWARENESS and this LEVEL of AWARENESS is not achievable until after the SPIRITUAL PERSON becomes a BODY of LIGHT. So therefor, the REQUIRED LIGHT for the BODY has to come from a LIGHT SOURCE, and the LIGHT SOURCE is JESUS CHRIST, THE LIGHT OF THE WORLD. The "WORLD" spoken of here is not just the Earth and its Solar System, but rather the entire UNIVERSE, for it ALL had COME from a SINGLE POINT of LIGHT, and that LIGHT is JESUS CHRIST.

> ***Revelation 3:14 AND UNTO THE ANGEL OF THE CHURCH OF THE LA-OD-I-CE'-ANS WRITE; THESE THINGS SAITH THE A-MEN', THE FAITHFUL AND TRUE WITNESS, THE BEGINNING OF THE CREATION OF GOD;***

NOTE: JESUS states in the last Scripture that HE is the BEGINNING of CREATION, and CREATION came forth from a SINGLE POINT of LIGHT, therefor, JESUS is the LIGHT of the WORLD!

To take you deeper into the LAYER of the Scriptures taken from the GOSPEL of John and the Book of Revelation; WE can tell you that JESUS not only provided the LIGHT for ALL of ***GOD'S*** CREATION, but HE also PROVIDED ***GOD'S*** *CHILDREN* with a SOUL.

JESUS was ADAM, and the FIRST BODY of FLESH to be GIVEN a SOUL, and it was HE who FATHERED all of MANKIND thereafter having a SOUL. Therefor anyone coming through the LINEAGE of ADAM RECEIVED a SOUL, and their SOUL came from JESUS CHRIST who is the KEEPER OF SOULS.

This is how JESUS could say that HE is both the ROOT and the OFFSPRING of DAVID, and the BRIGHT and MORNING STAR (Revelation 22:16). By JESUS being ADAM and the FIRST MAN with a SOUL, DAVID came through HIS LINEAGE, making JESUS the ROOT of DAVID. And, by

JESUS being the LIGHT of the WORLD, ALL things were MADE from HIM, thus making HIM the LIGHT for the BEGINNING of CREATION, called the MORNING STAR!

As WE go further into the GOSPEL of John, WE want you to start SEEING what JESUS has to say in the SCRIPTURES, in the SPIRITUAL SENSE, and not in a CARNAL sense. Once YOU start to SEE JESUS in this way, as John had SEEN HIM in the SPIRIT of ***GOD,*** YOU WILL RECEIVE the MESSAGE given by John in his GOSPEL.

John the Baptist

John the Baptist, (who is SOLOMON/ELIJAH in HEAVEN); was SENT by ***GOD*** to Earth to PREPARE the people of the Earth for JESUS' FIRST COMING. At the beginning of John's MINISTRY, forgiveness of sin could only be accomplished by the remission of sin to a Priest, and then providing the Priest with an animal sacrifice that the Priest would OFFER on behalf of the Sinner.

Except for THE ***HOLY SPIRIT (WHOSE SOUL IS REVERSED IN HIM),*** everything that ***GOD*** TEACHES in ***HIS*** *WORD* is done first in the flesh, and then in the SPIRIT. This is one of the reasons why there is both an OLD and a NEW COVENANT. MORAL LAWS GOVERNED the OLD COVENANT and the NEW COVENANT is GOVERNED by SPIRITUAL FAITH.

John the Baptist's RESPONSIBILITY was to teach in a MORAL FORM how one could repent of their sins DIRECTLY to ***GOD*** and be FORGIVEN of them by a WATER BAPTISM, without the need for a Priest or a sacrifice. The baptism however would have to be repeated if that person were to further sin, for unlike SPIRITUAL BAPTISM, water baptism is not an ETERNAL BAPTISM. However, the WATER BAPTISM gave Mankind the ability to go DIRECTLY to ***GOD*** for FORGIVENESS rather than to the Priests, WHO ***GOD*** had LOST CONFIDENCE IN. ***GOD*** also TIRED of the foul animal sacrifice that was being OFFERED to ***HIM*** for FORGIVENESS of SIN.

> ***Malachi 2:7*** *For the Priest's lips should keep knowledge, and should seek the LAW at his mouth: for he is the messenger of the* ***LORD of HOSTS.***

> ***Malachi 2:8*** *But ye are departed out of the way; ye have caused many to STUMBLE at the LAW; ye have CORRUPTED the COVENANT of Levi, saith the* ***LORD of HOSTS.***

NOTE: These Scriptures should give a CLEAR INDICATION of how THE LORD had lost ***HIS*** CONFIDENCE in the Priests to GUIDE ***HIS*** PEOPLE. So, when ***GOD*** could no longer TRUST the Priests, ***HE*** sent John the Baptist from HEAVEN to CHANGE the METHODOLOGY for FORGIVENESS of SIN. This NEW METHODOLOGY would no longer require the use of either Priests or Animal Sacrifices, but rather required REPENTANCE and BAPTISM for FORGIVENESS.

John the Baptist, being SWORN to the OATH of the NAZARITE by his parents, Zach-a-ri'-as and Elisabeth prior to his BIRTH, neither cut his hair nor did he eat or drink anything that grew of the vine; and all the LAWS governing the NAZARITE applied to John.

> ***Luke 1:15*** *For he shall be great in the sight of THE LORD, and shall drink neither wine nor strong drink; and he shall be filled with THE* ***HOLY GHOST,*** *even from his mother's womb.*

John studied the Holy Scriptures as a child, for he was the son of a Priest, and gathered some Disciples together beyond the Jordan River in the area of Beth-ab'-a-ra, where he began to baptize. It was rumored throughout the area that John was baptizing with water and many came to him to be baptized. Once the Pharisees had heard what John was doing, they sent out men to ask him if he were the MESSIAH; for they had heard that the MESSIAH would do such things as BAPTISM, but John told them he was not the CHRIST (the MESSIAH). They also asked John if he was ELIJAH; for they knew from the Scriptures of Malachi, that ELIJAH would come prior to the MESSIAH coming, but John denied that as well; even though John the Baptist was indeed ELIJAH, but was unaware of it.

GOD told John there would be a MAN who would come to him for the WATER BAPTISM, and he should recognize this PERSON once HE had been BAPTIZED, for THE ***HOLY SPIRIT*** would come down upon HIM and REMAIN. John was also TOLD THE ***HOLY SPIRIT*** would come in the FORM of a DOVE, and after the BAPTISM was completed the ***HOLY SPIRIT*** would REMAIN with this PERSON; FOR HE is the MESSIAH (CHRIST).

John was unaware that the MAN (the MESSIAH) ***GOD*** had TOLD him about, was his 2nd COUSIN JESUS, (for Mary the Mother of JESUS was John's Mother, Elizabeth's 1st Cousin), although John had never met JESUS, before the day of HIS BAPTISM.

Shortly after JESUS' 30th BIRTHDAY, HE was told by ***GOD*** to go down to the JORDAN and be BAPTIZED by the ONE who had been PREACHING in the WILDERNESS.

> ***John 1:23*** *He said, I am THE VOICE OF ONE CRYING IN THE WILDERNESS, MAKE STRAIGHT THE WAY OF THE LORD, as said the Prophet Isaiah.* **(Isaiah 40:3)**

JESUS had heard of John the Baptist, and went to him for the BAPTISM, just as ***THE LORD*** had so instructed HIM to do.

> ***John 1:32*** *And John bare record, saying, I saw the* ***SPIRIT*** *DESCENDING from HEAVEN like a DOVE, and it ABODE upon HIM.*

> ***John 1:33*** *And I KNEW HIM NOT: but* ***HE*** *that SENT me to BAPTIZE with WATER, the SAME said unto me, UPON WHOM THOU SHALT SEE THE* ***SPIRIT*** *DESCENDING, AND REMAINING ON HIM, THE SAME IS HE WHICH BAPTIZETH WITH THE* ***HOLY GHOST.***

> ***John 1:34*** *And I saw, and bare record that this is the SON of* ***GOD.***

So JESUS on that day was baptized with water by John the Baptist, and ALSO BAPTIZED IN ***THE NAME of THE LORD***; WITH THE ***HOLY SPIRIT of GOD,*** and the WORLD was forever CHANGED; and the NEW COVENANT of FAITH was INITIATED, by BAPTISM of THE LAMB of ***GOD.***

17.1 NO WASTED FOOTSTEPS

Although it appears in the Scriptures that JESUS waited until the following day to start gathering HIS Disciples, HE actually started gathering them IMMEDIATELY after HIS BAPTISM. In the 29th verse of the 1st Chapter of John's GOSPEL it says the following:

> ***John 1:29*** *The next day John SEETH JESUS coming unto him, and saith, BEHOLD the LAMB of* ***GOD,*** *which taketh away the sin of the world.*

"Behold the LAMB of ***GOD***", was the STATEMENT that John the Baptist had made to JESUS at their INITIAL MEETING, prior to him BAPTIZING JESUS. After JESUS' BAPTISM, the Apostle John "recalls" what John the Baptist had said, "Behold the LAMB of ***GOD***, so indicating that JESUS went out to gather HIS Disciples IMMEDIATELY after HIS BAPTISM. However, the way it is WORDED in the Scripture can be MISINTERPRETED to indicate that John had made the same statement again on the following day, however he did not. Let US review the Scriptures.

> ***John 1:35*** *Again the next day after John stood, and two of his disciples;*
>
> ***John 1:36*** *And looking upon JESUS as HE walked, he saith, BEHOLD, the LAMB of* ***GOD!***
>
> ***John 1:37*** *And the two disciples heard him speak, and they FOLLOWED JESUS.*

This is the Apostle John's way of saying, "on that same day when John the Baptist had said, BEHOLD the LAMB of ***GOD",*** (for JESUS had only met ONCE with John the Baptist, which was the DAY of HIS BAPTISM), that two of John's disciples followed JESUS to HIS home. They did this because they had heard John refer to JESUS as being the LAMB of ***GOD,*** and John had taught them, that the LAMB of ***GOD*** was the MESSIAH, the CHRIST that was to come.

NOTE: Without being able to SEE INTO the LAYER of the SCRIPTURE, the point being made by the SCRIPTURE can be easily OVERLOOKED. The Apostle John's POINT in the SCRIPTURE is that this EVENT happened on the SAME DAY of JESUS' BAPTISM, when John the Baptist had referred to JESUS as being the LAMB of ***GOD,*** even though it appears to be otherwise. Therefor the Scripture in John 1:35 and 1:36, merely repeats that which was said in John 1:29, adding to it; that two of John's disciples had heard the statement made by John about JESUS being the LAMB of ***GOD***. JESUS DID NOT RETURN TO JOHN AFTER HIS BAPTISM.

> ***John 1:38*** *Then JESUS turned, and saw them following, and saith unto them,* ***WHAT SEEK YE?*** *They said unto HIM, Rabbi (which is to say, being INTERPRETED MASTER,) where dwellest thou?*

***John 1:39** HE saith unto them, **COME AND SEE.** They came and saw where HE dwelt, and abode with HIM that day: for it was about the tenth hour.* **(4:00 PM)**

***John 1:40** One of the two which heard John speak, and followed HIM, was Andrew, Simon Peter's brother.*

***John 1:41** He first findeth his own brother Simon, and saith unto him, WE HAVE FOUND THE MESSIAH, which is, being INTERPRETED, the CHRIST.*

From the Scriptures it should be UNDERSTOOD that JESUS' MINISTRY started IMMEDIATELY after HIS BAPTISM, and that two of John the Baptist's disciples, out of curiosity followed JESUS home. It may also be noted, that of the two, only Andrew's name is mentioned, who is the brother to Simon, whom JESUS later renamed PETER. The reason the other disciple's name (who had followed JESUS to HIS house that day) is not mentioned, is because the very next day he returned to John the Baptist and followed John rather than JESUS; for he was not meant to be one of the TWELVE.

The CHURCH on EARTH is taken from PETER

Then on the same day, Andrew found his brother Simon, and told him that he had found the CHRIST, and Andrew brought Simon (Peter) to meet JESUS. When they meet, JESUS tells Simon that he will later be CALLED CE'-PHAS, however Simon is not referred to as CE'-PHAS further on in the Scriptures, but is rather renamed and called Peter. So, why did JESUS tell Simon that he would be called CE'-PHAS, meaning a STONE, rather than Peter which also means a "STONE"?

JESUS had told Simon that he would be called CE'-PHAS, because this is Simon Peter's name in HEAVEN, for CE'-PHAS is a SEVENTH LEVEL ANGEL and a PRINCE in HEAVEN. Simon was also told that he would be called CE'-PHAS, meaning a "STONE" because he is the ANGEL of the CHURCH of CHRIST in HEAVEN, and the CORNERSTONE of the CHURCH in HEAVEN.

The name Peter, also meaning a "STONE", applied to the Church on Earth, and Peter was to be its CORNERSTONE. But the Church on Earth was taken from Peter and given to the Apostle Paul. The Church was taken from Peter for his denying JESUS THREE TIMES after JESUS had been taken captive, and this is also why JESUS called Peter after HIS RESURRECTION by the name of Simon, and no longer by the name of Peter.

This is also why JESUS asked Simon THREE TIMES if he LOVED HIM, because Simon Peter had denied JESUS THREE TIMES after the Pharisees had taken HIM captive. These are the WORDS SPOKEN by JESUS to Simon (Peter) after HIS RESURRECTION:

> ***John 21:14*** *This is now the third time that JESUS shewed HIMSELF to HIS Disciples, after HE was RISEN from the dead.*
>
> ***John 21:15*** *So when they had dined, JESUS saith to Simon Peter,* ***SIMON, SON OF JO'-NAS, LOVEST THOU ME MORE THAN THESE?*** *He saith unto HIM, Yea, LORD; thou knowest that I LOVE thee. HE saith unto him,* ***FEED MY LAMBS.***
>
> ***John 21:16*** *HE saith unto him the SECOND TIME,* ***SIMON, SON OF JO'-NAS, LOVEST THOU ME?*** *He saith unto HIM, Yea, LORD; thou knowest that I LOVE thee. HE saith unto him,* ***FEED MY SHEEP.***
>
> ***John 21:17*** *HE saith unto him the THIRD TIME,* ***SIMON, SON OF JO'-NAS, LOVEST THOU ME?*** *Peter was grieved because HE said unto HIM the THIRD TIME,* ***LOVEST THOU ME?*** *And he said unto HIM, LORD, thou knowest ALL THINGS; thou knowest that I LOVE THEE, JESUS saith unto him,* ***FEED MY SHEEP.***

In the Scriptures up until the time of JESUS' being taken captive by the Pharisees, HE refers to Simon as Peter. However after Peter had denied JESUS THREE TIMES, JESUS called him again by his earthly name of Simon rather than Peter, thus indicating that the Church on earth would no longer be built on Simon Peter. Even though JESUS had prophesised to Peter while at the LAST SUPPER, that he would deny HIM THREE TIMES before the cock would crow (Matthew 26:34), HE did not say that Peter would be forgiven for it without REPENTANCE, and Peter had not REPENTED for denying JESUS. This is why JESUS made Peter REPENT THREE TIMES TO HIM after HIS RESURRECTION, for Peter had denied JESUS THREE TIMES.

NOTE: If Peter had been BAPTIZED in THE ***HOLY SPIRIT*** on the night of JESUS' CAPTIVITY, he could have NEVER DENIED that he had KNOWN

JESUS CHRIST, the SON of ***GOD***! However, because Peter's BAPTISM came on the day of PENTECOST, he had not yet been REBORN in CHRIST on the night he had denied knowing JESUS. If Peter had not denied JESUS on that fateful night, then the GOSPEL of MARK would have been called "THE GOSPEL ACCORDING TO PETER", and the Church on Earth would have been established on Peter rather than on the teachings of Paul. HOWEVER, ALBEIT THE WILL of ***GOD!***

The next day

On the day following JESUS' BAPTISM, HE gathers HIS THIRD Disciple, Philip, and Philip introduces JESUS to his friend Na-than'-a-el, who is a ***GOD*** FEARING man. When Philip sees Na-than'-a-el he tells him that he has found the MESSIAH, whose NAME is JESUS, and that JESUS is from the city of Nazareth. However, once Na-than'-a-el hears that JESUS is from Nazareth he becomes skeptical of HIM, because the Scriptures of Micah the Prophet had said that the MESSIAH would come forth from Bethlehem, and not out of Nazareth.

But JESUS KNEW who Na-than'-a-el was and that he was a good man, and when JESUS acknowledged that HE knew Na-than'-a-el, Na-than'-a-el asked how HE had come to know him?

> ***John 1:48*** *Na-than'-a-el saith unto HIM, Whence thou knowest me? JESUS answered and said unto him,* ***BEFORE THAT PHILIP CALLED THEE, WHEN THOU WAST UNDER THE FIG TREE, I SAW THEE.***

> ***John 1:49*** *Na-than'-a-el answered and saith unto HIM, RABBI, thou art the SON of* ***GOD;*** *thou art the KING of ISRAEL.*

> ***John 1:50*** *JESUS answered and said unto him,* ***BECAUSE I SAID UNTO THEE, I SAW THEE UNDER THE FIG TREE, BELIEVEST THOU? THOU SHALT SEE GREATER THINGS THAN THESE.***

> ***John 1:51*** *And HE saith unto him,* ***VERILY, VERILY, I SAY UNTO YOU, HEREAFTER YE SHALL SEE HEAVEN OPEN, AND THE ANGELS OF GOD ASCENDING AND DESCENDING UPON THE SON OF MAN.***

NOTE: Why is it that once Na-than'-a-el had heard JESUS say HE had saw him under the fig tree, that he cast aside his skepticism and BELIEVED that JESUS was the MESSIAH and the SON of ***GOD?*** The reason he then BELIEVED, was because the place where JESUS had said HE had seen Na-than'-a-el was a very SECRET place. It was a place where Na-than'-a-el would go to PRAY alone, and no one else knew of this place, but Na-than'-a-el. So he KNEW that JESUS had to have been SENT by ***GOD*** for HIM to have known about Na-than'-a-el's secret place for PRAYER.

In the FINAL Scripture (John 1:51), when JESUS tells Na-than'-a-el that he will see HEAVEN OPENED and the ANGELS ASCENDING and DESCENDING on the Son of MAN; JESUS was referring to the DAY of HIS RAPTURE. Na-than'-a-el was present at the sea of Ti-be'-ri-as (John 21:2) with James, John, Simon Peter, Thomas, Philip, and Andrew, when JESUS was TAKEN up to HEAVEN by RAPTURE. John was there as well, but he was uncertain as to what he had WITNESSED. What John saw was a MAN whom they BELIEVED was JESUS they were talking to, instantly disappear from sight. So being uncertain as to what he had WITNESSED, John omitted JESUS' RAPTURE from his GOSPEL. It was Na-than'-a-el who had been given the PROPHECY of that EVENT by JESUS, and ONLY he clearly SAW HEAVEN OPEN and the ANGELS DESCEND UPON JESUS and CARRY HIM BACK UP TO HEAVEN. And, it was Na-than'-a-el who described the EVENT to the other Disciples, even to those who were present at the time JESUS RECEIVED RAPTURE, for they were not sure as to what had happened. This EVENT was afterward recorded by both Mark and Luke and put into their GOSPELS (Mark 16:19 and Luke 24:51).[1]

17.2 MIRACLES BEGIN

WE have talked thus far about the FIRST and SECOND DAY of JESUS' MINISTRY. On the FIRST DAY (the day of HIS BAPTISM), JESUS met Andrew and Simon Peter, and on the SECOND day HE met Philip, and Philip introduced HIM to his friend Na-than'-a-el. Although the Scriptures in the GOSPEL of John do not chronicle it, JESUS also met with EIGHT other of HIS Disciples on the SECOND DAY, after HIS meeting with Philip. This brings the total

[1] Whenever you see in the Scriptures a STATEMENT made with the WORDS "VERILY, VERILY, I SAY UNTO YOU", this STATEMENT pertains to PROPHECY given specifically to the individuals there at that TIME! JESUS was telling Na-than'-a-el that "he alone" would SEE the ANGELS of HEAVEN ASCENDING AND DESCENDING on JESUS, and Na-than'-a-el did indeed CLEARLY SEE THAT EVENT, whereas no one else did.

NUMBER of HIS disciples to ELEVEN, TWO DAYS after HIS BAPTISM. HIS TWELFTH Disciple, Matthew, JESUS met on the NINTH DAY of HIS MINISTRY, after HE had returned home from JERUSALEM, for Matthew was the Tax Collector at the entrance to the City of Nazareth, where JESUS lived.

A GAP in TIME!

In the early chapters of John's GOSPEL, he chronicles the first THREE days of JESUS' MINISTRY. However, John does not speak about the FORTY DAYS and FORTY NIGHTS that JESUS SPENT in the WILDERNESS being TEMPTED by the Devil, as the other three GOSPELS do. This EVENT happened immediately after JESUS' BAPTISM, so what happened to that FORTY-DAY GAP in TIME? Also, why wasn't it WRITTEN into the Scriptures of John's GOSPEL, for the GOSPEL of John gives an accurate account of JESUS' time after HIS BAPTISM? Did it really HAPPEN?

The answer to these questions is really quite simple; no one saw that GAP in TIME, because the FORTY DAYS and FORTY NIGHTS took place in a MOMENT of TIME! Therefor, because John was with JESUS from the SECOND DAY forward in JESUS' MINISTRY, he did not witness JESUS' being gone for any PERIOD of TIME. The Scriptures in the GOSPEL of Luke can verify that the FORTY-DAY GAP in TIME took place in a MOMENT, for JESUS was in THE SPIRIT when HE was TEMPTED by the Devil in the WILDERNESS (THE GAP)!

> ***Luke 4:5*** *And the Devil, taking HIM up into an high mountain, shewed unto HIM all the Kingdoms of the World in a <u>MOMENT of TIME.</u>*

NOTE: JESUS was TAKEN IMMEDIATELY after HIS BAPTISM outside of the EARTH PLANE and into the FIFTH DIMENSION, the GAP DIMENSION, where TIME does not EXIST. The Disciples only knew of this EVENT by JESUS' TESTIMONY of it, for they could not have WITNESSED the EVENT. John WROTE only about what he had WITNESSED himself and therefor omitted it from his GOSPEL, even though he had known it had taken place!

The THIRD DAY and the BEGINNING of MIRACLES

On the THIRD DAY of JESUS' MINISTRY, HE and ELEVEN of HIS Disciples attended a marriage ceremony in Cana of Galilee that Mary HIS mother was hosting for one of the town Elders. When Mary saw that the wine had run out, she requested that JESUS do something to help her. JESUS, being put on the spot by Mary, and unsure as to what HE might be able do (as HE had not YET performed any MIRACLES), then said to Mary: "***WOMAN, WHAT HAVE I TO DO WITH THEE? MINE HOUR IS NOT YET COME". (John 2:4)***

JESUS had thought HE would have RECEIVED some sort SIGN from ***GOD*** prior to HIM performing any MIRACLES. However, the REQUEST made by Mary was the SIGN from above HE had been looking for! JESUS then had HIS Disciples who were acting as servants at the WEDDING, fill SIX waterpots with water. HE then CONVERTED the WATER into 153 gallons of WINE, and this was the FIRST MIRACLE PERFORMED by JESUS CHRIST; and ELEVEN of HIS Disciples witnessed the MIRACLE and BELIEVED in HIM!

> ***John 2:11*** *This BEGINNING of MIRACLES did JESUS in Cana of Galilee, and MANIFESTED forth HIS GLORY; and HIS Disciples BELIEVED on HIM.*

Attending the PASSOVER

On the 7th day of April (Abib) JESUS was BAPTIZED in the ***SPIRIT of GOD*** and on the 10th day of April HE PERFORMED HIS 1st MIRACLE. HE then on the 11th day of April journeyed with HIS Mother, brothers, and HIS Disciples to JERUSALEM, and they went by way of Ca-per'-na-um.

Once they arrive at the TEMPLE in JERUSALEM, JESUS sees various sorts of MERCHANDISE being sold out of the COURTYARD of the TEMPLE, and this TROUBLED HIM.

> ***John 2:14*** *And found in the TEMPLE those that sold oxen and sheep and doves, and the changers of money sitting:*

> ***John 2:15*** *And when HE had made a scourge of small cords, HE drove them all out of the TEMPLE, and the sheep, and the oxen; and poured out the changers money, and overthrew the tables;*

> ***John 2:16*** *And said unto them that sold doves,* ***TAKE THESE THINGS HENCE; MAKE NOT MY FATHER'S HOUSE AN HOUSE OF MERCHANDISE.***

> ***John 2:17*** *And HIS Disciples remembered that it was written, THE ZEAL OF THINE HOUSE HATH EATEN ME UP.*[2]

Back to the TEMPLE

Once the Jews had seen that JESUS had disrupted their courtyard MERCHANDISING, they questioned HIS ACTIONS. They said to HIM, by whose authority are YOU committing these acts, and asked what sign HE could give them to prove HE was the CHRIST? JESUS answered them by saying, if they were to DESTROY THIS TEMPLE (HE was referring to HIS OWN body), HE could raise it up in THREE DAYS. But the Jews laughed at HIM and being unaware of what HE had meant, said, how could HE build in three days a Temple that took hundreds of men forty-six years to build?

While in JERUSALEM (over a course of time) JESUS performed many MIRACLES, and many of them who had WITNESSED the MIRACLES, BELIEVED IN JESUS CHRIST, but the Pharisees and Scribes refused to believe HE was CHRIST!

> ***John 2:23*** *Now when HE was in JERUSALEM at the PASSOVER, in the FEAST DAY, many BELIEVED in HIS NAME, when they saw the MIRACLES which HE did.*

> ***John 2:24*** *But JESUS did not commit HIMSELF unto them, because HE KNEW ALL MEN,*

> ***John 2:25*** *And needed not that any should testify of man: for HE KNEW what was in man.*

---

[2] Shortly after THE LORD had come to ME on October 13th 1997, ***HE*** had me attend two Churches. While I attended these Churches for one year each, I observed both Churches doing the same things as the Pharisees were doing in the aforementioned Scriptures. As you would enter into either of these Churches, you could plainly see things such as, video and audiocassettes, books, CD-ROM's, and other various types of religious articles that were FOR SALE. There were also cash registers and credit card imprinters there and the religious things were all being sold out of the Church's lobby. I even attended one Church having a bicycle hanging from its ceiling that was to be given away in an upcoming raffle! THE LORD would CONTINUALLY REMIND ME each and every time I entered into those Churches of the SCRIPTURES, FORBIDDING the SALE of anything out of the HOUSE of ***GOD***. This type of behavior pushed JESUS CHRIST to the POINT of RAGE, and HE FORBIDS it; so why do the Churches do it?"

NOTE: In John 2:24 and 2:25, what is being said in the LAYER of the Scripture; is that JESUS neither introduced HIMSELF to men, nor did HE entrust in them to DEFEND HIS MESSAGE. The LAYER also tells you that JESUS KNEW ALL MEN SPIRITUALLY, and expected nothing from them PERSONALLY, except they should hear HIS MESSAGE. ***GOD*** had sent JESUS to DELIVER a MESSAGE and JESUS KNEW that only those who ***GOD*** had intended to RECEIVE IT could RECEIVE IT, and this is why the Pharisees and Scribes refused to BELIEVE in HIM!

Thus far WE have covered the FIRST NINE DAYS of the MINISTRY of JESUS CHRIST. In those NINE DAYS JESUS gathered to HIMSELF TWELVE DISCIPLES, and a following of THOUSANDS of weary SOULS looking for SPIRITUAL GUIDANCE. NO OTHER PERSON EVER WALKING THE EARTH, COULD DO EVEN IN A LIFETIME, WHAT JESUS HAD DONE IN ONLY NINE DAYS.

As WE progress further into the GOSPEL of John, I PRAY that you will start to not only SEE JESUS in the SPIRIT, but you WILL start to FEEL HIM in your SPIRIT. For those of CHRIST and those in CHRIST, SHALL FEEL THE POWER of CHRIST, ***SAITH THE LORD!***

> ***John 17:24 FATHER, I WILL THAT THEY ALSO, WHOM THOU HAST GIVEN ME, BE WITH ME WHERE I AM; THAT THEY MAY BEHOLD MY GLORY, WHICH THOU HAST GIVEN ME: FOR THOU LOVEST ME BEFORE THE FOUNDATION OF THE WORLD.***
>
> ***John 17: 25 O RIGHTEOUS FATHER, THE WORLD HATH NOT KNOWN THEE: BUT I HAVE KNOWN THEE, AND THESE HAVE KNOWN THAT THOU HAST SENT ME.***
>
> ***John 17:26 AND I HAVE DECLARED UNTO THEM THY NAME, AND WILL DECLARE IT: THAT THE LOVE WHEREWITH THOU HAST LOVED ME MAY BE IN THEM, AND I IN THEM.***

A-MEN'

17.3 SPIRITUAL CONVERSION & The 2nd MIRACLE

JESUS had been PREACHING the KINGDOM of ***GOD*** for only a few weeks, and there was a certain Pharisee by the name of Nic-o-de'-mus who would come to hear JESUS SPEAK. However Nic-o-de'-mus did so COVERTLY, for if the other Pharisees were to find out that he had followed the teaching of JESUS, he would have been put out of the Synagogue for doing so.

One evening, Nic-o-de'-mus came to JESUS wanting to further his UNDERSTANDING about HEAVENLY things, for he knew that JESUS had surely come out from ***GOD.*** So JESUS told him about SPIRITUAL REBIRTH. Nic-o-de'-mus, having difficulty in UNDERSTANDING what JESUS meant about REBIRTH, asked JESUS if HE meant that a person was to reenter their mother's womb a second time, and be born again. However, JESUS was SPEAKING about a SPIRITUAL REBIRTH and not about a physical one.

> ***John 3:5*** *JESUS ANSWERED,* ***VERILY, VERILY, I SAY UNTO THEE, EXCEPT A MAN BE BORN OF WATER AND OF THE SPIRIT, HE CANNOT ENTER INTO THE KINGDOM OF GOD.***

> ***John 3:6 THAT WHICH IS BORN OF FLESH IS FLESH; AND THAT WHICH IS BORN OF SPIRIT IS SPIRIT.***

The WATER spoken of by JESUS; REPRESENTS the LIVING WATERS of the *WORD of* ***GOD,*** and the SPIRIT REPRESENTS THE ***HOLY SPIRIT*** BAPTISM which one must RECEIVE to be SAVED. JESUS further tells Nic-o-de'-mus that a person cannot SEE the SPIRIT even though they may FEEL it, and it can be compared to the WIND that one can feel but cannot see, but Nic-o-de'-mus still didn't UNDERSTAND.

When JESUS SEES that Nic-o-de'-mus is still having difficulty understanding, HE is shocked; because a Pharisee is supposed to UNDERSTAND the *WORD of* ***GOD,*** and even at this very FUNDAMENTAL LEVEL of UNDERSTANDING, Nic-o-de'-mus cannot comprehend what JESUS is telling him. So JESUS says:

> ***John 3:11 VERILY, VERILY, I SAY UNTO THEE, WE SPEAK THAT WE DO KNOW, AND TESTIFY THAT WE HAVE SEEN; AND YE RECEIVE NOT OUR WITNESS.***

> ***John 3:12 IF I HAVE TOLD YOU EARTHLY THINGS, AND YE BELIEVE NOT, HOW SHALL YOU BELIEVE, IF I TELL YOU OF HEAVENLY THINGS?***

JESUS continues to tell Nic-o-de'-mus that only those who have come down from HEAVEN may ASCEND back to HEAVEN, and further says that even though HE, JESUS was here walking upon the earth, HE was yet still in HEAVEN; thus indicating HIS having OMNIPRESENCE. JESUS then tells of HIS pending CRUCIFIXION, and relates it to when MOSES had held up the serpent in the wilderness as a sign of medicinal healing.

> ***John 3:14 AND AS MOSES LIFTED UP THE SERPENT IN THE WILDERNESS, EVEN SO MUST THE SON OF MAN BE LIFTED UP:***[3]

> ***John 3:15 THAT WHOSOEVER BELIEVETH IN HIM SHOULD NOT PERISH, BUT HAVE ETERNAL LIFE.***

What JESUS is telling Nic-o-de'-mus, is that ANYONE who SEES JESUS' CRUCIFIXION as a SIGN FOR HEALING, (like the pole with the serpent MOSES had fashioned in the wilderness), they will be SPIRITUALLY HEALED BY BELIEVING IN IT! Whereas the pole fashioned in the wilderness was for the healing of the flesh, the CROSS represents, the HEALING of the SPIRIT; for it is FIRST in the FLESH and then in the SPIRIT ***SAITH THE LORD!***

> ***John 3:18 HE THAT BELIEVETH ON HIM IS NOT CONDEMNED: BUT HE THAT BELIEVETH NOT IS CONDEMNED ALREADY, BECAUSE HE HATH NOT BELIEVED IN THE NAME OF THE ONLY BEGOTTEN SON OF GOD.***

NOTE: After MOSES had fashioned the pole in the wilderness, HE told the people, if they were bitten by the serpent and would look upon the pole for their HEALING, they would be HEALED. But only those BELIEVING what MOSES had told THEM came to look upon the pole, and it was by their ***FAITH*** they were HEALED. JESUS was saying the very same thing as

---

[3] When the Children of ISRAEL were dying in the wilderness from the fiery serpent bite, ***GOD*** told MOSES to fashion a pole having the WINGS of an ANGEL on it, and a serpent wound around it. Then when MOSES were to raise up the pole for the Children of ISRAEL to SEE, those who had been bitten by the serpent would not die from its bite. JESUS in the last Scripture refers to the CROSS with HIM on it, as being the same as the pole MOSES had fashioned in the wilderness, thus indicating that the CROSS is a SYMBOL of SPIRITUAL HEALING.

MOSES had said; That for them BELIEVING that JESUS is CHRIST, THE SON OF ***GOD;*** the CROSS of crucifixion would represent the sign of HEALING for them in the NEW COVENANT.

JESUS tells Nic-o-de'-mus, ANYONE refusing to BELIEVE in HIM is already CONDEMNED, because they refuse to BELIEVE in the TRUTH. They are the children of DARKNESS who fear the LIGHT; for in the LIGHT they are EXPOSED. But the CHILDREN of the LIGHT will come to the LIGHT, because they have a SOUL (a PURPOSE) from ***GOD*** and therefor KNOW the TRUTH when they HEAR IT!

> ***John 3:21 BUT HE THAT DOETH TRUTH COMETH TO THE LIGHT, THAT HIS DEEDS MAY BE MADE MANIFEST, THAT THEY ARE WROUGHT IN GOD.***

Mission Accomplished by John the Baptist

With John the Baptist and his disciples still Baptizing with water, John's disciples ask John why all of the people are now coming to JESUS for their BAPTISM, rather than to him? John then explains to them, that he had come from above to PREPARE the way for JESUS CHRIST, as it was WRITTEN in the Scriptures (Malachi 4:5), and now his MISSION was COMPLETED. John further tells them that his ministry will now DECREASE, while JESUS' MINISTRY INCREASES, and that his reward was in his SERVING his PURPOSE in ***GOD***.

> ***John 3:30*** *HE must INCREASE, but I must DECREASE.*

> ***John 3:31*** *HE that cometh from ABOVE is ABOVE ALL: he that is of the earth is earthly, and speaketh of the earth: HE that cometh from HEAVEN is ABOVE ALL.*

> ***John 3:32*** *And what HE hath SEEN and HEARD, that HE testifieth; and no man receiveth HIS testimony.*

> ***John 3:33*** *He that hath RECEIVED HIS TESTIMONY hath SET his SEAL that* ***GOD*** *is TRUE.*

NOTE: What John the Baptist is telling his disciples, is that ONLY the CHILDREN of ***GOD*** will HEAR and UNDERSTAND what JESUS CHRIST has to say. And, that ***GOD*** sent JESUS to DEMONSTRATE without measure the POWER of the ***SPIRIT of GOD,*** withholding nothing from JESUS.

> ***JOHN 3:36*** *He that BELIEVETH on the SON hath EVERLASTING LIFE: and he that believeth NOT the SON shall not see life; but the WRATH of* ***GOD*** *abideth on him.*

The Samaritan Woman at the WELL

> ***John 4:1*** *When therefore the LORD knew how the Pharisees had heard that JESUS made and Baptized more disciples than John,*

> ***John 4:2*** *(Though JESUS HIMSELF Baptized not, but HIS Disciples,)*

> ***John 4:3*** *HE left Ju-dae'-a, and departed again into Galilee.*

On the way to Galilee, JESUS and HIS Disciples went through Samaria and stopped at the well that JACOB had given to his son JOSEPH. With it being about noon, JESUS sent HIS Disciples into town to buy some food while HE sat to rest at the well. While waiting, a Samaritan woman came to the well to draw some water and JESUS asked the woman for a DRINK. The woman being somewhat in shock that a Jew would speak to her, (because the Jews saw the Samaritans as inferior people), asked HIM why HE had asked her for a DRINK?

> ***John 4:10*** *JESUS answered and said unto her,* ***IF THOU KNEWEST THE GIFT OF GOD, AND WHO IT IS THAT SAYETH TO THEE, GIVE ME TO DRINK; THOU WOULDEST HAVE ASKED OF HIM, AND HE WOULD HAVE GIVEN THEE LIVING WATER.***

The woman then tells JESUS that the well is very deep, and HE hadn't anything to draw the water up from the well, so how was HE going to give her the LIVING WATERS HE had spoken of? She further tells JESUS how the well was at one time JACOB'S WELL and how JACOB had drank from it, and asked JESUS, did HE think HE was GREATER than JACOB?

> ***John 4:13*** *JESUS answered and said unto her,* ***WHOSOEVER***

DRINKETH OF THIS WATER SHALL THIRST AGAIN:

John 4:14 BUT WHOSOEVER DRINKETH OF THE WATER THAT I SHALL GIVE HIM SHALL NEVER THIRST; BUT THE WATER THAT I SHALL GIVE HIM SHALL BE IN HIM A WELL OF WATER SPRINGING UP INTO EVERLASTING LIFE.

NOTE: The WATER that JESUS is speaking about; is the LIVING WATERS, the *WORD of* ***GOD.*** ONCE a person RECEIVES the *WORD of* ***GOD,*** they will RECEIVE with it, ETERNITY.

The woman tells JESUS to give her some of the LIVING WATERS HE was SPEAKING of, and JESUS requests for her to first go and fetch her husband. But she says to JESUS, she does not have a husband, and JESUS says to her, she has spoken truthfully, for she had had FIVE HUSBANDS, and the man she is now living with was not her husband. Once the woman hears this, she says to JESUS that she PERCEIVES HIM to be a PROPHET, because HE knew these things about her past. She further tells JESUS that they worship ***GOD*** on this mountain they were now at, but she had heard, they should really be WORSHIPPING ***GOD*** at the TEMPLE in JERUSALEM.

But JESUS tells her that if she were to TRULY WORSHIP ***GOD*** it wouldn't be either here on the mountain or in JERUSALEM, for only the Jews WORSHIPPED the TRUE ***GOD.*** However, the Jews were not WORSHIPPING PROPERLY, for they were worshipping ***GOD*** in the FLESH, rather than in the SPIRIT.

John 4:23 BUT THE HOUR COMETH, AND NOW IS, WHEN THE TRUE WORSHIPPERS SHALL WORSHIP THE FATHER IN SPIRIT AND IN TRUTH: FOR THE FATHER SEEKETH SUCH TO WORSHIP HIM.

John 4:24 GOD IS A SPIRIT: AND THEY THAT WORSHIP HIM MUST WORSHIP HIM IN SPIRIT AND IN TRUTH.

The woman then tells JESUS, that when the MESSIAH whom is called CHRIST COMES, that HE WILL TEACH them of these things and how to WORSHIP ***GOD.***

John 4:26 *JESUS saith unto her,* ***I THAT SPEAK UNTO THEE***

AM HE.

Meanwhile, JESUS' Disciples return from buying some food in town, and when they SEE that HE is talking to a Samaritan woman they feel discomforted by it, for the Jews did not speak to Samaritans. But they didn't ask JESUS why HE had been SPEAKING to her. The woman after seeing the Disciples, leaves, leaving her water-pot at the well and hurriedly goes back to her town BELIEVING she had found the CHRIST who was to come. She then proceeds to tell the townsfolk how JESUS had told her things about herself, that only she had known.

The Disciples then try to get JESUS to eat for they were all very hungry, but HE tells them that HE has MEAT TO EAT already, SPEAKING OF HIS CRUCIFIXION and how many of the PEOPLE needed to be CONVERTED in a rather short period of time. But they had thought when HE had told them "HE had MEAT to EAT", that someone had already given JESUS some food and HE wasn't hungry.

> ***John 4:34*** *JESUS saith unto them,* ***MY MEAT IS TO DO THE WILL OF HIM THAT SENT ME, AND TO FINISH HIS WORK.***

JESUS tells them that HE has come to SOW the SEED and they will gather the HARVEST from that which HE has SOWN and from that which the Prophets have SOWN. JESUS further says, both the SOWER of the SEED and the GATHERERS of the HARVEST will REJOICE TOGETHER, ONCE THEIR WORK HAS BEEN COMPLETED.

After the woman had told the townspeople about JESUS, they came to HIM in DROVES wanting to HEAR HIM SPEAK, and when HE had SPOKEN, they BELIEVED that HE was the CHRIST who was to COME into the world. JESUS then stayed in the area for two days PREACHING to them, and then departed to Galilee, to the City of Cana, the place where HE had made the water into WINE.

The 2nd MIRACLE

While in Cana of Galilee there was an Official from the City of Ca-per'-na-um whose son had become seriously ill and feverish to the point of death. The Official had heard of JESUS and BELIEVED HE could HEAL his son, so he asked if JESUS would come back with him to Ca-per'-na-um and HEAL his son.

John 4:48** Then said JESUS unto him, **EXCEPT YE SEE SIGNS AND WONDERS, YE WILL NOT BELIEVE.

NOTE: JESUS knew that ***GOD*** was sending these people to HIM to HEAL, so those who had SEEN with their own eyes what HE had DONE could BELIEVE HE was CHRIST.

***John 4:49** The Nobleman saith unto HIM, SIR, come down ere my child die.*

***John 4:50** JESUS saith unto him, **GO THY WAY; THY SON LIVETH.** And the man BELIEVED the WORD SPOKEN unto him, and he went his way.*

When the Official had returned home, his servants told him that his son's fever had broken, and he was recovering from the illness. The man then asked at what time did the fever break? They told him it was at about the seventh hour (1:00PM in the afternoon) and the man knew this was the TIME when JESUS had said to him, ***"GO THY WAY; THY SON LIVETH".*** The Official then and his entire household BELIEVED in JESUS from that time forward.

This was the SECOND MIRACLE JESUS had PERFORMED since the TIME of HIS BAPTISM, and ALL them that had EYES to SEE, DID SEE, and BELIEVED. But the Jews and the Pharisees still refused to believe, even though they had seen with their own eyes what JESUS could do.

17.4 Troubled Waters

The POOL

Nearly six months into HIS MINISTRY, and the time being near to the Day of Atonement (October 10th), JESUS decides to take HIS TWELVE and go back to JERUSALEM. While at JERUSALEM they went to a place called the "Gate of the Sheep" (a place where sheep were bought and sold), and at the GATE there was a POOL of WATER, called Be-thes'-da. This POOL was unique, as it was said; an ANGEL (ASAPH) would come down periodically from HEAVEN and SANCTIFY the water in the pool.

Around the POOL you would see many ill and maimed people waiting, for they believed if they were to get into the WATER immediately after the ANGEL had SANCTIFIED it, they would be HEALED of whatever affliction they had suffered from. So the people would stay close to the POOL, not knowing at what time the ANGEL would come down; for it was said, only the FIRST to enter the POOL after it had been SANCTIFIED, would be HEALED.

JESUS, passing by the POOL, noticed a man who had been waiting there to be HEALED for thirty-eight years. The man suffered from a severe illness and he had brought his bed to the POOL and lay there for many years, waiting for the opportunity to be HEALED. JESUS asked the man, if he wanted to be HEALED, and the man answered, yes, but told JESUS, every time the ANGEL would come down, someone else would get into the WATER before him, and he hadn't anyone there to put him in FIRST.

JESUS told the man, "***RISE, TAKE UP THY BED, AND WALK***" (John 5:8), and the man was IMMEDIATELY HEALED, so he picked up his bed and walked away. When the Jews saw the man carrying his bed, and it was on the SABBATH DAY, they told him he was breaking the law; for it was forbidden to do any sort of work on the SABBATH.

But the man told those accusing him of breaking the law, the MAN who had HEALED him of his affliction told him to take up his bed and walk, so he did as he was told. So they asked the man, who was it that told him to carry his bed away? But the man wasn't sure who it was for there were many people there and JESUS had moved on and out of the immediate area. The man then left and went off to the TEMPLE to thank ***GOD*** for his HEALING, for JESUS had told him to THANK ***GOD.***

> ***John 5:14*** *Afterward JESUS findeth him in the TEMPLE, and said unto him,* ***BEHOLD, THOU ART MADE WHOLE: SIN NO MORE, LEST A WORSE THING COME UNTO THEE.***

> ***John 5:15*** *The man departed, and told the Jews that it was JESUS, which had made him whole.*

The REBUKING

So the Jews came to JESUS to accuse HIM of violating the SABBATH, and wanted to stone HIM for doing so. But JESUS told them that HIS ***FATHER, GOD,*** worked on the SABBATH DAY and so does HE.

> ***John 5:18*** *Therefore the Jews sought the more to kill HIM, because HE had not only broken the SABBATH, but said also that* ***GOD*** *was HIS* ***FATHER****, making HIMSELF equal with* ***GOD.***

JESUS then tells those accusing HIM, that HE on HIS own can do nothing; but what HE sees HIS ***FATHER*** do, HE does the same; and that ***GOD*** had EMPOWERED HIM to do the same things ***GOD*** can do. JESUS says, as HIS ***FATHER*** can RAISE UP the dead, so can HE also RAISE UP the dead, and tells them that ***GOD*** had GIVEN HIM JUDGMENT over ALL mankind, and ALL mankind should also HONOR the SON, as should they HONOR ***THE FATHER.***

> ***John 5:24 VERILY, VERILY, I SAY UNTO YOU, HE THAT HEARETH MY WORD, AND BELIEVETH ON HIM THAT SENT ME, HATH EVERLASTING LIFE, AND SHALL NOT COME INTO CONDEMNATION; BUT IS PASSED FROM DEATH UNTO LIFE.***

> ***John 5:25 VERILY, VERILY, I SAY UNTO YOU, THE HOUR IS COMING, AND NOW IS, WHEN THE DEAD SHALL HEAR THE VOICE OF THE SON OF GOD: AND THEY THAT HEAR SHALL LIVE.***

JESUS further tells the Jews that ***GOD*** has GIVEN HIM POWER OVER LIFE and DEATH, and also the AUTHORITY to exercise JUDGMENT. HE says, those who have led GOOD LIVES HE will RAISE UP on the LAST DAY to have an EVERLASTING LIFE, and those who have led EVIL LIVES will be RAISED UP to STAND in JUDGMENT of their EVIL ACTS, and receive ETERNAL DAMNATION.

JESUS says again to them, HE alone can do nothing, but it is ***GOD*** who has EMPOWERED HIM to PERFORM the MIRACLES HE has done. Also, it isn't HIM who DECIDES what shall be done or who should be HEALED, it is ***GOD*** WHO DETERMINES BOTH HIS ACTIONS and HIS JUDGMENTS, for ALL that HE DOES is by the WILL of ***THE FATHER.*** Therefor, HE need not look for the APPROVAL of men to JUSTIFY HIS ACTIONS; for HIS ACTIONS are JUSTIFIED by ***GOD,*** and not by men. Nor does HE need to justify HIMSELF to men, for WHATSOEVER HE DOES, THE MIRACLES WILL JUSTIFY THEMSELVES.

> ***John 5:37 AND THE FATHER HIMSELF, WHICH HATH SENT ME, HATH BORNE WITNESS OF ME. YE HAVE NEITHER HEARD HIS VOICE, NOR SEEN HIS SHAPE.***

John 5:38 AND YE HAVE NOT HIS WORD ABIDING IN YOU: FOR WHOM HE HATH SENT, HIM YE BELIEVE NOT.

John 5:39 SEARCH THE SCRIPTURES; FOR IN THEM YE THINK YE HAVE ETERNAL LIFE: AND THEY ARE THEY WHICH TESTIFY OF ME.

John 5:40 AND YE WILL NOT COME TO ME, THAT YE MIGHT HAVE LIFE.

John 5:41 I RECEIVE NOT HONOUR FROM MEN.

NOTE: This was a STRONG REBUKING of the JEWS put forth by JESUS CHRIST for their denial of HIM. As you were previously told, the WORDS, "VERILY, VERILY, I SAY UNTO YOU", implies that what is being said in the Scripture applies SPECIFICALLY to them it is being ADDRESSED TO. The JEWS JESUS had REBUKED in the Scriptures, were at that TIME CONDEMNED by HIS JUDGMENT to ETERNAL DAMNATION ***SAITH THE LORD.*** For by their rebuking the ACTIONS of JESUS CHRIST they were BLASPHEMING THE ***HOLY SPIRIT of GOD*** WHO WAS PERFORMING THE MIRACLES THROUGH JESUS CHRIST. And those, who were in dispute with JESUS, unknowingly were CONDEMNING THEMSELVES TO HELL by SINNING AGAINST THE ***HOLY SPIRIT!***

CONDEMNATION of the ACCUSERS

JESUS then tells HIS ACCUSERS they are NOT of ***GOD,*** and had NOT ***GOD'S LOVE*** abiding in them; and HE need not ACCUSE them before ***GOD,*** for MOSES (the PERSON of THE ***HOLY SPIRIT***) had already ACCUSED THEM before ***GOD*** and they were FOUND GUILTY and CONDEMNED.

NOTE: The JEWS believed because they were the DESCENDANTS of ABRAHAM they were BLESSED, and by the BLESSING they would receive eternity. But SAVING (ETERNAL LIFE) COMES BY GRACE and not by BLESSING ***SAITH THE LORD***, and GRACE COMES BY WAY OF JESUS CHRIST, whom they had REFUSED.

Gathering the Multitudes

Some period of time after leaving JERUSALEM, JESUS takes HIS Disciples and crosses over the Sea of Galilee, and a great multitude of people followed. They followed JESUS because they had WITNESSED many of HIS MIRACLES and saw many people HEALED. Being nearly one year into HIS MINISTRY, and the time of the PASSOVER FEAST approaching, JESUS went up into the mountains with HIS Disciples and the MULTITUDES of people followed.

> ***John 6:5*** *When JESUS then lifted up HIS EYES, and saw a great company come unto HIM, HE saith unto Philip,* ***WHENCE SHALL WE BUY BREAD THAT THESE MAY EAT?***

When JESUS looked around and saw the thousands of people who had followed HIM, HE asked Philip where could they go to buy enough food to feed them ALL. But Philip, seeing the thousands of people in their company, tells JESUS there wasn't anyplace where they could get enough food to FEED a group of that size. But JESUS wanted to BROADEN HIS Disciples FAITH and SHOW them that ***GOD WOULD PROVIDE THEM WITH WHAT WAS NEEDED.***

Andrew, overhearing the conversation between JESUS and Philip, tells JESUS there is a boy in their company having FIVE LOAVES of BREAD, and TWO LITTLE FISH. However, Andrew says he realizes with only that small amount of food they wouldn't be able to feed them all.

NOTE: GOD was AGAIN setting the STAGE for JESUS to PERFORM another MIRACLE, so JESUS MIGHT PROVE to HIS Disciples that NOTHING is to DIFFICULT for ***THE LORD!***

Where they were situated in the mountain there were grassy fields, so JESUS has the MULTITUDE (roughly FIVE THOUSAND PEOPLE) set themselves down in the grass. HE then took up the Basket of FIVE LOAVES of BREAD and TWO FISHES, and HELD THEM UP BEFORE ***THE ALMIGHTY*** and GAVE THANKS. JESUS then told HIS Disciples to pass out the food, and give each PERSON as much as they wanted to EAT of the BREAD and of the FISHES. So the Disciples passed out the FOOD to the MULTITUDE and they ALL ATE and they were FILLED.

After ALL had eaten, JESUS tells HIS Disciples to gather up that which had not been EATEN so that no leftovers were LOST. When the Disciples gathered up the leftover FOOD they FILLED TWELVE FULL BASKETS.

NOTE: The TWELVE BASKETS that each of the DISCIPLES had to gather up the remaining food in, represented the TWELVE MINISTRIES each Disciple would ESTABLISH for JESUS CHRIST. By each of the TWELVE BAS-

KETS being FILLED UP with the remaining FOOD, this REPRESENTED that ALL of ***GOD'S*** CHILDREN would be GATHERED, leaving not a ONE BEHIND.

> ***Amos 9:9*** *For, lo, I will COMMAND, and I will SIFT the HOUSE of ISRAEL among ALL nations, like as corn is SIFTED in a sieve, yet shall NOT the LEAST GRAIN fall upon the EARTH.*

> ***John 6:14*** *Then those men, when they had SEEN the MIRACLE that JESUS did, said, THIS IS OF A TRUTH THAT PROPHET THAT SHOULD COME INTO THE WORLD.*

> ***John 6:15*** *When JESUS therefore PERCEIVED that they would come and take HIM by FORCE, to make HIM a KING, HE departed again into a mountain HIMSELF ALONE.*

WALKING on WATER

JESUS after FEEDING the MULTITUDE then went away by HIMSELF further up into the mountains. HIS Disciples then leaving JESUS behind, got back into their boat and started across the sea of Galilee towards Ca-per'-na-um. Shortly after their departure, the sea arose and created large swells and they were also fighting a head wind causing them to have to row. After rowing for some period of time and only being out a little over three miles, the Disciples see JESUS walking towards them on the SEA, and they became frightened because they thought it was a GHOST.

> ***John 6:20*** *But HE saith unto them,* ***IT IS I; BE NOT AFRAID.***

Then once they knew it was JESUS they RECEIVED HIM into the boat. As SOON as HE had stepped onboard, the Disciples LOOKED UP and they had already reached the far side of the SEA, whereas they were only three miles out when HE had come aboard.

The next day when the people whom HE had FED saw that JESUS was gone, they took boats and crossed the sea to look for HIM. They had searched the mountain and could not find HIM and recalled seeing the night before, HIS Disciples leave without HIM, crossing back over the sea towards Ca-per'-na-um. So they went to see if the Disciples knew where JESUS had gone. When they arrive at the bank of Ca-per'-na-um, they see that JESUS is with HIS Disciples, and in amazement ask HIM how he had gotten there?

> ***John 6:26*** *JESUS answered them and said,* ***VERILY, VERILY, I SAY UNTO YOU, YE SEEK ME, NOT BECAUSE YE SAW THE MIRACLES, BUT BECAUSE YE DID EAT OF THE LOAVES, AND WERE FILLED.***

> ***John 6:27 LABOR NOT FOR THE MEAT WHICH PERISHETH, BUT FOR THAT MEAT WHICH ENDURETH UNTO EVERLASTING LIFE, WHICH THE SON OF MAN SHALL GIVE UNTO YOU: FOR HIM HATH GOD THE FATHER SEALED.***

NOTE: The FOOD JESUS is SPEAKING of in the SCRIPTURES, is the *WORD of* ***GOD,*** this is the FOOD that JESUS came DOWN from HEAVEN with to FEED the PEOPLE. This is the SPIRITUAL NOURISHMENT WE HAVE DISCUSSED PREVIOUSLY, THAT WHICH IS NEEDED TO KEEP THE SPIRIT ALIVE!

The PEOPLE then ask JESUS how might they SERVE ***GOD*** and JESUS tells them ALL that is NEEDED is for them to BELIEVE HE had been sent by ***GOD*** to FEED them. In reply they ask JESUS, what sign would be given to them so they might BELIEVE? They further say that their forefathers received MANNA from HEAVEN to eat when they were in the wilderness with MOSES. (However, they were unaware that JESUS was speaking about SPIRITUAL FOOD and not carnal food.)

> ***John 6:32*** *Then JESUS said unto them,* ***VERILY, VERILY, I SAY UNTO YOU, MOSES GAVE YOU NOT THAT BREAD FROM HEAVEN; BUT MY FATHER GIVETH YOU THE TRUE BREAD FROM HEAVEN.***

> ***John 6:33 FOR THE BREAD OF GOD IS HE WHICH COMETH DOWN FROM HEAVEN, AND GIVETH LIFE UNTO THE WORLD.***

> ***John 6:34*** *Then said they unto HIM, LORD, evermore GIVE US THIS BREAD.*

NOTE: JESUS was trying to explain to them that the bread (MANNA) that

MOSES gave their forefathers in the wilderness was for their FLESH. Whereas the BREAD HE had brought DOWN FROM HEAVEN was from ***GOD*** to FEED their SPIRITS. AS WE HAVE PREVIOUSLY SAID, what was done in the OLD COVENANT was the SERVING of ***GOD*** in the FLESH, and ***GOD*** sent MANNA to the people while in the wilderness to feed their FLESH. However, in the NEW COVENANT, ONE must serve ***GOD*** in the SPIRIT, so ***HE*** PROVIDES JESUS CHRIST (the *WORD of* ***GOD***) to FEED THE SPIRIT. ***FIRST IN THE FLESH, AND THEN IN THE SPIRIT SAITH THE LORD!***

JESUS then tells them that HE is BOTH the BREAD and the WATER of LIFE, and anyone BELIEVING in HIM will PRESERVE THEIR LIFE. But JESUS also WARNS them that because they had SEEN with their own eyes the MIRACLES HE had performed, and they STILL REFUSE TO BELIEVE, they were giving up their only chance to be RECEIVED into HEAVEN.

HE tells them that only those who are sent by ***GOD*** to HIM, can RECEIVE HIM, and they will never be turned away, because it is the WILL of ***THE FATHER.*** JESUS says and it is the WILL of ***THE FATHER*** that NONE of them ***HE*** has CHOSEN should be LOST, and THEY SHALL be gathered and RESURRECTED on the LAST DAY UNTO ETERNAL LIFE.

Once the JEWS who are heckling JESUS hear HIM say that HE IS THE BREAD of LIFE THAT HAS COME DOWN FROM HEAVEN, they say amongst themselves; isn't this person speaking, JESUS, the son of JOSEPH and Mary whom we know? If so then, how could HE have come down from HEAVEN?

> ***John 6:43*** *JESUS therefore answered and said unto them,* ***MURMUR NOT AMONG YOURSELVES.***
>
> ***John 6:44 NO MAN CAN COME TO ME, EXCEPT THE FATHER WHICH HATH SENT ME DRAW HIM: AND I WILL RAISE HIM UP AT THE LAST DAY.***
>
> ***John 6:45 IT IS WRITTEN IN THE PROPHETS, "AND THEY SHALL BE ALL TAUGHT OF GOD". EVERY MAN THEREFORE THAT HATH HEARD, AND HATH LEARNED OF THE FATHER, COMETH UNTO ME.***

NOTE: JESUS is saying in the SCRIPTURES, HE is ***THE BREAD of LIFE,*** and ALL who are to COME UNTO ***GOD,*** must FIRST LEARN ABOUT ***GOD,*** and they can only do so through HIM, for HE is the *WORD of* ***GOD!***

The MANNA from HEAVEN

John 6:48 I AM THE BREAD OF LIFE.

John 6:49 YOUR FATHERS DID EAT MAN'-NA IN THE WILDERNESS, AND ARE DEAD.

John 6:50 THIS IS THE BREAD WHICH COMETH DOWN FROM HEAVEN, THAT A MAN MAY EAT THEREOF, AND NOT DIE.

John 6:51 I AM THE LIVING BREAD WHICH CAME DOWN FROM HEAVEN: IF ANY MAN EAT OF THIS BREAD, HE SHALL LIVE FOR EVER: AND THE BREAD THAT I WILL GIVE IS MY FLESH, WHICH I WILL GIVE FOR THE LIFE OF THE WORLD.

NOTE: The JEWS further heckled JESUS and said, how could HE give them HIS FLESH to eat, for they did not UNDERSTAND that if JESUS had not DIED upon the CROSS for the *WORD of **GOD,*** the GOSPELS would have never been WRITTEN nor the BIBLE PUBLISHED. JESUS came to die upon the CROSS, so those BELIEVING in HIM MIGHT LIVE through HIS WORDS.

John 6:53** Then JESUS said unto them, **VERILY, VERILY, I SAY UNTO YOU, EXCEPT YE EAT THE FLESH OF THE SON OF MAN, AND DRINK HIS BLOOD, YE HAVE NO LIFE IN YOU.

NOTE: JESUS is saying in the last Scripture that until YOU can UNDERSTAND and ACCEPT that HE WILLINGLY DIED FOR THE SINS OF THE WORLD YOU CANNOT BE SAVED, FOR YOU WILL NOT BELIEVE IN THE *WORD of **GOD.*** JESUS' LIFE was the PRICE that had to be PAID for the BIBLE to be PUBLISHED, thus making the *WORD of **GOD*** PRICELESS for those RECEIVING IT! JESUS TELLS how HIS FLESH and HIS BLOOD went into the WRITING of the HOLY BIBLE, and HOW HIS WORDS IS THE FOOD NEEDED for the SPIRIT to LIVE.

John 6:57 AS THE LIVING FATHER HATH SENT ME, AND I

LIVE BY THE FATHER: SO HE THAT EATETH ME, EVEN HE SHALL LIVE BY ME.

John 6:58 THIS IS THAT BREAD WHICH CAME DOWN FROM HEAVEN: NOT AS YOUR FATHERS DID EAT MAN'-NA, AND ARE DEAD: HE THAT EATETH OF THIS BREAD SHALL LIVE FOR EVER.

JESUS gave this SERMON in the Synagogue at Ca-per'-na-um, and many of those who followed HIM found HIS WORDS to be offensive and no longer followed HIM. But JESUS knew who they were that could not BELIEVE in HIM, and also KNEW who it was to BETRAY HIM. For they were looking for something to benefit their bodies and not their Spirits and did not UNDERSTAND what had made them UNIQUE were their Spirits and not their flesh. HE then asked them what they would do if they were to see HIM ASCEND back to HEAVEN before their very eyes, but they did not answer HIM. And HE said:

John 6:63 IT IS THE SPIRIT THAT QUICKENETH; THE FLESH PROFITETH NOTHING: THE WORDS THAT I SPEAK UNTO YOU, THEY ARE SPIRIT, AND THEY ARE LIFE.

JESUS then reminded them in attendance, HE is the GIFT of LIFE sent by ***GOD,*** and ***GOD*** has already DETERMINED who would come to HIM, and who would REFUSE HIM. And them REFUSING to believe in JESUS and HIS WORDS have been DOOMED from the BEGINNING, even prior to their life on earth. After telling the congregation this, JESUS SEES large groups of people starting to leave for they were OFFENDED by HIS WORDS, and HE TURNS to HIS TWELVE Disciples and asks, if they were also going to leave HIM?

John 6:68 *Then Simon Peter answered HIM, LORD, to whom shall we go? Thou hast the WORDS of ETERNAL LIFE.*

17.5 Return to JERUSALEM

JESUS, being one and one-half years into HIS MINISTRY, taught the *WORD of* ***GOD*** primarily in the area of Galilee, while staying out of JERUSALEM. HE didn't go into JERUSALEM because the Pharisees there wanted to kill HIM. With the Feast of Tabernacles (October 15th / Booths) nearing, HIS sibling brothers came to HIM and asked why HE wasn't teaching openly in JERUSALEM, like the Rabbis did, for they didn't BELIEVE HE was CHRIST and routinely challenged HIM. But JESUS told them that HIS HOUR had not yet come, thus meaning the TIME for HIS CRUCIFIXION. For HE knew the Jews in JERUSALEM if given the opportunity, would have HIM killed. HE told HIS brothers that HE would not go with them into JERUSALEM, so HE stayed behind in Galilee while they went up to the FEAST.

Shortly after HIS brothers had left for the FEAST, JESUS went secretly into JERUSALEM, and while there overheard the Jews say they had been looking for HIM, so they might kill HIM. And, while listening to the murmurs of the crowds, JESUS heard some say HE was a GOOD MAN and the CHRIST, while others were saying HE was a liar and deceiving the people with HIS TEACHING.

After being covert in JERUSALEM for a couple of days, and during the middle of the FEAST, JESUS went back into the TEMPLE AGAIN to PREACH. The Jews at the TEMPLE listening to HIM SPEAK were amazed as to how HE could both READ and WRITE, for at that time only the Pharisees, Scribes and the very wealthy were literate. They had also heard that JESUS was just a Carpenter's SON, and said amongst themselves, HE is a SELF-PROCLAIMED PROPHET and HIS DOCTRINE is a falsity.

Once JESUS started to SPEAK, HE spoke with GREAT AUTHORITY, and the Jews immediately starting to criticize and heckle HIM. They accused JESUS of being self GLORIFIED by HIS PROCLAIMING to be the MESSIAH (CHRIST), and JESUS said to them;

John 7:17 IF ANY MAN WILL DO HIS WILL, HE SHALL KNOW OF THE DOCTRINE, WHETHER IT BE OF GOD, OR WHETHER I SPEAK OF MYSELF.

John 7:18 HE THAT SPEAKETH OF HIMSELF SEEKETH HIS OWN GLORY: BUT HE THAT SEEKETH HIS GLORY THAT SENT HIM, THE SAME IS TRUE, AND NO UNRIGHTEOUSNESS IS IN HIM.

John 7:19 DID NOT MOSES GIVE YOU THE LAW, AND YET NONE OF YOU KEEPETH THE LAW? WHY GO YE ABOUT TO KILL ME?

In reply the Jews tell JESUS that HE was possessed with a devil, and it was the devil in HIM causing HIM to speak HIS foul WORDS and VIOLATE the SABBATH DAY. But JESUS asked them how they could condemn HIM for doing the GOOD things HE had done? And, how could they fault HIM for HEALING the SICK, whether it be on the SABBATH or any other day? JESUS asks them, when they circumcise in accordance with MOSES' Law on the SABBATH DAY, aren't they as well violating the SABBATH? So why is it a sin for HIM to HEAL on the SABBATH and not a sin for them to circumcise on the SABBATH?

After JESUS said these things to them, the Jews in attendance started to say to each other, isn't this the MAN who the Pharisees seek to kill, and why is it HE speaks openly at the TEMPLE without anyone trying to arrest HIM? Could the Pharisees possibly know that HE is CHRIST and has not told us? But some of them said; they knew that this MAN had come from Galilee with HIS Disciples, and when CHRIST was to come, they weren't suppose to know where HE had come from.

> ***John 7:28*** *Then cried JESUS in the TEMPLE as HE taught, saying,* ***YE BOTH KNOW ME, AND YE KNOW WHENCE I AM: AND I AM NOT COME OF MYSELF, BUT HE THAT SENT ME IS TRUE, WHOM YE KNOW NOT.***
>
> ***John 7:29 BUT I KNOW HIM: FOR I AM FROM HIM, AND HE HATH SENT ME.***

The Jews then tried to take JESUS, but HE slipped away from them. Then some of them in attendance said in defense of JESUS; will CHRIST when HE comes do more MIRACLES than this MAN, for they BELIEVED that JESUS was the CHRIST.

Once the Pharisees hear how some of the people were starting to BELIEVE that JESUS was the CHRIST, they sent out officers to arrest HIM. But JESUS told the officers when they had come for HIM that now HE was easy to find for HE openly taught at the TEMPLE. But in the not so distant future they would no longer be able to find HIM, for HE was going back to ***THE FATHER*** and where HE was going they could not come.

The Jews didn't UNDERSTAND what JESUS was saying to them. They thought HE was saying that HE was going to leave JERUSALEM and go off to teach the GENTILES elsewhere, when HE said, "***YE SHALL SEEK ME, AND SHALL NOT FIND ME: AND WHERE I AM, THITHER YE CANNOT***

COME". However at this time they did not try to ARREST JESUS.

On the final DAY of the FEAST, JESUS stood up at the TEMPLE again and CRIED OUT TO THE PEOPLE: ***"IF ANY MAN THIRST LET HIM COME UNTO ME, AND DRINK".***

> ***John 7:38 HE THAT BELIEVETH ON ME, AS THE SCRIPTURE HATH SAID, OUT OF HIS BELLY SHALL FLOW RIVERS OF LIVING WATER.***

> ***John 7:39*** *(BUT THIS SPAKE HE OF THE* ***SPIRIT,*** *which they that BELIEVE on HIM should RECEIVE: for THE* ***HOLY GHOST*** *was not yet GIVEN; because that JESUS was not yet GLORIFIED.)*

NOTE: At that TIME no ONE had yet been SAVED, because SAVING comes by way of ***HOLY SPIRIT*** BAPTISM. This could not occur until AFTER JESUS' RESURRECTION and GLORIFICATION BY ***GOD,*** for that EVENT MARKED the ***BEGINNING of the NEW COVENANT.*** As WE had spoken about earlier in this BOOK, even JESUS' Disciples were not SAVED prior to HIS RESURRECTION, for they at that time had only received a water baptism and had not yet RECEIVED SPIRITUAL BAPTISM.

After the people heard JESUS speak on that day there was a division in them, with some BELIEVING and some not. The PRIMARY concern of those who didn't believe was in their thinking that JESUS was BORN in Nazareth of Galilee, whereas the Scriptures had said that the MESSIAH would come out of BETHLEHEM. They were unaware that JESUS had been born in BETHLEHEM and were also unaware of HIS LINEAGE. For JESUS came through the LINEAGE of KING DAVID, from both HIS mother's and HIS ***FATHER'S*** sides of the family. JESUS kept this from HIS DISCIPLES and it wasn't until after HIS RESURRECTION; when JESUS' LINEAGE was traced, and Mary disclosed the details on JESUS' IMMACULATE BIRTH that it was made known to them.

There was also a DIVISION in BELIEF amongst the Pharisees; as to whether JESUS was the CHRIST. But those like Nic-o-de'-mus who had BELIEVED, had to do so covertly. For if the Pharisees found them out they would have been put out of the SYNAGOGUE. When Nic-o-de'-mus (who was a BELIEVER) tried to DEFEND JESUS, he was challenged by the other Pharisees, and asked why he was going against the Scriptures of the Prophets by PROCLAIMING a MAN from Galilee could be the CHRIST?

Judgment of the Adulteress

JESUS while in JERUSALEM would get up in the middle of the night and go up to the Mount of Olives to PRAY, while HIS Disciples slept within the confines of the city. Early one morning after HIS PRAYERS, JESUS went down to the TEMPLE to meet with HIS Disciples. There was already a large group of people gathered at the TEMPLE waiting to HEAR JESUS SPEAK, when JESUS arrived. Shortly after HIS arrival, the Pharisees trying to trick JESUS, brought a woman who had been caught in the act of ADULTERY to HIM, and asked JESUS as to what her punishment should be?

NOTE: ADULTERY was a crime that was punishable by death (stoning), in accordance with the LAWS given by MOSES. However, it was against the Roman law for any Jew to take a life; regardless of the crime; and only the Romans could sentence a person to death. So when the Jews brought the woman to JESUS, they thought to trick HIM and put HIM into a "NO WIN SCENARIO", by asking HIM what the woman's punishment should be. If HE were to say, "STONE HER", then HE would be breaking the Roman law, whereas if HE were to say "SPARE HER", HE would be breaking the Jewish law.

But JESUS knew exactly what they were up to, and after PONDERING their question for a minute or two, HE said, ***"HE THAT IS WITHOUT SIN AMONG YOU, LET HIM FIRST CAST A STONE AT HER".*** After they had thought for awhile about what HE had said, their own GUILT took HOLD of them. They then started leaving the area one by one, until only JESUS and the woman remained. JESUS then asked the woman, where were her ACCUSERS now, and she said, they had all left; and JESUS said; ***HATH NO MAN CONDEMNED THEE?***

> ***John 8:11*** *She said, NO MAN, LORD. And JESUS said unto her,* ***NEITHER DO I CONDEMN THEE: GO, AND SIN NO MORE.***

NOTE: The first eleven verses of the 8th Chapter of the GOSPEL of John is dedicated to JESUS' REBUKING of CAPITAL PUNISHMENT. By the woman committing ADULTERY, she had broken one of ***GOD'S TEN COMMANDMENTS,*** and this wasn't any different in the EYES of ***GOD*** than if she had COMMITTED MURDER. When JESUS SAID to the woman, THAT SHE SHOULD GO, AND SIN NO MORE; HE indicated that she had been FORGIVEN for HER SIN! The NEW COVENANT is a COVENANT of FAITH rather than a COVENANT of LAW, and by having FAITH for FORGIVENESS,

NO SIN IS WORTHY OF DEATH. FOR ONE MAY REPENT OF THEIR SINS UP UNTIL THE TIME OF THEIR DEATH, AND IT SHOULD BE ***GOD*** WHO DETERMINES WHEN THAT SHALL BE, AND NOT MAN![4]

HIS SERMON

After the woman had left the TEMPLE, JESUS went on to PREACH HIS SERMON.

> ***John 8:12*** *Then spake JESUS again unto them, saying,* ***I AM THE LIGHT OF THE WORLD: HE THAT FOLLOWETH ME SHALL NOT WALK IN DARKNESS, BUT SHALL HAVE THE LIGHT OF LIFE.***

After hearing JESUS say these things, the Pharisees again accuse HIM of lying by proclaiming HIMSELF to be someone who HE is not, and say to HIM that HE is deceiving the people with HIS WORDS. But JESUS said; although HE was BEARING a RECORD of HIMSELF, all HE had said had been the TRUTH. JESUS continues on to say, HE knew where HE had come from and also knew where HE was to GO, when it was TIME for HIM to leave this world. JESUS said, they judge man by their moral standards, whereas HE doesn't JUDGE any man for anything. However, if HE were to JUDGE, HIS JUDGMENT would be a RIGHTEOUS JUDGMENT. For HIS ***FATHER,*** who GIVES HIM HIS GUIDANCE IN HIS JUDGMENT, BEARS THE TRUTHFUL and RIGHTEOUS JUDGMENT.

The Pharisees then asked HIM where is HIS ***FATHER***, and JESUS replies to them, they NEITHER KNOW HIM nor HIS ***FATHER,*** for if they had KNOWN HIM, they would BELIEVE HIM, and would also know where HIS ***FATHER*** is. Through the course of that entire day, JESUS and the Pharisees debated, but no one tried to apprehend JESUS because they could not DISPUTE the TRUTH in HIS WORDS!

JESUS again tells the Jews as HE had done before that where HE was GO-

---

[4] If the Jews were to only seek JESUS' APPROVAL of the woman being incarcerated for the CRIME, rather than her being killed for the CRIME, HE WOULD HAVE GIVEN IT, for she had broken the LAW. JESUS SAID; HE HAD NOT COME TO CHANGE THE LAW, BUT RATHER TO FULFILL IT! IN THE NEW COVENANT, THE LAW STILL APPLIES, HOWEVER; DEATH IS NO LONGER AN ACCEPTABLE OPTION for the PENALTY, FOR JESUS ABOLISHED ALL CAPITAL PUNISHMENT WHEN HE SAID, ***"HE THAT IS WITHOUT SIN AMONG YOU, LET HIM FIRST CAST A STONE AT HER"!***

ING they could not come, and they were going to die in their SINS, because they REFUSED to BELIEVE in HIS WORDS. The Jews were still unaware of what JESUS was talking about when HE said, where HE is GOING they could not come and think that JESUS is threatening suicide. Then JESUS tells them they are from BENEATH (the SEED of Lucifer) and HE was from ABOVE (HEAVEN), and they were from this world (being a product of the Earth), but HE was NOT from this world. Thus trying to explain to them that HE had come from HEAVEN to EARTH, and was going back to HEAVEN. But the Jews still didn't UNDERSTAND what HE was saying.

So the Pharisees said again to JESUS; who are you? And, JESUS said I AM WHO I have said I AM. But you didn't BELIEVE ME then, and if I tell you once more, what difference will it make; for you will still not BELIEVE ME!

> ***John 8:26 I HAVE MANY THINGS TO SAY AND TO JUDGE OF YOU: BUT HE THAT SENT ME IS TRUE; AND I SPEAK TO THE WORLD THOSE THINGS WHICH I HAVE HEARD OF HIM.***

> ***John 8:27*** *They understood NOT that HE spake to them of* ***THE FATHER.***

NOTE: The reason JESUS keeps referring to HIS ***FATHER*** as being TRUE, is because HIS ***FATHER*** is THE ***HOLY SPIRIT of GOD,*** who is CALLED THE ***SPIRIT of TRUTH,*** and it was THE ***HOLY SPIRIT*** who was GIVING JESUS BOTH HIS WORDS and HIS JUDGMENT.

> ***John 8:30*** *As HE spake these WORDS, many BELIEVED on HIM.*

> ***John 8:31*** *Then said JESUS to those Jews which BELIEVED on HIM,* ***IF YE CONTINUE IN MY WORD, THEN ARE YE MY DISCIPLES INDEED;***

> ***John 8:32 AND YE SHALL KNOW THE TRUTH, AND THE TRUTH SHALL MAKE YOU FREE.***

But those who even had BELIEVED in JESUS as well as HIS MOCKERS said, we are of the seed of ABRAHAM, and we have never been bound to any man, so who are YOU going to free us from? JESUS in reply says, those who commit SINS are servants to their SINS, and the servant of SIN will die and have only a carnal life. But those WHO ABIDE in CHRIST will LIVE and have an ETERNAL LIFE, and will be FREE from the SIN that binds them to the EARTH.

NOTE: JESUS SPEAKS ABOUT THOSE OF CHRIST BEING FREED FROM THEIR SINS, FOR HE SHALL BE THE SACRIFICE TO ***GOD*** FOR THEIR SINS. THIS OCCURS AT THE TIME OF JESUS' DEATH, INDICATED IN THE SCRIPTURES BY THE TEARING (RENTING) OF THE VEIL, thus allowing ACCESS to THE ***HOLY SPIRIT.*** Then after JESUS' RESURRECTION UNTO LIFE, for them BELIEVING in CHRIST, ***HOLY SPIRIT*** BAPTISM TAKES PLACE and ALL SIN is FOREVER FORGIVEN!

JESUS confronts the Jews again about their continually trying to kill HIM, and tells them they do this because they cannot bear to hear the TRUTH. And, although they are the children of ABRAHAM, as they had so stated, they don't behave like ABRAHAM; for ABRAHAM would not try to kill HIM. But the Jews try to tell JESUS that they are not born out of fornication but have rather come forth from ***GOD.***

> ***John 8:42*** *JESUS said unto them,* ***IF GOD WERE YOUR FATHER, YE WOULD LOVE ME: FOR I PROCEED FORTH AND CAME FROM GOD; NEITHER CAME I OF MYSELF, BUT HE SENT ME.***

> ***John 8:43 WHY DO YE NOT UNDERSTAND MY SPEECH? EVEN BECAUSE YE CANNOT HEAR MY WORD.***

NOTE: These Scriptures show JESUS' FRUSTRATION with the Jews. Regardless of what HE would try to tell them, they REFUSED to BELIEVE HIM. ***GOD*** had SHUT their EARS so they could not HEAR the TRUTH, and closed their EYES so they could not SEE IT. They neither could SEE WHO JESUS WAS or acknowledge HIS GREAT MIRACLES; thus fulfilling the Scriptures.

> ***Isaiah 6:9*** *And* ***HE*** *said, GO, and tell this people, HEAR YE INDEED but UNDERSTAND NOT; and SEE YE INDEED, but PERCEIVE NOT.*

> ***Isaiah 6:10*** *Make the HEART of this people fat, and make their EARS HEAVY, and SHUT their EYES; lest they SEE with their EYES, and HEAR with their EARS, and UNDERSTAND with their HEART, and* ***CONVERT****, and be HEALED.*

NOTE: These last two Scriptures taken from the Book of Isaiah were written nearly 1200 years before the BIRTH of JESUS. IT WAS THE WILL OF ***GOD*** that the JEWS WOULD NOT BELIEVE IN JESUS OR WHAT HE WAS TO TELL THEM. AND, EVEN THOUGH JESUS KNEW THIS FROM THE SCRIPTURES, IT WAS NEVERTHELESS FRUSTRATING FOR HIM!

JESUS tells the Jews REFUSING to BELIEVE:

> ***John 8:44 YE ARE OF YOUR FATHER THE DEVIL, AND THE LUSTS OF YOUR FATHER YE WILL DO. HE WAS A MURDERER FROM THE BEGINNING, AND ABODE NOT IN THE TRUTH, BECAUSE THERE IS NO TRUTH IN HIM. WHEN HE SPEAKETH A LIE, HE SPEAKETH OF HIS OWN: FOR HE IS A LIAR, AND THE FATHER OF IT.***
>
> ***John 8:45 AND BECAUSE I TELL YOU THE TRUTH, YE BELIEVE ME NOT.***
>
> ***John 8:46 WHICH OF YOU CONVINCETH ME OF SIN? AND IF I SAY THE TRUTH, WHY DO YE NOT BELIEVE ME?***
>
> ***John 8:47 HE THAT IS OF GOD HEARETH GOD'S WORDS: YE THEREFORE HEAR THEM NOT, BECAUSE YE ARE NOT OF GOD.***

The Jews still unable to rebut HIS WORDS then accuse JESUS of being a Samaritan, and being possessed with a devil (for the Samaritans were looked at as GENTILES (unbelievers in ***GOD***)). But JESUS told them that HE had no devil in HIM, and was only fulfilling the WILL of HIS ***FATHER,*** and they were DISCREDITING HIM and DISHONORING HIS ***FATHER.*** JESUS then asks why they can't seem to understand that if they will BELIEVE in HIM they will never DIE.

But the Jews tell JESUS they are now certain HE is lying, for ABRAHAM and the Prophets were greater than HIM and they are all dead. But JESUS tells them that ABRAHAM lived to REJOICE in the DAY when CHRIST would come to the Earth and FREE the people from their SINS. But the Jews did not UNDERSTAND that JESUS was referring to ABRAHAM being alive in HEAVEN, so they say to JESUS, how could YOU have known ABRAHAM, for YOU are not yet even fifty years old?

> ***John 8:58*** *JESUS said unto them,* ***VERILY, VERILY, I SAY UNTO YOU, BEFORE ABRAHAM WAS, I AM.***

Once the Jews had realized that JESUS was making them look like FOOLS and they could no longer rebut HIM, they took up stones to throw at HIM, but HE suddenly disappeared into the crowd, and passed by them being unnoticed.

Making the Blind to SEE

Shortly after escaping the angry mob of Jews, JESUS and HIS Disciples come across a man who had been blind since his birth. The Disciples ask JESUS why the man had been born blind; was it because he had sinned prior to his birth, or was it his parents who had sinned thus causing him to be born blind? JESUS then explained to the Disciples that the blind man had been born blind, so JESUS could HEAL him that day, and both the blind man and them SEEING the MIRACLE could SEE the POWER of ***GOD*** and BELIEVE in HIM.

NOTE: Reincarnation is spoken about throughout the Scriptures, and the Disciples comments to JESUS are indicative of another example of reincarnation. How could the blind man have sinned prior to his birth, if he had not been spiritually reincarnated? And, why is it the Church never speaks about REINCARNATION? Is it because they want you to BELIEVE in their RELIGIOUS DOCTRINE rather than in the TRUTH?

After telling HIS Disciples this, JESUS takes some of HIS spit and mixes it with some dirt from the ground and makes it into clay. HE then ANOINTS the EYES of the blind man with the clay and tells him to go and wash his eyes in the pool of Si-lo'-am (meaning, SENT). Once the blind man does as JESUS had told him to do, he RECEIVES his vision and can SEE for the FIRST TIME in his life.

Once the blind man's neighbors saw that he could SEE, they were AMAZED. But some of them said it wasn't the same man who had been born blind, and that this man only looked like the blind man. However, there were others who said, it is he who had been born blind but was now able to SEE, so they asked him how he had RECEIVED his sight?

> ***John 9:11*** *He answered and said, A man that is called JESUS made CLAY and ANOINTED mine eyes, and said unto me,* ***GO TO THE POOL OF SI-LO'-AM, AND WASH:*** *and I went and washed, and I RECEIVED my SIGHT.*

They asked the blind man, where this MAN JESUS was now, and he told them he didn't know, so they brought the man before the Pharisees for interrogation, for JESUS had done this MIRACLE on the SABBATH DAY. The Jews had all been warned by the Pharisees to tell them if JESUS had PERFORMED any MIRACLES on the SABBATH DAY, for they were looking for a reason to arrest HIM.

So the Pharisees asked the man who had been born blind how he had RECEIVED his SIGHT, and he tells them the same thing he had told his neighbors. The Pharisees then tell the man, that JESUS had broken the law, and even though JESUS had said HE was of ***GOD,*** HE WAS A SINNER.

But some other men who had witnessed the HEALING said how could a sinner be able to perform such GREAT MIRACLES, for no one who was born blind had ever received their sight? So there was further division in the Jews with some of them BELIEVING that JESUS was the MESSIAH (CHRIST), while others and the Pharisees were saying HE was not!

The Pharisees then asked the man who he thought JESUS was, and he said; HE is a Prophet. But the Pharisees refused to believe that the man had been born blind, so they summoned his parents. Once the parents arrive, they confirm to the Pharisees the man was their son and he had been blind from his birth. But they further tell the Pharisees that they hadn't any idea as to why he was now able to see. (They told them this because they feared being put out of the Synagogue if they were to say it was JESUS CHRIST who had given their son his sight.) So they tell the Pharisees to ask their son how he had been healed because he was old enough to speak for himself. So the Pharisees again summoned the man to them.

> ***John 9:24*** *Then again called they the man that was blind, and said unto him, Give* **GOD** *the PRAISE: we know that this MAN is a sinner.*

> ***John 9:25*** *He answered and said, Whether HE be a sinner or no, I know not: one thing I know, that, whereas I was blind, now I see.*

Again they ask the man how JESUS had HEALED him, and he tells them he has already said what JESUS had done, so why should he tell them again? Would they now BELIEVE and become Disciples of JESUS? The Pharisees then in their frustration with the man accuse him of being a Disciple of JESUS, and tell him that they are disciples of MOSES. For they knew that ***GOD*** had spoken to MOSES, but they didn't believe in JESUS or what HE had done was an act of ***GOD.***

The man then tells the Pharisees, they had seen with their own eyes that JESUS had GIVEN him his SIGHT, so why couldn't they BELIEVE that the MIRACLE came from ***GOD.*** The man further says that ***GOD*** does not do these things for sinners, but ***HE*** only hears those who HEAR ***HIM.*** No MAN before has ever made a person who was born blind to see, and if JESUS were not from ***GOD,*** how could HE have done such a thing! The Pharisees then unable to answer the man, tell him that he is a sinner and knew nothing about ***GOD,*** and then threw him out of the Synagogue.

> ***John 9:35*** *JESUS heard that they had cast him out; and when HE had found him, HE said unto him,* ***DOST THOU BELIEVE ON THE SON OF GOD?***

> ***John 9:36*** *He answered and said, who is HE, LORD, that I might BELIEVE on HIM?*

> ***John 9:37*** *And JESUS said unto him,* ***THOU HAST BOTH SEEN HIM, AND IT IS HE THAT TALKETH WITH THEE.***

> ***John 9:38*** *And he said, LORD, I BELIEVE. And he WORSHIPPED HIM.*

> ***John 9:39*** *And JESUS said,* ***FOR JUDGMENT I HAVE COME INTO THIS WORLD, THAT THEY WHICH SEE NOT MIGHT SEE; AND THAT THEY WHICH SEE MIGHT BE MADE BLIND.***

> ***John 9:40*** *And some of the Pharisees which were with them heard these WORDS, and said unto HIM, Are we blind also?*

> ***John 9:41*** *JESUS said unto them,* ***IF YE WERE BLIND, YE SHOULD HAVE NO SIN: BUT NOW YE SAY, WE SEE; THEREFORE YOUR SIN REMAINETH.***

NOTE: What JESUS was telling the Pharisees was that because they had SEEN the MARVELOUS WORKS of ***GOD,*** and REFUSED to BELIEVE in ***HIS*** SON who had PERFORMED the MIRACLES, they could not be forgiven of their SIN, for they had denied the SACRIFICE for their SIN. JESUS

CHRIST is the CORNERSTONE of LIFE, and any REFUSING HIM is denying himself of his own LIFE. But this again only CONFIRMS that which is WRITTEN in the SCRIPTURES ***SAITH THE LORD of HOSTS:***

> ***Psalm 118:22*** *The STONE which the builders REFUSED is become the HEAD STONE of the CORNER.*

NOTE: Before WE go any further into the GOSPEL of John, ***THE LORD*** wants ME to clarify something for YOU. In the PREVIOUS BOOK it was told to YOU that CAIN was the seed of the DEVIL, and ***THE LORD*** has told ME that many of YOU refuse to BELIEVE this. If JESUS CHRIST were to tell YOU the SAME THING and also CONFIRM by HIS WORDS that all of the people coming through the lineage of CAIN were of the DEVIL, would YOU still refuse to believe? In the HOLY BIBLE it is said that CAIN MURDERED his brother ABEL, thus making him the FIRST MURDERER of a SOUL BEARING MAN, and a MURDERER from the very beginning. The following Scripture taken from the GOSPEL of John will clearly show YOU that CAIN was the OFFSPRING of Lucifer, the Devil, and that anyone coming through CAIN'S lineage is a child of the Devil!

> ***John 8:44 YE ARE OF YOUR FATHER THE DEVIL, AND THE LUSTS OF YOUR FATHER YE WILL DO. HE WAS A MURDERER FROM THE BEGINNING, AND ABODE NOT IN TRUTH, BECAUSE THERE IS NO TRUTH IN HIM. WHEN HE SPEAKETH A LIE, HE SPEAKETH OF HIS OWN: FOR HE IS A LIAR, AND THE FATHER OF IT.***

In this Scripture JESUS is telling them who refuse to BELIEVE HIS WORDS, that they are of the SEED of CAIN, the FIRST MURDERER, who is the SEED and the OFFSPRING of the DEVIL! When ***GOD*** asked Cain where his brother ABEL was, Cain lied to ***GOD*** by saying "*I know not: Am I my brother's keeper?*" (Genesis 4:9) and by Cain being the first MAN in the BIBLE to LIE, makes him the Father of LIES!

17.6 The GOOD SHEPHERD

Being one year and two months since JESUS had last PREACHED in JERUSALEM, and two years and eight months into HIS MINISTRY, JESUS decided to go up to JERUSALEM again for the Feast of Dedication (December

25th). While at the TEMPLE in SOLOMON'S Porch, JESUS PREACHED to the multitudes that had come to hear HIM SPEAK:

> ***John 10:1 VERILY, VERILY, I SAY UNTO YOU, HE THAT ENTERETH NOT BY THE DOOR INTO THE SHEEPFOLD, BUT CLIMBETH UP SOME OTHER WAY, THE SAME IS A THIEF AND A ROBBER.***

> ***John 10:2 BUT HE THAT ENTERETH IN BY THE DOOR IS THE SHEPHERD OF THE SHEEP.***

JESUS speaks in the Scriptures about the DOOR to HEAVEN, which WE had discussed earlier in this BOOK. This DOOR is referred to in the Scriptures as the EAST GATE, the GATE that RECEIVES FIRST LIGHT, or the MORNING STAR. This EAST GATE is the gate in which THE ***HOLY SPIRIT*** enters in and exits HEAVEN, as do ALL ENTERING IN or EXITING HEAVEN, and the GATE is CALLED, JESUS CHRIST.

> ***John 10:3 TO HIM THE PORTER OPENETH; AND THE SHEEP HEAR HIS VOICE: AND HE CALLETH HIS OWN SHEEP BY NAME, AND LEADETH THEM OUT.***

> ***John 10:4 AND WHEN HE PUTTETH FORTH HIS OWN SHEEP, HE GOETH BEFORE THEM, AND THE SHEEP FOLLOW HIM: FOR THEY KNOW HIS VOICE.***

> ***John 10:5 AND A STRANGER THEY WILL NOT FOLLOW, BUT WILL FLEE FROM HIM: FOR THEY KNOW NOT THE VOICE OF STRANGERS.***

JESUS is saying in these last three Scriptures that only BY HIM can ONE either ENTER IN or EXIT HEAVEN. HE also states that it is HE who BOTH goes out and COMES in FIRST before the SHEEP (***GOD'S*** CHILDREN), as HE had done as ADAM (in the flesh) or as HE had done as JESUS CHRIST (in the SPIRIT), and ALL who follow HIM RECOGNIZE HIS VOICE. This is to say, anyone either leaving or entering into HEAVEN is LED by JESUS and cannot be DECEIVED into following anyone else, for ***GOD*** WILL NOT ALLOW IT.

But on that day when JESUS had SPOKEN these WORDS to HIS audience, they did not UNDERSTAND and RECEIVE HIS MESSAGE. So, to make the MESSAGE simpler for them to UNDERSTAND:

> ***John 10:7*** *Then said JESUS unto them again,* ***VERILY, VERILY, I SAY UNTO YOU, I AM THE DOOR OF THE SHEEP.***

> ***John 10:8 ALL THAT EVER CAME BEFORE ME ARE THIEVES AND ROBBERS: BUT THE SHEEP DID NOT HEAR THEM.***

> ***John 10:9 I AM THE DOOR: BY ME IF ANY MAN ENTER IN, HE SHALL BE SAVED, AND SHALL GO IN AND OUT AND FIND PASTURE.***

The last three Scriptures basically say the same thing HE had already said, in the preceding five Scriptures. Once JESUS had realized the audience had not RECEIVED HIS MESSAGE the FIRST TIME, HE simply rephrased it and said it AGAIN. The MESSAGE is CLEAR, it simply states that NO ONE can either ENTER INTO or EXIT HEAVEN without going THROUGH JESUS CHRIST, and anyone who had CLAIMED to be the DOOR to HEAVEN before HIM, were LIARS. The Scriptures further state, anyone PREACHING anything other than HIS WORD (the TRUE *WORD of* ***GOD***), is both a THIEF and a ROBBER, because they are doing it for their own personal gain (THE HIRELING).

> ***John 10:10 THE THIEF COMETH NOT, BUT FOR TO STEAL, AND TO KILL, AND TO DESTROY: I AM COME THAT THEY MIGHT HAVE LIFE, AND THAT THEY MIGHT HAVE IT MORE ABUNDANTLY.***

> ***John 10:11 I AM THE GOOD SHEPHERD: THE GOOD SHEPHERD GIVETH HIS LIFE FOR THE SHEEP.***

> ***John 10:12 BUT HE THAT IS AN HIRELING, AND NOT THE SHEPHERD, WHOSE OWN THE SHEEP ARE NOT, SEETH THE WOLF COMING, AND LEAVETH THE SHEEP, AND FLEETH: AND THE WOLF CATCHETH THEM, AND SCATTERETH THE SHEEP.***

> ***John 10:13 THE HIRELING FLEETH, BECAUSE HE IS AN***

HIRELING, AND CARETH NOT FOR THE SHEEP.

This is a WARNING GIVEN by JESUS to HIS FOLLOWING; to BEWARE of them who will appear to be Pastors, Ministers, Priests, or Church Organizations (THE GREAT WHORE); that minister only for the MONEY and personal gain, who care not about one's SPIRITUAL well being. These are the ones who will STEAL, KILL and DESTROY YOU, both in the flesh and in the Spirit, for they are a PRODUCT of HELL and are serving the Devil!

John 10:14 I AM THE GOOD SHEPHERD, AND KNOW MY SHEEP, AND AM KNOWN OF MINE.

John 10:15 AS THE FATHER KNOWETH ME, EVEN SO KNOW I THE FATHER: AND I LAY DOWN MY LIFE FOR THE SHEEP.

John 10:16 AND OTHER SHEEP I HAVE, WHICH ARE NOT OF THIS FOLD: THEM ALSO I MUST BRING, AND THEY SHALL HEAR MY VOICE; AND THERE SHALL BE ONE FOLD, AND ONE SHEPHERD.

JESUS says HE is the only TRUE SHEPHERD, who will willingly LAY DOWN HIS LIFE for HIS SHEEP; and HE KNOWS who HIS SHEEP are and they KNOW who HE IS. JESUS also states in the Scripture that HE and ***THE FATHER*** have a NEVER ENDING RELATIONSHIP, KNOWING EACH OTHER FROM THE BEGINNING of CREATION. HE further says that HE also has another GROUP of PEOPLE who are not Jews, but are also HIS SHEEP (the GENTILE), and they too will become part of HIS FLOCK, and in HIS FLOCK there will be NO DIVISION.

John 10:17 THEREFORE DOTH MY FATHER LOVE ME, BECAUSE I LAY DOWN MY LIFE, THAT I MIGHT TAKE IT AGAIN.

JESUS speaks about HIS pending CRUCIFIXION and HIS RESURRECTION.

John 10:18 NO MAN TAKETH IT FROM ME, BUT I LAY IT DOWN OF MYSELF. I HAVE POWER TO LAY IT DOWN,

AND I HAVE POWER TO TAKE IT AGAIN. THIS COMMANDMENT I RECEIVED OF MY FATHER.

JESUS states that HE has been EMPOWERED by ***GOD*** to GIVE LIFE UNTO HIMSELF, both in the flesh and in the SPIRIT; and HE can do this OVER AND OVER, AGAIN and AGAIN throughout ETERNITY.

After hearing JESUS' WORDS, there is again a division among the Jews. Some say HE is crazy and that no one should listen to HIM. While others say, HIS WORDS were not the words of a mad man or a devil, for devils and crazy people cannot OPEN the EYES of the BLIND.

Then while still on SOLOMON'S PORCH, the Jews who had MOCKED HIS WORDS came and asked HIM to again say WHO HE WAS; and if HE were the CHRIST HE should say so!

John 10:25 *JESUS answered them,* ***I TOLD YOU AND YE BELIEVED NOT: THE WORKS THAT I DO IN MY FATHER'S NAME, THEY BEAR WITNESS OF ME.***

John 10:26 BUT YE BELIEVE NOT, BECAUSE YE ARE NOT OF MY SHEEP, AS I SAID UNTO YOU.

John 10:27 MY SHEEP HEAR MY VOICE, AND I KNOW THEM, AND THEY FOLLOW ME:

John 10:28 AND I GIVE UNTO THEM ETERNAL LIFE; AND THEY SHALL NEVER PERISH, NEITHER SHALL ANY MAN PLUCK THEM OUT OF MY HAND.

John 10:29 MY FATHER, WHICH GAVE THEM ME, IS GREATER THAN ALL; AND NO MAN IS ABLE TO PLUCK THEM OUT OF MY FATHER'S HAND.

John 10:30 I AND MY FATHER ARE ONE.

After JESUS had told the Jews these things, they started to pick up stones to stone HIM, and JESUS asked; for which one of the MIRACLES HE HAD PERFORMED were they going to stone HIM? The Jews then said they weren't going to stone HIM for what HE had done, but rather for what HE had said; because HE had said ***"I AND MY FATHER ARE ONE",*** thus making HIM-

SELF to be in the similitude of ***GOD.***

NOTE: JESUS CHRIST is referred to in the Scriptures as "IMMANUEL", thus meaning, ***AS ONE WITH GOD.*** The Jews did not understand that WHEN a PERSON is THE LIVING HOST to THE ***HOLY SPIRIT of GOD,*** as JESUS is, THEY ARE HONORING ***GOD*** by their saying they are ONE WITH ***HIM,*** whereas the Jews thought it to be a BLASPHEMY against ***GOD.*** But then JESUS QUOTES the Scripture from the 82nd Psalm to the mockers:

> ***Psalm 82:6*** *I have said, YE ARE GODS; and all of you are the CHILDREN of* ***THE MOST HIGH.***

And JESUS then SAYS:

> ***John 10:35 IF HE CALLED THEM*** *GODS,* ***UNTO WHOM THE WORD OF GOD CAME, AND THE SCRIPTURE CANNOT BE BROKEN;***

> ***John 10:36 SAY YE OF HIM, WHOM THE FATHER HAD SANCTIFIED, AND SENT INTO THE WORLD, THOU BLASPHEMEST; BECAUSE I SAID, I AM THE SON OF GOD?***

NOTE: JESUS asks why they believe HE had blasphemed ***GOD*** for what HE had said, when the Scriptures indicate those whom are SERVING ***GOD*** are to be referred to as GODS, and the CHILDREN of the ***MOST HIGH.*** And furthermore, why after seeing the MIRACLES HE had PERFORMED do they still refuse to believe HE had been sent down from HEAVEN, and was SANCTIFIED to PERFORM those MIRACLES, in the NAME of ***GOD?*** So therefor, why shouldn't HE be able to REFER to HIMSELF as being the SON of ***GOD?***

The Jews being made fools of then try to arrest JESUS, but HE manages to escape. So both HE and HIS Disciples returned to the Jordan River, the place where JESUS had been BAPTIZED by John the Baptist and resided there. Then while at the Jordan, many people came to HEAR JESUS SPEAK, and those that heard HIM speak said; all that John the Baptist had said about JESUS was TRUE. For at the Jordan they saw the many MIRACLES HE had PERFORMED and many of them BELIEVED HE was the CHRIST who was to COME.

17.7 Raising Lazarus

JESUS made many friends during HIS travels throughout the region while PREACHING the KINGDOM of ***GOD.*** Near to JERUSALEM in the small town of Bethany there lived a brother and two sisters, and their names were Lazarus, Martha, and Mary Magdalene. Whenever JESUS passed through the area HE would stop at the house where they lived and spend time with them, and over the course of JESUS' MINISTRY Lazarus and his two sisters became very close to JESUS. Lazarus being the eldest of the three managed the family and looked after his two sisters after the death of their parents. The youngest, Mary Magdalene was at the time of her meeting JESUS a Prostitute, because the family was in need of money for food and shelter.

At the beginning of JESUS' MINISTRY when making HIS first trip to JERUSALEM, HE and HIS Disciples stopped at Bethany for some food. While at the marketplace HE met Mary Magdalene and there CONVERTED her to Discipleship. JESUS told Mary to REPENT and no longer sell her body for money and if she were to follow HIM, ***GOD*** would SEE to the family's NEEDS. On the day of their first meeting, Mary took JESUS and HIS Disciples to her home to meet her brother Lazarus and her sister Martha, and they also that day became Disciples of JESUS. Thereafter JESUS became very close to the three, and whenever HE was in the area HE would stop and visit with them.

Shortly after being chased out of JERUSALEM by the Jews and PREACHING at the Jordan River, JESUS received an urgent message. Mary and Martha sent word to JESUS by way of a messenger, telling HIM that their brother Lazarus had become ill and was near to death.

> ***John 11:4*** *When JESUS heard that, HE said,* ***THIS SICKNESS IS NOT UNTO DEATH, BUT FOR THE GLORY OF GOD, THAT THE SON OF GOD MIGHT BE GLORIFIED THEREBY.***

But JESUS didn't immediately leave after receiving the message and stayed in the Jordan area for another two days. This surprised HIS Disciples for the message they had received from Martha and Mary in regard to Lazarus, appeared to be one of urgency and DESPERATION. They knew how JESUS LOVED the family and thought surely HE would go immediately to them, but JESUS stayed and continued to PREACH at the Jordan.

> ***John 11:7*** *Then after that saith HE to HIS Disciples,* ***LET US GO***

INTO JU-DAE'-A AGAIN.

The Disciples asked JESUS why HE should go back to JERUSALEM (Judae'-a) after having such a bad experience there with the Jews on HIS last visit? They reminded JESUS how the Jews wanted to stone HIM when HE was there, and thought it would be unsafe for HIM to return to the area.

> ***John 11:9*** *JESUS answered,* ***ARE THERE NOT TWELVE HOURS IN THE DAY? IF ANY MAN WALK IN THE DAY, HE STUMBLETH NOT, BECAUSE HE SEETH THE LIGHT OF THIS WORLD.***

> ***John 11:10 BUT IF A MAN WALK IN THE NIGHT, HE STUMBLETH, BECAUSE THERE IS NO LIGHT IN HIM.***

NOTE: JESUS was telling HIS Disciples in the last two Scriptures how HE had WORK yet to do in JERUSALEM, and how nothing should interfere with HIS WORK. JESUS knew it was not yet HIS time to die but knew HIS time was running out and HE had to make GOOD use of it. The TWELVE HOURS of LIGHT JESUS referred to in the Scripture indicated the short time HE had left on the EARTH, and HE stressed to HIS Disciples how HE must COMPLETE HIS WORK in that time.

After telling them this, JESUS then tells HIS Disciples that HIS FRIEND Lazarus was now SLEEPING, and they thought Lazarus' sleeping meant that he was getting better. However JESUS was referring to Lazarus being dead and not to him recovering. So when JESUS saw that HIS Disciples did not UNDERSTAND what HE had meant about Lazarus' sleeping, HE said plainly to them; Lazarus is dead.

JESUS, seeing how the Disciples were shocked at what HE had said, tells the Disciples it was GOOD that HE had not been there with Lazarus, for if HE had been there HE would have HEALED Lazarus and kept him from death. However it was the WILL of ***GOD*** that Lazarus should die, so HE could raise Lazarus from the dead for all to SEE and BELIEVE!

> ***John 11:15 I AM GLAD FOR YOUR SAKES THAT I WAS NOT THERE, TO THE INTENT YOU MAY BELIEVE; NEVERTHELESS LET US GO UNTO HIM.***

Thomas then tells JESUS that they would all go up to Bethany with HIM, and if need be, die there with HIM; knowing how the Jews sought to kill JESUS. Thomas said they were all willing to die to defend JESUS from the Jews. So JESUS and HIS Disciples journeyed towards JERUSALEM by way of Bethany, which was only about one and one-half miles outside of JERUSALEM.

By the time JESUS and HIS Disciples get near to Lazarus' house in Bethany, Lazarus had already been dead for four days. Many of the local people had come to Mary and Martha's house to comfort them and mourn with the two sisters over their brother's death. Once Martha hears THE LORD had come into the area, (for JESUS would draw large crowds of people and they would spread the word that JESUS was in the area), she runs out to meet HIM, leaving Mary behind in the house.

> ***John 11:21*** *Then said Martha unto JESUS, LORD, if thou hadst been here, my brother had not died.*

> ***John 11:22*** *But I know that even now, whatsoever thou will ask of* ***GOD, GOD*** *will give thee.*

> ***John 11:23*** *JESUS saith unto her,* ***THY BROTHER SHALL RISE AGAIN.***

NOTE: The reason why ***GOD*** had Martha run out to meet JESUS rather than Mary (for Mary was closer to JESUS than Martha), was because Martha had the FAITH NEEDED for JESUS to PERFORM the MIRACLE. Although Mary LOVED JESUS, she was disappointed that HE had not come and spared her brother's life, and was at that time lacking the FAITH needed for the MIRACLE to HAPPEN.

> ***John 11:24*** *Martha saith unto HIM, I know that he shall rise again in the resurrection at the LAST DAY.*

> ***John 11:25*** *JESUS saith unto her,* ***I AM THE RESURRECTION, AND THE LIFE: HE THAT BELIEVETH IN ME, THOUGH HE WERE DEAD, YET SHALL HE LIVE:***

> ***John 11:26 AND WHOSOEVER LIVETH AND BELIEVETH IN ME SHALL NEVER DIE. BELIEVEST THOU THIS?***

***John 11:27** She saith unto HIM, Yea, LORD: **I BELIEVE** THAT THOU ART THE CHRIST, THE SON OF **GOD,** WHICH SHOULD COME INTO THE WORLD.*

NOTE: This last statement made by Martha to JESUS CONFIRMS ***THE FAITH*** that was needed for JESUS to PERFORM the MIRACLE of RAISING LAZARUS FROM THE DEAD.

After Martha had told JESUS she had BELIEVED that HE WAS the CHRIST, the SON of ***GOD,*** she then runs back to the house to tell her sister Mary that THE LORD had arrived. As soon as Mary hears that JESUS was near, she runs out to meet HIM, for HE had not yet entered the town of Bethany. When the local people see Mary run out of the house to MEET JESUS they think she is going to the grave-site of Lazarus, so they followed her.

***John 11:32** Then when Mary was come where JESUS was, and saw HIM, she fell down at HIS FEET, saying unto HIM, LORD, if thou hadst been here, my brother had not died.*

***John 11:33** When JESUS therefore saw her weeping, and the Jews also weeping which came with her, HE GROANED in the SPIRIT, and was TROUBLED.*

***John 11:34** And said, **WHERE HAVE YE LAID HIM?** They said unto HIM, LORD, come and see.*

***John 11:35** JESUS wept.*

***John 11:36** Then said the Jews, BEHOLD HOW HE LOVED HIM!*

Then some of them questioned; if JESUS LOVED Lazarus so much and could even make the BLIND to SEE, why couldn't HE have kept HIS FRIEND Lazarus from dying? JESUS, still grieving over HIS friend's death is then taken by Mary to the grave-site and sees that they have put Lazarus into a cave, and rolled a large stone in front of it to cover its opening.

***John 11:39** JESUS said, **TAKE YE AWAY THE STONE.** Martha the sister of him that was dead, saith unto HIM, LORD, by this time he stinketh: for he hath been dead four days.*

John 11:40 *JESUS saith unto her,* ***SAID I NOT UNTO THEE, THAT, IF THOU WOULDEST BELIEVE, THOU SHOULDEST SEE THE GLORY OF GOD?***

John 11:41 *Then they took away the stone from the place where the dead was laid. And JESUS lifted up HIS EYES, and said,* ***FATHER, I THANK THEE THAT THOU HAST HEARD ME.***

John 11:42 AND I KNEW THAT THOU HEAREST ME ALWAYS: BUT BECAUSE OF THE PEOPLE WHICH STAND BY I SAID IT, THAT THEY MAY BELIEVE THAT THOU HAST SENT ME.

John 11:43 *And when HE thus had SPOKEN, HE cried with a LOUD VOICE,* ***LAZ'-A-RUS COME FORTH.***

John 11:44 *And he that was dead came forth, bound hand and foot with graveclothes: and his face was bound about with a napkin. JESUS saith unto them,* ***LOOSE HIM AND LET HIM GO.***

John 11:45 *Then many of the Jews which came to Mary, and had seen the things which JESUS did, BELIEVED on HIM.*

But there were others that saw the MIRACLE who still maintained their allegiance to the religious leaders, and went to the Pharisees and told them what JESUS had done. After hearing these things the Pharisees gathered together the Chief Priests and the Scribes for council. The Council concluded, if JESUS were allowed to continue with these kinds of MIRACLES the people would no longer listen to them. Then the Romans would take away their charter and they would lose their control over the people.

NOTE: The Romans allowed the Pharisees to remain in power so they could be used to control the people. If the people were to refuse to listen to the Pharisees, then the Romans would no longer have any use for them, and they would be taken out of power.

One of the Chief Priests by the name of Ca'-ia-phas that same year had RECEIVED a prophecy, in the prophecy Ca'-ia-phas was told that ONE MAN must die for the Jewish nation to exist, and he said to the others that JESUS was the MAN who was to die. The PROPHECY also said that JESUS must die for ALL of ***GOD'S*** CHILDREN and not just those who lived in Ju-dae'-a.

NOTE: The PROPHECY that the High Priest Ca'-ia-phas RECEIVED was not fully UNDERSTOOD by him, for he thought it applied only to the preservation of the Jewish Nation, rather than to the SAVING GRACE for ALL of ***GOD'S*** CHILDREN (ISRAEL). Ca'-ia-phas believed that the MAN who was to DIE, namely JESUS CHRIST, was to die to preserve the Jewish Nation, and to keep the Priests, Pharisees and Scribes in power. However, he didn't understand that the PROPHECY ONLY applied to those who BELIEVED that JESUS was the CHRIST and the SON of ***GOD.***

So as of that day when Ca'-ia-phas told the Council this, they then plotted to kill JESUS, so HE no longer openly moved about in the area. JESUS then took HIS Disciples and went into the land of E'-phra-im and PREACHED and stayed out of JERUSALEM for several months.

When it was time for the PASSOVER again, the Pharisees and Chief Priests wondered whether JESUS would come back into JERUSALEM for the FEAST. So they spread the word that if anyone were to know JESUS' whereabouts, they were to inform the Chief Priests and the Pharisees immediately so they could apprehend HIM.

17.8 Anointing @ Bethany

> ***John 12:1*** *Then JESUS six days before the PASSOVER came to Beth'-a-ny, where Laz'-a-rus was which had been dead, whom HE raised from the dead.*

That afternoon, JESUS and HIS Disciples dined with Lazarus, Martha and Mary at the house of Simon the Leper. While Martha prepared and served the food, Mary Magdalene took very expensive ointment she had bought and anointed JESUS' FEET with the ointment, while weeping all the time. As her tears would fall upon the FEET of JESUS, she wiped HIS FEET with her hair and the room was filled with the fragrance of the ointment.

It was unbeknown to Mary at that time, she was anointing JESUS for HIS burial which would occur exactly SEVEN DAYS from that day. Although JESUS had told the family of Lazarus and HIS Disciples, HIS TIME to DIE was nearing HE was somewhat vague about exactly when it would take place. JESUS KNEW it would happen on the first DAY of PASSOVER, however HE had not yet told anyone of the date for HE wanted HIS Disciples to stay focused on the EVENTS that were about to take place, rather than them being concerned about HIS well being.

Judas Iscariot (the BETRAYER) was also present with them that day and complained about Mary's spending so much money for the ointment she used to ANOINT JESUS. He said to the other Disciples the money used to buy the ointment should have been given to the poor or put into the treasury, because he was the treasurer and managed the funds for the Disciples. It was Judas' love of money that caused him to betray JESUS in the first place, however it was always DESTINED by ***GOD*** for him to do so, for he was of the seed of the Devil. After Judas had made the comment, JESUS replied to him:

> ***John 12:7*** *Then said JESUS,* ***LET HER ALONE: AGAINST THE DAY OF MY BURYING HATH SHE KEPT THIS.***

> ***John 12:8 FOR THE POOR ALWAYS YE HAVE WITH YOU; BUT ME YE HAVE NOT ALWAYS.***

There were many people there that day round about the house belonging to Simon the Leper, to see both JESUS and Lazarus whom HE had raised from the dead. It was rummored that the Pharisees also wanted to kill Lazarus, because many of the people who had seen him raised from the dead, considered Lazarus to be LIVING PROOF that JESUS was CHRIST. Also, Lazarus was a Disciple of JESUS, and by his living so close to the TEMPLE in JERUSALEM, many left the synagogue to come and hear Lazarus speak about JESUS. Other than just the TWELVE Disciples, JESUS had many other Disciples aiding in HIS MINISTRY, and Lazarus, Mary, and Martha certainly MINISTERED for THE LORD.

Many of the people coming into the area for the PASSOVER heard that JESUS was at Simon the Leper's house with Lazarus and came to SEE both JESUS and the one HE had raised from the dead. JESUS had HIS Disciples find an ass's colt for HIM to ride on that day into JERUSALEM, so the Scriptures so stating the EVENT of HIS TRIUMPHAL ENTRY into JERUSALEM would be FULFILLED. When JESUS left Bethany and was en route to JERUSALEM, the people laid Palm Branches on the path HE was to take.

> ***Zechariah 9:9*** *Rejoice greatly, O daughter of ZION; shout O daughter of JERUSALEM: behold, thy KING cometh unto thee: HE is JUST, and having SALVATION; lowly, and riding upon an ass, and upon a colt the foal of an ass.*

Even the people on that day fulfilled Scripture Prophecy by their laying the Palm Branches before JESUS' entry into JERUSALEM, and SHOUTING; HO-

SANNA: BLESSED IS THE KING OF ISRAEL THAT COMETH IN THE NAME OF THE LORD.

> ***Psalm 118:25*** *SAVE NOW, I beseech thee, O LORD: O LORD, I beseech thee, send now PROSPERITY.*
>
> ***Psalm 118:26*** *Blessed be HE that cometh in the NAME of THE LORD: we have BLESSED YOU out of the HOUSE of THE LORD.*
>
> ***Psalm 118:27 GOD*** *is THE LORD, which hath shewed us* ***LIGHT****: bind the* ***SACRIFICE*** *with cords, even unto the HORNS of the ALTAR.*

NOTE: The word "HOSANNA" is a Jewish word meaning: "SAVE US NOW", however; in the HEBREWAH LANGUAGE it is a tagged WORD, "HO'-SO'-UN-AH", meaning; "THE SAVING LIGHT"! It was unbeknown by the PEOPLE or the DISCIPLES at the TIME, that the things they were doing were FULFILLING SCRIPTURE PROPHECY. It wasn't until afterwards that the Disciples realized they had PARTICIPATED in the PROPHECY written thousands of years before the EVENT had taken place. What the people had done by laying down the PALM BRANCHES was indicative of the GLORIFICATION of the SACRIFICE and the riding into JERUSALEM on the ass's colt verified the COMING of the KING of ISRAEL into JERUSALEM.

GOD GLORIFIES JESUS

Once in JERUSALEM, there were some Greeks who had come up to celebrate the FEAST of the PASSOVER that had heard about JESUS, and when they saw the Disciple Philip they asked him if they might be able to meet JESUS. Then after consulting with Andrew about introducing the Greeks to JESUS, they both went to HIM to make the request.

> ***John 12:23*** *And JESUS answered them, saying,* ***THE HOUR IS COME THAT THE SON OF MAN SHOULD BE GLORIFIED.***
>
> ***John 12:24 VERILY, VERILY, I SAY UNTO YOU, EXCEPT A CORN OF WHEAT FALL INTO THE GROUND AND DIE, IT ABIDETH ALONE: BUT IF IT DIE, IT BRINGETH FORTH MUCH FRUIT.***

John 12:25 HE THAT LOVETH HIS LIFE SHALL LOSE IT; AND HE THAT HATETH HIS LIFE IN THIS WORLD SHALL KEEP IT UNTO LIFE ETERNAL.

NOTE: JESUS was telling Andrew, Philip, and those around HIM, that HIS TIME to DIE for the SINS of the world had come, and by HIS DEATH the world (including the Greeks) would BENEFIT. But JESUS reminds them that once they had TRULY followed in HIS FOOTSTEPS they would come to HATE the world, for the world had HATED JESUS.

John 12:26 IF ANY MAN SERVE ME, LET HIM FOLLOW ME; AND WHERE I AM, THERE SHALL ALSO MY SERVANT BE: IF ANY MAN SERVE ME, HIM WILL MY FATHER HONOUR.

John 12:27 NOW IS MY SOUL TROUBLED; AND WHAT SHALL I SAY? FATHER SAVE ME FROM THIS HOUR: BUT FOR THIS CAUSE CAME I UNTO THIS HOUR.

NOTE: In the Scriptures JESUS was telling HIS Disciples, HE hadn't much time left, and although they wanted to introduce HIM to the Greeks wanting to meet him, the time would not allow it. JESUS wanted ALL to know that if they were to SERVE HIM, they should follow after HIS TEACHINGS, and by them following HIS TEACHINGS, ***GOD*** would HONOR them for it. HE also tells them that now the time is nearing for HIM to DIE and HE WAS FRIGHTENED by it, but HE had come into the world to SERVE that PURPOSE, therefor HE would not ASK ***GOD*** to SPARE HIM from it.[5]

JESUS then said:

John 12:28 FATHER, GLORIFY THY NAME. *Then came there a VOICE from HEAVEN, saying,* ***I HAVE BOTH GLORIFIED IT AND WILL GLORIFY IT AGAIN.***

---

[5] ALTHOUGH JESUS CHRIST IS THE SON of ***GOD,*** HE WAS STILL IN THE FORM OF A MAN AND COULD SUFFER LIKE ANY OTHER MAN. JESUS KNEW THAT NOT ONLY WOULD HE FEEL THE PHYSICAL PAIN ENDURED BY HIS CRUCIFIXION, BUT HE MUST ALSO SUFFER THE ***WRATH of GOD*** THAT WOULD BE LEVIED ON HIM AFTER HE HAD RECEIVED THE SINS OF THE WORLD. BUT JESUS ALSO KNEW THAT ONLY HE COULD ENDURE THE ***WRATH of GOD*** AND NO ONE ELSE COULD DO THAT FOR HIM!

NOTE: In the LAYER of the last SCRIPTURE the statement made FROM ***GOD*** about the GLORIFYING of the NAME of ***GOD,*** refers to the reoccurring of this EVENT throughout ETERNITY. It also refers to the GLORIFICATION of the NAME of ***GOD*** by both JESUS CHRIST and the PERSON of THE ***HOLY SPIRIT,*** the TWO PERSONS where ***GOD HAS PUT HIS NAME.*** There are TWO FROM THE OLD COVENANT and TWO FROM THE NEW COVENANT: THE FOUR SERAPHIM, the SONS of ***GOD,*** they REPRESENT ***GOD*** in the FORM of ***MAN.***

When the people HEARD the VOICE from HEAVEN some thought that they had heard thunder, while others said that it was the VOICE of an ANGEL that had spoken to JESUS.

> ***John 12:30*** *JESUS answered and said,* ***THIS VOICE CAME NOT BECAUSE OF ME, BUT FOR YOUR SAKES.***

> ***John 12:31 NOW IS THE JUDGMENT OF THIS WORLD: NOW SHALL THE PRINCE OF THIS WORLD BE CAST OUT.***

> ***John 12:32 AND I, IF I BE LIFTED UP FROM THE EARTH, WILL DRAW ALL MEN UNTO ME.***

NOTE: In the LAYER of the LAST TWO Scriptures the Scripture speaks about the CASTING OUT of Lucifer from Heaven and how he no longer has access to ***GOD.*** This refers only to the SAVED, for anyone RECEIVING SAVING GRACE by way of ***HOLY SPIRIT*** BAPTISM can NO LONGER be ACCUSED to ***GOD*** for SIN. Only those who have not been SAVED can be ACCUSED by the Devil to ***GOD*** for their SIN, for they are still of this world! This also MARKS the LAST SERAPHIM to DIE upon the EARTH, for the FOURTH SERAPHIM, the ***182 PERSON,*** neither DIES of the FLESH or the ***SPIRIT SAITH THE LORD*** throughout ETERNITY, for ***HE*** is the FIRST DESCENDANT and the ***SEVEN SPIRITS of GOD, PROCEEDING FROM THE THRONE of GOD!*** The LIFTING UP FROM the EARTH refers to JESUS' CRUCIFIXION, for HE was raised up from the Earth on the CROSS. ONCE the people found out that JESUS was to die by CRUCIFIXION, some became doubtful of HIM, because it was said that the MESSIAH would LIVE FOREVER. HOWEVER they were unaware that there are TWO MESSIAH'S that are referred to in the Scriptures (Zechariah 11:7) as BEAUTY (JESUS CHRIST) and BANDS (THE DELIVERER, the ***182 PERSON***). For the Scriptures say that BEAUTY (JESUS CHRIST) was to be sold for THIRTY pieces of

SILVER (Zechariah 11:13), whereas BANDS JUDGES the EARTH (Isaiah 42:4).

> ***John 12:34*** *The people answered HIM, We have heard that CHRIST abideth for ever: and how sayest thou,* ***THE SON OF MAN MUST BE LIFTED UP?*** *Who is the SON of MAN?*

> ***John 12:35*** *Then JESUS said unto them,* ***YET A LITTLE WHILE IS THE LIGHT WITH YOU. WALK WHILE YE HAVE LIGHT, LEST DARKNESS COME UPON YOU: FOR HE THAT WALKETH IN DARKNESS KNOWETH NOT WHETHER HE GOETH.***

> ***John 12:36 WHILE YE HAVE LIGHT, BELIEVE IN THE LIGHT, THAT YE MAY BE CHILDREN OF LIGHT.*** *These things spake JESUS, and departed, and did HIDE HIMSELF from them.*

Even though JESUS PERFORMED so many MIRACLES before them, they still refused to BELIEVE that HE was CHRIST. The Scripture then reiterates what WE had said earlier in regard to ***GOD*** shutting their eyes so they could not SEE, and closing their ears so they could not HEAR.

However there were many of the Pharisees that BELIEVED in JESUS, but they could not openly CONFESS HIM in fear of being put out of the synagogue, for they loved their religion more than they LOVED ***GOD,*** and this TROUBLED JESUS.

> ***John 12:44*** *JESUS cried and said,* ***HE THAT BELIEVETH ON ME, BELIEVETH NOT ON ME, BUT ON HIM THAT SENT ME.***

> ***John 12:45 AND HE THAT SEETH ME, SEETH HIM THAT SENT ME.***

> ***John 12:46 I AM COME A LIGHT INTO THE WORLD, THAT WHOSOEVER BELIEVETH ON ME SHOULD NOT ABIDE IN DARKNESS.***

> ***John 12:47 AND IF ANY MAN HEAR MY WORDS, AND BE-***

LIEVE NOT, I JUDGE HIM NOT: FOR I CAME NOT TO JUDGE THE WORLD, BUT TO SAVE THE WORLD.

John 12:48 HE THAT REJECTETH ME, AND RECEIVETH NOT MY WORDS, HATH ONE THAT JUDGETH HIM: THE WORD THAT I HAVE SPOKEN, THE SAME SHALL JUDGE HIM IN THE LAST DAY.

John 12:49 FOR I HAVE NOT SPOKEN OF MYSELF; BUT THE FATHER WHICH SENT ME, HE GAVE ME A COMMANDMENT, WHAT I SHOULD SAY, AND WHAT I SHOULD SPEAK.

John 12:50 AND I KNOW THAT HIS COMMANDMENT IS LIFE EVERLASTING: WHATSOEVER I SPEAK THEREFORE, EVEN AS THE FATHER SAID UNTO ME, SO I SPEAK.

NOTE: In these last few Scriptures JESUS is telling HIS audience that ANYONE BELIEVING in HIM is BELIEVING in ***GOD,*** and those who are REJECTING HIM are REJECTING ***GOD.*** JESUS also states that ALL of HIS WORDS have come forth from THE ***HOLY SPIRIT of GOD;*** and those refusing to BELIEVE in HIS WORDS WILL BE JUDGED BY THE SAME WORDS, AND BY THE ONE WHO HAD GIVEN HIM HIS WORDS (THE ***HOLY SPIRIT***). JESUS also says that only by HIS WORDS could ONE RECEIVE ETERNITY. Therefor, anyone refusing to BELIEVE HIS WORDS is DENYING ***GOD,*** and also DENYING their own ETERNITY. As explained in the PREVIOUS BOOK, ONE must be able to see at least FOUR LAYERS deep into the SCRIPTURES before they can RECEIVE ETERNITY. The OLD TESTAMENT has only THREE LAYERS of DEPTH, so ONLY by the NEW TESTAMENT (the FOUR GOSPELS and the REVELATION of JESUS CHRIST) can one RECEIVE the LIVING WATERS deep enough to SWIM in and be HEALED (Ezekiel 47:9). Therefor ONLY by the WORDS of JESUS CHRIST (given to HIM by THE ***HOLY SPIRIT***) can ONE RECEIVE ETERNITY. For no other WORDS spoken on the EARTH has SUFFICIENT DEPTH to them for ONE to SWIM in, be HEALED, and RECEIVE ETERNITY!

17.9 The LAST SUPPER

Two days prior to the PASSOVER JESUS sent HIS Disciples out to reserve a specific room where they could gather and eat one last meal together prior to HIS DEPARTURE. After gathering there and finishing their meal, JESUS rose from the table, removed HIS clothes, and wrapped a towel around HIM.

> ***John 13:4*** *HE riseth from supper, and laid aside HIS garments; and took a towel, and girded HIMSELF.*

> ***John 13:5*** *After that HE poureth water into a bason, and began to wash the Disciples feet, and wipe them with the towel wherewith HE was girded.*

NOTE: JESUS' washing the Disciples feet was similar to the CLEANSING MOSES had done with Aaron and the Priests prior to their entering into Priesthood and SERVING ***GOD***. The Levite Priests would be bathed outside of the TABERNACLE and put into their Priest's Garments by MOSES, prior to them being allowed to enter the TABERNACLE. JESUS performed the same ceremony at the LAST SUPPER, by HIS CLEANSING the Disciples feet. Whereas MOSES cleansed the Priests physically, JESUS' cleansed them SPIRITUALLY, thus preparing the Disciples for their MINISTRIES.

When JESUS came around the table to Simon Peter, Peter refused to let JESUS wash his feet by his thinking that JESUS was to GOOD to do such a thing:

> ***John 13:7*** *JESUS answered and said unto him,* ***WHAT I DO THOU KNOWEST NOT NOW; BUT THOU SHALT KNOW HEREAFTER.***

> ***John 13:8*** *Peter saith unto HIM, Thou shalt never wash my feet. JESUS answered him,* ***IF I WASH THEE NOT, THOU HAST NO PART WITH ME.***

NOTE: JESUS was telling Peter that by HIM washing his feet he was being CLEANSED SPIRITUALLY, and if HE did not CLEANSE Peter in this way he would remain SPIRITUALLY UNCLEAN and not fit for MINISTRY.

After Peter hears this from JESUS he tells HIM to not only wash his feet, but also his hands and head. JESUS tells Peter that after his feet have been cleaned (thus meaning Peter's being made SPIRITUALLY clean), not only would his feet be clean but his SPIRITUAL BODY would be CLEAN. Then JESUS said after HE had washed all the Disciples feet that not all of the Disciples were clean, for HE was referring to Judas Iscariot who was about to BETRAY HIM.

JESUS then set back down at the CENTER of the table and asked the Disciples if they had realized what HE had just done and explains to them how HE had been sent to earth to set an EXAMPLE for them to FOLLOW. JESUS says that although HE is their LORD, HE was sent to CARE for them rather than them caring for HIM. JESUS tells the Disciples that they are to LOOK after one another as HE had looked after them, and to remember that the servant is not greater than his LORD, thus meaning, if HE had done it, they should do it as well.

> ***John 13:16 VERILY, VERILY, I SAY UNTO YOU, THE SERVANT IS NOT GREATER THAN HIS LORD; NEITHER HE THAT IS SENT GREATER THAN HE THAT SENT HIM.***

JESUS says that they must learn to follow before they can LEAD, and know how to SERVE before they can be served, and if they were to follow this example their MINISTRIES would be successful. JESUS says however, not all present at the table could follow this doctrine, for Judas Iscariot still sat among them. JESUS then tells the Disciples that one of them would BETRAY HIM, and after HE says this to them, the Disciples start looking around the table to see which one of them it might be.

> ***JOHN 13:26*** *JESUS answered,* ***HE IT IS, TO WHOM I SHALL GIVE A SOP, WHEN I HAVE DIPPED IT.*** *And when HE had dipped the sop, HE gave it to Judas Is-car'-i-ot, the son of Simon.*

After giving the sop to Judas (bread dipped in wine and olive oil) JESUS whispers to Judas, "do what you must do and do it quickly". Judas then hurriedly leaves the room, but the Disciples were not aware of where Judas had gone, and some thought that maybe JESUS had sent Judas off to buy more food, for he was the Treasurer and held the Disciple's money bag.

NOTE: Even though JESUS had said aloud that the one HE would give the sop to was the one who would BETRAY HIM, ONLY JUDAS ISCARIOT knew who JESUS was referring to; for it was meant for only Judas' ears to hear.

And, although JESUS had spoken these WORDS openly at the table and while John and Simon Peter both sat near to HIM, neither they nor anyone at the table (other than Judas) realized that JESUS had IDENTIFIED Judas as the BETRAYER.

> ***John 13:27*** *And after the sop Satan entered into him. Then said JESUS unto him,* ***THAT THOU DOEST, DO QUICKLY.***

> ***John 13:28*** *Now NO MAN at the table knew for what intent HE spake this unto him.*

> ***John 13:29*** *For some of them thought, because Judas had the bag, that JESUS had said unto him, Buy those things that we have need of against the feast; or, that he should give something to the poor.*

After Judas left the room JESUS tells the Disciples that HE would soon be GLORIFIED, and ***GOD*** would also be GLORIFIED by what HE was about to do. JESUS says HE will soon be leaving them and going to a place where they could not follow, and after HE has left them, they were to express their LOVE for one another, just as HE had done with them. Then, by their expressing their LOVE towards one another, all the people seeing their COMPASSION would KNOW they were DISCIPLES of JESUS CHRIST.

NOTE: JESUS tells HIS Disciples this because ALL of them, who had either seen or heard JESUS, saw the COMPASSION HE had for the people. ANYONE who had come to HIM for HELP had not been DENIED, and JESUS wanted the Disciples to continue on in this way, DEMONSTRATING LOVE towards ONE ANOTHER.

Simon Peter then asked, where was JESUS going that he could not follow? And JESUS tells Simon Peter, where HE was going Peter could not go yet, but at a later time he could, referring to HEAVEN. Peter now knowing that JESUS was speaking about HIS dying and going to HEAVEN then asks HIM why he could not come with HIM now; for Peter said, he would willingly lay down his life for JESUS.

> ***John 13:38*** *JESUS answered him,* ***WILT THOU LAY DOWN THY LIFE FOR MY SAKE? VERILY, VERILY, I SAY UNTO THEE, THE COCK SHALL NOT CROW, TILL THOU HAST DENIED ME THRICE.***

NOTE: While JESUS was here on earth HE was the LIVING HOST to THE ***HOLY SPIRIT,*** therefor making HIM the REPRESENTATIVE of ***GOD.*** When Peter had made the VOW of laying down his life for JESUS he was making a COMMITMENT to ***GOD*** that he could not KEEP. This is why the CHURCH was taken away from Simon Peter and given to the Apostle Paul, for Simon Peter broke his VOW to ***GOD.***

> ***Ecclesiastes 5:4*** *When thou VOWEST a VOW unto* ***GOD,*** *defer not to pay it; for* ***HE*** *hath no pleasure in fools: pay that which thou hast VOWED.*

> ***Ecclesiastes 5:5*** *Better is it that thou shouldest not VOW, than thou shouldest VOW and not pay.*

Many Mansions in HEAVEN

After JESUS tells Peter this, HE tells HIS Disciples if they BELIEVE in ***GOD*** then they should also BELIEVE in HIM, for HE had COME OUT from ***GOD*** (being a DESCENDANT of ***GOD***). HE further says, in HEAVEN there are many MANSIONS, and HE was going there FIRST to PREPARE a place for them to LIVE. JESUS tells the Disciples that HE will later RETURN and gather them up, and bring them to where HE is. But most of the Disciples don't UNDERSTAND what HE is saying.

So Thomas tells JESUS he neither knows where HE is going nor how to get there. JESUS then says to Thomas, I AM the WAY, the TRUTH and the LIFE, and no man can come into HEAVEN or to the ***FATHER (THE HOLY SPIRIT)*** except by ME. JESUS further tells Thomas, if you have KNOWN ME you have also KNOWN MY ***FATHER***, for THE ***FATHER (THE HOLY SPIRIT)*** and I are ONE.

NOTE: JESUS CHRIST is the DESCENDING NATURE of ***GOD (YESHUA)*** in the form of a MAN, and what JESUS was telling Thomas is that if Thomas knew HIM SPIRITUALLY, he also had known ***GOD,*** for the ***SPIRIT of GOD*** was in HIM.

> ***John 14:11 BELIEVE ME THAT I AM IN THE FATHER, AND THE FATHER IN ME: OR ELSE BELIEVE ME FOR THE VERY WORKS' SAKE.***

NOTE: JESUS asks Thomas in the Scripture as to why he didn't understand that both HE and THE ***FATHER*** SHARE the SAME ***SPIRIT?*** JESUS reminds Thomas how he had SEEN with his own eyes the MIRACLES PERFORMED, and asks why he couldn't UNDERSTAND IT WAS ***GOD*** who had PERFORMED THOSE MIRACLES. JESUS SAYS, YOU HAVE HEARD ME SAY, BY MYSELF I CAN DO NOTHING, AND EVEN THE WORDS THAT I SPEAK ARE GIVEN TO ME BY ***GOD,*** SO WHY CAN'T YOU BELIEVE THAT I HAVE COME OUT FROM ***GOD***?

JESUS then tells all the Disciples that if they will BELIEVE in ***GOD*** and HIM, they will also be able to PERFORM the SAME MIRACLES HE had done; and also GREATER ONES than those, because HE would SEE that their PRAYERS were ANSWERED in HEAVEN.

> ***John 14:12 VERILY, VERILY, I SAY UNTO YOU, HE THAT BELIEVETH ON ME, THE WORKS THAT I DO SHALL HE DO ALSO; AND GREATER WORKS THAN THESE SHALL HE DO; BECAUSE I GO UNTO MY FATHER.***
>
> ***John 14:13 AND WHATSOEVER YE SHALL ASK IN MY NAME, THAT WILL I DO, THAT THE FATHER MAY BE GLORIFIED IN THE SON.***
>
> ***John 14:14 IF YE SHALL ASK ANY THING IN MY NAME, I WILL DO IT.***[6]

JESUS tells HIS Disciples that after HE leaves the EARTH HE will send to them another COMFORTER, and the COMFORTER to COME is called "THE SPIRIT of TRUTH" (THE ***HOLY SPIRIT***). However ONLY THEM who are SAVED by the GRACE of ***GOD*** can RECEIVE the COMFORTER. For ***HE*** cannot be seen and ***HIS PRESENCE*** can only be FELT in the SPIRIT after RECEIVING SPIRITUAL BAPTISM. JESUS says when THE COMFORTER COMES ***HE*** will DWELL with them in both SPIRIT and TRUTH.

JESUS also says, although HE is about to LEAVE the EARTH, HE will still remain with them, for HE in the SPIRIT will manifest HIMSELF to them. Then they who BELIEVE in HIM will follow HIS DOCTRINE, and BOTH HE and

---

[6] The name "DID'-Y-MUS" given to Thomas in the Scriptures, means "DOUBTFUL" in the Hebrew Language, as does also the word "THOMAS" mean "DOUBTFUL" in the English Language; thus giving Thomas a NAME befitting his PERSONALITY. It may also be noted in TONGUES (HEBREWAH) the WORD "DOUBT" or "DOUBTFUL" is the WORD "TO'-MA-SAH", which is where the name THOMAS was derived.

GOD (THE ***HOLY SPIRIT***) WILL DWELL WITHIN THEM. Then, after THE ***HOLY SPIRIT*** has come, ***HE*** will help them to REMEMBER the things they had experienced with HIM while HE was yet on the EARTH, and also, THE ***HOLY SPIRIT*** will TEACH them NEW THINGS.

HE then promises to LEAVE HIS PEACE (THE ***HOLY SPIRIT***) WITH THEM, for JESUS KNEW the Disciples would be TROUBLED by HIS LEAVING. But HE tells them that they shouldn't be saddened by it, but they should rather be HAPPY for HIM, for HE was going back to THE ***FATHER.*** HE said that HE was telling them these things now so when they came to pass they would remember HE had told them of them.

> ***John 14:30 HEREAFTER I WILL NOT TALK MUCH WITH YOU: FOR THE PRINCE OF THIS WORLD COMETH, AND HATH NOTHING IN ME.***

NOTE: In the last Scripture JESUS KNEW HE would soon be taken captive, and refers to Judas, as being the Devil (the Prince of this world), for Judas was now POSSESSED. JESUS says to them that Judas is not a Disciple and will not minister for HIM.[7]

17.10 The VINE of TRUTH

After JESUS had washed the feet of HIS DISCIPLES and told them that one of them would betray HIM, HE gets up from the table and leaves the room where they had their supper, and as HE walks and they follow HE SAYS:

> ***John 15:1 I AM THE TRUE VINE, AND MY FATHER IS THE HUSBANDMAN.***

> ***John 15:2 EVERY BRANCH IN ME THAT BEARETH NOT FRUIT HE TAKETH AWAY: AND EVERY BRANCH THAT BEARETH FRUIT, HE PURGETH IT, THAT IT MAY BRING FORTH MORE FRUIT.***

---

[7] JESUS said all these things while at the table during the LAST SUPPER, and although HIS Disciples heard HIS every WORD they didn't UNDERSTAND. It wasn't until after they had been BAPTIZED in the SPIRIT and REBORN in CHRIST that they BEGAN to UNDERSTAND JESUS' MESSAGE!

NOTE: What is being said in these last two Scriptures? JESUS refers to HIMSELF as being a VINE, and refers to them who will follow in HIS FOOT-STEPS as being the BRANCHES growing out of that VINE. This is REL-EVANT to those who will be PARTAKERS in the NEW COVENANT by PREACHING the GOSPELS; for they are the BRANCHES growing out of JESUS continuing on in the NEW COVENANT. Some of the BRANCHES (HIS DISCIPLES) will not bear fruit; meaning, they will NOT conduct meaningful MINISTRIES, and those BRANCHES ***GOD*** will remove from the VINE because their MINISTRIES have FAILED. While other BRANCHES will be PRODUCTIVE, and ***GOD*** will continually PRUNE and NURTURE them to make certain those BRANCHES FLOURISH.

John 15:3 NOW YE ARE CLEAN THROUGH THE WORD WHICH I HAVE SPOKEN UNTO YOU.

John 15:4 ABIDE IN ME, AND I IN YOU. AS THE BRANCH CANNOT BEAR FRUIT OF ITSELF, EXCEPT IT ABIDE IN THE VINE; NO MORE CAN YE, EXCEPT YE ABIDE IN ME.

John 15:5 I AM THE VINE, YE ARE THE BRANCHES: HE THAT ABIDETH IN ME, AND I IN HIM, THE SAME BRINGETH FORTH MUCH FRUIT: FOR WITHOUT ME YE CAN DO NOTHING.

John 15:6 IF A MAN ABIDE NOT IN ME, HE IS CAST FORTH AS A BRANCH, AND IS WITHERED; AND MEN GATHER THEM, AND CAST THEM INTO THE FIRE, AND THEY ARE BURNED.

John 15:7 IF YOU ABIDE IN ME, AND MY WORDS ABIDE IN YOU, YE SHALL ASK WHAT YE WILL, AND IT SHALL BE DONE UNTO YOU.

John 15:8 HEREIN IS MY FATHER GLORIFIED, THAT YE BEAR MUCH FRUIT; SO SHALL YE BE MY DISCIPLES.

NOTE: JESUS is saying that HE NOW has given HIS Disciples an UN-DERSTANDING of the *WORD of **GOD***, and they can USE it TRUTHFULLY, for they have been made CLEAN by it. The NEW COVENANT being a COV-

ENANT GOVERNED by FAITH rather than LAW, requires a CLEANSING by SPIRITUAL BAPTISM to have FAITH; and that BAPTISM can only COME by way of JESUS CHRIST (THE *WORD of* ***GOD***). Therefor those made CLEAN by the WORD, will be BAPTIZED in the SPIRIT and abide in JESUS and HIS DOCTRINE. JESUS says that those being BAPTIZED and ANOINTED to TEACH the *WORD of* ***GOD*** will do so in accordance with HIS DOCTRINE, and by following HIS DOCTRINE will GLORIFY ***GOD,*** for they have BELIEVED in JESUS CHRIST, THE SON of ***GOD***.

However JESUS also WARNS them who will try to teach the *WORD of* ***GOD*** without being BAPTIZED in the SPIRIT and therefor lacking the ANOINTING to PREACH; for they will not ABIDE in JESUS or HIS DOCTRINE and will be cast into HELL for their FALSE TEACHING.

> ***John 15:9 AS THE FATHER HATH LOVED ME, SO HAVE I LOVED YOU: CONTINUE YE IN MY LOVE.***

> ***John 15:10 IF YE KEEP MY COMMANDMENTS, YE SHALL ABIDE IN MY LOVE; EVEN AS I HAVE KEPT MY FATHER'S COMMANDMENTS, AND ABIDE IN HIS LOVE.***

> ***John 15:11 THESE THINGS HAVE I SPOKEN UNTO YOU, THAT MY JOY MIGHT REMAIN IN YOU, AND THAT YOUR JOY MAY BE FULL.***

> ***John 15:12 THIS IS MY COMMANDMENT, THAT YE LOVE ONE ANOTHER, AS I HAVE LOVED YOU.***

> ***John 15:13 GREATER LOVE HATH NO MAN THAN THIS, THAT A MAN LAY DOWN HIS LIFE FOR HIS FRIENDS.***

NOTE: JESUS reminds HIS Disciples they are to LOVE one another as HE has LOVED them, and that HIS LOVE for them is a GREATER LOVE than any man's love for his friends. For JESUS says HE will even LAY DOWN HIS LIFE for the ones HE LOVES, and what more can a MAN do to EXPRESS HIS LOVE for HIS FRIENDS.[8]

> ***John 15:14 YE ARE MY FRIENDS, IF YE DO WHATSOEVER I COMMAND YOU.***

John 15:15 HENCEFORTH I CALL YOU NOT SERVANTS; FOR THE SERVANT KNOWETH NOT WHAT HIS LORD DOETH: BUT I HAVE CALLED YOU FRIENDS; FOR ALL THINGS I HAVE HEARD OF MY FATHER I HAVE MADE KNOWN UNTO YOU.

John 15:16 YE HAVE NOT CHOSEN ME, BUT I HAVE CHOSEN YOU, AND ORDAINED YOU, THAT YE SHOULD GO AND BRING FORTH FRUIT, AND THAT YOUR FRUIT SHOULD REMAIN: THAT WHATSOEVER YE SHOULD ASK OF THE FATHER IN MY NAME, HE MAY GIVE IT YOU.

John 15:17 THESE THINGS I COMMAND YOU THAT YOU LOVE ONE ANOTHER.

NOTE: JESUS looks at them who are SERVING HIM in MINISTRY as HIS FRIENDS rather than HIS SERVANTS. HE WANTS YOU TO BE A PARTAKER RATHER THAN A SPECTATOR, AND A PARTNER RATHER THAN A HIRED HAND. BUT IT IS KEY TO ALL WHO ARE SERVING JESUS THAT THEY LOVE ONE ANOTHER. AS ***GOD*** LOVES THEM WHO ARE SERVING JESUS CHRIST, SO SHALL YOU ALSO LOVE THEM ***SAITH THE LORD.*** JESUS says that it is HE WHO CHOOSES them to SERVE HIM, and it is HE who ORDAINS for MINISTRY. This is SOMETHING the CHURCH has OVERLOOKED and CONTINUALLY DISOBEYS, for they believe they may choose and ordain on their own.

John 15:18 IF THE WORLD HATE YOU, YE KNOW THAT IT HATED ME BEFORE IT HATED YOU.

John 15:19 IF YE WERE OF THE WORLD, THE WORLD WOULD LOVE HIS OWN: BUT BECAUSE YE ARE NOT OF THE WORLD, BUT I HAVE CHOSEN YOU OUT OF THE

[8] Throughout time, MANKIND has always preferred to SERVE another MAN rather than ***GOD.*** JESUS expresses throughout HIS GOSPELS, that while YOU SERVE HIM, HE SERVES ***GOD.*** JESUS does this because of MAN'S unwillingness to SERVE ***GOD*** on his own, so JESUS SERVES ***GOD*** on YOUR BEHALF because HE LOVES YOU. However, ONCE YOU have RECEIVED ***HOLY SPIRIT*** BAPTISM, JESUS no longer needs to INTERCEDE on YOUR BEHALF, because after BAPTISM YOU WILL SERVE ***GOD*** on YOUR OWN ACCORD!

WORLD, THEREFORE THE WORLD HATETH YOU.

John 15:20 REMEMBER THE WORD I SAID UNTO YOU, THE SERVANT IS NOT GREATER THAN HIS LORD. IF THEY HAVE PERSECUTED ME, THEY WILL ALSO PERSECUTE YOU; IF THEY HAVE KEPT MY SAYING, THEY WILL KEEP YOUR'S ALSO.

John 15:21 BUT ALL THESE THINGS WILL THEY DO UNTO YOU FOR MY NAME'S SAKE, BECAUSE THEY KNOW NOT HIM THAT SENT ME.

NOTE: JESUS is forewarning HIS Disciples before their MINISTRIES begin that the world as a whole will HATE them, because of their PREACHING the TRUTH, for the world HATES the TRUTH, and they will be hated just as HE had been HATED. The Devil is called the Prince of the world and also the Father of LIES; therefor, anyone of this world is a PARTAKER in LIES and will HATE anyone TEACHING or PREACHING the TRUTH. JESUS tells the Disciples that they will be PERSECUTED for their PREACHING in HIS NAME, because those of this world HAVE REFUSED to BELIEVE in HIM and haven't any KNOWLEDGE of ***GOD.***

John 15:22 IF I HAD NOT COME AND SPOKEN UNTO THEM, THEY HAD NOT HAD SIN: BUT NOW THEY HAVE NO CLOAK FOR THEIR SIN.

John 15:23 HE THAT HATETH ME HATETH MY FATHER ALSO.

John 15:24 IF I HAD NOT DONE AMONG THEM THE WORKS WHICH NONE OTHER MAN DID, THEY HAD NOT HAD SIN: BUT NOW HAVE THEY BOTH SEEN AND HATED BOTH ME AND MY FATHER.

John 15:25 BUT THIS COMETH TO PASS, THAT THE WORD MIGHT BE FULFILLED THAT IS WRITTEN IN THEIR LAW, THEY HATED ME WITHOUT A CAUSE.

REFERENCE:

> ***Psalm 69:4*** *They that HATE ME without a cause are more than the hairs of MINE HEAD: they that would DESTROY ME, being MINE enemies wrongfully, are mighty: then I restored that which I took not away.*[9]

NOTE: The Scriptures of John 15:22 through 15:25 speak about how ***GOD*** gave the people the opportunity to SEE ***HIS*** GREAT WORKS through JESUS CHRIST, and yet they still refused to BELIEVE, just as it had been PROPHESISED in the Scriptures. Most of what JESUS CHRIST had done was RECORDED and provided in the BOOK WE call the ***HOLY BIBLE*** and even to this day the people refuse to BELIEVE in HIM. This is why the NEW COVENANT is a COVENANT of FAITH, for ONE MUST HAVE FAITH to BELIEVE that which is WRITTEN in the ***HOLY BIBLE***. Therefor, by ***GOD*** providing the TRUTH through JESUS CHRIST, the *WORD of* ***GOD,*** one can no longer SIN through IGNORANCE, for the TRUTH has been made AVAILABLE to ALL and they no longer have a CLOAK for their SIN!

The COMING of the SPIRIT of TRUTH

> ***John 15:26 BUT WHEN THE COMFORTER IS COME, WHOM I WILL SEND UNTO YOU FROM THE FATHER, EVEN THE SPIRIT OF TRUTH, WHICH PROCEEDETH FROM THE FATHER, HE SHALL TESTIFY OF ME:***
>
> ***John 15:27 AND YE ALSO SHALL BEAR WITNESS, BECAUSE YE HAVE BEEN WITH ME FROM THE BEGINNING.***

NOTE: The COMFORTER that is to come to the earth, is THE ***HOLY SPIRIT of GOD,*** who is called THE SPIRIT of TRUTH. ***HE*** first COMES in THE ***SPIRIT*** to GUIDE the Disciples in their MINISTRY, and they RECEIVE both ***HIM*** and ***HIS*** GIFTS at the TIME of their ***HOLY SPIRIT*** BAPTISM (the DAY of PENTECOST). Then from the TIME of PENTECOST thereafter, anyone be-

[9] This Scripture taken from the 69th Psalm PROPHESISED how JESUS was to be HATED, and how the leaders of the world would want to see HIM DESTROYED, even though all that HE did was GOOD. It also speaks to JESUS' DEATH and RESURRECTION and HOW HE RESTORED HIS OWN LIFE AFTER THE WORLD HAD TAKEN FROM HIM!

ing BAPTIZED in THE ***HOLY SPIRIT*** will also RECEIVE ***HIM*** and ***HIS*** GIFTS continuing on up until the TIME of ***HIS*** COMING as THE ***DELIVERER.*** The LAYER of the Scripture not only refers to THE ***HOLY SPIRIT*** who in the ***SPIRIT*** COMES FIRST, but ALSO refers to THE ***HOLY SPIRIT*** COMING at THE END, in the FLESH. WE have TOLD you of this both in this BOOK and in the PREVIOUS BOOK. THIS is ***GOD'S*** APPEARANCE as the ***DELIVERER*** and the FULFILLMENT of the PROPHECY given to NOAH in GENESIS.

> ***Genesis 6:3*** *And THE LORD said,* ***MY SPIRIT*** *shall not always strive with man, FOR* ***HE*** *ALSO IS FLESH: yet HIS days shall be an hundred and twenty years.*

THE ***HOLY SPIRIT*** WILL COME JUST PRIOR TO THE FIRST RAPTURE, and WILL GATHER ***HIS SPIRIT BACK UNTO HIMSELF,*** and any who were HOST to ***HIM*** AT THAT TIME, WILL BE MARKED AND SEALED AND WILL RETAIN THE GIFTS THEY HAD RECEIVED OF ***HIM.*** THEN FROM THAT POINT IN TIME FORWARD, NO ONE WILL RECEIVE ***HOLY SPIRIT*** BAPTISM, BUT RATHER THE SEAL OF THE ***LIVING GOD*** for their PROTECTION and PRESERVATION.

17.11 Coming of THE *HOLY SPIRIT*

> ***John 16:1 THESE THINGS HAVE I SPOKEN UNTO YOU, THAT YE SHOULD NOT BE OFFENDED.***

> ***John 16:2 THEY SHALL PUT YOU OUT OF THE SYNAGOGUES: YEA, THE TIME COMETH, THAT WHOSOEVER KILLETH YOU WILL THINK HE DOETH GOD SERVICE.***

> ***John 16:3 AND THESE THINGS WILL THEY DO UNTO YOU, BECAUSE THEY HAVE NOT KNOWN THE FATHER, NOR ME.***

NOTE: Throughout the GOSPELS JESUS WARNS HIS Disciples about the consequences associated with MINISTERING for HIM. HE tells them they should not be OFFENDED by the treatment they will receive, because it will not be through any fault of their own. HE says the Disciples will not be allowed in the synagogues and that all CHRISTIANS will be HATED and PERSE-

CUTED throughout the world. Then those who are mistreating and killing them will claim they are doing ***GOD*** a service. JESUS says that those who partake in their PERSECUTIONS will do so because they neither have a relationship with ***GOD,*** nor do they believe in HIM.

JESUS says HE tells them these things now so they would REMEMBER HE had forewarned them of the difficulties they were to face. HE explains that HE hadn't previously told them about these things, because HE was with them and could PROTECT them. But now the time had come for HIM to LEAVE, and HE wanted to make certain they UNDERSTOOD the CHALLENGES ahead. HE says HE knows they are troubled and saddened by HIS leaving them, but if HE were not to leave, THE ***HOLY SPIRIT*** would not come. So it is GOOD for them that HE LEAVES, for HE will send THE ***HOLY SPIRIT*** to them.

> ***John 16:8 AND WHEN HE HAS COME, HE WILL REPROVE THE WORLD OF SIN, AND OF RIGHTEOUSNESS, AND OF JUDGMENT:***
>
> ***John 16:9 OF SIN, BECAUSE THEY BELIEVE NOT ON ME;***
>
> ***John 16:10 OF RIGHTEOUSNESS, BECAUSE I GO TO MY FATHER, AND YE SEE ME NO MORE;***
>
> ***John 16:11 OF JUDGMENT, BECAUSE THE PRINCE OF THIS WORLD IS JUDGED.***

NOTE: The last FOUR SCRIPTURES apply to THE ***HOLY SPIRIT*** COMING FIRST in the SPIRIT (2nd LAYER, PRESENT) and then in the FLESH (3rd LAYER, FUTURE). In the FIRST LAYER JESUS speaks about THE ***HOLY SPIRIT*** coming to HIS Disciples in the SPIRIT to aid in their MINISTRIES. In the SECOND LAYER of the SCRIPTURE, JESUS speaks about all those being BAPTIZED after them also RECEIVING THE ***HOLY SPIRIT*** in the SPIRIT just as the Disciples had.

However, YOU are about to enter into the 3rd LAYER of the SCRIPTURE ***SAITH THE LORD,*** and THE ***HOLY SPIRIT*** is about to make ***HIS*** APPEARANCE in the FLESH. THE ***HOLY SPIRIT,*** in SPIRIT, has already REPROVED the world of SIN, RIGHTEOUSNESS, and JUDGMENT, and ***HE*** will SOON do AGAIN in the FLESH what ***HE*** has already done in the SPIRIT. ***HE*** will do this just prior to the BEGINNING of THE GREAT TRIBULA-

TION.

NOTE: When The PERSON of THE ***HOLY SPIRIT (182 PERSON)*** COMES in FLESH, ***HE*** will criticize (REPROVE) and JUDGE any person or organization claiming to PREACH the GOSPELS, and will CONDEMN any of them that are teaching a FALSE DOCTRINE of JESUS CHRIST. ***HE*** will also JUDGE all that REFUSE to BELIEVE in JESUS CHRIST and WILL DELIVER the RIGHTEOUS from this world to a PLACE of PROTECTION, while the world ENDURES the GREAT TRIBULATION. ***HE*** WILL JUDGE the Prince of this world (the Devil), along with those PARTAKING in the Prince's BUSINESS, who at that time will also be in FLESH. By them being in FLESH and a PRODUCT of the earth, they will be JUDGED in FLESH, just as they already had been JUDGED in Spirit ***SAITH THE LORD.***

> ***Zechariah 11:16*** *For, lo,* ***I*** *will raise up a SHEPHERD in the land, which shall not visit those that be CUT OFF, neither shall seek the YOUNG ONE, nor HEAL that that is BROKEN, nor FEED that that standeth still: but* ***HE*** *SHALL EAT THE FLESH OF THE FAT, and TEAR THEIR CLAWS IN PIECES.*

JESUS tells HIS Disciples that there were MANY more things HE would like to tell them about THE ***HOLY SPIRIT***. However, HE knew they WOULDN'T UNDERSTAND these things yet. The Disciples were not yet BAPTIZED in THE ***HOLY SPIRIT*** and had not yet RECEIVED the GIFTS GIVEN by ***HIM***, therefor their UNDERSTANDING was limited, and they couldn't at that time comprehend the SPIRITUAL TRUTHS JESUS wanted to give them.

> ***John 16:13 HOWBEIT WHEN HE, THE SPIRIT OF TRUTH, IS COME, HE WILL GUIDE YOU INTO ALL TRUTH: FOR HE SHALL NOT SPEAK OF HIMSELF; BUT WHATSOEVER HE SHALL HEAR, THAT SHALL HE SPEAK: AND HE WILL SHEW YOU THINGS TO COME.***

> ***John 16:14 HE SHALL GLORIFY ME: FOR HE SHALL RECEIVE OF MINE, AND SHALL SHEW IT UNTO YOU.***

> ***John 16:15 ALL THINGS THAT THE FATHER HATH ARE MINE: THEREFORE SAID I, THAT HE SHALL TAKE OF MINE, AND SHALL SHEW IT UNTO YOU.***

NOTE: What JESUS is saying in the Scriptures is that the Disciples UNDERSTANDING and GUIDANCE would COME by way of THE ***HOLY SPIRIT,*** after HE has left the earth; and JESUS refers to THE ***HOLY SPIRIT*** in both SPIRIT, and in FLESH. The UNDERSTANDING and GUIDANCE for the Disciples of yesteryear and up till now, came by way of THE ***SPIRIT,*** whereas for HIS FUTURE DISCIPLES, it will come by way of FLESH (***182 PERSON of THE HOLY SPRIT***). JESUS refers to THE ***HOLY SPIRIT*** in the Scripture as HIS ***FATHER,*** WHO WILL TAKE THOSE THINGS ***HE*** HAD GIVEN TO ***HIS*** SON (JESUS), AND SHOW THEM TO THE WORLD. THUS PROCLAIMING THE ***HOLY SPIRIT PERSON*** HAS TAKEN THE WORLD FROM THE DEVIL AND HAS GIVEN IT TO ***HIS*** SON, JESUS CHRIST.

JESUS tells HIS Disciples that soon they will no longer be able to see HIM, but shortly thereafter they will see HIM again. (HE is referring to HIS DEATH and RESURRECTION). However, the Disciples fail to UNDERSTAND what JESUS is saying.

> ***John 16:20 VERILY, VERILY, I SAY UNTO YOU, THAT YE SHALL WEEP AND LAMENT, BUT THE WORLD SHALL REJOICE: AND YE SHALL BE SORROWFUL, BUT YOUR SORROW WILL BE TURNED INTO JOY.***

> ***John 16:21 A WOMAN WHEN SHE IS IN TRAVAIL HATH SORROW, BECAUSE HER HOUR HAS COME: BUT AS SOON AS SHE IS DELIVERED OF THE CHILD, SHE REMEMBERETH NO MORE THE ANGUISH, FOR JOY THAT A MAN IS BORN INTO THE WORLD.***

> ***John 16:22 AND YE NOW THEREFORE HAVE SORROW: BUT I WILL SEE YOU AGAIN, AND YOUR HEART SHALL REJOICE, AND YOUR JOY NO MAN TAKETH FROM YOU.***

NOTE: JESUS refers to HIS DEATH as being similar to a woman having HARD LABOR PAINS while giving BIRTH to a CHILD. HE says, although the woman endures a great deal of pain giving BIRTH, once the CHILD is BORN she quickly forgets about the PAIN and REJOICES over the NEWBORN PERSON. This ALL relates to SPIRITUAL REBIRTH as WE have explained throughout this BOOK. JESUS had to DIE in the FLESH so those BELIEVING IN HIM could be BAPTIZED and RE-BORN IN THE SPIRIT of TRUTH. When a PERSON RECEIVES SAVING GRACE by ***HOLY SPIRIT***

BAPTISM, their ***GOD*** GIVEN SPIRIT LITERALLY SEPARATES from their Spirit of FLESH (earth given Spirit), just like a CHILD separates from its mother during BIRTH. While enduring this SEPARATION, a great deal of EMOTIONAL PAIN is experienced, similar to the LABOR PAIN a woman endures while giving birth. But once the PROCESS is COMPLETED, a CHILD is BORN into ETERNITY; and that CHILD can no longer die!

After REBIRTH (SPIRITUAL BAPTISM) ANYTHING asked for in the NAME of JESUS will be GIVEN by ***GOD*** to YOU. For JESUS will ASK ***GOD*** on your BEHALF and ***GOD*** WILL always ANSWER HIS PRAYERS. JESUS then tells HIS Disciples that after they RECEIVE their GIFTS given by THE ***HOLY SPIRIT***, they no longer would need to PRAY in HIS NAME. For one of their GIFTS would be the GIFT of TONGUES, and ONCE they could PRAY in TONGUES (HEBREWAH), they would no longer need HIM to INTERCEDE. This is because they could then PRAY DIRECTLY to ***GOD*** and to THE THRONE on their OWN in TONGUES (the HEBREWAH LANGUAGE).

> ***John 16:28 I CAME FORTH FROM THE FATHER, AND AM COME INTO THE WORLD: <u>AGAIN</u>, I LEAVE THE WORLD, AND GO TO THE FATHER.***

NOTE: The FIRST THREE LAYERS of the SCRIPTURE indicates that JESUS routinely COMES OUT FROM ***GOD,*** and then after JESUS COMPLETES HIS MINISTRY HE LEAVES the world. The WORD "AGAIN" is the "TRIGGER WORD"; for in the Scripture LAYER JESUS SAYS, HE HAD DONE THIS SAME THING BEFORE, and HE WILL DO IT **<u>AGAIN</u>**, as HE had done it in the PAST, in the PRESENT, and in the FUTURE!

Once JESUS had explained these things to HIS Disciples, ***GOD*** then opens the Disciples EARS and for the FIRST TIME they begin to UNDERSTAND what JESUS is SAYING. It appears to the Disciples as though HE wasn't any longer SPEAKING in PARABLES, however JESUS hadn't changed HIS METHODOLOGY, but rather ***GOD*** improved their ability to SPIRITUALLY HEAR and UNDERSTAND. This was the FIRST time JESUS' Disciples hadn't any DOUBT that HE was CHRIST, and had CAME OUT from ***GOD*** as the SCRIPTURES had said.

> ***John 16:31*** *JESUS answered them,* ***DO YE NOW BELIEVE?***

> ***John 16:32 BEHOLD, THE HOUR COMETH, YEA, IS NOW COME, THAT YE SHALL BE SCATTERED, EVERY MAN TO***

HIS OWN, AND SHALL LEAVE ME ALONE: AND YET I AM NOT ALONE, BECAUSE THE FATHER IS WITH ME.

John 16:33 THESE THINGS I HAVE SPOKEN UNTO YOU, THAT YE MIGHT HAVE PEACE. IN THE WORLD YE SHALL HAVE TRIBULATION: BUT BE OF GOOD CHEER; I HAVE OVERCOME THE WORLD.

NOTE: After JESUS sees the FAITH of HIS Disciples has INCREASED, and they were UNANIMOUS in BELIEVING HE was CHRIST, HE tells them about what will soon take place. JESUS says shortly thereafter, they will flee from HIM, while the Pharisees take HIM CAPTIVE. JESUS says however, they should not hold themselves accountable or feel guilty for not defending HIM, for they are fulfilling SCRIPTURE.

Zechariah 13:7 *AWAKE, O sword, against* ***MY*** *SHEPHERD, and against the MAN that is* ***MY*** *FELLOW,* ***SAITH THE LORD of HOSTS:*** *SMITE the SHEPHERD, and the SHEEP shall be SCATTERED: and* ***I*** *will turn MINE HAND upon the little ones.*

Not wanting the Disciples to be discouraged for what they are about to do, JESUS offers them PEACE rather than GUILT ("THAT YE MIGHT HAVE PEACE"), and tells them in this world there is TROUBLE (TRIBULATION). BUT JESUS says that HE HAS OVERCOME THE WORLD, and will soon be OUT OF IT! JESUS then PRAYED for HIS DISCIPLES, and for ALL them who will PREACH ***GOD'S WORD*** after HIM.

THE PRAYER

John 17:1 *These WORDS spake JESUS, and LIFTED UP HIS EYES to HEAVEN, and said,* ***FATHER, THE HOUR IS COME; GLORIFY THY SON, THAT THY SON ALSO MAY GLORIFY THEE:***

John 17:2 AS THOU HAS GIVEN HIM POWER OVER ALL FLESH, THAT HE SHOULD GIVE ETERNAL LIFE TO AS MANY AS THOU HAST GIVEN HIM.

John 17:3 AND THIS IS LIFE ETERNAL, THAT THEY

MIGHT KNOW THEE THE ONLY TRUE GOD, AND JESUS CHRIST, WHOM THOU HAS SENT.

John 17:4 I HAVE GLORIFIED THEE ON THE EARTH: I HAVE FINISHED THE WORK WHICH THOU GAVEST ME TO DO.

NOTE: JESUS states in the OPENING of HIS PRAYER that HIS CRUCIFIXION will GLORIFY both HIM and ***GOD.*** IT GLORIFIES ***GOD*** by ***GOD'S*** RECEIVING the FINAL SACRIFICE for man, by MAN, and it GLORIFIES JESUS CHRIST by HIM BEING THE FINAL SACRIFICE, THE ***LAMB of GOD*** WITHOUT BLEMISH. The POWER over all flesh GIVEN to JESUS, REPRESENTS JESUS' ABILITY to DEFEAT DEATH of the FLESH, and HIS ABILITY to GIVE LIFE after DEATH to them who ***GOD*** has SENT that BELIEVE in HIM.

JESUS said in HIS PRAYER, HE had GLORIFIED ***GOD*** on the earth, and had FINISHED the WORK HE had been sent to do. JESUS GLORIFIED ***GOD*** by HIS DEMONSTRATING ***GOD'S*** GREAT POWER by MIRACLES HE performed in the NAME of ***GOD.*** The WORK JESUS had COMPLETED was HIS GIVING the people the TRUTH through the *WORD of* ***GOD,*** SPOKEN by HIS MOUTH, and RECORDED in THE GOSPELS and the Book of REVELATION by HIS Disciples.

JESUS then ASKED ***THE LORD*** AGAIN, to GLORIFY HIM, as ***HE*** had DONE prior to the CREATION of the world.[10]

JESUS tells THE LORD HE has given to HIS Disciples the *WORD of* ***GOD*** that had been GIVEN to HIM and they have RETAINED it, and NOW they BELIEVE HIS WORDS and ***GOD'S*** *WORD* are the SAME WORDS. JESUS stresses in HIS PRAYER that it APPLIES to ALL of them that ***GOD*** has GIVEN HIM. JESUS says HE has NOW come out of the world even though HIS Disciples remain, and PRAYS for ***GOD*** to KEEP them being left behind from EVIL in the world. JESUS then tells ***THE LORD*** HE has retained ELEVEN of the TWELVE that were given to HIM, and only Judas Iscariot has been lost so the SCRIPTURE could be fulfilled.

---

[10] The FIRST GLORIFICATION refers to the LIGHT SOURCE (JESUS CHRIST) who provided the LIGHT for the WORLD needed for THE BEGINNING of PHYSICAL LIFE OUTSIDE of HEAVEN. By JESUS BEING GLORIFIED AGAIN, JESUS REFERS TO THAT SAME LIGHT SOURCE (JESUS CHRIST) providing the LIGHT of LIFE needed for SPIRITUAL AFTERLIFE and ACCESS TO HEAVEN, FOR THEM BELIEVING IN HIM.

REFERENCE:

Psalm 41:9 *Yea, MINE own familiar friend, in whom I trusted, which did* ***eat of my bread,*** *hath lifted up his heel against ME.*

NOTE: When JESUS had said to the Disciples, the one HE would give the SOP of BREAD to, was the one who would betray HIM, HE was fulfilling the PROPHECY of the Scripture in verse 9 of the 41st Psalm.

JESUS PRAYS that HIS Disciples may SHARE in HIS JOY; thus meaning they COULD NOW RECEIVE ***HOLY SPIRIT*** BAPTISM, and be as ONE with ***GOD*** as HE is ONE in ***GOD*** by way of THE ***HOLY SPIRIT.*** JESUS says HE fears for HIS Disciples lives, for they have now RECEIVED the *WORD of* ***GOD*** and will be HATED by the world, just as HE had been hated by the world. However JESUS doesn't ask ***GOD*** to take the Disciples out of the world, for HE knows they must carry on HIS MINISTRY. But HE does ask ***GOD*** to PROTECT them from the EVIL in the world because they are no longer of the world, though they remain in it.

JESUS PRAYS that HIS WORD will SANCTIFY HIS Disciples by the TRUTH and FAITH in it, and anyone BELIEVING in HIS WORD will also be SANCTIFIED by it. HE further PRAYS that ALL BELIEVERS may PARTAKE in the NEW COVENANT, RECEIVE ***HOLY SPIRIT*** BAPTISM and by that BAPTISM, RECEIVE both HE and ***GOD***, so they may SHARE in HIS GLORY, and in ***GOD'S LOVE,*** and be RECEIVED into HEAVEN to DWELL with HIM.

John 17:22 AND THE GLORY WHICH THOU GAVEST ME I HAVE GIVEN THEM; THAT THEY MAY BE ONE, EVEN AS WE ARE ONE:

John 17:23 I IN THEM, AND THOU IN ME, THAT THEY MAY BE MADE PERFECT IN ONE; AND THAT THE WORLD MAY KNOW THAT THOU HAST SENT ME, AND HAST LOVED THEM, AS THOU HAST LOVED ME.

John 17:24 FATHER, I WILL THAT THEY ALSO, WHOM THOU HAST GIVEN ME, BE WITH ME WHERE I AM; THAT THEY MAY BEHOLD MY GLORY, WHICH THOU HAST GIVEN ME: FOR THOU LOVEST ME BEFORE THE FOUNDATION OF THE WORLD.

NOTE: You should see from the Scriptures that the MAIN TOPIC of the PRAYER is in the BELIEF that JESUS CHRIST had come from HEAVEN to earth to be the SACRIFICE for the SIN of the world. The PRAYER indicates that only those BELIEVING in JESUS CHRIST can EVER BEHOLD the GLORY of ***GOD*** and be RECEIVED into HEAVEN. For one cannot KNOW ***GOD*** without SPIRITUAL BAPTISM, and that comes only by way of JESUS CHRIST. JESUS CHRIST came forth from ***GOD*** and by HIS FAITH IN ***GOD*** DEFEATED DEATH, and ONLY by HIS FAITH can DEATH BE DEFEATED, and that FAITH comes only by way of THE ***HOLY SPIRIT!***

> ***John 17:25 O RIGHTEOUS FATHER, THE WORLD HATH NOT KNOWN THEE: BUT I HAVE KNOWN THEE, AND THESE HAVE KNOWN THAT THOU HAST SENT ME.***

> ***John 17:26 AND I HAVE DECLARED UNTO THEM THY NAME, AND WILL DECLARE IT: THAT THE LOVE WHEREWITH THOU HAST LOVED ME MAY BE IN THEM, AND I IN THEM.***

17.12 CAPTURE and CRUCIFIXION

After JESUS had told HIS Disciples how they would be persecuted for carrying on HIS MINISTRY, and PRAYED for their well being to ***THE FATHER,*** they crossed over the Brook of Ce'-dron and went into the GARDEN called Geth-sem'-a-ne. This was a place where JESUS often went to with HIS Disciples when HE wanted to SPEAK to them in private. Judas Iscariot also knew about this place, because while in JERUSALEM JESUS often took them there. So after leaving the house where they had had their SUPPER, Judas Iscariot went to Pharisees to tell them where JESUS could be found.

The Pharisees then quickly gathered up the Chief Priests and some Officers, and paid Judas the thirty pieces of silvers he had been promised for his BETRAYAL of JESUS. Once gathered, they took up lanterns and torches and armed themselves with swords and spears. They then headed off towards the Garden of Geth-sem'-a-ne where JESUS and HIS Disciples were.

While in the Garden JESUS tells HIS Disciples to keep watch, while HE PRAYED. However, the Disciples being very tired, for it was well passed midnight, fell fast asleep. JESUS tries to awaken them several times, but shortly after HE awakens them they again fall back to sleep.

When the Pharisees, Priests, and Officers, along with Judas Iscariot arrive at the entrance to the Garden, Judas tells them that he would go up and kiss JESUS so they would know for certain which one HE was; for many of them had never seen JESUS. JESUS, being told by ***GOD*** that HIS time had come, was aware of their arrival, and even before they could see HIM, calls out to them.

> ***John 18:4*** *JESUS therefore, knowing ALL THINGS that should come upon HIM, went forth, and said unto them,* ***WHOM SEEK YE?***

> ***John 18:5*** *They answered HIM, JESUS of Nazareth, JESUS saith unto them.* ***I AM HE.*** *And Judas also, which BETRAYED HIM, stood with them.*

> ***John 18:6*** *As soon then as HE had said unto them,* ***I AM HE,*** *they went backward, and fell to the ground.*

NOTE: The POWER in the WORDS of JESUS when HE had spoken, ***"I AM HE";*** DEMONSTRATED the POWER in the *WORD of* ***GOD (THE ROD of IRON).*** This is why the Scriptures say that when the Pharisees and those in company with them heard HIS WORDS, they all fell backwards to the ground. The Scripture also DEMONSTRATES that JESUS had POWER over HIS Captors, for by HIS WORDS ALONE HE could have defeated them, if it had been the WILL of ***GOD.***

> ***John 18:7*** *Then asked HE them again,* ***WHOM SEEK YE?*** *And they said, JESUS of Nazareth.*

> ***John 18:8*** *JESUS answered,* ***I HAVE TOLD YOU THAT I AM HE: IF THEREFORE YOU SEEK ME, LET THESE GO THEIR WAY:***

JESUS requested that the Pharisees let HIS Disciples go, so HIS PROMISE to ***GOD*** in keeping ELEVEN Disciples from harms way, would be KEPT. For JESUS had said in HIS PRAYER to ***GOD***, "***OF THEM WHICH THOU GAVEST ME HAVE I LOST NONE (John 17:12)***".

Hearing the commotion, the Disciples awaken and gather around JESUS, and Simon Peter draws his sword and cuts off the right ear of Mal'-chus who was an armed servant for the High Priest. But JESUS rebukes Peter for doing it, and tells him to put his sword away and into its sheath. JESUS takes the ear that had been cut off and puts it back onto Mal'-chus' head, and it was instantly HEALED. JESUS then says to Simon Peter, "SHOULD I NOT FULFILL THAT WHICH I WAS SENT BY ***THE FATHER*** TO DO"?

The Officers then bind JESUS' hands in front of HIM with a CORD, and lead HIM off to An'-nas, who was the father-in-law of Ca'-ia-phas, the High Priest. Ca'-ia-phas, the High Priest, was the one who had RECEIVED the PROPHECY and said that ONE MAN WOULD DIE FOR ALL THE PEOPLE. It was also Ca'-ia-phas who had told the Pharisees that the MAN in the PROPHECY was JESUS of Nazareth, and how JESUS must die to SAVE ISRAEL.

An'-nas then led JESUS by the cord to the synagogue where Ca'-ia-phas was, and Simon Peter and Joseph of Ar-i-ma-thae'-a (who was a very wealthy man and also a SECRET Disciple) followed covertly behind them. Once at the Synagogue, Joseph of Ar-i-ma-thae'-a went in with JESUS and HIS captors; for he had known Ca'-ia-phas, but Simon Peter waited outside and was not allowed in. But Joseph of Ar-i-ma-thae'-a talked with the woman minding the door and she then let Simon Peter in. Once the woman sees Simon Peter's face she recognizes him as one of JESUS' Disciples. But when confronted by the woman, Peter denies ever knowing JESUS, and moves over to the fireplace to warm his hands.

Meanwhile, Ca'-ia-phas interrogates JESUS and asks HIM about HIS Disciples, and also about the DOCTRINE HE had been TEACHING to the people. But JESUS tells him that ALL of HIS TEACHING was done OPENLY in the TEMPLE or at the Synagogues and not in secret, and there were many of the Jews in attendance. JESUS says to Ca'-ia-phas, HE had TAUGHT openly in front of the Jews and hid nothing from them, and if he wanted to know what was said, he should ask the Jews.

After telling Ca'-ia-phas this, one of the Officers standing next to JESUS slaps JESUS across the face, accusing HIM of being disrespectful to the High Priest.

> ***John 18:23*** *JESUS answered him,* ***IF I HAVE SPOKEN EVIL, BEAR WITNESS OF THE EVIL: BUT IF WELL, WHY SMITEST THOU ME?***

While warming himself at the fire, Simon Peter stood next to a couple of men who thought they had seen him with JESUS, and they said to Peter; he looked like one of JESUS' Disciples. But Simon Peter again denied that he knew JESUS, and said, I am not a Disciple of HIS. Then shortly thereafter Mal'-chus, whom Simon Peter had cut off his ear in the GARDEN, sees Simon Peter, and he too asks Peter if he wasn't one of the Disciples with JESUS in the GARDEN? But Simon Peter again denies that he knows JESUS, and at that moment of Peter's THIRD DENIAL of JESUS CHRIST the cock crew. Peter then REMEMBERED what JESUS had told him, of how he would DENY HIM THREE TIMES PRIOR TO THE COCK CROWING.

Still being bound, JESUS was then taken from the Synagogue and led to the Roman Judgment Hall. But the Jews didn't want to enter the Judgment Hall for fear of defiling themselves by being in a heathen place for judgment. Their being there concerned them that they would make themselves unclean and not fit to celebrate the PASSOVER. So they summoned the Governor, Pon'-tius Pilate, and he came out to see what they wanted.

When Pilate sees JESUS bound like a prisoner, he asks HIS captors what they were accusing HIM of? The Jews then tell Pilate, JESUS was a criminal and worthy to be put to death. But Pilate tells them they should judge JESUS themselves and punish HIM according to their own law. But the Jews remind Pilate that it is against Roman law for the Jews to kill anyone. So Pilate agrees to give JESUS a hearing and summonses HIM to the Judgment Hall.

Pilate then asks JESUS if HE were a KING of the Jews, and JESUS replies; ***IS THIS SOMETHING YOU HAVE CONCLUDED ON YOUR OWN, OR DID SOMEONE TELL YOU I AM THE KING OF THE JEWS?***

> ***John 18:35*** *Pilate answered, Am I a Jew? Thine own nation and the Chief Priests have delivered thee unto me: what hast thou done?*

> ***John 18:36*** *JESUS answered,* ***MY KINGDOM IS NOT OF THIS WORLD: IF MY KINGDOM WERE OF THIS WORLD, THEN WOULD MY SERVANTS FIGHT, THAT I SHOULD NOT BE DELIVERED TO THE JEWS: BUT NOW IS MY KINGDOM NOT FROM HENCE.***

> ***John 18:37*** *Pilate therefore said unto HIM, art thou a KING then? JESUS answered,* ***THOU SAYEST THAT I AM A KING. TO THIS END WAS I BORN, AND FOR THIS CAUSE CAME I INTO THE WORLD, THAT I SHOULD BEAR WITNESS UNTO THE TRUTH. EVERY ONE THAT IS OF THE TRUTH HEARETH MY VOICE.***

NOTE: JESUS tells Pilate, HIS KINGDOM is not of this world, for if it were HIS servants would fight to FREE HIM and would not have allowed the Jews to take HIM captive. HE further tells Pilate, at this time HIS KINGDOM is not on the earth (BUT **NOW** IS MY KINGDOM NOT FROM HENCE). JESUS says, for this reason (meaning HIS CRUCIFIXION) HE had come into the world, thus signifying HE had come to DIE on the CROSS. HE further tells Pilate HE had come to TEACH ***GOD'S*** CHILDREN the TRUE UNDERSTANDING of the *WORD of **GOD,*** and only those that ***GOD*** had INTENDED to RECEIVE HIS MESSAGE have RECEIVED IT!

After hearing what JESUS had to say, Pilate sees the situation as being an internal power struggle between the Jewish Religion and those preferring to follow JESUS and HIS DOCTRINE. So Pilate goes out and tells the Jews, he cannot find anything wrong that JESUS had done worthy of criminal punishment. Pilate further tells them that he has agreed by their custom to free one prisoner for the PASSOVER, and asks if they want him to free JESUS. Then showing his arrogance toward the Jews, Pilate refers to JESUS as being their KING, but the crowd shouts back to Pilate to release Bar-ab'-bas, who was a convicted robber, rather than JESUS.

The Whipping and Humiliation

After hearing the angry crowd shout back that they had wanted Bar-ab'-bas released rather than JESUS, Pilate took JESUS down to the stocks, and had HIM WHIPPED. The Centurions then braided a crown from a vine of thorns and pushed the crown down onto JESUS' HEAD causing BLOOD to stream down HIS FACE. They also removed HIS ROBE and put HIM into a PURPLE ROBE, one like a King would have worn, and brought HIM out on to the terrace for ALL the people to see how HE had been HUMILIATED.

NOTE: Although Pilate had thought what he was doing was of his own accord, it was NOT! ALL he had done to JESUS was a reenactment of Scripture, to fulfill the PROPHECY GIVEN about JESUS and how HE was to be TREATED. These things were done to VERIFY JESUS as being the CHRIST, the MESSIAH. The following Scriptures taken from the Book of Isaiah were WRITTEN approximately ONE THOUSAND YEARS before the BIRTH OF JESUS CHRIST. Review the detail in the Scriptures regarding how JESUS was to be treated and YOU will see that ***GOD*** had PLANNED it ALL!

> ***Isaiah 53:5*** *But HE was WOUNDED for our transgressions, HE was BRUISED for our iniquities, the CHASTISEMENT of our*

peace was upon HIM; and with HIS STRIPES we are HEALED.

Isaiah 53:6 *All we like SHEEP have gone astray; we have turned every one to his own way; and* ***THE LORD*** *hath laid upon HIM the iniquity of us all.*

Isaiah 53:7 *HE was oppressed, and HE was afflicted, yet HE opened not HIS mouth: HE is brought as a LAMB to the slaughter, and as a SHEEP before her shearers is dumb, so HE openeth not HIS mouth.*

Isaiah 53:8 *HE was taken from prison and from JUDGMENT: and who shall DECLARE HIS GENERATION? For HE was cut off out of the land of the living: for the transgression of my people was HE stricken.*

When the crowd sees JESUS plated with a crown of thorns and in a purple robe they cry out to Pilate, "CRUCIFY HIM, CRUCIFY HIM". But Pilate again tells the angry crowd of Jews he cannot find any fault in JESUS and if they want HIM crucified they should do it themselves. The Jews then tell Pilate that JESUS proclaimed HIMSELF to be the SON of ***GOD*** and for doing so by Jewish Law HE should be put to death.

After hearing that JESUS had said HE was the SON of ***GOD*** Pilate becomes concerned, and asks JESUS again who HE was? But JESUS doesn't answer him, and Pilate says to JESUS, "Don't you realize I have the power to either CRUCIFY YOU or RELEASE YOU"?

John 19:11 *JESUS answered,* ***THOU COULDEST HAVE NO POWER AT ALL AGAINST ME, EXCEPT IT WERE GIVEN THEE FROM ABOVE: THEREFORE HE THAT DELIVERED ME UNTO THEE HATH THE GREATER SIN.***

NOTE: JESUS tells Pilate if it were not the DIVINE WILL of ***GOD*** for HIM to be CRUCIFIED, Pilate would be powerless against HIM. HE also tells Pilate, the JEWS and Judas who have BETRAYED HIM had committed the GREATER SIN than he, for they had delivered HIM to Pilate.

Pilate then wanted to release JESUS, but the Jews cried out all the more, "CRUCIFY HIM". The Jews then told Pilate that JESUS was a self proclaimed KING, and if Pilate were to release JESUS he would be dishonoring Caesar, for

Caesar was their King. After hearing this, Pilate decides to CONDEMN JESUS to DEATH by CRUCIFIXION, so he brings JESUS once more into the Judgment Hall before the Judgment Seat, a place called Gab'-ba-tha by the Jews, meaning, "PAVEMENT", for the Judgment Seat sat upon a slab of pavement.

The CRUCIFIXION

It was about noon (the sixth hour) and Pilate shouted out to the crowd, "BEHOLD YOUR KING"! The crowd then shouted back to Pilate, "CRUCIFY HIM, CRUCIFY HIM", and Pilate said, "SHALL I CRUCIFY YOUR KING"? The Chief Priests replied, "We have no King but Caesar", so Pilate ORDERED JESUS to be CRUCIFIED and they led HIM away carrying HIS CROSS upon HIS BACK to a place called in HEBREWAH, GOL'-GO-THA; meaning the place of the skull. There they CRUCIFIED JESUS and two other men with HIM, placing JESUS in the MIDDLE of two thieves, further fulfilling Scripture about JESUS, by HIM being amidst two TRANSGRESSORS at the time of HIS DEATH.

> ***Isaiah 53:12*** *Therefore will **I** divide HIM a portion with the GREAT, and HE shall divide the spoil with the STRONG; because HE hath poured out HIS SOUL unto DEATH: and HE was numbered with the TRANSGRESSORS; and HE bare the SIN of MANY, and made INTERCESSION for the TRANSGRESSORS.*

Pilate placed a plaque on the top of the CROSS of CRUCIFIXION that said, "JESUS OF NAZARETH THE KING OF THE JEWS", and it was written in three languages, Hebrew, Greek, and Latin.[11]

When the Chief Priests and the Pharisees saw the title above the CROSS; they asked Pilate to change the plaque to say, "HE SAID, I AM KING OF THE JEWS" rather than "THE KING OF THE JEWS". But Pilate said the WORDS would remain as they had been WRITTEN.

The four Centurions who nailed JESUS to the CROSS, ripped JESUS' under garment into four pieces so each of them could take a piece for themselves. However when they got to JESUS' ROBE it hadn't any seam for it was woven of a SINGLE THREAD and couldn't be torn apart. So the Centurions decided to cast lots for the ROBE; thus further fulfilling SCRIPTURE PROPHECY.

---

[11] These are the same three languages that the GOSPELS were WRITTEN in!

> ***Psalm 22:18*** *They part MY GARMENTS among them, and CAST LOTS upon MY VESTURE.*

At the CROSS stood THREE women, and all three had the name of MARY; Mary the mother of JESUS, Mary the wife of Clopas, and Mary Magdalene. When JESUS saw HIS mother standing there in shock looking at HIM, HE said, ***"WOMAN, BEHOLD THY SON"!*** Then JESUS looked DIRECTLY into the EYES of HIS Disciple John, and again back at HIS mother Mary, HE said to John, ***"BEHOLD THY MOTHER"!*** Thus meaning JESUS had chosen John to look after Mary as if she were John's own mother. From that very day forward, Mary, the mother of JESUS, lived with John until the day of her death.

About the ninth hour (3:00 PM) JESUS said HE was thirsty and asked for a drink, so one of the soldiers dipped a sponge on the end of a hyssop reed into a vial of vinegar and put it up to JESUS' MOUTH. After HE had tasted the vinegar HE BOWED HIS HEAD AND SAID, ***"IT IS FINISHED",*** thus meaning all SCRIPTURE regarding HIS DEATH had been FULFILLED and that the *WORD of* ***GOD*** had been COMPLETED. JESUS then GAVE UP THE ***HOLY SPIRIT.***

> ***Psalm 69:21*** *They gave ME also gall for MY meat; and in MY THIRST gave ME VINEGAR to DRINK.*

At the time of JESUS' DEATH, the sky became BLACK and it THUNDERED, and the GROUND QUAKED, and ALL that were in attendance suddenly became FRIGHTENED and they looked at one another with concern upon their faces; saying among themselves, SURELY THIS MAN MUST BE THE SON of ***GOD!***

The Jews not wanting the three CROSSES to remain up during the PASSOVER FEAST and it was also the SABBATH DAY, go to Pilate to ask him to remove the CROSSES. Pilate agrees and sends out his Centurions to break the legs of them who had been crucified. This was done to hasten the death of them that had been crucified by causing them to suffocate. However; once they had broken the legs of the two on either side of JESUS, much to their surprise, the Centurions saw that JESUS was already dead. So to make certain of it, they pierced HIS side with a spear, and WATER and BLOOD gushed out of HIS SIDE.

> ***Zechariah 12:10*** *And I will pour upon the HOUSE of DAVID, and upon the inhabitants of JERUSALEM, the* ***SPIRIT of GRACE*** *and*

of SUPPLICATIONS: and they shall LOOK upon ME whom they have PIERCED, and they shall mourn for HIM, as one mourneth for HIS ONLY SON, and shall be in bitterness for HIM, as one that is in bitterness for HIS FIRSTBORN.

John 19:38 *And after this Joseph of Ar-i-ma-thae'-a, being a Disciple of JESUS, but secretly for fear of the Jews, besought Pilate that he might take away the BODY of JESUS: and Pilate gave him leave. He came therefore and took the BODY of JESUS.*

After Joseph of Ar-i-ma-thae'-a took JESUS' BODY down from the CROSS, Nic-o-de'-mus came with ointments used for burial, and they wrapped JESUS in linen burial clothes after they anointed HIS BODY with the ointments (SPICES of cloves and MYRRH and ALOE). They then put JESUS' BODY into a tomb belonging to Joseph of Ar-i-ma-thae'-a that was in a GARDEN very near to where JESUS had been crucified. Then they and the other Disciples rolled a very large stone over the mouth of the tomb closing it off, in fear that the Jews would come and steal the BODY of JESUS.

17.13 The RESURRECTION of JESUS CHRIST

JESUS was CRUCIFIED shortly after noon on a Friday, the 14th day of April, and removed from the CROSS and placed into a sepulchre (tomb) by 9:00PM on that same day. However for the Jews the new day (Saturday the SABBATH) had begun, because the new day begins at EVEN (6:00PM in the evening) when the sun goes down and the first three stars are visible.

On Sunday the 16th of April, the SECOND DAY of PASSOVER, Mary Magdalene went to the TOMB of JESUS prior to daylight. When Mary arrived at the TOMB that morning she noticed that the very large stone that had been placed at its opening had been rolled away, and the opening to the TOMB was now accessible. Mary's first thoughts were that the Jews had come and taken JESUS' BODY from the TOMB. So before looking into the TOMB she ran off to find the Disciples and tell them what had happened.

Mary first finds John and Simon Peter and tells them that someone had come and removed the BODY of JESUS from the TOMB. They immediately then started running towards the TOMB and John was the first to arrive; but he didn't enter the TOMB but rather looks inside and sees only the linen grave clothes lying where JESUS had been laid. When Simon Peter arrives at the TOMB he enters and sees the grave clothes wadded up in one place, and the hood (the napkin) lying in another, and there is significance as to why the Scriptures so noted how the grave clothes were found laying in the TOMB.

NOTE: If someone (such as the Jews) were to come and take the BODY of JESUS from the tomb they **would not** have removed the grave clothes from HIS BODY. However, if JESUS were to be RISEN from the DEAD and ASSISTED by the ANGELS to remove HIS grave clothes, the ANGELS would have FIRST removed the hood from off HIS HEAD so JESUS could SEE them, therefor tossing the hood aside. The remaining grave clothes HE was wrapped in would then be removed and left to lie where they were taken off. The Scriptures so indicate that the ANGELS ASSISTED JESUS in the removal of HIS grave clothes, and they afterwards came back to the tomb to be seen by Mary so she could CONFIRM their APPEARANCE.

> ***John 20:6*** *Then cometh Simon Peter following him, and went into the sepulchre, and seeth the linen clothes lie,*
>
> ***John 20:7*** *And the napkin, that was about HIS HEAD, not lying with the linen clothes, but wrapped together in a place by itself.*
>
> ***John 20:8*** *Then went in also that other Disciple, which came first to the sepulchre, and he SAW, and BELIEVED.*

NOTE: Once Simon Peter and John had seen that someone had come and rolled away the large stone from the mouth of the tomb and JESUS' BODY had been removed, they realized that HE had RISEN from the DEAD and had not been taken by the JEWS. They knew if anyone were to steal the BODY of JESUS, they would not have removed HIS grave clothes and embalming ointments from HIM, for fear of contracting a disease from HIS decomposing BODY.

John and Simon Peter then left the tomb and went to their homes, but Mary Magdalene stayed at the tomb and mourned over the loss of JESUS, as she, (unlike John and Simon Peter), was unaware of HIS RESURRECTION.

As Mary kneeled in the front of the tomb and wept, she looked inside of the tomb and saw two ANGELS sitting where the body of JESUS had lain. The ANGELS then say to Mary, "why do you weep"? And Mary replies; they have taken away the BODY of my LORD and I do not know where they have put HIM. As soon as Mary had replied to the ANGELS, she then turned and saw JESUS standing behind her, but she didn't recognize HIM and thinks HE is the Gardener.

John 20:15 *JESUS saith unto her,* ***WOMAN, WHY WEEPEST THOU? WHOM SEEKEST THOU?*** *She, supposing HIM to be the Gardener, saith unto HIM. Sir, if thou have borne HIM hence, tell me where thou hast laid HIM, and I will take HIM away.*

John 20:16 *JESUS saith unto her,* ***MARY,*** *She turned herself, and saith unto HIM, Rab-bo'-ni; which is to say, MASTER.*

John 20:17 *JESUS saith unto her,* ***TOUCH ME NOT; FOR I AM NOT YET ASCENDED TO MY FATHER: BUT GO TO MY BRETHREN, AND SAY UNTO THEM, I ASCEND UNTO MY FATHER, AND YOUR FATHER; AND TO MY GOD, AND YOUR GOD.***[12]

JESUS tells Mary to go and tell the Disciples, whom HE then refers to as HIS BROTHERS, that she has seen HIM and HE is about to ASCEND to HIS ***FATHER,*** and JESUS says that HIS ***FATHER*** is also their ***FATHER.*** HE also says that HIS ***GOD*** is their ***GOD,*** thus making the Disciples an EQUIVALENCY to HIM.

NOTE: JESUS does this SPECIFICALLY, because the Disciples were soon to BECOME ONE IN CHRIST through MARRIAGE (UNITY). Once the BRIDE is MARRIED to the GROOM, SHE takes on the GROOM'S SURNAME, CHRIST; and in the EYES of ***GOD*** and in the EYES of THE ***HOLY SPIRIT*** the BRIDE and the GROOM are then EQUIVALENT (the ONLY BEGOTTEN of the ***FATHER***)! JESUS also instructs Mary to not TOUCH HIM, for HE hadn't yet ASCENDED to HEAVEN. HE does this for TWO REASONS; the FIRST reason is that HE was NOW in a SPIRITUAL FORM and Mary would not be able to FEEL HIM. The SECOND and most important REASON; is that Mary had not yet been BAPTIZED in THE ***HOLY SPIRIT*** and was UNCLEAN, and even though she would not be able to FEEL JESUS, if she were to TOUCH HIM, HE WOULD HAVE ALSO BECAME UNCLEAN.

---

[12] When Mary Magdalene first SEES JESUS, she doesn't recognize HIM because HE had taken on another APPEARANCE, therefor she assumes HE is the Gardener. But as soon as JESUS SPEAKS to Mary, she then realizes it is JESUS that is speaking to her, because she KNOWS ***HIS VOICE***. What did JESUS say in regard to HIS SHEEP KNOWING HIS VOICE? (***John 10:4 AND WHEN HE PUTTETH FORTH HIS OWN SHEEP, HE GOETH BEFORE THEM, AND THE SHEEP FOLLOW HIM: FOR THEY KNOW HIS VOICE.***)

Mary then goes to the Disciples and tells them what she had just SEEN, and also tells them what JESUS had said to her, but not all of them believe her. Then on that very same DAY, the Disciples gathered where they had often met with JESUS, and when they were all in attendance, except for Thomas, they locked the DOORS fearing the Jews would come looking for them. After the area had been secured, JESUS then appeared to them and SAID, ***"PEACE BE UNTO YOU".***

> ***John 20:21*** *Then said JESUS to them again,* ***PEACE BE UNTO YOU: AS MY FATHER HATH SENT ME, EVEN SO SEND I YOU.***
>
> ***John 20:22*** *And when HE had said this, HE BREATHED on them, and saith unto them,* ***RECEIVE YE THE HOLY GHOST:***
>
> ***John 20:23 WHOSE SOEVER SINS YE REMIT, THEY ARE REMITTED UNTO THEM; AND WHOSE SO EVER SINS YE RETAIN, THEY ARE RETAINED.***

NOTE: These Scriptures DENOTE JESUS' ORDAINING of HIS DISCIPLES to carry on HIS MINISTRY by way of THE ***HOLY SPIRIT.*** JESUS tells them that anyone who comes to them and remits their SINS, and RECEIVES ***HOLY SPIRIT*** BAPTISM, WILL BE SAVED. This is because the DISCIPLES will be HOST to THE ***HOLY SPIRIT*** WHO PRESIDES OVER JUDGMENT. He also says, anyone who they have REFUSED, will not be SAVED; and, those REFUSED will also be a DETERMINATION made by ***HOLY SPIRIT*** JUDGMENT.

Afterwards the DISCIPLES tell Thomas about them SEEING and SPEAKING to JESUS, for he was absent from their MEETING, but Thomas refuses to believe them. Thomas says; unless he could put his fingers into the nail prints on JESUS' HANDS, and stick his hand into the SIDE of JESUS where HE had been pierced by the spear, he would not believe that JESUS was ALIVE.

On the following MONDAY, the DISCIPLES meet again at the same place where they had SPOKEN to JESUS eight days prior; only this time Thomas was with them. Once the doors were shut and secured, JESUS again appears to them, and SAYS, ***PEACE BE UNTO YOU.***[13]

---

[13] This is another way of SAYING, LET THE ***HOLY SPIRIT*** BE WITH YOU, for PEACE comes by way of THE COMFORTER: WHOM IS THE ***HOLY SPIRIT.***

JESUS then tells Thomas to stick his fingers into the nail prints on HIS HANDS, and to ALSO put his hand into HIS SIDE that had been pierced, so Thomas could BELIEVE it was indeed JESUS standing AMIDST them. After Thomas had done so and seen that it was JESUS CHRIST standing with them, he says:

> ***John 20:28*** *And Thomas answered and said unto HIM, MY LORD and MY GOD.*

> ***John 20:29*** *JESUS saith unto him,* ***THOMAS, BECAUSE THOU HAST SEEN ME, THOU HAST BELIEVED: BLESSED ARE THEY THAT HAVE NOT SEEN, AND YET HAVE BELIEVED.***

NOTE: This is why the NEW COVENANT is a COVENANT governed by FAITH. For only a FEW witnessed the RESURRECTION of JESUS CHRIST, and ONLY BY FAITH SHALL THEY WHO HAVE NOT SEEN, BELIEVE! This is why the FIRST GIFT GIVEN BY THE ***HOLY SPIRIT*** is ALWAYS the GIFT of FAITH.

> ***John 20:30*** *And many other signs TRULY did JESUS in the presence of HIS DISCIPLES, WHICH ARE NOT WRITTEN IN THIS BOOK:*

> ***JOHN 20:31*** *But these are WRITTEN, that ye might BELIEVE that JESUS is the CHRIST, the SON of* ***GOD;*** *and that BELIEVING ye might have LIFE through HIS NAME.*

17.14 Final MIRACLE and RAPTURE

> ***John 21:1*** *After these things JESUS shewed HIMSELF again to the DISCIPLES at the sea of Ti-be'-ri-as; and on this wise shewed HE HIMSELF.*

> ***John 21:2*** *There were together Simon Peter, and Thomas called Did'-y-mus, and Na-than'-a-el of Cana in Galilee, and the sons of Zeb'-e-dee, and two other of HIS DISCIPLES.*

The sons of Zeb'-e-dee are James and John, and the two other DISCIPLES spoken of in the Scripture are Philip and Andrew, thus making the group consist of

SEVEN DISCIPLES. These are them who THE LORD had chosen to WITNESS HIS FINAL MIRACLE, and RAPTURE, although it was only Na-than'-a-el who clearly saw what had taken place at the TIME of RAPTURE. This is a list of the SEVEN:

1) Simon Peter
2) Thomas
3) James
4) John
5) Philip
6) Andrew
7) Na-than'-a-el

NOTE: Wherever in the GOSPELS it is noted by Scripture that JESUS was taken up to HEAVEN in the presence of HIS DISCIPLES, it is so WITNESSED by the TESTIMONY of Na-than'-a-el alone. Although there were SIX other DISCIPLES present at the time of JESUS' RAPTURE, it was unclear to all but Na-than'-a-el as to what had actually taken place. It was Na-than'-a-el who saw HEAVEN OPEN and the ANGELS ASCENDING and DESCENDING on JESUS CHRIST, just as JESUS had told him he would during their very first meeting. The other DISCIPLES only saw that JESUS had suddenly DISAPPEARED out of the MIDST of them and did not SEE the RAPTURE take place as Na-than'-a-el had WITNESSED! This is what JESUS had told Na-than'-el when they first met:

> ***John 1:51*** *And HE saith unto him,* ***VERILY, VERILY, I SAY UNTO YOU, HEREAFTER YE SHALL SEE HEAVEN OPEN, AND THE ANGELS OF GOD ASCENDING AND DESCENDING UPON THE SON OF MAN.***

When the SEVEN DISCIPLES had gathered together at the Sea of Ti-be'-ri-as, Simon Peter suggested they all go fishing; so they got into a boat and went out to sea. That night they hadn't caught any fish, and on the following morning as they were returning to the shore, JESUS stood on the beach and asked them if they had caught any fish; and they said they had not. Although they were not out more than a few hundred feet from the shoreline and could see the MAN who had spoken to them CLEARLY, they did not realize the MAN they were SPEAKING to was JESUS CHRIST.

> ***John 21:6** And HE said unto them, **CAST THE NET ON THE RIGHT SIDE OF THE SHIP, AND YE SHALL FIND.** They cast therefore, and now they were not able to draw it for the multitude of fishes.*

Once the DISCIPLES had heard the MAN say, "Cast the Net on the RIGHT SIDE of the Ship, and YE SHALL FIND", they then REALIZED it WAS THE VOICE of JESUS, and the DISCIPLE John said to Simon Peter, the MAN on the SHORE is THE LORD. So Simon Peter, being naked, immediately put on his fisher's coat and jumped overboard so he could hastily swim to shore.

Once Simon Peter gets to the shore he sees that the MAN who had spoken to them has a fire going with fish cooking on it, and also has BREAD for them to eat. JESUS, who is the MAN, tells the DISCIPLES to bring to shore the net full of fish. As they drag the net up onto the shore they count the fish and the number of them is ONE HUNDRED and FIFTY-THREE. The NUMBER "153" REPRESENTS the FIRST and the LAST MIRACLE of JESUS CHRIST on EARTH, for HE had CONVERTED ONE HUNDRED and FIFTY-THREE gallons of water into WINE for HIS FIRST MIRACLE.

The MAN on the shore did not look like JESUS but they knew it was HIM by the sound of HIS VOICE, and by what HE had said to them. When JESUS had FIRST met the Disciples, HE told them if they wanted to catch fish they needed to cast their nets on the other side of the boat (Luke 5:4) just as HE had done on this day. But more so, the DISCIPLES recognized JESUS' VOICE; and even though this MAN did not look like JESUS, they KNEW it was HE.

> ***John 21:12** JESUS saith unto them, **COME AND DINE.** And none of the DISCIPLES durst ask HIM, WHO ART THOU? Knowing that it was THE LORD.*

JESUS then gave them all both the BREAD and the FISH HE had cooked to eat, and this was the THIRD TIME after HIS RESURRECTION HE had APPEARED. After they had eaten, JESUS then asks Simon the son of Jo'-nas (formerly called Simon Peter by JESUS) if he LOVED HIM; and Simon Peter answers YES, and JESUS tells him to FEED HIS LAMBS. Then JESUS asks Simon Peter TWICE more the exact same thing, and Simon Peter TWICE more says that he does LOVE JESUS, and he becomes annoyed by JESUS' asking him THREE TIMES the same question. JESUS says to Simon Peter the SECOND and THIRD time after Simon Peter replied, "FEED MY SHEEP".

NOTE: JESUS had Simon Peter CONFIRM his LOVE for HIM THREE

TIMES, because THREE TIMES Peter DENIED knowing JESUS; after JESUS had been taken captive by the Jews.

After Simon, son of Jo'-nas had confirmed he LOVED JESUS, JESUS tells Simon how he was to die. The Scripture (John 21:18) is a bit difficult to INTERPRET, but what JESUS is telling Simon in the Scripture, is that he was to be CRUCIFIED while hanging upside down, and this is how Simon Peter met his death, SEVENTY-SEVEN YEARS after JESUS had told him of it. After Simon Peter hears how he was going to die, he then asks JESUS how the DISCIPLE John would die and JESUS replied to PETER in this way:

> ***John 21:22*** *JESUS saith unto him,* ***IF I WILL THAT HE TARRY TILL I COME, WHAT IS THAT TO THEE? FOLLOW THOU ME.***

> ***John 21:23*** *Then went this saying abroad among the BRETHREN, that that DISCIPLE should not die: yet JESUS said not unto him, He shall not die;* ***IF I WILL THAT HE TARRY TILL I COME, WHAT IS THAT TO THEE?***

NOTE: What JESUS was telling Simon, son of Jo'-nas (Simon Peter), was that the SPIRIT of the DISCIPLE John would continue on the earth, until JESUS' SECOND COMING. The ANGEL in the Revelation of JESUS CHRIST tells John this very same thing again, and this is why John refers to himself in the Book of Revelation as a BROTHER and COMPANION in the TRIBULATION. For the SPIRIT of the DISCIPLE John remains on earth, even until this very day, and he will endure the GREAT TRIBULATION being the LEADER of the TRIBULATION SAINTS. When the PERSON bearing the SPIRIT of John dies, that very same SPIRIT enters into a NEWBORN CHILD, and continues to PREACH upon the earth, up until the RETURN of JESUS. Many of the GREAT PREACHERS of the GOSPELS since JESUS had walked with John, were of the SPIRIT of John.

> ***Revelation 10:11*** *And he said unto me, THOU MUST PROPHESY AGAIN BEFORE MANY PEOPLES, AND NATIONS, AND TONGUES, AND KINGS.*

NOTE: In this last Scripture, the ANGEL is telling John, he will continue to PREACH upon the earth to many different people, in many different nations, in different languages, and will even PREACH before Kings. The man bearing the

SPIRIT of John this day is a well-known PREACHER living in America, but having his ROOTS in the Middle East!

> ***John 21:24*** *This is the DISCIPLE which testifieth of these things, and WROTE these things: and we know that his TESTIMONY is TRUE.*

> ***John 21:25*** *And there are also many other things which JESUS did, the which, if they should be WRITTEN every one, I suppose that even the world itself could not contain the BOOKS that should be WRITTEN. A-MEN'*

This concludes the MESSAGE of JOHN'S GOSPEL. MAY THE GRACE of ***GOD*** and the LOVE of JESUS CHRIST BE WITH YOU ALL; ***A-MEN'***

Chapter 18

END TIME Prophecy

END TIME PROPHECY is woven throughout the FABRIC of the entire HOLY BIBLE. The HISTORY of the EARTH from its beginning to its end and every major EVENT to take place in the world, is denoted within the Bible's SCRIPTURES. The LIFE CYCLE of the EARTH continues to go on throughout ETERNITY and is NEVER ENDING SAITH THE LORD; yet the PROPHECY of the EARTH'S DESTRUCTION is made quite CLEAR. Is this a CONTRADICTION in the Scriptures, or just a misunderstanding of them?

This Chapter will EXPLAIN how the Earth continues on and is yet DESTROYED in its ENTIRETY every SEVEN THOUSAND YEARS. However, before WE can EXPLAIN this phenomena, WE must FIRST give a CLEAR definition of what the WORD "Earth" means; and WE will do so by SCRIPTURE.

> ***Genesis 1:2*** *And the EARTH was without form and VOID; and darkness was upon the face of the deep. And THE* ***SPIRIT of GOD*** *moved upon the FACE of the WATERS.*

> ***Genesis 1:3*** *And* ***GOD*** *SAID, LET THERE BE LIGHT: and there was LIGHT.*

From these last two Scriptures it can be SEEN, that even before CREATION, the HOLY BIBLE speaks about the EARTH, saying that it was VOID and without FORM. So what is the EARTH? In the FOLLOWING Scriptures, the HOLY BIBLE DEFINES what the WORD "EARTH" means:

> ***Genesis 1:9*** *And* ***GOD*** *SAID, LET THE WATERS UNDER THE HEAVEN BE GATHERED TOGETHER UNTO ONE PLACE, AND LET THE DRY LAND APPEAR: and it was so.*

> ***Genesis 1:10*** *And* ***GOD*** *called the DRY LAND "EARTH"; and the*

gathering together of the WATERS called ***HE*** *"SEAS": and* ***GOD*** *saw that it was GOOD.*

According to the Scriptures, the BIBLE DEFINES the EARTH as a place where there is "DRY LAND", and DOES NOT specifically refer to the EARTH as being a single PLANET, such as the PLANET in this Solar System called Earth. Therefor; anyplace having DRY LAND that will support LIFE, by it having LIGHT and WATER in the BIBLICAL SENSE, is EARTH. This is why the BIBLE in its SCRIPTURES refers to "THE EARTH" (being two WORDS) rather than simply saying only the WORD "Earth", when it refers to the dwelling place of MANKIND.

Relative DESTRUCTION

In the beginning of the PREVIOUS BOOK (Revealing the Bible's TRUTH), The BOOK speaks of the DESTRUCTION of the UNIVERSE at the CONCLUSION of the world.

However, at the END of the same BOOK, it states; rather than the entire UNIVERSE being DESTROYED, only the EARTH and its SOLAR SYSTEM is DESTROYED. When the PREVIOUS BOOK had been completed, and I had been informed by ***GOD*** that only the EARTH and its SOLAR SYSTEM is DESTROYED, I could have simply went back and changed it in the BOOK. All references made to the DESTRUCTION of the "UNIVERSE" could have been changed to say the DESTRUCTION of the "SOLAR SYSTEM". However, THE LORD wanted it to remain as it had initially been WRITTEN! THE LORD had ME leave it this way because it more accurately fit the MINDSET of the SCRIPTURES regarding the DESTRUCTION of the Heavens and the Earth.

Although this may seem to be a bit CONFUSING to you, it really serves a PURPOSE being this way, and is not CONFLICTING with the SCRIPTURES. This is because the BIBLE Scriptures regarding the "WORLD", refers only to THE EARTH and its SOLAR SYSTEM, and not to the UNIVERSE in its ENTIRETY. Therefor, when READING in the Scriptures, and seeing the use of the WORD "WORLD" or "Heavens", realize that the Scriptures are referring to an independent SOLAR SYSTEM and not the UNIVERSE. Furthermore, any references made to "THE EARTH", relate to any place where there is DRY LAND, WATER, and LIGHT being SUPPORTIVE of CARNAL LIFE, and not only to the planet Earth. There are MANY EARTH-LIKE planets within the UNIVERSE, more than the SANDS of the SEAS.

When one EARTH is DESTROYED, then another is CREATED. There have been MANY PLANETS called EARTH, and the WORD EARTH does not just apply to this particular planet; for there was an EARTH before it, and there will be an EARTH again, after it! THE LORD CAN MAKE A NEW EARTH OR THE LORD CAN RE-NEW THE FACE of the EARTH ***HE*** HAD PREVIOUSLY DESTROYED. The Scriptures tell us of BOTH of these SCENARIOS:

> ***Psalm 104:30*** *Thou sendest forth thy **SPIRIT,** they are CREATED: and thou RENEWEST the FACE of the EARTH.*

This is why the Scriptures can SPEAK about a TOTAL DESTRUCTION of the EARTH, and yet say, the EARTH will ENDURE forever, without being CONTRADICTORY.

THE EARTH'S TOTAL DESTRUCTION:

> ***Isaiah 24:19*** *The EARTH is utterly BROKEN DOWN, the EARTH is clean DISSOLVED, the EARTH is MOVED exceedingly.*

> ***Isaiah 24:20*** *The EARTH shall REEL to and fro like a drunkard, and shall be REMOVED like a cottage; and the TRANSGRESSION thereof shall be heavy upon it; AND IT SHALL FALL, and **<u>NOT RISE AGAIN.</u>***

THE EARTH'S CONTINUANCE and RENEWAL:

> ***Ecclesiastes 1:4*** *One GENERATION passeth away, and another GENERATION COMETH: but the **<u>EARTH ABIDETH FOR EVER.</u>***

The BIBLE Scripture is WRITTEN to so indicate that the EARTH and its SOLAR SYSTEM is an independent WORLD of its own, being SUPPORTIVE of LIFE, and everything outside of that SOLAR SYSTEM, is IRRELEVANT to it and cannot INFLUENCE it. Therefor the DESTRUCTION of the WORLD consists of the DESTRUCTION of the LIGHT SOURCE (the Sun) and all that is DEPENDENT on that LIGHT SOURCE for its existence; thus making the DESTRUCTION, a RELATIVE DESTRUCTION of the Heavens and the Earth and not a DESTRUCTION of all of ***GOD'S CREATION.***

Destruction of a Star called the Sun, which is a STAR that gives LIGHT to any WORLD, is spoken about throughout the Scriptures. This is done throughout ETERNITY and does not only apply to the Sun that gives LIGHT to this WORLD, but to ALL STARS providing LIGHT to planets suitable for carnal life. The BIBLE speaks of the SUPER NOVA that occurs prior to the DEATH of a STAR giving LIGHT to a planet having WATER and DRY LAND. The Star prior to its NOVA intensifies in LIGHT and increases the HEAT it gives off, as explained in the Book of Revelation.

> ***Revelation 16:8*** *And the fourth ANGEL poured out his vial upon the SUN; and POWER was given unto him to SCORCH men with FIRE.*

> ***Revelation 16:9*** *And men were SCORCHED with GREAT HEAT, and blasphemed the NAME of* ***GOD,*** *which have POWER over these PLAGUES: and they repented not to give* ***HIM*** *GLORY.*

> ***Isaiah 30:26*** *Moreover the LIGHT of the MOON shall be as the LIGHT of the SUN, and the LIGHT of the SUN shall be SEVEN-FOLD, as the LIGHT of SEVEN DAYS, in the DAY that THE LORD bindeth up the BREACH of* ***HIS*** *PEOPLE, and healeth the stroke of their wound.*

The BIBLE also speaks about the changing of the COLOR of a STAR such as the SUN when it DIMS, to the COLOR RED, prior to its DEATH. It may also be NOTED that references in the BIBLE to those STARS being affected by the EVENTS of the SUN, are references to the other planets in that SOLAR SYSTEM.

> ***Revelation 8:12*** *And the FOURTH ANGEL sounded, and the third part of the SUN was smitten, and the third part of the MOON, and the third part of the STARS; so as the third part of them was DARKENED, and the day shone not for a third part of it, and the night likewise.*

> ***Revelation 6:12*** *And I beheld when he had opened the SIXTH SEAL, and lo, there was a great EARTHQUAKE; and the SUN became BLACK as sackcloth of hair, and the MOON became as BLOOD;*

Revelation 6:13 *And the stars of heaven fell unto the EARTH, even as a fig tree casteh her untimely figs, when she is shaken of a mighty wind.*

All these BIBLICAL references apply to the DESTRUCTION of the SUN and the EARTH and not to the entire UNIVERSE. The references to the STARS falling to the EARTH refer to a METEOR SHOWER that violently hits the EARTH. THE LORD DESTROYS the SUN and its SOLAR SYSTEM at the CONCLUSION of the LAST DAY, and then ***GOD*** provides the LIGHT for ***HIS*** PEOPLE from that TIME forward.

Isaiah 60:19 *The SUN shall be no more thy LIGHT by day; neither for brightness shall the MOON give light unto thee: but THE LORD shall be unto thee an EVERLASTING LIGHT, and thy* **GOD** *thy GLORY.*

Isaiah 60:20 *Thy SUN shall no more go down; neither shall thy MOON withdraw itself: for THE LORD shall be thine EVERLASTING LIGHT, and the DAYS of thy MOURNING shall be ENDED.*

Highlighting Isaiah's END TIME Prophecy of the WORLD

Throughout this Chapter WE will discuss the various SCRIPTURES that relate to PROPHECY of END TIME EVENTS. WE will name but a few of the BIBLICAL Chapters covering the EVENTS and will only list the MORE obvious ones; although throughout its ENTIRETY the BIBLE speaks about the EVENTS taking place at the END TIMES. Without the ability to SEE into the 3rd LAYER of the Scripture (the FUTURE), the EVENTS within the 3rd LAYER are not DISCERNIBLE. Therefor to inform you of them, ***GOD*** has CLEARLY described the OUTCOME of the WORLD at its CONCLUSION in various Scriptures of the BIBLE. This is a PARTIAL listing of the Books whose Chapters describe the END TIME EVENTS:

1. Chapter 24 and 66 of the Book of Isaiah
2. Chapter 24 of the GOSPEL of Matthew
3. Chapter 13 of the GOSPEL of Mark
4. Chapter 21 of the GOSPEL of Luke
5. Chapters 12,13, and 14 of the Book of Zechariah
6. Chapter 3 of the Book of Joel

7. Chapters 5 and 7 of the Book of Micah
8. Chapters 11 and 12 of the Book of Daniel
9. Chapters 8,9,10, and 11 of the Book of Ezekiel
10. Chapter 8 of the Book of Amos
11. ALL 5 Chapters of the Book of Lamentations (looking at references made to JERUSALEM as meaning; to the EARTH)
12. ALL 22 Chapters of the Book of Revelation

The Books Chapters from the aforementioned list should be READ in their entirety, for they will give you a FUNDAMENTAL UNDERSTANDING of the END TIME EVENTS. What is described in these Chapters Scriptures, should be taken MOST literally.

MINDFULLY, the Scriptures will be somewhat confusing and INCOMPREHENSIBLE. However, SPIRITUALLY, YOU WILL UNDERSTAND the MESSAGE GIVEN. In this Chapter WE will only HIGHLIGHT the 24th Chapter of the Book of the Prophet Isaiah, but WE strongly recommend that the other Chapters listed be READ by you as well.

Chapter 24 of the Book of *ISAIAH*

> ***Isaiah 24:1*** *BEHOLD, THE LORD maketh the EARTH empty, and maketh it WASTE, and turneth it UPSIDE DOWN, and scattereth abroad the inhabitants thereof.*

Let US shed some LIGHT of UNDERSTANDING on the PREVIOUS Scripture taken from the 24th Chapter of the Book of the Prophet Isaiah. The opening WORD; **"BEHOLD",** means to SEE, to BELIEVE, and to SPIRITUALLY EXPERIENCE what is about to be DESCRIBED in the SCRIPTURES. The Scripture starts by saying, "THE LORD maketh the EARTH EMPTY". The English definition of the WORD "EMPTY" means, something that is LACKING contents that could or should be present. But the SCRIPTURE uses the WORD "EMPTY" more so to mean **"VOID",** thus making the EARTH no longer VALID in support of LIFE.

The Scripture further says that THE LORD "MAKETH IT WASTE". The WORD "WASTE" as used in the Scripture, refers to the EARTH as being made **"BARREN", or "LIFELESS".** It then says, THE LORD "TURNETH IT UPSIDE DOWN". This refers to a MAGNETIC POLE REVERSAL of the EARTH'S magnetic polarity, thus making the EARTH'S North Pole magnetically the South Pole, and visa versa.

The balance of the Scripture says; THE LORD "SCATTERETH ABROAD THE INHABITANTS THEREOF"; this refers to the GREAT EARTHQUAKES caused by the EVENT. When the MAGNETIC POLE REVERSAL takes place, it will be so ABRUPT it will cause the dislodging of ALL MAJOR FAULT LINES in the EARTH. This will cause ALL the remaining people on the EARTH to be VIOLENTLY TOSSED ABOUT, and physically SCATTERED throughout the EARTH. The next Scripture in the 24th Chapter of Isaiah, tells you of who left on the EARTH, will be AFFECTED by the EVENT:

> ***Isaiah 24:2*** *And it shall be, as with the PEOPLE, so with the PRIEST; as with the SERVANT, so with his MASTER; as with the MAID, so with her MISTRESS; as with the BUYER, so with the SELLER: as with the LENDER, so with the BORROWER; as with the TAKER of usury, so with the GIVER of usury to him.*

The previous Scripture clearly STATES the EVENT will AFFECT each and every person REMAINING on the EARTH without EXCEPTION, therefor saying that all of the inhabitants of the EARTH will undergo this CALAMITY.

> ***Isaiah 24:3*** *The land shall be UTTERLY EMPTIED, and UTTERLY SPOILED: for THE LORD HATH SPOKEN THIS WORD.*

The Prophet Isaiah says in the last Scripture, ***GOD*** will DESTROY the EARTH by the EVENT, thus causing its PERMANENT and FINAL DESTRUCTION. Isaiah also notes in the Scripture that the EVENT will most CERTAINLY take PLACE for the ***ALMIGHTY GOD*** had TOLD him it would.

The next few Scriptures tell as to why ***GOD*** does this to the EARTH. The Scriptures also say there will be a few people that will TEMPORARILY SURVIVE the EVENT, as DESCRIBED in the 1st verse.

> ***Isaiah 24:4*** *The EARTH mourneth and fadeth away, the WORLD languisheth and fadeth away, the HAUGHTY PEOPLE of the EARTH languisheth.*

NOTE: As WE have previously mentioned in this Chapter, the EARTH and its SOLAR SYSTEM represent the WORLD as an ENTITY, and this is why the Prophet says that both the Earth and the World will languish and fade away, thus meaning the entire Solar System will be DESTROYED!

> ***Isaiah 24:5*** *The EARTH also is DEFILED under the INHABITANTS thereof; because they have TRANSGRESSED the LAWS, CHANGED the ORDINANCE, BROKEN the EVERLASTING COVENANT.*

> ***Isaiah 24:6*** *Therefore hath the CURSE DEVOURED the EARTH, and they that dwell therein are DESOLATE: therefore the INHABITANTS of the EARTH are BURNED, and FEW MEN LEFT.*

NOTE: The Scripture says the people have DEFILED the EARTH by their SINNING, and they have CHANGED THE *WORD of **GOD*** with their many TRANSLATIONS of the HOLY BIBLE ("Changed the Ordinance"). It also says they have BROKEN the NEW COVENANT of FAITH; thus bringing a CURSE upon the EARTH. Therefor, the CURSE will BURN many (meaning they will die quickly), and the FEW who SURVIVE the EVENTS of the CURSE will be CUT OFF from ***GOD*** and SUFFER; with them wishing they had DIED with the others.

The next few Scriptures show how the SURVIVORS that remain on the EARTH will FEEL, after the CALAMITY has occurred.

> ***Isaiah 24:7*** *The new wine MOURNETH, the vine languisheth, ALL the merry hearted do SIGH.*

> ***Isaiah 24:8*** *The mirth of the tabrets ceaseth, the noise of them that rejoice endeth, the joy of the harp ceaseth.*

> ***Isaiah 24:9*** *They shall not drink wine with a song; strong drink shall be bitter to them that drink it.*

> ***Isaiah 24:10*** *The city of CONFUSION is broken down: every house is shut up, that no man may come in.*

> ***Isaiah 24:11*** *There is a crying for wine in the streets; all joy is darkened, the mirth of the land is gone.*

> ***Isaiah 24:12*** *In the city is left DESOLATION, and the gate is smitten with DESTRUCTION.*

> ***Isaiah 24:13*** *When thus it shall be in the midst of the land among*

the PEOPLE, there shall be as the shaking of an olive tree, and as the gleaning grapes when the vintage is done.[1]

The SCRIPTURES clearly state that those who SURVIVE the EVENT spoken of in the 1st verse, will have nothing left to enjoy or live for; for there will not be any joy left in the world. The Scripture says; neither wine nor any type of alcoholic beverage will ease the burden of the SORROW the survivors will ENDURE. The EARTH will be full of CONFUSION, and the people will not look to each other for comfort or friendship; and will ISOLATE themselves from the other SURVIVORS of the EARTH. The EARTH at this point in time has become a place exhibiting only DESTRUCTION, and VOID of happiness; and one can only look forward to DEATH, rather than LIFE.

These PEOPLE will BEG ***GOD*** for MERCY, but it will then be TOO LATE for any SALVATION, for ***GOD*** will no longer hear their PLEAS. But to no avail they will continually cry out for ***GOD'S*** help, while ENDURING the PAIN being inflicted upon the EARTH.

Isaiah 24:14 *They shall lift up their voice, they shall sing for the MAJESTY of THE LORD, they shall cry ALOUD from the sea.*

Isaiah 24:15 *Wherefore GLORIFY ye THE LORD in the FIRES, even the NAME of THE LORD* ***GOD*** *of ISRAEL in the isles of the sea.*

Those left to SUFFER the GREAT TRIBULATION on EARTH will HEAR the REJOICING of them who have RECEIVED the RAPTURE, and will have heard how the RIGHTEOUS who had SERVED ***GOD*** have been put into a PLACE of PROTECTION. The DEMONS causing the EVENTS taking place on the EARTH cannot HARM the RIGHTEOUS, although they can freely TORMENT them who remain on EARTH.

Isaiah 24:16 *From the uttermost part of the EARTH have we heard songs, even glory to the RIGHTEOUS. But I said, MY LEANNESS, MY LEANNESS, WOE UNTO ME! The treacherous dealers have dealt treacherously; Yea, the treacherous dealers*

---

[1] The Scripture in Isaiah 24:13, refers to the SURVIVORS being equivalent to grapes that have been left on the vine to ROT, after the 1st picking. This refers to the 1st REAPING of the GRAPES spoken of in the Book of Revelation, verses 14:14 – 14:16. These are the PEOPLE who have been left behind on the EARTH to SUFFER the *WRATH of* ***GOD.***

have dealt very treacherously.

Isaiah 24:17 *FEAR, and the PIT, and the SNARE, are upon thee, O INHABITANT of the EARTH.*

The Scriptures explain what the SURVIVORS remaining on EARTH must undergo, and how the Devil, Demons, and the Plagues brought to bear on the EARTH, are inescapable!

Isaiah 24:18 *And it shall come to pass, that he who fleeth from the NOISE of the FEAR shall FALL INTO the PIT; and he that cometh up out of the midst of the PIT shall be TAKEN by the SNARE: for the WINDOWS from on HIGH are OPEN, and the foundations of the EARTH do SHAKE.*

Isaiah 24:19 *The EARTH is utterly BROKEN DOWN, the EARTH is clean DISSOLVED, the EARTH is MOVED exceedingly.*

Isaiah 24:20 *The EARTH shall reel to and fro like a drunkard, and shall be REMOVED like a cottage; and the TRANSGRESSION thereof shall be HEAVY upon it; and it shall FALL, and* ***NOT RISE AGAIN****.*

After the EARTH is nearly DESTROYED, THE LORD then PUNISHES the Devil, the Beast (Antichrist) and the FALSE Prophet, along with those of the EARTH who have SINNED against ***HIM.*** They will all be LOCKED UP in HELL for ONE THOUSAND YEARS (during the MILLENNIUM), and then Resurrected from the DEAD at the END of the LAST DAY for JUDGMENT. Only the Devil, Lucifer is released from HELL five months prior to the END of the LAST DAY, for he will gather those whom have not served ***GOD*** together, so they may SUFFER the FIRST DEATH (carnal death) prior to their JUDGMENT.

Isaiah 24:21 *And it shall come to pass in that day, that THE LORD shall PUNISH the Host of the High Ones that are on High, and the Kings of the EARTH upon the EARTH.*

Isaiah 24:22 *And they shall be GATHERED together, as PRISONERS are GATHERED in the PIT, and shall be shut up in the*

PRISON, and after MANY days shall they be VISITED.

After the JUDGMENT of them who had been raised from the DEAD, THE LORD will DESTROY COMPLETELY ALL of the EARTH and its SOLAR SYSTEM that REMAINS. The BEHEADED SOULS will then return to the DUST of the EARTH, while the GUESTS of the WEDDING SUPPER and the BRIDE, ASCEND UP to HEAVEN in CHRIST.

> ***Isaiah 24:23*** *Then the MOON shall be confounded, and the SUN ashamed, when THE **LORD of HOSTS** shall REIGN in MOUNT ZION, and in JERUSALEM, and before **HIS** Ancients GLORIOUSLY.*

Chapter 19
KNOWING

There are certain things ONE must KNOW in order to RECEIVE JESUS CHRIST as their LORD and SAVIOR, and through HIM RECEIVE ***HOLY SPIRIT*** BAPTISM and SAVING GRACE. ONE'S only CONNECTION to ***GOD*** comes by way of THE ***HOLY SPIRIT,*** and THE ***HOLY SPIRIT*** comes only by WAY of JESUS CHRIST, and JESUS CHRIST can only come to them who ***GOD*** has SENT HIM to.

The WORD "KNOWING" is defined as, to perceive directly or to UNDERSTAND, or to be FAMILIAR WITH that which would otherwise be UNKNOWN. It also means to be mentally keen or quick, having or exhibiting a CAPACITY for DISCERNMENT and the INTELLIGENT APPLICATION of KNOWLEDGE. HAVING KNOWLEDGE of CERTAIN KEY ELEMENTS is this Chapter's topic of DISCUSSION.

KNOWING YOUR *GOD*

Although YOU may not know ***GOD, HE*** certainly KNOWS YOU. BIBLE Scripture tells YOU that ***GOD*** KNOWS ALL THINGS, for ***HE*** is "ALL KNOWING". JESUS CHRIST says that ***GOD*** even numbers the hairs on your head, thus meaning that ***GOD*** KNOWS everything there is to KNOW about YOU at any particular TIME in your LIFE. Isn't it NOW TIME for YOU to KNOW YOUR ***GOD*** for ***HE*** already KNOWS YOU?

WE KNOW the Church would like to TEACH YOU how to DEVELOP a RELATIONSHIP with ***GOD,*** however this is something that CANNOT be taught for there are NO TWO RELATIONSHIPS the SAME, SAITH THE LORD. What THE LORD will allow one person to do, ***HE*** WILL DISALLOW another to do the SAME. One CANNOT share THEIR RELATIONSHIP WITH ***GOD*** with another, nor can they provide a GUIDELINE for another to FOLLOW. Only JESUS CHRIST and THE ROD of IRON (the *WORD of* ***GOD***) can PROVIDE the GUIDANCE needed to acquire a RELATIONSHIP with ***GOD.***

This is not to say a person should not witness to another ABOUT ***GOD,*** for it is a GOOD thing to SHARE YOUR EXPERIENCES with others. But YOUR EXPERIENCE hasn't anything in COMMON whatsoever with someone else's, for NO TWO RELATIONSHIPS with ***GOD*** WILL be the SAME. Other than the GUIDELINES GIVEN to YOU in SCRIPTURE, only THE LORD can determine what YOU should or shouldn't do, for ***HE*** WILL SET YOUR PATH, and each and every PERSON'S PATH is a DIFFERENT ONE.

Having a RELATIONSHIP with ***GOD*** can only come by way of ***GOD,*** for it is ***HIS CHOICE*** and not YOURS that a RELATIONSHIP EXIST between YOU and ***HE***. You cannot compare yourself to another person who is SERVING ***GOD,*** for there is but only one COMMON TRAIT among THOSE who SERVE ***GOD,*** and that is THEIR LOVE for ***GOD*** and for the others who ALSO LOVE and SERVE ***GOD.***

In summary; what is being told to YOU, is that neither I nor anyone else can tell YOU how you must SERVE ***GOD,*** for ***GOD*** can only TELL YOU THAT, and ***HE*** does so through ***HIS** WORD and **HIS SPIRIT.***

The only TANGIBLE CONNECTION in this world to THE LORD is through ***GOD'S** WORD,* and ONLY through ***HIS** WORD* can a RELATIONSHIP BE INITIATED. Anyone who is SEEKING to have a RELATIONSHIP with ***GOD*** must READ the HOLY BIBLE regularly. This is the BEGINNING of the CONVERSION PROCESS, and ONE MUST FIRST be CONVERTED before a RELATIONSHIP with ***GOD*** can be ACHIEVED. JESUS CHRIST told HIS DISCIPLES, their DIRECTION would come by way of THE ***HOLY SPIRIT*** and not by way of the Church, although the Church Leaders will try to tell you otherwise.

There are many believing, that by them going to Church on Sundays, and giving both time and money to charities, they have fulfilled their obligation to ***GOD;*** but this is a FALSEHOOD, SAITH THE LORD. SERVING ***GOD*** CANNOT be a GROUP AFFAIR or done simply on Sundays. This isn't about ***GOD*** getting to KNOW YOU while you're at Church; but it is rather about YOUR getting to KNOW ***GOD*** and making ***HIM*** a part of YOUR daily LIFE; and this must be done on an INDIVIDUAL BASIS.

The PROMISE made by JESUS CHRIST of SAVING GRACE only comes to those who diligently SEARCH for it by PRAYER and by READING the HOLY BIBLE. However, PRAYER is only answered when it is within the WILL of ***GOD,*** and the WILL of ***GOD*** can only be KNOWN by KNOWING the SCRIPTURES.

Entry into HEAVEN

There are only two ways for ONE to enter into HEAVEN, by ***DIVINE RIGHT*** or by being a GUEST of CHRIST. The Angel who has come down from HEAVEN to be a man or a woman has a DIVINE RIGHT back to HEAVEN. HOWEVER, those of YOU who are of the ANGELIC REALM haven't any RECOLLECTION of ever being an Angel, and it would be RISKY BUSINESS for one to ASSUME they are of the Angel.

The BRIDE of CHRIST also SHARES in the DIVINE RIGHT of JESUS CHRIST through MARRIAGE, so THEIR ACCESS TO HEAVEN WILL NEVER BE DENIED. HOWEVER, these are the ONES who HAVE BEEN CHOSEN by ***GOD*** to be the BRIDE, and THEIR BAPTISM and SAVING GRACE may not COME until they have DRAWN THEIR FINAL BREATH on EARTH. But by BELIEVING that YOU are of the BRIDE and YOUR BAPTISM will come automatically has even a lower probability than believing you are of the Angel; and this is ALSO RISKY BUSINESS. The NUMBERS of the BRIDE consists of only ONE HUNDRED AND FOUR MILLION, out of the TWENTY-ONE BILLION people having a life on EARTH. This NUMBER represents less than one-half of one percent of all the people who have ever lived in this world.

If an ASSUMPTION were to be made by you at all, it should be the ASSUMPTION that YOU are one of the WEDDING GUESTS of CHRIST, and if you are, YOUR BAPTISM will not come automatically. Therefor there are CERTAIN REQUIREMENTS that MUST be fulfilled for YOU to be INCLUDED as a WEDDING GUEST of CHRIST and have YOUR NAME put into the GUEST REGISTER.

The FIRST and MOST important REQUIREMENT is that YOU are BAPTIZED in THE ***HOLY SPIRIT***, and this must happen before your NAME can be added to the GUEST REGISTER. WE had covered this SUBJECT earlier in this BOOK, so you might want to go back and READ about it again.

There is a PROCESS to follow for the WEDDING GUESTS, if by the WILL of ***GOD*** you are a GUEST. The FIRST thing that MUST be done before ***HOLY SPIRIT*** BAPTISM can even be considered, is YOUR REPENTANCE of SIN to ***GOD.*** This is done OPENLY, PERSONALLY, and PRIVATELY before ***GOD*** in PRAYER. This SHOULD NOT be done in the PRESENCE of other people, for it is a PRIVATE MATTER between you and THE LORD.

If THE LORD ACCEPTS your REPENTANCE, ***HE*** THEN TAKES YOU TO THE CROSS of CRUCIFIXION, and there YOU WILL LEAVE YOUR

SIN. ONCE at the CROSS, ***GOD*** WILL REMIND YOU of each and every SIN YOU had ever COMMITTED, and give YOU the OPPORTUNITY to REPENT of them. After YOUR REPENTANCE has been ACCEPTED in its ENTIRETY by ***GOD***, ***HOLY SPIRIT*** BAPTISM WILL TAKE PLACE and YOUR NAME will be entered into THE GUEST REGISTER. There will not be any DOUBT in YOUR MIND that the BAPTISM had taken place, for THE ***HOLY SPIRIT of GOD*** WILL COME OVER YOU, and the FEELING you will EXPERIENCE will be like no other feeling YOU have ever had. This is the BEGINNING of CONVERSION, and NOW you will be GUIDED in ALL that YOU do by THE ***HOLY SPIRIT.***

Anything in YOUR previous life (life prior to CONVERSION) that THE LORD had OPPOSED WILL BE REMOVED from it. However, the things being REMOVED from YOUR LIFE will not BE MISSED or will YOU FEEL DEPRIVED of them.

Knowing who YOU are

It has been mentioned earlier in this BOOK, and more explicitly in the PREVIOUS BOOK, that there are THREE distinct types of people on the Earth. The FIRST TYPE is called "the BEAST" (***GOD'S*** SIXTH DAY CREATION), the SECOND TYPE is "the BLESSED" (the OFFSPRING of ADAM) and THIRD TYPE is "the DAMNED" (the Devil's offspring). These THREE TYPES of people are referred to in the BIBLE as the "GENTILE" who are the BEAST, the "HEBREW" who are the BLESSED, and the "CANAANITE", who are the DAMNED.

These THREE FORMS of LIFE on EARTH can be looked at in principle as being similar to the particles making up an ATOM. In this case, the GENTILE can be viewed as the NEUTRON, the HEBREW as the PROTON, and the CANAANITE as the ELECTRON. Whereas the GENTILE much like the NEUTRON of an ATOM isn't either POSITIVELY or NEGATIVELY charged within the NUCLEUS, when being moved outside of the NUCLEUS, it can take on either a POSITIVE or NEGATIVE CHARACTERISTIC. The HEBREW on the other hand, will always exhibit a POSITIVE CHARACTERISTIC like that of the PROTON, and the CANAANITE will always be NEGATIVE like the ELECTRON.

This is to say, whereas the PEDIGREE of the HEBREW will always be BLESSED and the PEDIGREE of the CANAANITE will always be DAMNED, the GENTILE can be MOVED in either of the TWO DIRECTIONS. Then depending on where it may finally be LOCATED and come to REST it will have taken on either a POSITIVE or a NEGATIVE CHARACTERISTIC. As with the NEUTRON of an ATOM, the GENTILE MUST be MOVED outside of the NUCLEUS in order for it to become either a POSITIVELY or NEGATIVELY CHARGED BODY, and therefor it needs an EXTERNAL INFLUENCE for the PHENOMENA to take place.

The GENTILE remaining in his or her ORIGINAL STATE (NEUTRAL) over the course of THEIR LIFE will simply RETURN to the DUST of the EARTH. This happens when the LIFE CYCLE of the WORLD or that person's life has been completed. But, if the GENTILE were to be moved and take on the CHARACTERISTIC of either the HEBREW or the CANAANITE, it will then either ASCEND to HEAVEN like the HEBREW, or descend to HELL like the CANAANITE, depending on its CHARACTERISTIC. This phenomenon was described in detail in the PREVIOUS BOOK, when WE addressed the meaning of the TREE of LIFE that sat in the middle of the Garden of Eden, and now sits in the MIDDLE of PARADISE.

The vast majority of the WEDDING GUESTS in HEAVEN (of whom WE had spoken about earlier) are comprised of GENTILES. Therefor it is IMPORTANT to know what EXTERNAL FORCE is NECESSARY to MOVE the GENTILE into a POSITIVE CHARACTERISTIC so they MIGHT take on the CHARACTERISTIC of the HEBREW (THE BLESSED).

It should be obvious that the external influence of the Devil will move the GENTILE in the NEGATIVE DIRECTION, whereas it should be equally as OBVIOUS that THE ***HOLY SPIRIT*** will move the GENTILE in a POSITIVE ONE. As explained earlier in this Chapter, ALL people SEEKING to KNOW their TRUE IDENTITY and their DESTINY should ASSUME (if an ASSUMPTION can be made), they are of the WEDDING GUESTS. The WEDDING GUESTS by far outnumber both the Angel and the BRIDE, therefor of the THREE GROUPS who WILL ASCEND to HEAVEN the HIGHEST PROBABILITY is that YOU will be ONE of the WEDDING GUESTS.

With all this being said, WE are once again back to the SAME scenario that was FACED earlier in YOUR KNOWING ***GOD.*** Until YOU are REBORN in CHRIST and have RECEIVED ***HOLY SPIRIT*** BAPTISM, YOU cannot KNOW ***GOD*** or who you are, or what YOUR DESTINY HOLDS. This is WHY JESUS CHRIST says; HE is the DOOR of the SHEEP. For ONE cannot KNOW ***GOD*** or THEMSELVES, or their DESTINY without ***HOLY SPIRIT*** BAPTISM, and that can only come by way of JESUS CHRIST. Therefor, the SAME conditions APPLYING to YOUR coming to KNOW ***GOD*** also APPLY to YOUR being able to KNOW both who YOU are, and what YOUR DESTINY may be.

Knowing the LIGHT SOURCE

GOD'S CHILDREN are CHILDREN of LIGHT. If WE again look to the ATOM as WE had just previously done, it can be said that the HEBREW (the PROTON) exhibits POSITIVE LIGHT. It can also be said that the CANAANITE (the ELECTRON) exhibits NEGATIVE LIGHT or DARKNESS. Whereas the GENTILE (the NEUTRON) neither has a POSITIVE LIGHT or a NEGATIVE LIGHT (DARKNESS) they therefor must RECEIVE LIGHT from either the POSITIVE or NEGATIVE EXTERNAL SOURCE of LIGHT (KNOWING that either FORM of LIGHT is an ETERNAL LIGHT).

While on EARTH in a CARNAL form of Life, the THREE ingredients necessary for Carnal Life is PROVIDED externally; the Light comes from the Sun, and the Water and Dry Land come from the EARTH. However the TRUE ESSENCE of LIFE comes from the ***GOD*** given SPIRIT that has LIFE in ITSELF. The LIGHT needed for ETERNAL LIFE comes from CHRIST, who is the ORIGINAL SOURCE of LIGHT that ALL BLESSED LIFE has come from. This is why JESUS CHRIST refers to HIMSELF as the BRIGHT and MORNING STAR, and also the LIGHT of the WORLD.

> ***Revelation 22:16 I JESUS HAVE SENT MINE ANGEL TO TESTIFY UNTO YOU THESE THINGS IN THE CHURCHES, I AM THE ROOT AND THE OFFSPRING OF DAVID, AND THE BRIGHT AND MORNING STAR.***

> ***John 8:12*** *Then spake JESUS again unto them, saying,* ***I AM THE LIGHT OF THE WORLD: HE THAT FOLLOWETH ME SHALL NOT WALK IN DARKNESS, BUT SHALL HAVE THE LIGHT OF LIFE.***

The SECOND ingredient necessary for AFTERLIFE is the WATERS needed for ETERNAL LIFE. These are the LIVING WATERS SPRINGING FORTH from the *WORD of* ***GOD,*** COMING by way of JESUS CHRIST; for ONLY the FOUR GOSPELS and the Book of Revelation have the NECESSARY DEEPER WATERS to SWIM IN, and both the GOSPELS and the Book of REVELATION came forth from JESUS CHRIST. In the Book of GENESIS, these LIVING WATERS are expressed by MOSES as the WATERS that are ABOVE the FIRMAMENT; that were divided from the waters below the firmament.

Genesis 1:6 *And* ***GOD*** *said, LET THERE BE A FIRMAMENT IN THE MIDST OF THE WATERS, AND LET IT DIVIDE THE WATERS FROM THE WATERS.*

Genesis 1:7 *And* ***GOD*** *made the firmament, and divided the waters which were under the firmament from the WATERS which were ABOVE the firmament: and it was so.*

The THIRD ingredient needed for ETERNAL LIFE is the DRY LAND. This DRY LAND can be referred to as a piece of REAL ESTATE or a PARCEL of LAND providing ONE with a DWELLING PLACE, and that DWELLING PLACE is ONE'S PLACE in HEAVEN. This ALSO comes by way of JESUS CHRIST, for THE ***FATHER*** has GIVEN to JESUS CHRIST all that ***HE*** has, and JESUS will SHARE what has been GIVEN to HIM with the WORTHY (the STRONG).

Isaiah 53:12 *Therefore will* ***I*** *divide HIM a portion with the GREAT, and HE shall divide the spoil with the STRONG; because HE hath POURED OUT HIS SOUL unto death: and HE was numbered with the TRANSGRESSORS; and HE BARE the SIN of MANY, and made INTERCESSION for the TRANSGRESSORS.*

KNOWING what is REQUIRED

WE KNOW that most of you believe that your GOOD WORKS will benefit you in YOUR RELATIONSHIP with ***GOD*** and get you into HEAVEN, but this is a FALSE BELIEF. Even being RIGHTEOUS in all that YOU do will not BENEFIT YOU in your AFTERLIFE, for GOOD WORKS and RIGHTEOUS ACTIONS are MORAL TITHES. MORAL TITHES are not SPIRITUAL TITHES and therefor they can only benefit you in your CARNAL Life. ***GOD*** does not become overly impressed with ONE'S good MORAL behavior for it is YOUR SPIRITUAL BEHAVIOR that MUST BE ALIGNED with the ***HOLY***.

Isaiah 64:6 *But we are all as an UNCLEAN thing, and all our RIGHTEOUSNESSES are as FILTHY RAGS; and we all do FADE as a leaf; and our INIQUITIES, like the wind, have taken us away.*

Isaiah 64:7 *And there is NONE that calleth upon thy NAME, that stirreth up himself to TAKE HOLD of THEE: for thou hast HID thy*

FACE from us, and hast CONSUMED us, because of our INIQUITIES.

Isaiah 64:8 *But now, O LORD, thou art our* ***FATHER;*** *we are the CLAY, and THOU our POTTER; and we all are the work of thy HAND.*

These last three Scriptures tell YOU that your good works and your righteousness' are WORTHLESS in the EYES of ***GOD,*** and while YOU have been so busy trying to do what is believed to be right, YOU haven't bothered ASKING ***GOD*** what is RIGHT? Furthermore, by NOT routinely calling UPON THE LORD for ***HIS*** DIRECTION, when YOU finally REALIZE YOU need ***HIS*** DIRECTION, ***HE*** WILL NOT LISTEN TO YOUR PLEAS and turn ***HIS BACK*** towards YOU!

The last Scripture (Isaiah 64:8) is an ACKNOWLEDGMENT by the Prophet, that only BY ***GOD*** CAN ONE DO ***GOD'S*** WORK; and only by ***HIS DIRECTION*** can RIGHTEOUSNESS be achieved. But you will see when READING the balance of the Scriptures WRITTEN in the 64th Chapter of Isaiah; the people had not come to REALIZE their FAULTS until after it had become TOO LATE!

GOD makes it very CLEAR throughout the ENTIRE HOLY BIBLE that YOU must have an ONGOING RELATIONSHIP with ***HIM,*** and allow ***GOD*** to RULE over YOUR ENTIRE LIFE, and not just a portion of it. The HOLY BIBLE describes the LIVES of them who had SERVED ***GOD*** throughout time, and when READING about these PEOPLE, you will SEE that there weren't any TWO that were the SAME (except for those who had been reincarnated). Therefor, it MUST be KNOWN that there isn't any particular model to follow (except for JESUS CHRIST) that will ENSURE YOU that YOU'RE TRULY SERVING ***GOD*** in all of your WAYS.

This is why it is said in the Scriptures that you must walk HUMBLY with ***GOD*** being of a CONTRITE (WILLING) SPIRIT. By walking HUMBLY, you are ACKNOWLEDGING that ALL of YOUR DIRECTION must come from ***GOD,*** and by YOUR WILLINGNESS of SPIRIT you ADHERE to ***HIS DIRECTION.*** In many cases this DIRECTION may appear to be RISKY, but by YOUR FAITH IN ***GOD, HE WILL NEVER ALLOW YOU TO FAIL IN ALL THAT YOU DO TO SERVE HIM!***

Micah 6:8 HE *hath shewed thee, O MAN, what is GOOD; and what doeth THE LORD require of thee, but to do JUSTLY, and to*

*LOVE MERCY, and to WALK HUMBLY with thy **GOD?***

***Micah 6:9** THE LORD'S VOICE crieth unto the city, and the MAN of WISDOM shall SEE thy NAME: hear ye **THE ROD,** and WHO hath APPOINTED it.*

Chapter 20
The CHURCH

The CHURCH was NEVER intended to be an ORGANIZATION or an ENTERPRISE, but it was rather meant to be a BODY of PEOPLE sharing in the COMMON BELIEF that JESUS CHRIST is THE SON of ***GOD.*** These PEOPLE were to carry on with the TEACHING of the *WORD of* ***GOD*** as JESUS CHRIST had TAUGHT it to HIS DISCIPLES. The CHURCH was neither meant to be a building nor a method of WORSHIP, but rather a COMMON PLACE for WORSHIPPING ***GOD*** through ***HOLY SPIRIT*** BAPTISM, which comes only by way of JESUS CHRIST.

Its Beginning

The CHURCH began SEVEN days after the RAPTURE of JESUS CHRIST back to HEAVEN, on the DAY of PENTECOST. The ELEVEN remaining DISCIPLES gathered one hundred and eight of the other Disciples (who had also followed JESUS) together, making the total NUMBER of PEOPLE one hundred and nineteen in attendance.

Even on the FIRST DAY of the CHURCH, it began by making ERRORS. The Disciples had thought that because they had lost one of the Disciples, namely Judas Iscariot, they should appoint a TWELFTH to Discipleship. They then chose two from the one hundred and eight other Disciples of JESUS, and the two picked were Joseph Justus who was called Barsabas, and Matthias. After the TWO were selected, they then cast lots to see which one of them should be picked, and it was Matthias.

NOTE: The MISTAKE made by the DISCIPLES on that day, was TWO-FOLD. The 1st mistake made was in the DISCIPLES taking it upon themselves to appoint the TWELFTH DISCIPLE replacing Judas Iscariot, for they were NEVER EMPOWERED to ORDAIN. The 2nd mistake made was in their casting lots to see which of the two chosen would be the TWELFTH, rather than the TWELFTH being chosen by a VOTE. In either case, what they did was WRONG, for they were ASSUMING they had the power to ORDAIN. If the

DISCIPLES would have waited to SEE who ***GOD*** would send them, and for JESUS CHRIST to APPOINT the TWELFTH, they would have seen that the TWELFTH was INTENDED to be the APOSTLE Paul, and NOT Matthias whom they had selected.

Division in the CHURCH

The APOSTLE John was only twenty-two years old at the time of JESUS' RESURRECTION, making him one hundred and twelve years old when he was GIVEN the REVELATION of JESUS CHRIST. It can be seen from the OPENING Scriptures in the Book of Revelation, that in only ninety years of its existence, the CHURCH had already become divided into SEVEN DENOMINATIONS. These SEVEN DENOMINATIONS related to seven DIFFERENT methods of worship, supposedly ALL coming from the SAME TEACHER, JESUS CHRIST. This is why John was TOLD to write SEVEN LETTERS into the Book of Revelation regarding the SEVEN CHURCHES in Asia Minor. These Letters are meant to be a WARNING to ALL of the CHRISTIAN CHURCHES throughout the WORLD about their establishing their own DOCTRINE, rather than following the DOCTRINE given by JESUS CHRIST. The WARNINGS not only applied to those Churches of yesteryear, but more so SPECIFICALLY to the CHURCHES of TODAY!

The THREAT given in the Book of Revelation to the Churches was, if they were to continue in their methodology of RELIGION that they would suffer the GREAT TRIBULATION. The GREAT TRIBULATION can only be suffered by those who are alive at the time of it, so the WARNINGS apply to the CHURCHES existing at the TIME of the GREAT TRIBULATION, and that time is NOW!

When JESUS taught the *WORD of* ***GOD*** throughout the land, HE didn't adopt a different philosophy on how HE taught in the various areas. HE always taught the SAME MESSAGE and taught it in the SAME WAY. However, once the CHURCH had begun, those LEADING the Church found that by altering the *WORD of* ***GOD*** and making it more suitable to fit the local peoples belief in worship; they met with less opposition from the Pagans and could increase their revenues by getting more people to attend. This was the Beginning of the CHURCH'S DOWNFALL!

By the CHURCH'S bending to the people's demands, it INFLUENCED the Church's BEHAVIOR. The CHURCH then started to allow the CONGREGATION to bring into it articles of IDOLATRY and RELIGIOUS ARTIFACTS which the Pagans used, many of which still remain in the Churches today. ALL

CHURCH FACILITIES calling themselves a PLACE of WORSHIP should be FREE from having any such articles within their confines. This IDOLATRY is inclusive of STATUES, PAINTINGS, FIGURINES, CRUCIFIXES, IMAGERY and BASINS, whether they are of glass, wood, metal or stone; replicating any IMAGE of any sort; for it is a BLASPHEMY to ***MY*** HOUSE of WORSHIP ***SAITH THE LORD***.

JESUS CHRIST said, a HOUSE DIVIDED AGAINST ITSELF CANNOT STAND, therefor, if the CHURCH has DIVISION within it, how can it STAND? How can a BODY of PEOPLE using the SAME *WORD of* ***GOD*** as their DOCTRINE to follow, and the SAME ***SPIRIT of GOD*** for its GUIDANCE, have so many DIFFERENCES in its BELIEFS and METHODOLOGY? The answer to these QUESTIONS are ALL the SAME, the CHURCH and its LEADERSHIP lack the ANOINTING to be a CHURCH ***SAITH THE LORD!***

These are NOT CHURCHES at all; but they are rather ORGANIZATIONS created by men to be ENTERPRISES for PROFIT. This is why the Church and its RELIGION is CALLED "THE GREAT WHORE": For what it does it does for MONEY and POWER!

> ***Revelation 17:2*** *With whom the Kings of the EARTH have COMMITTED FORNICATION, and the INHABITANTS of the EARTH have been made DRUNK with the wine of HER FORNICATION.*

A House of MERCHANDISING

I have yet to walk into a Church Facility where there hadn't been anything sold from within its confines. This is ALSO a BLASPHEMY SAITH THE ***HOLY SPIRIT of GOD. GOD'S*** HOUSE of PRAYER is intended to be a HOUSE of WORSHIP and PRAYER, and not a place where goods are to be BOUGHT or SOLD for any reason whatsoever! These are supposed to be CHURCHES that represent the TEACHINGS of JESUS CHRIST, and JESUS FORBIDS that anything be BOUGHT or SOLD in a PLACE of WORSHIP and PRAYER.

> ***John 2:13*** *And the Jews PASSOVER was at hand, and JESUS went up to JERUSALEM,*

> ***John 2:14*** *And found in the TEMPLE those that SOLD oxen and sheep and doves, and the CHANGERS of MONEY sitting:*

John 2:15 *And when HE had made a scourge of small cords, HE drove them all out of the TEMPLE, and the sheep and the oxen; and poured out the CHANGERS' money, and overthrew the tables;*

John 2:16 *And said unto them that SOLD doves,* ***TAKE THESE THINGS HENCE; MAKE NOT MY FATHER'S HOUSE AN HOUSE OF MERCHANDISE.***

Doesn't the CHURCH READ from these SAME SCRIPTURES? What is so DIFFICULT for them to UNDERSTAND about what JESUS CHRIST SAYS WITHIN THEM; HE SAYS, NOTHING is to be either BOUGHT or SOLD in ***GOD'S*** HOUSE of PRAYER! This also includes RAFFLES, LOTTERIES, and BINGO, for NO sort of TRANSACTION, other than the COLLECTION of TITHES and OFFERINGS is ALLOWED in the HOUSE of THE LORD. This PERTAINS to any PART of the CHURCH FACILITY, even if it were to be a PROPERTY located elsewhere. Any PROPERTY having been PURCHASED with CONGREGATION FUNDS belongs to the CHURCH, and the CHURCH belongs to ***GOD,*** and JESUS CHRIST FORBIDS any buying or selling on HIS PROPERTIES.

THE LORD wants ME to make this SUBJECT quite CLEAR to ALL that READ this BOOK. The CHURCH'S **ONLY** source of INCOME **MUST** come from either TITHES or OFFERINGS and **CANNOT** come from any other means of raising money! THE LORD also SAYS, although the CHURCH LEADERSHIP may RECEIVE GIFTS, and may USE the GIFTS for themselves, they MUST REMEMBER that those GIFTS BELONG TO ***GOD,*** and not them. ***ALL THAT COMES INTO THE CHURCH BELONGS TO GOD, SAITH THE LORD.***

This means ALL TANGIBLE ARTICLES and MONEY coming into the CHURCH'S POSSESSION by way of TITHING or OFFERING belong to ***GOD,*** and not to the Church's Leadership, although they may make use of the TITHES and OFFERINGS in the NAME of THE LORD. FURTHERMORE, ANY gathering of the CONGREGATION whether it is on or off the PREMISES of the CHURCH FACILITY MUST be PAID FOR out of the CHURCH'S GENERAL FUND, and cannot be a considered a CHURCH FUNCTION if any other means of paying the COST of the gathering is used. The CHURCH is intended to be a MEANS of the DISPERSAL of ***GOD'S*** FUNDS to the CONGREGATION, and NOT a means of the RAISING of ***GOD'S*** FUNDS for personal gain.

When JESUS FED the thousands HE was PREACHING to, HE PRO-

VIDED ALL that was EATEN by them. HE didn't take up a COLLECTION prior to their feeding the PEOPLE, but rather DISPERSED that which was DONATED for the cause. THE LORD tells ME that TOO MUCH of the TITHES and OFFERINGS made by the CONGREGATION go into the CHURCH FACILITY, and not enough go into the CHURCH'S MINISTRY and to the NEEDY. JESUS CHRIST didn't have a FACILITY, but HE rather made USE of what was AVAILABLE, and the CHURCH of JESUS CHRIST should be DOING the SAME!

The FUNCTION of the CHURCH

The FUNCTION of the CHURCH is to TEACH the *WORD of* ***GOD*** and PROVIDE a PLACE of WORSHIP, and as DISCUSSED throughout this BOOK this can only be done by ***GOD'S*** ANOINTED. If this PRACTICE had been followed over the COURSE of YEARS, there would be only ONE CHURCH EXISTING TODAY and MANY MORE SOULS WOULD HAVE BEEN SAVED ***SAITH THE LORD!***

One of the GREATEST ERRORS being made by the CHURCH today, is the CHURCH'S belief that it can take the place of THE ***HOLY SPIRIT.*** The CHURCH does this by its trying to PROVIDE the GUIDANCE to its MEMBERS that can only be MINISTERED by THE ***HOLY SPIRIT.*** The CHURCH'S PURPOSE is to TEACH the *WORD of* ***GOD*** as JESUS CHRIST had taught, and to only provide COUNSELING in regard to that TEACHING. This COUNSELING is not inclusive of the GOVERNING of ONE'S BEHAVIOR or by the CHURCH'S trying to provide guidance regarding LIFE STYLE or METHOD of WORSHIP. These things are JUDGMENTAL, and the CHURCH is not EMPOWERED to JUDGE!

Those Churches who are doing this exhibit the epitome of RELIGION, and are not following the TEACHINGS of JESUS CHRIST. For JESUS said, HE had not COME to JUDGE the world, but rather to SAVE IT. The BASIS of the CHURCH is to FOLLOW the TEACHINGS of JESUS, and not to make up their own set of RELIGIOUS RULES for the CONGREGATION to live by. Neither is the CHURCH to JUSTIFY their bizarre RULES of MORALITY by their distorted interpretation of the *WORD of* ***GOD.***

The BIBLE gives the RULES that are to be followed; however the CONGREGATION is insistent on following the DOCTRINE of MEN rather than the *WORD of* ***GOD.*** The HOLY BIBLE makes it VERY CLEAR that SATURDAY (the SEVENTH DAY) is the SABBATH, yet nearly all CHRISTIAN CHURCHES gather on Sunday, and fail to OBEY ***GOD'S 4th COMMAND-***

MENT, HONORING the SABBATH. ***GOD*** didn't change ***HIS COMMANDMENT,*** but yet the CHURCH does not HONOR IT! The BREAKING of any of ***GOD'S COMMANDMENTS*** is a SIN, whether it be ADULTERY, MURDER, or dishonoring the SABBATH, ALL ARE SINS ***SAITH THE LORD!***

GOD also FORBIDS the WORSHIPPING of IDOLS, and the bringing of such articles into ***HIS*** HOUSE of PRAYER. Yet the Churches are full of these articles and the CONGREGATION kneels before them, and kisses them, and treats them as though they are Holy even though they were made by the hands of men.

If YOU could only SEE what THE LORD has SHOWN ME as to what is going to HAPPEN to these Churches and their followings, YOU would CEASE from following after them, and FOLLOW the *WORD of **GOD.*** ***GOD*** HOLDS each and every INDIVIDUAL responsible for their ACTIONS, and has PROVIDED a BOOK of TRUTH called THE HOLY BIBLE for each of YOU to READ. ***HE*** has done this so NO EXCUSES can be made on YOUR DAY of JUDGMENT; so READ and be NOT DECEIVED!

Chapter 21
The False Prophet

The WORDS, "False Prophet", represent both a TITLE and a TERM given to a PERSON or PERSONS who MISUSE, MISINTERPRET, or MISREPRESENT the TRUE MEANING of the *WORD of* ***GOD.*** Starting with the writings of MOSES, THE LORD warned ***HIS*** CHILDREN to beware of False Prophets, and since there have been Prophets, there have also been False Prophets. For ONE to UNDERSTAND what a False Prophet is they must first UNDERSTAND what the WORD "Prophet" means, in a ***GODLY*** *SENSE.*

A Prophet is a GIFTED PERSON who has a UNIQUE CONNECTION to ***GOD,*** and ***GOD*** WILL SPEAK DIRECTLY to the PROPHET and THROUGH the PROPHET to others. A Prophet can be either male or female, and can either be BORN a PROPHET, or become ONE later on in Life. HOWEVER, it is ***GOD*** who has determined who will be a PROPHET and when the PROPHET'S MINISTRY shall begin. Once becoming a Prophet, the PROPHET will generally separate themselves from family and friends and will maintain somewhat of an isolated LIFE, for they will only be able to relate to others who are also Prophets or to those in the SERVICE to ***GOD***. This is why the OLD TESTAMENT speaks about ROVING BANDS of PROPHETS who CONGREGATED TOGETHER and traveled throughout ISRAEL prophesying. The PROPHET has DEDICATED his or her LIFE to the SERVICE of ***GOD,*** and will not allow ANYTHING to compromise their RELATIONSHIP with ***GOD.***

Although PROPHECY is still GIVEN to ***GOD'S*** ANOINTED, no person after JESUS CHRIST can be referred to as a Prophet, for JESUS was the LAST PROPHET and the LAST KING of ISRAEL. The CHURCH routinely misuses the WORD "Prophet" by referring to someone who has been GIVEN PROPHECY as being a PROPHET, whereas they are NOT! When THE ***HOLY SPIRIT*** COMES to EARTH in the form of a MAN, ***HE*** will be referred to as a PROPHET by many, although ***HE*** is MORE than a PROPHET; for ***HE*** is the SPIRIT of TRUTH. This subject will be further discussed later on in this BOOK.

The Person of the False Prophet

The entire 23rd Chapter of the Book of Jeremiah is DEDICATED to giving a GENERAL description of the False Prophet, and YOU should READ the DESCRIPTION given in those Scriptures. However, the WORDS "False Prophet" have also a whole host of other MEANINGS, other than just being a TITLE given to them who TEACH and PREACH FALSELY the *WORD of* ***GOD,*** and claim to be doing so in the ***NAME of GOD.***

As explained in detail in the PREVIOUS BOOK, the Book of Revelation is WRITTEN in SEVEN LAYERS, and ALL that is CONTAINED within the Book of Revelation's LAYERS, have SEVEN LEVELS of UNDERSTANDING to them. The MESSAGE being conveyed here is that the WORDS "False Prophet", refer to more than to just a person or persons who MISREPRESENT ***GOD*** and ***HIS*** *WORD.* However in this Chapter, WE will ONLY cover the GENERAL UNDERSTANDING of the WORDS "False Prophet" as they relate to them who both PREACH and TEACH a FALSE MESSAGE and claim to do so in the ***NAME of GOD.***

> ***Jeremiah 23:1*** *WOE be unto the Pastors that DESTROY and SCATTER the SHEEP of* ***MY*** *pasture! SAITH THE LORD.*

The PERSON of the False Prophet can be EASILY IDENTIFIED, for this PERSON is one who ministers for the BENEFIT of MONEY, POWER and for PERSONAL GAIN, ***SAITH THE LORD***. The False Prophet can bear a title such as; Priest, Pastor, Minister, Reverend, or have a Leadership Role in any Christian Organization or Church. However, the Book of Revelation has given them the TITLE of the "GREAT WHORE", for this title best fits them. Although other Religions are also led by False Prophets, they are not referred to as such in the NEW TESTAMENT, as it only refers to them as being False Prophets that claim themselves to be CHRISTIANS.

One of the typical trademarks of the False Prophet is the misuse of Scripture to further the collection of money. The Pastor or Church Leader will most often tell YOU that you will receive a greater blessing by YOUR making a LARGER donation to the Church, and then will try to support that LIE, by MISQUOTING SCRIPTURE. The typical Scripture used will be taken from the Book of Malachi.

> ***Malachi 3:8*** *Will a man rob* ***GOD?*** *Yet ye have robbed* ***ME.*** *But ye*

say, Wherein have we robbed thee? In TITHES and OFFERINGS?

Malachi 3:9 *Ye are CURSED with a CURSE: for ye have robbed* ***ME****, even this whole nation.*

Malachi 3:10 *Bring ALL the TITHES into the STOREHOUSE, that there may be meat in MINE HOUSE, and prove* ***ME*** *now herewith, SAITH THE* ***LORD of HOSTS,*** *if* ***I*** *will not OPEN you the WINDOWS of HEAVEN, and POUR you out a BLESSING, that there shall not be room enough to receive it.*

At first glance of these Scriptures it appears that the MESSAGE given in them, is a MESSAGE in regard to MONEYS being withheld from ***GOD*** by the people, by their not properly TITHING and OFFERING to the Church, and this is PARTIALLY TRUE. It also appears that if the MONEY would be returned to ***GOD, HE*** would then BLESS those who had returned the MONEY in some GREATER MEASURE, and this is also PARTIALLY TRUE. However this is NOT the MESSAGE in its ENTIRETY, for ***GOD*** in these SCRIPTURES is not REFERRING to MONEY being withheld by the people to the CHURCH, but rather MONEY that is being taken from the Church by its LEADERSHIP.

NOTE: One MUST REMEMBER that the Devil is quite clever, and he speaks most often in HALF-TRUTHS, such as he did to EVE in the Garden of Eden. The Devil told EVE in the Garden, if she ate of the fruit of the Tree of the KNOWLEDGE of GOOD and EVIL, she would become LIKE ***GOD,*** and this was the TRUTH. But he also told EVE that she would not DIE for doing so, and this was a LIE.

If you read the prior Scriptures in Malachi to those WE had previously quoted, you will SEE that the MESSAGE of the Scripture does not refer to the people, as being the one's who were not giving to the Church. It rather refers to the TITHES and OFFERINGS that were given by the people to the Church, that were being MISUSED. The Scriptures are also saying, what was being given by the people to THE LORD was not being properly dispersed to the NEEDY, but was rather being taken by the Priests and those OVERSEEING the FUNDS and used for other purposes.

Malachi 3:5 *And* ***I*** *will come near to you to JUDGMENT; and* ***I*** *will be a swift WITNESS against the SORCERERS, and against the ADULTERERS, and against FALSE SWEARERS, and against those that oppress the hireling in his wages, the widow, and the father-*

*less, and that turn aside the stranger from his right, and FEAR NOT **ME,** SAITH THE **LORD of HOSTS.***

YOU should SEE from the Scripture, the MESSAGE is directed to the False Prophet and the People's Leadership, and not to the people of the CONGREGATION. So when it was asked of the Prophet by the Religious Leadership as to how they were ROBBING ***GOD,*** the Prophet speaking in the ***NAME of THE LORD*** answered them by saying; the TITHES and the OFFERINGS given to them were being inappropriately used. And, if the Church Leaders would see to ensuring that ALL the TITHES and OFFERINGS were properly put into THE LORD'S TREASURY, then the people, would benefit by it. The Scripture also says that the TITHES and OFFERINGS was intended to be used for the PEOPLE, and not given to the Leadership for their PERSONAL use.

The CHURCH most often uses these SAME Scriptures of Malachi to induce GUILT within the CONGREGATION by implying they're not donating enough to the CHURCH. However, the Scriptures are being MISUSED, for they are MEANT to be a WARNING to the CHURCH about them MISUSING the CHURCH FUNDS!

GOD does not NEED your MONEY but rather WANTS your LOVE, and if you GIVE ***HIM*** ALL of YOUR LOVE, ***HE*** *will surely BLESS YOU for it.* However, the NEEDY do NEED your HELP and the money given by you to the Church is suppose to go into that effort. The MESSAGE being given in the Scriptures pertains to both the Nation's Leaders and to the Church's Leaders of that time, to not misappropriate the FUNDS being given to them by the people for the NEEDY. The PROPHET was telling them, if they were to follow this ORDER, THE LORD would see that the FUNDS within the TREASURY would continually grow, and their crops would be fruitful and free from disease and pests.

The Scripture does not speak about one personally gaining by donating more, but rather speaks to the appropriation of the TITHES and OFFERINGS. So, when you see these Scriptures being quoted by a Pastor or Priest to imply that if you give MORE money, you will RECEIVE more in return from ***GOD***, BELIEVE IT NOT, for BLESSINGS cannot be BOUGHT!

Yet another common sign of a Church being led by a False Prophet, is when it passes the OFFERING PLATE around more than ONCE per SERVICE. This is a CLEVER way to increase the revenue by causing intimidation or guilt within the Congregation for not giving MORE. There are many excuses given for the SECOND or THIRD passing of the COLLECTION plate, such as the expanding of the Church's facility, or the need for newer or better Church equipment, musical instruments, new furniture, and so forth. This all seems well intended, but if THE LORD approves of what is being requested by the Church's Leadership, ***HE*** will provide the Church with the money needed in the FIRST COLLECTION, without the need of additional COLLECTIONS.

A Church being led by a False Prophet will also have the COLLECTION PLATE go around more than once to pay visiting Guest Speakers or Performers for their appearances. If these people are doing so in the ***NAME of GOD,*** they needn't receive any pay for their services, for ***GOD*** will see to their PAYMENT. If it is a matter of merely covering the Guest's travel costs, or lodging, their PAYMENT should come from the Host Church's General Fund, and not be the BURDEN of the CONGREGATION.

NOTE: While I had been attending a local Church, I asked a friend (whom didn't attend any Church) to attend one of the Church's Evening Services, even though on that particular evening I could not attend. So she and her daughter attended the evening service and there was some sort of play or movie presentation being staged that night. The COLLECTION PLATE was passed around TWICE during the regular service and my friend gave generously both times, first by giving cash, and then having to write a check for the second passing of the plate. Prior to the main event, the OFFERING PLATE was sent around once more and when my friend saw that the Church still wanted MORE MONEY from her, it turned her off to it, so she and her daughter got up and left. After already giving all she could afford, she felt embarrassed that she hadn't anymore to give. This INTIMIDATION and GUILT factor brought about by the Church's GREEDY behavior was UNSCRUPULOUS. Once I found out what had happened that evening, it upset ME to see a person being turned away from ***GOD*** by the Church's GREED. Shortly after that occurrence I was told by THE LORD to no longer ATTEND that Church. JESUS CHRIST WARNS about this type of BEHAVIOR:

> ***Matthew 18:5 AND WHOSO SHALL RECEIVE ONE SUCH LITTLE CHILD IN MY NAME RECEIVETH ME.***
>
> ***Matthew 18:6 BUT WHOSO SHALL OFFEND ONE OF THESE LITTLE ONES WHICH BELIEVE IN ME, IT WERE BETTER FOR HIM THAT A MILLSTONE WERE HANGED ABOUT HIS NECK, AND THAT HE WERE DROWNED IN THE DEPTH OF THE SEA.***

In further regard to MISUSE of the CHURCH, the Church facility should

NEVER be used as a place for entertainment, for its PURPOSE is to be a HOUSE of WORSHIP and PRAYER and not a Center for the Performing Arts. Even the Christmas plays depicting the BIRTH and Crucifixion of JESUS CHRIST, generally put on by the Church during the holidays, is a MISUSE of ***GOD'S*** HOUSE of PRAYER. By whose AUTHORITY is this practice being ALLOWED in MY HOUSE, ***SAITH THE LORD***, and why are they not FEARFUL of the PUNISHMENT they will RECEIVE?

Variations in the False Prophet

There are various types of False Prophets and not all of them are a PRODUCT of the Devil. The only COMMON trait shared by ALL False Prophets, is the LACKING of ANOINTING to PREACH the *WORD of* ***GOD***. Some False Prophets have been CONVERTED and SAVED ***SAITH THE LORD***, but HAVE NOT RECEIVED the THREE GIFTS NECESSARY to PREACH the *WORD of* ***GOD.*** A PREACHER of the WORD must be absolutely certain they have RECEIVED by way of THE ***HOLY SPIRIT*** at LEAST THREE of the NINE GIFTS GIVEN. To refresh MEMORIES, WE will list the NINE GIFTS again below so YOU might review YOUR status to SEE if YOU are QUALIFIED to PREACH. KEEP in MIND, the 1st GIFT GIVEN is always the GIFT of FAITH, and any TWO of the other EIGHT GIFTS GIVEN may be used in addition to the GIFT of FAITH, thus making up the THREE GIFTS NEEDED to PREACH.

The NINE GIFTS of THE ***HOLY SPIRIT:***

1. The GIFT of the ***WORD of WISDOM*** (The ability to ACCURATELY APPLY SCRIPTURE)
2. The GIFT of the ***WORD of KNOWLEDGE*** (The ability to UNDERSTAND SCRIPTURE to at least 4 LAYERS of DEPTH)
3. The GIFT of ***FAITH*** (The ability to FEEL and KNOW the PRESENCE of THE ***HOLY SPIRIT***)
4. The GIFT of ***HEALING*** (The ability to HEAL the BODY and the SPIRIT by PRAYER and by TOUCH)
5. The GIFT of ***WORKING MIRACLES*** (The ability to PERFORM SUPERNATURAL EVENTS)
6. The GIFT of ***PROPHECY*** (The ability to ACCURATELY SEE and FORETELL FUTURE EVENTS)
7. The GIFT of ***DISCERNING SPIRITS*** (The ability to SEE and IDENTIFY SPIRITUAL MATTER)

8. The GIFT of ***SPEAKING IN TONGUES*** (The ability to SPEAK in the HEBREWAH LANGUAGE)
9. The GIFT of ***THE INTERPRETATION OF TONGUES*** (The ability to INTERPRET the HEBREWAH LANGUAGE into YOUR common language)

NOTE: For those of YOU who READ this list and are CURRENTLY PREACHING the *WORD of* ***GOD,*** it is PARAMOUNT YOU are certain, that YOU are in POSSESSION of at LEAST THREE of these NINE GIFTS. IF YOU ARE NOT ABSOLUTELY CERTAIN, CEASE IN YOUR MINISTRIES IMMEDIATELY ***SAITH THE LORD of HOSTS,*** for YOU ARE of the False Prophet!

SIGNS of the Hireling

Of all the variations of the False Prophet the Hireling is the most common among them. The Hireling is rather obvious in his ways and can be readily IDENTIFIED, ***SAITH THE LORD***. This type of False Prophet views his or her Ministry as a JOB rather than as a SERVICE to ***GOD,*** and looks towards the EARTH for rewards of MONEY and PRESTIGE for their service.

This is a MOST SERIOUS OFFENSE, as ***GOD*** SEES this type of False Prophet as being the GREAT WHORE, one who PERFORMS their service for MONEY! One of the trademarks for this type of False Prophet is their CONTINUALLY SEEKING further income from their Ministry, and can do it rather cleverly; for they are the PRODUCT of the Devil. One such example of this type of behavior would be a Pastor, Minister, or Priest who continually reminds the Congregation that the 10% TITHES they give to the Church should be based on their GROSS rather than their NET INCOME, even though this is UNTRUE!

NOTE: The 10% TITHES YOU are to GIVE should be based on what is yours, and whatever may be taken from you in taxes is no longer yours, but rather the government's.

The "HIRELINGS" will always look to expand and grow their Ministries for the benefit of INCOME, and will have seemingly never ending projects requiring further DONATIONS from the Congregation. They will seek to acquire all the LUXURIES of Life they personally desire, by use of Church funds. They will always be driving a fancy new car, own a big house, and have plenty of spending money; and this will be their TRADEMARK.

You will find that the Hireling will most often speak of his or her own personal experiences in Life, rather than giving the explanation of Scripture, for they themselves don't UNDERSTAND SCRIPTURE. They will try to express Scripture most often by showing you how the Scripture has applied to them personally, for they are SELF-CENTERED and relate everything to themselves. This type of False Prophet will NEVER go out of their way to help anyone, unless they at a later time may benefit from it. Then when they do extend themselves, their ulterior motivation will be for the PAYMENT of the services rendered.

Chapter 22

THE PERSON of THE *HOLY SPIRIT*

Before Creation there was only ***GOD,*** and ***GOD*** was a ***FATHER*** and a ***SON.*** The ***FATHER'S NAME*** is ***YAHWEH*** and the ***SON'S NAME*** is ***IXOTE,*** and only they were in existence, for THEY were ALWAYS and shall ALWAYS BE, ***SAITH THE LORD of HOSTS.*** There was neither a HEAVEN nor a UNIVERSE, nor TIME of any measurement; and the ANGELS had not yet been CREATED. After trillions upon trillions of YEARS if the TIME could be MEASURED, ***YAHWEH*** had ***HIS SON IXOTE*** CREATED a KINGDOM and ***GOD*** called the KINGDOM HEAVEN. ***YAHWEH*** also had ***IXOTE*** CREATE the HOSTS of HEAVEN who were to be SERVANTS to ***GOD,*** and ***GOD*** called the SERVANTS, ANGELS.

IXOTE being the FIRST DESCENDANT of ***GOD*** was to RULE ALL of HEAVEN, and the ANGELS called ***IXOTE,*** the ***LORD of HOSTS*** and also called ***HIM,*** THE ANCIENT of DAYS. Many ANGELS were CREATED to SERVE ***GOD*** and they did so for trillions upon trillions of YEARS, if TIME could be MEASURED. There still was not a UNIVERSE, or planets, or any LIGHTS whatsoever in the HEAVENS, for ***GOD*** was the LIGHT thereof, and the ANGELS and ***GOD*** lived in PEACE and HARMONY for trillions upon trillions of YEARS, if TIME could be MEASURED.

GOD then wanted to EXPAND ***HIS*** KINGDOM so ***HE*** established a HIERARCHY in HEAVEN, and certain ANGELS were made to be PRINCES; and the PRINCES RULED over all the ANGELS in HEAVEN, and ***IXOTE,*** the ***LORD of HOST*** and the ANCIENT of DAYS RULED over the PRINCES. ***GOD*** then CHANGED the HIERARCHY in HEAVEN, and ***IXOTE*** CREATED for ***HIMSELF*** a ***SON*** and ***HE*** CALLED ***HIS SON YESHUA,*** and ***YESHUA*** CREATED for ***HIMSELF*** FOUR SONS and THEY were CALLED SERAPHIM. The FIRST SERAPHIM was CALLED THE ***DELIVERER*** and THE ***SEVEN SPIRITS of GOD,*** for ***HE*** PROCEEDED FROM THE THRONE of ***GOD.*** The NEXT THREE SERAPHIM came FORTH from ***HIM,*** and the FIRST ONE coming from ***HIM*** was called JESUS, and JESUS was to be the LIGHT SOURCE for ALL FURTHER CREATION. Then from JESUS came forth SOLOMON the THIRD SERAPHIM, and from SOLOMON came DAVID the FOURTH.

Each of the FOUR SERAPHIM were to come into ***GOD'S*** NEW CREATION which ***GOD*** CALLED EARTH, with the FIRST DESCENDANT of the ***SEVEN SPIRITS of GOD*** called JESUS, being the ONE who was to BRING a SOUL to the EARTH in the FORM of a MAN. The MAN BEARING the SOUL on the EARTH was called ADAM, and ADAM was to be the FIRST DESCENDANT of JESUS on EARTH to be a LIVING SOUL. Then from ADAM'S GENERATIONS were to COME FORTH ALL of ***GOD'S*** CHILDREN, with ADAM'S SOUL being passed down from GENERATION to GENERATION continuously over a TIME PERIOD of SEVEN THOUSAND EARTH YEARS, after the GREAT FLOOD.

Once JESUS had RETURNED to HEAVEN from the EARTH and had left HIS SOUL on EARTH, the DESCENDING ORDER of the FOUR SERAPHIM to the EARTH from that TIME forward, was to be in the REVERSE ORDER from that of THEIR DESCENDING ORDER from ***GOD.*** The FOURTH SERAPHIM out from ***GOD,*** called DAVID, was to come FIRST to the EARTH, and the FIRST SERAPHIM DESCENDING from ***GOD*** was to COME LAST, thus making the LAST to be FIRST, and the FIRST, LAST. The SERAPHIM were then renumbered in accordance with their appearances on EARTH rather than in their DESCENDING ORDER from ***GOD***, thus making the FIRST SERAPHIM out from ***GOD*** to be KNOWN as the FOURTH SERAPHIM, rather than the FIRST!

Shortly after the CREATION of the FOUR SERAPHIM there was a REVOLT in HEAVEN, and LUCIFER being one of the THREE PRINCES, LED the REVOLT. LUCIFER believed that the MAN (ADAM) bearing a SOUL, by being a DESCENDANT from ***GOD,*** would be placed above him, and feared the loss of his POWER. For the ANGEL was a CREATION of ***GOD*** and not a DESCENDANT. However, LUCIFER was assured by ***IXOTE*** that the MAN would not be CLASSIFIED above the ANGEL, but LUCIFER still saw the MAN to be a threat.

After a few short years of ADAM'S existence, LUCIFER came into the GARDEN where the MAN was kept, and caused the MAN, ADAM and his wife EVE to SIN. He did this in trying to PROVE to ***GOD*** that the MAN was UNWORTHY for HEAVEN because he had SINNED, for if he could keep the MAN out of HEAVEN, the THREAT of the MAN would no longer be VALID. However this backfired on Lucifer and he and his following were cast out of HEAVEN. They were then given their own dominion, and ***GOD*** called Lucifer's domain HELL for it was FAR from HEAVEN, and this was the BE-

GINNING of the CREATION of HEAVEN and HELL!

IXOTE DESCENDS

It wasn't until the time of NOAH that ***IXOTE*** DESCENDED to EARTH in THE ***SPIRIT of GOD,*** to DWELL with the MAN whom ***GOD*** found to be WORTHY. The EARTH, being corrupted by men and void of THE ***HOLY SPIRIT,*** became so EVIL that ***GOD*** DETERMINED ITS DESTRUCTION. So ***GOD*** sent ***IXOTE*** whom ***HE CALLED HIS HOLY SPIRIT*** to the EARTH to COUNSEL and GUIDE NOAH in his efforts to BUILD an ARK. NOAH, being in the ***SPIRIT of GOD*** was the FIRST MAN upon the EARTH to be the HOST to ***IXOTE,*** and this is why the SCRIPTURES say that NOAH walked with ***GOD.*** Even though ENOCH, NOAH'S great grandfather (who is DAVID the FOURTH SERAPHIM) also had walked with ***GOD,*** HE was not HOST to ***HIM,*** whereas NOAH was.

IXOTE, THE ***DELIVERER,*** between the time of NOAH until the COMING of JESUS CHRIST, came to the EARTH to be JOSEPH, MOSES, and JOSEPH again, to GIVE BIRTH to JESUS CHRIST, thus passing down to JESUS the BIRTHRIGHT of JOSEPH. And, by JOSEPH being the LIVING HOST to THE ***HOLY SPIRIT,*** this MADE JESUS the ONLY BEGOTTEN of THE ***FATHER*** and the SON of ***GOD.*** Although THE ***HOLY SPIRIT, IXOTE,*** came to be WITH several other men other than just NOAH, JOSEPH and MOSES, the others however were not ***HIS*** HOST, but ***HE*** was rather theirs, whereas NOAH, MOSES, and JOSEPH were ***HIS*** LIVING HOSTS. Even DAVID, who had RECEIVED THE ***HOLY SPIRIT,*** was NOT HOST to ***HIM;*** and ONLY JESUS CHRIST after HIS FATHER JOSEPH, was a LIVING HOST TO THE ***HOLY SPIRIT of GOD.***

After the RESURRECTION

It wasn't until after the RESURRECTION of JESUS CHRIST that THE ***HOLY SPIRIT*** was left on EARTH to BAPTIZE them who had BELIEVED in JESUS, after being DIRECTED by JESUS to them. After BAPTISM, THE ***HOLY SPIRIT,*** by having OMNIPRESENCE, can DWELL with as many people as ***GOD*** so CHOOSES, however, the BAPTIZED are not HOST to ***HIM,*** as JESUS was.

For a person to be the HOST to THE ***HOLY SPIRIT,*** that person MUST BE IN POSSESSION OF ALL NINE GIFTS GIVEN BY ***HIM,*** and ONLY THE FOUR SERAPHIM CAN BE GIVEN ALL NINE GIFTS. The DWELLING

TIME of THE ***HOLY SPIRIT*** with any one person will vary depending on that person's ANOINTING, and all but the GIFT of FAITH will be periodic and only AVAILABLE when THE ***HOLY SPIRIT'S PRESENCE*** is with the ANOINTED.

As spoken about earlier in this BOOK, at the TIME of ONE'S BAPTISM, that person's SCRIBE ANGEL is no longer needed to record their behavior, so the SCRIBE ANGEL is sent back to HEAVEN. Then after the NAME of the BAPTIZED has been recorded into the GUEST REGISTER in HEAVEN, the ANGEL RAPHAEL comes to them and OVERSEES their well being while they remain on EARTH. RAPHAEL also has OMNIPRESENCE and can be in ALL PLACES at the same time. When a person needs the PRESENCE of THE ***HOLY SPIRIT,*** it is RAPHAEL who will summons ***HIM*** for assistance, and aside from the GIFT of FAITH, the other EIGHT GIFTS will not be AVAILABLE for the BAPTIZED without the ASSISTANCE of THE ***HOLY SPIRIT.***

The reason the GIFT of FAITH remains PERMANENTLY with the BAPTIZED is to ENABLE them to FEEL and KNOW the PRESENCE of THE ***HOLY SPIRIT;*** and to also help them in a TIME of DOUBT, when ***HE*** is NOT PRESENT with them. This is also why the NEW COVENANT is called a ***COVENANT of FAITH***, for the GIFT of FAITH NEVER LEAVES THOSE HAVING RECEIVED BAPTISM. Therefor it is FAITH that becomes the CORNERSTONE anchoring ONE'S CONNECTION TO ***GOD,*** and the FAITH NEEDED can only be RECEIVED from ***IXOTE,*** THE ***HOLY SPIRIT of GOD.*** This is why it is said in the SCRIPTURES, *"But the JUST shall LIVE by **HIS FAITH** (Habakkuk 2:4)"*.

HOST to THE *HOLY SPIRIT*

When the THIRD and FOURTH SERAPHIM (JESUS CHRIST and ***THE DELIVERER***) are on the EARTH, THEY are both HOST to THE ***HOLY SPIRIT*** and take on the PERSONALITY of THE ***HOLY SPIRIT.*** This is why JESUS CHRIST had told HIS Disciple Thomas, if he had known HIM, he had also known ***THE FATHER,*** for JESUS CHRIST was as ONE with ***THE FATHER,*** THUS MEANING, THE HOST to THE ***HOLY SPIRIT.***

> ***John 14:5*** *Thomas saith unto HIM, LORD, we know not whither thou goest; and how can we know the way?*

> ***John 14:6*** *JESUS saith unto him,* ***I AM THE WAY, THE TRUTH, AND THE LIFE: NO MAN COMETH UNTO THE FATHER,***

BUT BY ME.

John 14:7 IF YE HAD KNOWN ME, YE SHOULD HAVE KNOWN MY FATHER ALSO: AND FROM HENCEFORTH YE KNOW HIM, AND HAVE SEEN HIM.

JESUS was telling Thomas, that by his KNOWING JESUS SPIRITUALLY, he also knew THE ***HOLY SPIRIT,*** who is JESUS' ***FATHER;*** for after JESUS' BAPTISM, HE WAS IN THE ***SPIRIT of GOD,*** HAVING ALL NINE GIFTS and in the LIKENESS of ***GOD*** by THE ***SPIRIT.***

THE *HOLY SPIRIT* in the FORM of a MAN

When the BIBLE refers to THE ***REDEEMER,*** it means ***THE DELIVERER,*** for the ***REDEEMER*** and ***THE DELIVERER*** are ***ONE.***

Isaiah 44:6 *Thus saith* ***THE LORD,*** *the KING of ISRAEL, and HIS* ***REDEEMER*** *the* ***LORD of HOSTS; I AM THE FIRST, AND I AM THE LAST; AND BESIDE ME THERE IS NO GOD.***

What is this SCRIPTURE saying? **Answer:** The Scripture says that ***GOD*** is the *KING of ISRAEL,* and that ***HE*** and ***HIS SON,*** the ***REDEEMER,*** (***THE DELIVERER***) ARE ***GOD.*** Within ***THE TRINITY,*** JESUS CHRIST is ***YESHUA,*** and ***YESHUA*** is the ***SON of IXOTE,*** and ***IXOTE*** is the ***SON of GOD. THE DELIVERER*** who is the FOURTH SERAPHIM, when within ***THE TRINITY,*** is ***IXOTE,*** THE ***HOLY SPIRIT of GOD,*** and the ***SON TO YAHWEH, WHO IS GOD.***

The FIRST referred to in the SCRIPTURE is ***YAHWEH*** who had come down FIRST as ***GOD*** to the EARTH on Mount Sinai, to GIVE MOSES and ISRAEL ***THE LAW!*** The LAST referred to in the SCRIPTURE is the FOURTH SERAPHIM and ***HE*** will come down to the EARTH as ***THE DELIVERER,*** being in the FORM of a MAN. This is one of the reasons why in the GOSPELS, JESUS refers to HIMSELF as the SON of ***MAN,*** because HIS ***FATHER*** is a ***MAN.***

This is also why in the book of Habakkuk 2:4 ***THE DELIVERER*** is said to have ***HIS SOUL*** REVERSED (*not upright in* ***HIM***), for ***HE*** COMES FIRST in ***THE SPIRIT*** (as ***GOD*** did on Sinai) and then in the FLESH, as ***THE DELIVERER.*** For anyone else EVER having come to the EARTH from HEAVEN had come FIRST in the FLESH, and then in the SPIRIT, thus making ***THE DELIVERER*** to be REVERSED from all the others.

Unlike any other MAN to EVER walk the EARTH, ***THE DELIVERER WILL BE THE LIVING HOST TO GOD; BEING THE FATHER, THE SON, AND THE HOLY SPIRIT,*** and this is why ***GOD*** SAYS in the SCRIPTURES:

> ***Isaiah 41:4*** *Who hath wrought and done it, calling the generations from the BEGINNING?* ***I THE LORD,*** *the FIRST, and* ***WITH*** *the LAST;* ***I AM HE.***

This is also why ***GOD*** says that ***ONLY HE IS THE KING, THE SAVIOR, THE DELIVERER (THE REDEEMER), AND THE HOLY ONE of ISRAEL.***

> ***Isaiah 43:10*** *Ye are MY witnesses, saith THE LORD, and MY SERVANT whom* ***I*** *have chosen: that ye may KNOW and BELIEVE* ***ME,*** *and UNDERSTAND that* ***I AM HE:*** *before* ***ME*** *there was no* ***GOD*** *formed, neither shall there be after* ***ME.***

> ***Isaiah 43:11 I,*** *even* ***I,*** *am* ***THE LORD;*** *and beside* ***ME*** *there is no SAVIOUR.*

> ***Isaiah 43:12 I*** *have declared, and have SAVED, and* ***I*** *have shewed, when there was no strange god among you: therefore ye are my witnesses, saith* ***THE LORD,*** *that* ***I AM GOD.***

> ***Isaiah 43:13*** *Yea, before the DAY was* ***I AM HE;*** *and there is none that can deliver out of* ***MY HAND, I*** *WILL WORK, and who shall let it?*

> ***Isaiah 43:14*** *Thus saith* ***THE LORD,*** *your* ***REDEEMER,*** *the* ***HOLY ONE of ISRAEL;*** *For your sake* ***I*** *have sent to Babylon, and have brought down all their nobles, and the Chal-de'-ans, whose cry is in the ships.*

> ***Isaiah 43:15 I AM THE LORD,*** *your* ***HOLY ONE,*** *the CREATOR of ISRAEL, your* ***KING.***

When JESUS CHRIST came to SAVE the WORLD, HE came on behalf of THE ***HOLY SPIRIT,*** the ***SON of GOD.*** When ***THE DELIVERER*** COMES, ***HE SHALL COME IN THE NAME OF GOD, TO DELIVER and JUDGE THE WORLD; AND THEN DESTROY IT!***

Chapter 23

Influence versus Control

Throughout this BOOK and in the PREVIOUS BOOK as well, WE have spoken about ***HOLY SPIRIT*** BAPTISM and also about the CONVERSION that takes place in a person's LIFE as a result of it. In this Chapter WE will explain what exactly happens in an individual's LIFE as a RESULT of SPIRITUAL CONVERSION. There are some things within the CONVERTED PERSON'S LIFE that will undergo IMMEDIATE CHANGE, while there are others that will be GRADUALLY altered and changed over a course of TIME.

Although the Dictionary views CONVERSION as being CHANGE, SPIRITUALLY the two WORDS "CONVERSION" and "CHANGE" have different meanings. Whereas a Spiritual Change entails an ABRUPT course of action, SPIRITUAL CONVERSION is somewhat GRADUAL with SUBTLE TRANSITIONS taking place during the CONVERSION PROCESS. The two can be compared somewhat like the comparison of a DIMMER LIGHT SWITCH to a TOGGLE LIGHT SWITCH. Whereas the DIMMER SWITCH allows for a GRADUAL CHANGE in the LIGHT INTENSITY, the TOGGLE SWITCH CHANGES from either the LIGHT being on, to the LIGHT being off, with no in between state.

The SPIRITUAL CONVERSION that takes place at the TIME of ONE'S BAPTISM can be COMPARED to a DIMMER SWITCH that is being GRADUALLY turned so it slowly increases the INTENSITY of the LIGHT. It can also be said that the DIMMER SWITCH gradually INFLUENCES the STATE of the LIGHT, whereas the TOGGLE SWITCH abruptly CONTROLS the STATE of LIGHT, allowing it to be either OFF or ON.

The REASON the PROCESS of SPIRITUAL CHANGE is called "CONVERSION" rather than "CHANGE", is because the changes taking place SPIRITUALLY within the NEWBORN CHILD of ***GOD*** are gradually INFLUENCED CHANGES, rather than abrupt and CONTROLLED changes. ***GOD*** does this PURPOSELY so the PERSON going through the CHANGES never feels as though they have LOST CONTROL over themselves.

After BAPTISM takes place, an EVALUATION is performed by THE

HOLY SPIRIT to determine what deficiencies existing within the INDIVIDUAL'S LIFE must be changed FIRST during the CONVERSION PROCESS. THE ***HOLY SPIRIT*** then sets priorities and the CRITICAL DEFICIENCIES are ALTERED FIRST. These CHANGES will be rather ABRUPT and will not only be apparent to the INDIVIDUAL undergoing the CHANGES, but will also be quite apparent to other people who have known that INDIVIDUAL prior to his or her CONVERSION.

At the TIME of BAPTISM there will be certain BEHAVIOR CHANGES that will IMMEDIATELY transpire in the NEWBORN CHILD of ***GOD,*** and all the people who had known that PERSON prior to their CONVERSION would notice the CHANGES in their BEHAVIOR. Although the CHANGES will be obvious, those observing the CHANGES will not SEE any CHANGE in the INDIVIDUAL'S BASIC PERSONALITY, for they will only identify the CHANGES SPIRITUALLY and not MINDFULLY. If the person SEEING the CHANGES is meant to REMAIN in the NEWBORN CHILD'S LIFE, then he or she will SEE the CHANGES as being POSITIVE ONES, and will want to have even a CLOSER RELATIONSHIP with the CHILD of ***GOD.*** On the other hand, if the person SEEING the CHANGES is not meant to be a part of the NEWBORN CHILD'S LIFE, they will find them to be NEGATIVE and will feel as though they can no longer RELATE to that PERSON.

These FEELINGS toward one another of PAST RELATIONSHIPS, will be MUTUAL, with BOTH the NEWBORN CHILD and their ACQUAINTANCES SEEING their RELATIONSHIPS as either POSITIVE, if it is meant to CONTINUE, or NEGATIVE if it is NOT! This is CALLED the WEANING PROCESS, and ALL PERSONS and CHARACTERISTICS needing to be REMOVED from the NEWBORN CHILD'S LIFE WILL BE REMOVED; ***SAITH THE LORD of HOSTS!***

In some cases, the people needing to be REMOVED from the NEWBORN'S LIFE will be FAMILY MEMBERS. It can be a wife or a husband, a brother or a sister, an aunt or an uncle, cousins or friends, and it can even be a mother or father. JESUS explains this PROCESS in the Scriptures, and HE says it in varying ways.

> ***Matthew 19:29 AND EVERY ONE THAT HATH FORSAKEN HOUSES, OR BRETHREN, OR SISTERS, OR FATHER, OR MOTHER, OR WIFE, OR CHILDREN, OR LANDS, FOR MY SAKE, SHALL RECEIVE AN HUNDREDFOLD, AND SHALL INHERIT EVERLASTING LIFE.***

JESUS also REMINDS them who LOVE HIM that they must be willing to endure significant CHANGES in their LIVES, allowing nothing to COME BEFORE HIM. THIS IS A SET CONDITION BY ***GOD,*** and this is why THE ***HOLY SPIRIT*** does it on a GRADUAL BASIS minimizing the EFFECTS, otherwise it would be very DIFFICULT to endure.

The people who are to be REMOVED from the NEWBORN CHILD'S LIFE are not all necessarily bad people, however they will in some way be an OBSTACLE in that INDIVIDUAL'S CONVERSION PROCESS. None of the people REMOVED will have been SAVED at the time of their REMOVAL, although they, at some later TIME, may be SAVED and then allowed to return to their LOVED ONE as a NEWBORN BROTHER or SISTER.

> ***Matthew 10:37 HE THAT LOVETH FATHER OR MOTHER MORE THAN ME IS NOT WORTHY OF ME: AND HE THAT LOVETH SON OR DAUGHTER MORE THAN ME IS NOT WORTHY OF ME.***
>
> ***Matthew 10:38 AND HE THAT TAKETH NOT HIS CROSS, AND FOLLOWETH AFTER ME, IS NOT WORTHY OF ME.***
>
> ***Matthew 10:39 HE THAT FINDETH HIS LIFE SHALL LOSE IT: AND HE THAT LOSETH HIS LIFE FOR MY SAKE SHALL FIND IT.***

During and after the WEANING PROCESS, ***GOD*** will put NEW PEOPLE into the NEWBORN'S LIFE. These could be renewed OLD FRIENDSHIPS or NEW ONES, and these people will not in any way jeopardize the CONVERSION PROCESS for the NEWBORN and both will be made to BENEFIT by their RELATIONSHIP.

The Influence of THE *HOLY SPIRIT*

From the TIME of BAPTISM onward THE ***HOLY SPIRIT*** will INFLUENCE ONE'S thoughts and behavior, thus REMOVING ALL SIN from the NEWBORN SPIRIT'S LIFE. After the CONVERSION PROCESS has been COMPLETED (and this might be from a few months to several years), the NEWBORN CHILD will live a SIN FREE LIFE, and will no longer be capable of committing SIN; ***SAITH THE LORD of HOSTS***. This will be somewhat difficult to BELIEVE for them READING this BOOK who have been attending

Church for a long time; for many things taught by the Church to be sins, are not sins at all, but rather rules made by men. So when a person may catch him or herself, doing some of these things the Church teaches to be sins, they might believe they have SINNED, however, they have not, for a SAVED SOUL is SINLESS in CHRIST!

I was quite surprised to find out that many things I thought to be SINS were NOT SINS. ***THE LORD***, JESUS and also the ANGELS, have spent a GREAT DEAL of TIME teaching ME of those misconceptions of SIN being taught by the Church, and THEY have shown me by Scripture where the Church's FALSEHOOD lies; and these errors come most often from the Epistles of the Apostles. There are FAR TOO MANY RULES BEING MADE BY THE CHURCHES ***SAITH THE LORD OF HOSTS,*** AND THIS HAS MOVED MANY PEOPLE AWAY FROM ***THE LORD***.

The INFLUENCES of THE ***HOLY SPIRIT*** are UNIQUE in the SENSE that the PERSON being INSPIRED by them, never feels as though they are BEING CONTROLLED, even though they ARE, and BELIEVE the choices being made by them are of their own doing, although they ARE NOT! Anything having been an OBSTACLE for the NEWBORN CHILD of ***GOD*** will be removed by the INFLUENCE of THE ***HOLY SPIRIT***, and this is done in such a way that the PERSON never feels they are being DEPRIVED of that which has been taken out of their LIVES. This INFLUENCE is CALLED, ***HOLY SPIRIT*** GUIDANCE or COUNSELING, and even when THE ***HOLY SPIRIT*** is not present with the NEWBORN, the GUIDANCE still REMAINS by ANGELIC OVERSEEING.

> ***Psalm 91:11*** *For **HE** shall give **HIS** ANGELS charge over thee, to KEEP thee in ALL thy ways.*

> ***Psalm 91:12*** *They shall BEAR thee up in THEIR HANDS, lest thou dash thy foot against a stone.*

NOTE: The entire 91st Psalm should be READ for it is DEDICATED to ***GOD'S ANOINTED*** (THE BAPTIZED), and within the SCRIPTURES lie the TRUTH GIVEN in this CHAPTER. The Psalm MAKES PROMISES that are KEPT by ***GOD,*** of ONE'S PROTECTION and RECEIPT of ETERNAL LIFE; ***SAITH THE LORD of HOSTS.*** It should be READ routinely so YOU CAN SEE the BENEFIT of ***HOLY SPIRIT*** BAPTISM.

CONTROL versus POSSESSION

THE ***HOLY SPIRIT*** both CONTROLS and INFLUENCES, whereas the Devil and his Demons POSSESS. When a PERSON is BAPTIZED in THE ***HOLY SPIRIT*** there is a CERTAIN PARTNERSHIP that takes place between the BAPTIZED and THE ***HOLY SPIRIT.*** BY MUTUAL TRUST the NEWBORN and THE ***HOLY SPIRIT*** UNITE, and there is NEVER any OPPOSITION between the TWO, what the ONE WANTS, the OTHER also WANTS.

HOWEVER, when the Devil or his Demons POSSESS a PERSON, the actions and the behavior of the person will be in opposition to what the person really wants. Whereas ***HOLY SPIRIT*** BAPTISM is a PARTNERSHIP, Devil and Demon POSSESSION is an OWNERSHIP!

When a PERSON first RECEIVES ***HOLY SPIRIT*** BAPTISM, for the FIRST FORTY DAYS and FORTY NIGHTS the TEMPTER (the Devil) still has ACCESS to them. This is why by Scripture the GOSPELS SPEAK about the TEMPTATION PERIOD that JESUS went through for HIS FIRST FORTY DAYS and NIGHTS (although for JESUS this took place in an INSTANT) after HIS BAPTISM.

This PERIOD of SUSCEPTIBILITY does not apply to the Angel or to the BRIDE, for they HAVE a DIVINE RIGHT to HEAVEN, whereas it does PERTAIN to the WEDDING GUESTS. JESUS spoke about this in the GOSPELS as if HE had gone through it, to indicate that MOST will go through this period of TEMPTATION, but HE did this to only SIMPLIFY MATTERS. However, JESUS KNEW that the WEDDING GUESTS would endure the FORTY DAYS and NIGHTS of TEMPTATION, and, because they will make up the bulk of the SAVED, it is implied by Scripture that the EVENT applies to everyone.

JESUS CHRIST gives a WARNING in the GOSPELS about the fate of them who are of the GUESTS who have RECEIVED ***HOLY SPIRIT*** BAPTISM and have FAILED during the FIRST FORTY DAYS. As YOU were told earlier in this BOOK, once YOUR NAME has been entered into the GUESTS REGISTER in HEAVEN, it CANNOT BE REMOVED. However what YOU were NOT TOLD at that time, is that there is a FORTY-DAY LAG in the ENTRY of YOUR NAME. So during those FORTY DAYS and FORTY NIGHTS, the TEMPTER will try to DECEIVE YOU into BELIEVING that you have not been SAVED, and will try to catch you in his SNARE. And if YOU FALL during this period of TIME there will not be any REDEMPTION for you, for you will have SINNED against THE ***HOLY SPIRIT.*** THIS IS YOUR TRIAL AND TRIBULATION PERIOD ***SAITH THE LORD of HOSTS!***

This is the WARNING given by JESUS CHRIST about what happens to them who FAIL during their TIME of TRIAL and TRIBULATION. The following Scriptures refer to the WEDDING GUEST who has RECEIVED SPIRITUAL BAPTISM (MADE CLEAN) and fails the FORTY DAY TEST prior to their CONVERSION.

> ***Matthew 12:43 WHEN THE UNCLEAN SPIRIT IS GONE OUT OF A MAN, HE WALKETH THROUGH DRY PLACES, SEEKING REST, AND FINDETH NONE.***

> ***Matthew 12:44 THEN HE SAITH, I WILL RETURN UNTO MY HOUSE FROM WHENCE I CAME OUT; AND WHEN HE IS COME, HE FINDETH IT EMPTY, SWEPT, AND GARNISHED.***

> ***Matthew 12:45 THEN GOETH HE, AND TAKETH WITH HIMSELF SEVEN OTHER SPIRITS MORE WICKED THAN HIMSELF, AND THEY ENTER IN AND DWELL THERE: AND THE LAST STATE OF THAT MAN IS WORST THAN THE FIRST. EVEN SO SHALL IT BE ALSO UNTO THIS WICKED GENERATION.***

NOTE: What JESUS is saying in these Scriptures, is that ONCE BAPTISM has occurred and ALL evilness is REMOVED from a PERSON, if that PERSON allows the evilness to return (during their TIME of TRIAL and TRIBULATION) there is no further hope for them. FURTHERMORE, their CONDITION will be WORSE than it had been prior to their BAPTISM.

During the "GREAT TRIBULATION", the FORTY-DAY PERIOD of TRIAL and TRIBULATION will be shortened to TEN DAYS for both the WEDDING GUESTS and the "Beheaded Souls". ***GOD*** allows the time to be SHORTENED because during the GREAT TRIBULATION there is no longer a BALANCE between GOOD and EVIL, and only the STRONGEST will be able to ENDURE even the TEN-DAY PERIOD of TIME. These PEOPLE must endure it on their OWN; for THE ***HOLY SPIRIT*** will have already left the EARTH and those left behind will not have a COUNSELOR. Those of the WEDDING GUESTS that ENDURE will RECEIVE RAPTURE with the TRIBULATION SAINTS. However those of the "Beheaded Souls" must GIVE UP their LIVES by REFUSING to take the "Mark of the BEAST".

Revelation 2:10 FEAR NONE OF THOSE THINGS WHICH THOU SHALT SUFFER: BEHOLD, THE DEVIL SHALL CAST SOME OF YOU INTO PRISON, THAT YE MAY BE TRIED; AND YE SHALL HAVE TRIBULATION TEN DAYS; BE THOU FAITHFUL UNTO DEATH, AND I WILL GIVE THEE A CROWN OF LIFE.

Revelation 2:11 HE THAT HATH AN EAR, LET HIM HEAR WHAT THE SPIRIT SAITH UNTO THE CHURCHES; HE THAT OVERCOMETH SHALL NOT BE HURT OF THE SECOND DEATH.

NOTE: What JESUS is SAYING in the last Scriptures is; that those who survive the TEN-DAY PERIOD of TRIAL and TRIBULATION during the time of the "Mark of the BEAST", and do not RECEIVE RAPTURE, will be RESURRECTED to LIVE again in the MILLENNIUM. JESUS also says, those who are Resurrected will return to the dust of the EARTH after the MILLENNIUM, rather than being CAST into HELL and SUFFERING the SECOND DEATH.

Chapter 24

World Power and the VISIONS of Daniel

The Prophet Daniel was GIVEN VISIONS by ***GOD*** of the PENDING changes in World Power. These changes were to take place from the TIME of Daniel on through to the END of the WORLD. Even though the Book of Daniel has but THREE LAYERS of DEPTH to it, it still becomes very DIFFICULT to UNDERSTAND. This is because many of the COMING EVENTS spoken about in the Scriptures by Daniel relate to EVENTS that have already happened, and those EVENTS are LAYERED in with the END TIME EVENTS that are yet to HAPPEN!

Furthermore, the ANOINTING required to UNDERSTAND the EVENTS written about by the Prophet Daniel, require the PERSON disseminating the EVENTS have at least SEVEN of the NINE GIFTS GIVEN by THE ***HOLY SPIRIT***. Until NOW, ***GOD*** has withheld the CLARITY of Daniel's PROPHECIES, and the many explanations given in the past of them are for the most part INCORRECT. In this Chapter WE will DISCLOSE much of the PROPHECY GIVEN to Daniel, and point out many things to you that the Church has misunderstood in regard to the INTERPRETATION of the SCRIPTURES.

In this Chapter WE will cover all TWELVE chapters of the Book of Daniel, and start with the Kingdom of JUDAH'S CAPTIVITY by Neb-u-chad-nez'-zar, King of Babylon. However, it must be understood prior to OUR going into the Scriptures of Daniel, that even though ***GOD*** allowed ISRAEL and JUDAH to be taken under control by the King of Babylon, ***HE*** NEVER RELINQUISHED ***HIS AUTHORITY*** over them! ***GOD*** only allowed Neb-u-chad-nez'-zar to brutally RULE over the Children of ISRAEL so they might be taught a LESSON for their turning their backs to ***GOD,*** and refusing to LISTEN to ***HIM.*** However, whatever lesson they learned was only temporary, for they returned again to their old ways ***SAITH THE LORD.***

NOTE: It might be INTERESTING to note, that in all the Scriptures of Daniel there isn't any mentioning whatsoever about the ARK of the COVENANT, or of its whereabouts. After the King of Babylon took JUDAH captive, the Scriptures tell of how all the HOLY ARTICLES were brought into

Babylon and put into the King's Treasury. However, there isn't any mentioning whatsoever about what had happened to the ARK of the COVENANT. Even after Ezra and Nehemiah were given permission to rebuild the WALL and the TEMPLE in JERUSALEM, and all of the HOLY ARTICLES were brought back into the TEMPLE from Babylon, nothing is mentioned in regard to where the ARK was. So what happened to the ARK of the COVENANT? Later on in this CHAPTER WE WILL TELL YOU WHERE THE ARK IS, WHEN IT WAS TAKEN FROM THE TEMPLE, AND WHO TOOK IT!

Timeline

After the death of KING SOLOMON, ***GOD*** divided the Kingdom of ISRAEL into two separate Kingdoms. The First Kingdom was the Kingdom of Judah, which consisted of two tribes, the tribe of Judah and the tribe of Benjamin. However at that time there were also Levites living in Judah, who looked after the TEMPLE and the HOLY ARTICLES.

SOLOMON'S son Re-ho-bo'-am was made King over Judah after his father had died, and Re-ho-bo-am RULED in JERUSALEM which was the Capitol City of Judah. The other ten tribes formed an allegiance and made Jer-o-bo'-am, the son of Ne'-bat their King, and Jer-o-bo'-am made Samaria, Israel's Capitol City.

After approximately four hundred and thirty years of Israel's independent existence, and its being ruled by mostly corrupt Kings, ***GOD*** allowed Neb-u-chad-nez'-zar the King of Babylon to seize and take control of Israel. Israel's Capitol, Samaria, was rifled and dismantled by the King of Babylon, and those who did not flee to another country were taken captive and brought into the Babylonian Empire.

Although Israel had been taken captive, Judah still remained intact; and Zed-e-ki'-ah reigned as King of Judah after Je-hoi'-a-kim in JERUSALEM. Zed-e-ki'-ah fortified the city making it nearly impenetrable and he also made many secret passages beneath its streets so he and his regime could move about the city in secrecy, fearing a pending battle over the city with the Chal'-de-ans.

A few short years after Israel's captivity, the Kingdom of Judah was also taken under control by King Neb-u-chad-nez'-zar. At that time the King appointed Je-hoi'-a-kim as King over Judah. After three years of Je-hoi'-a-kim's rule, he rebelled against Neb-u-chad-nez'-zar, and Neb-u-chad-nez'-zar attacked JERUSALEM and took it back under his control, and then Zed-e-ki'-ah was made King. However shortly thereafter, Zed-e-ki'-ah also rebelled against Neb-u-chad-nez'-zar, and Zed-e-ki'-ah's sons were killed as a result of it, and Zed-e-ki'-ah's eyes were put out and he was taken out of power. The invading forces of the Chal-de'-ans who were under the control of Neb-u-chad-nez'-zar DESTROYED then both JERUSALEM and SOLOMON'S TEMPLE, and took the people, all of the TEMPLE'S artifacts, and the King's treasures back to Babylon, leaving only a few people such as Jeremiah the Prophet behind in JERUSALEM.

Daniel the Prophet

Shortly after the captivity of Judah, King Neb-u-chad-nez'-zar decided to choose some servants from the young men of Judah and Israel to serve him in his palace. The instructions given to the Chief Servant by the King, was that he should choose from the Children of Israel the finest looking of all the young men. They were to be free from any type of physical defect and have also unique skills. The ones chosen were to be well educated and capable of learning the Chal'-de-an language, which was the King's language, for the King wanted to use the HEBREW SLAVES as Advisors and Consultants to him.

NOTE: Neb-u-chad-nez'-zar knew that there were Prophets among the Children of Israel, and he had heard how these Prophets could foretell the future and could provide him with wise consultation. He wasn't quite sure how to go about selecting them, so he assumed that the best looking young men would be the most likely to be Prophets. This search for Prophets by the King became an obsession with him, for it was ***GOD*** who had INSPIRED the King to seek a HEBREW PROPHET.

The King also directed his Chief servant to feed the ones he had chosen with the King's finest food and wine for a period of time. Then after the lot had been fed, made healthy, and cleaned up, (for they had been living under very poor conditions), they were to be brought before the King for an interview.

There were four young men who were all from the tribe of Judah, whose names were Daniel, Han-a-ni'-ah, Mish'-a-el, and Az-a-ri'-ah. The Chief Servant found these four to be the best looking and most intelligent among the young men he had chosen. He was so impressed by the four he even gave the four new Chal'-de-an names. He called Daniel, Bel-te-shaz'-zar, Han-a-ni'-ah he called Sha'-drach, Mish'-a-el he called Me'-shach; and Az-a-ri'-ah he called A-bed'-ne-go.

Daniel, not wanting to eat the King's food (for he found it to be offensive), asked the Chief Servant if he and his three friends could be given beans and water rather than having to eat and drink what the King had offered? At first, the Chief Servant refused Daniel's request for he feared they would become weak and ill looking by them eating only beans and drinking water. But Daniel assured the Chief Servant that their requested diet would improve their appearances and not degrade them. To further assure the Chief Servant, Daniel told him that after ten days of eating only beans and drinking water, the Chief Servant could come and look them over. Then at that time if they appeared to be unhealthy or in anyway lacking in nutrition, they would then agree to eat the King's food. The Chief Servant then agreed to grant Daniel his request.

After the ten days had passed, the Chief Servant came to the four who had only eaten beans and drank water to view their condition, and he was amazed to see how healthy they looked. Daniel and his companions looked by far healthier than those who had been eating the King's food.[1]

When the time had come for the four young men to go before the King, Daniel, Han-a-ni'-ah, Mish'-a-el, and Az-a-ri'-ah were brought along with several other men chosen for the interview, and when the King talked with the four he was amazed to see how intelligent they were. He found them to be quite attractive and significantly more intelligent than his Magicians and Astrologers. So the King immediately selected the four Hebrews to serve him in his palace.

The King's 1st DREAM

One night the King had a DREAM and the DREAM troubled him because he didn't know the meaning of it. In the King's DREAM he saw a large statue of a man that was made of several different types of materials. The head of the statue was made of gold, the arms and chest were made of silver, the belly and thighs were made of brass, its legs were made of iron and its feet were made of both iron and clay.

In the DREAM the King saw a large stone appear seemingly from out of nowhere, and the stone struck the feet of the statue that were made from iron and clay, and when struck by the stone they crumbled. The entire statue then began to crumble as well, and it fell to the ground like dust, and was then blown away by the wind. Furthermore, the STONE that had struck the statue began to grow, and it grew into a LARGE MOUNTAIN and the MOUNTAIN became the size of the entire EARTH.

The next morning when the King arose, being unable to sleep all night be-

[1] ***GOD*** had given all four of these young men skills in several areas. Daniel was GIVEN SIX GIFTS by THE ***HOLY SPIRIT*** and the other three men were GIVEN THREE GIFTS, and when all four of them were together, ALL NINE GIFTS were PRESENT. ***GOD*** had GIVEN Daniel the ability to UNDERSTAND and INTERPRET both DREAMS and VISIONS, for Daniel was chosen by ***GOD*** to SPEAK on ***HIS*** behalf to King Neb-u-chad-nez'-zar.

cause of his DREAM, he summoned his Magicians, Astrologers, and Sorcerers. The King then told them how he had had a DREAM that past evening that had troubled him, and wanted them to give to him the interpretation of the DREAM. But the King refused to tell them what the DREAM was about, for he didn't trust them; and said, if they could truly INTERPRET the DREAM, they should know what the dream entailed, and refused to tell anything further pertaining to it.

But the King's Magicians, Astrologers and Sorcerers said to him, no man can INTERPRET a DREAM without being told first what the DREAM was about. But the King still refused to give them details of the DREAM, saying, if you can INTERPRET the DREAM you should also know what the DREAM is about. The Magicians, Astrologers, and Sorcerers tell the King that he was being unfair, saying, only the gods could do such a thing he was requesting. After hearing what they had to say, the King became very angry, and being enraged by their inability to help him, decrees that ALL of the wise men in Babylon be put to death.

A'-ri-och, the Captain of the Guard, was then sent out by the King to kill all the Wise Men of Babylon, and when he gets to Daniel's house, A'-ri-och tells Daniel what the King has ordered. So Daniel asks A'-ri-och as to why the King would order such a thing? And A'-ri-och tells Daniel how the King had had a DREAM and how the King's Wise Men were unable to interpret it, causing the King to order; all of the Wise Men in Babylon be put to death. Daniel then asks A'-ri-och as to why he had not been given the opportunity to INTERPRET the King's DREAM, and request to see King Neb-u-chad-nez'-zar.

After being brought before the King, Daniel tells the King how his ***GOD*** can INTERPRET ANY DREAM. But Daniel says to him, that he must first PRAY to his ***GOD*** in HEAVEN that evening, and then his ***GOD*** would give him the INTERPRETATION for the King. After considering Daniel's request, the King consents to allowing Daniel time to PRAY that evening, and stays his decree to kill the Wise Men of Babylon until after he has heard what Daniel has to say about his DREAM.

Daniel then goes to his house and tells his friends Han-a-ni'-ah, Mish'-a-el, and Az-a-ri'-ah about the King's order to have them all killed, if they couldn't INTERPRET the King's DREAM. Being in fear for their lives all four PRAYED to ***GOD*** for MERCY, and that night ***GOD*** answered their PRAYERS and REVEALED to Daniel the INTERPRETATION of the King's DREAM; and Daniel THANKED THE LORD for ***HIS*** HELP.

Daniel 2:20 *Daniel answered and said, Blessed be the NAME of*

> ***GOD** for ever and ever: for WISDOM and MIGHT are **HIS:***
>
> ***Daniel 2:21** And **HE** changeth the times and the seasons: **HE** removeth Kings, and **HE** setteh up Kings: **HE** giveth WISDOM unto the wise, and KNOWLEDGE to them that know UNDER-STANDING:*
>
> ***Daniel 2:22 HE** REVEALETH the deep and secret things: **HE** KNOWETH what is in the darkness, and LIGHT dwelleth with **HIM.***
>
> ***Daniel 2:23** I thank thee, and PRAISE thee, O thou **GOD** of my fathers, who hast given me WISDOM and MIGHT, and hast made known unto me now what we desired of thee: for thou hast now made known unto us the King's matter.*

After Daniel had THANKED ***GOD*** for the INTERPRETATION of the DREAM, he returned to A'-ri'-och, the Captain of the Guard; and once again requests an audience with the King. Unbeknown to Daniel that the King had stayed his decree; he requests that A'-ri-och delay the killing of the King's Wise Men until after he has spoken to the King. Daniel also informs A'-ri-och that he would tell the King that morning what his DREAM was about, and also give him the INTERPRETATION of it; therefor, the Wise Men of Babylon needn't be put to death.

When Daniel meets with the King, he tells him, even though none of the Wise Men of Babylon could tell the King about his DREAM, nor give the INTERPRETATION of it, his ***GOD*** can and Daniel proceeds on to describe the DREAM to King Neb-u-chad-nez'-zar. He tells the King how in his DREAM he had seen an IMAGE (STATUE) whose head was made of GOLD, chest and arms made of SILVER, belly and thighs made of BRASS, legs made of IRON and the feet were made of both IRON and CLAY.

Daniel further explains how each one of the materials making up the IMAGE represented a Kingdom of the world, with the head of GOLD representing the King and the Kingdom of Babylon. He tells the King, after him will come forth a King who would be less powerful than he, and this was represented by the IMAGE'S arms and chest being made of SILVER, rather than GOLD. Daniel says, after this second Kingdom shall come a third Kingdom, and this Kingdom had been indicated by the IMAGE'S thighs and belly being made of BRASS; and this third Kingdom shall rule over the entire world. Then after the

Kingdom of BRASS will come a Kingdom made of IRON; and out of the Kingdom of iron will come yet another Kingdom, made also from IRON, but the iron will be mixed with CLAY. Daniel further tells the King, because the two materials (the IRON and the CLAY) do not mix well, they will eventually separate into two Kingdoms, one of IRON and the one of CLAY. And these two Kingdoms will coexist, and will not RECOMBINE.

Daniel tells the King, the GREAT STONE he had seen in the DREAM that seemingly came from out of nowhere and grew into a MOUNTAIN, represented ***GOD'S KINGDOM,*** and that KINGDOM would be the FINAL KINGDOM. For it was ***GOD'S KINGDOM*** represented by the GREAT STONE in the King's DREAM that had DESTROYED all the others in the DREAM. Daniel then says, ***GOD'S KINGDOM,*** is an EVERLASTING KINGDOM, and it can NEVER be destroyed for it shall stand FOREVER!

Once told this, King Neb-u-chad-nez'-zar fell upon his knees before Daniel and tried to worship him, because he had not only told the King about the DREAM accurately, but also gave him the INTERPRETATION of it. The King knew then what Daniel had said to him was the TRUTH, for Daniel's ***GOD*** had REVEALED both his DREAM and the FUTURE to him.

NOTE: THE LORD will now have ME explain the King's DREAM to you in further detail. The GOLD head of the IMAGE in Neb-u-chad-nez'-zar's DREAM represented the Kingdom of the Babylonian Empire. The SILVER chest and arms represented the Kingdoms of the MEDES and the PERSIANS who would eventually overthrow the Babylonian Empire and rule after them with King DARIUS being the FIRST KING of the MEDES and PERSIANS. The IMAGE'S thighs and belly made of BRASS represented the Kingdom of the GREEKS led by Alexander the Great. They would conquer the known world and rule over that region after the MEDES and PERSIANS. The legs of IRON represented the Roman Empire and Europe, for out of Europe would come forth several nations who each would rule the world for some period of time. The FEET made of both the IRON and CLAY, represent both GREAT BRITAIN (Europe), and the UNITED STATES of AMERICA (North America) who came forth from the BRITISH EMPIRE (Europe). The Scriptures also say that after the United States of America and the other Kingdoms of the world have FALLEN, the ***KINGDOM of GOD*** will PREVAIL. This will make ***GOD'S KINGDOM*** the SEVENTH and FINAL KINGDOM of the WORLD.

> ***Daniel 2:42*** *And as the toes of the feet were part of IRON, and part of CLAY, so the Kingdom shall be partly STRONG, and partly BROKEN.*

> ***Daniel 2:43*** *And whereas thou sawest IRON mixed with miry CLAY, they shall MINGLE THEMSELVES with the SEED of MEN: but they SHALL NOT CLEAVE one to another, even as IRON is not MIXED with CLAY.*

NOTE: The first Scripture says; although the ALLIANCE between GREAT BRITAIN and the UNITED STATES will be strongly tied to one another, they will not be under the same RULING GOVERNMENT. The second Scripture states that both of the PEOPLES of those nations (Britain (IRON) and the USA (CLAY) will be of the SAME LINEAGE (*Mingle themselves with the SEED of MEN*), however, they will be SEPARATED into two different NATIONS (*SHALL NOT CLEAVE ONE TO ANOTHER*).

> ***Daniel 2:44*** *And in the days of these Kings shall the* ***GOD of HEAVEN*** *set up a KINGDOM, which shall NEVER be destroyed: and the KINGDOM shall NOT be left to other people, but it shall break in pieces and CONSUME all these kingdoms, and it shall stand for EVER.*

After receiving the INTERPRETATION of the DREAM, King Neb-u-chad-nez'-zar placed Daniel in charge of ALL the Wise Men in Babylon, and made him a Ruler over the province he lived in, and also made Daniel the Chief of the Babylonian Governors. The King also permitted Daniel's three companions, Han-a-ni'-ah, called Sha'-drach, Mish'-a-el, called Me'-shach, and Az-a-ri'-ah, called A-bed-ne-go, to support Daniel in his Governorship.

NOTE: THE LORD says the time is now come to DISCLOSE the whereabouts of the ARK of the COVENANT, and the details surrounding its initial and FINAL REMOVAL from SOLOMON'S TEMPLE in JERUSALEM!

It is known that the ARK of the COVENANT resided in SOLOMON'S TEMPLE in JERUSALEM up until the time of the DESTRUCTION of JERUSALEM and its TEMPLE by Neb-u-chad-nez'-zar, King of Babylon. Before being named Babylon, the area of Babylon was called the Land of Shi'-nar. It was foreseen and foretold by the Prophet Zechariah as to how the Land of Shi'-nar would ultimately play a role in the taking of the ARK of the COVENANT.

The 5th and 6th Chapters of the book of Zechariah tell of how the HOLY ARTICLES of the TEMPLE were to be taken into the Land of Shi'-nar (Babylon), and how JERUSALEM and its TEMPLE would be REBUILT again after its DESTRUCTION by Neb-u-chad-nez'-zar. The Scriptures also tell of how a

CURSE would be placed upon the Land of Shi'-nar and upon anyone involved in the theft of the HOLY ARTICLES. The CURSE also applied to any FALSE BEARERS of the *WORD of* ***GOD,*** and also to the place where the HOLY ARTICLES are made to reside!

> ***Zechariah 5:4 I*** *will bring it forth,* ***SAITH THE LORD of HOSTS,*** *and it shall enter into the HOUSE of the THIEF, and into the house of him that sweareth falsely by* ***MY NAME:*** *and it shall remain in the midst of his house, and shall CONSUME it with the timber thereof and the stones thereof.*

NOTE: This Scripture tells of how the HOLY ARTICLES were stolen and taken into the HOUSE of the THIEF (referring to Babylon, now called Iraq). It also pertains to the Muslim people who claim to be doing things in the name of ***ALLAH*** (*"him that sweareth falsely by* ***MY NAME"***), although ***GOD*** hadn't taken ANY PART in their ACTIONS.

The Scriptures in Zechariah 5:5 through 5:11 speak of how the ARK (referred to in the Scriptures as an "e'-phah") will be removed by the ANGELS and placed in the Land of Shi'-nar. As with ALL SCRIPTURE, this event happens in the PAST, the PRESENT and in the FUTURE.

> ***Zechariah 5:5*** *Then the ANGEL that talked with me went forth, and said unto me, Lift up now thine eyes, and see what is this that goeth forth.*

> ***Zechariah 5:6*** *And I said, What is it? And he said, This is an e'-phah that goeth forth. He said moreover, This is their RESEMBLANCE through all the EARTH.*

> ***Zechariah 5:7*** *And, behold, there was lifted up a talent of LEAD: and this is a WOMAN that sitteth in the midst of the e'-phah.*

NOTE: The WOMAN spoken of in the Scripture refers to the FALSE PROPHET who claims to be a partaker in ***GOD'S COVENANT*** with MAN, but is NOT, and SWEARS FALSELY by ***HIS NAME.***

> ***Zechariah 5:8*** *And he said, This is WICKEDNESS. And he cast it into the midst of the e'-phah; and he cast the weight of LEAD upon the mouth thereof.*

Zechariah 5:9 *Then lifted I up mine eyes, and looked, and, behold, there came out TWO WOMEN, and the wind was in their WINGS; for they had WINGS like the WINGS of a STORK; and they LIFTED up the e'-phah between the EARTH and the HEAVEN.*

NOTE: The TWO WOMEN spoken about in the Scriptures refers to the COVENANT ANGELS, ZARALL and CHAMUEL. These are the TWO ANGELS of the OLD COVENANT, which the ARK of the COVENANT (the e'-phah) REPRESENTS.

Zechariah 5:10 *Then said I to the ANGEL that talked with me, Whither do these bear the e'-phah?*

Zechariah 5:11 *And he said unto me, to build it an house in the Land of Shi'-nar: and it shall be established, and set there upon her own base.*

The Scriptures tell you that the ARK of the COVENANT was brought into Babylon, and resided there (upon its own base) until the TEMPLE was REBUILT, and then it was brought back again into the TEMPLE in JERUSALEM.

So the questions still remain as to, when was the ARK of the COVENANT permanently REMOVED from the TEMPLE, and where was it taken? WE will FIRST address the WHEREABOUTS of the ARK, and do so by SCRIPTURE:

Revelation 11:19 *And the TEMPLE of* ***GOD*** *was opened in HEAVEN, and there was seen in* ***HIS*** *TEMPLE the ARK of* ***HIS*** *TESTAMENT: and there were lightnings, and voices, and thunderings, and an earthquake, and great hail.*

NOTE: The Scripture taken from the Book of Revelation clearly states that the ARK of the COVENANT, called in the Scripture, the "ARK of ***HIS*** TESTAMENT", now RESIDES in HEAVEN!

So, the only question still remaining is when was the ARK removed from the TEMPLE in JERUSALEM and brought to HEAVEN? WE know from the Scriptures that it was the ANGELS ZARALL and CHAMUEL who removed the ARK; so when did they take it? WE will give YOU this answer shortly, but first you must know a little about the history of the ARK.

After the Jews had lost the ARK TWICE, first to the Philistines (1 Samuel 6:1) and then to the Chaldeans (Babylonians); when it was finally brought back to the TEMPLE in JERUSALEM, it was GUARDED twenty-four hours a day by the Levite Priests. This guarding of the ARK continued on up until the DESTRUCTION of the TEMPLE by the Romans in 60AD, even though the ARK had already been missing for SIXTY YEARS. The ARK being MISSING was a GUARDED SECRET by the Jewish Priests for the SIXTY YEARS after the RESURRECTION of JESUS CHRIST.

At the TIME of JESUS' crucifixion, it says in the Scripture that the VEIL in the TEMPLE was TORN (RENT), thus indicating the BREAKING of the OLD COVENANT and the MAKING of the NEW COVENANT. The TEARING of the VEIL further represented MAN'S NEW ACCESS to ***GOD*** by way of JESUS CHRIST, for before JESUS, only the High Priest had ACCESS to the ARK of the COVENANT, the place where ***GOD*** SAT, BEHIND the VEIL.

> ***Luke 23:45*** *And the sun was darkened, and the VEIL of the TEMPLE was RENT in the midst.*

ONCE the NEW COVENANT was made there wasn't any further need for the ARK, because ***GOD*** NOW DWELLS within the HEART of MAN and no longer SITS UPON the MERCY SEAT of the ARK BEHIND the VEIL.

At the TIME of JESUS' crucifixion, the ANGELS ZARALL and CHAMUEL RIPPED the VEIL and REMOVED the ARK of the COVENANT from the TEMPLE. When the HIGH PRIEST Ca'-ia-phas found that the ARK was gone, and that it happened at the TIME of JESUS' CRUCIFIXION, he made a pact with the other Priests looking after the ARK, to never let it be known to the people that the ARK had been taken. For if they had made it public knowledge, it would have CONFIRMED JESUS to be the SON of ***GOD,*** and they would be blamed by the people for the DEATH of the MESSIAH!

This SECRET was kept by the Priests up until the TIME the ROMANS DESTROYED JERUSALEM and its TEMPLE in 60AD. After its DESTRUCTION, the people ASSUMED that the ARK had either been taken by the Romans or was destroyed in the fire when the city was burnt to the ground. This is why the WHEREABOUTS of the ARK and the records regarding its movement have never been found.

The King's IMAGE of GOLD

After receiving the INTERPRETATION of his DREAM from Daniel, King Neb-u-chad-nez'-zar decides to construct in the province of Du'-ra an IMAGE of himself made of GOLD; thus representing him and his Kingdom's greatness.

Once finished, the IDOL (IMAGE) stood ninety feet tall and was nine feet wide. The King then summoned all his officials throughout the Kingdom of Babylon to come to Du'-ra for the dedication of the IDOL.

During the dedication, a Herald of the King announces; when the people of the land hear the sound of instruments playing in the streets, all the people were then to bow down immediately and worship the IDOL. It was also decreed; if anyone were to refuse to worship the IDOL, them in refusal were to be cast into the burning furnace used to fire the bricks, and their punishment would come in the same hour of their crime. After the dedication, whenever the people would hear the sound of the instruments playing, they did as they were told to do by the King's Decree, and bowed themselves to the ground and worshipped the IDOL.

After some period of time, the people noticed that there were certain Hebrews who were not following after the order of the King, so they went to the King to complain about it. The King when hearing the complaints, asked, who were they that had refused to follow his commandment? It was then told to the King, it was Daniel's companions, Sha'-drach, Me'-shach, and A-bed'-ne-go. The King in anger then ordered the three to be brought before him.

> ***Daniel 3:14*** *Neb-u-chad-nez'-zar spake and said unto them, is it true, O Sha'-drach, Me'-shach, and A-bed'-ne-go, do not ye serve my gods, nor worship the golden image which I have set up?*

After the three admitted they had not worshipped the King's idol, the King tells them he will give them another chance. He said he would forget the matter, if the next time when hearing the instruments play they would bow down and worship the IDOL made of GOLD. But warns, if they do not, neither their ***GOD*** nor anyone else could deliver them out of his hand. But the three answered the King by saying; they would not serve the King's false god, and their ***GOD*** could indeed both DELIVER them out of the hand of the King and also out of the BURNING FURNACE, if ***HE*** so desired.

After hearing this, the King became infuriated with them and orders the BURNING FURNACE to be heated to a temperature SEVEN TIMES GREATER than its normal temperature. He then commanded that Sha'-drach, Me'-shach, and A-bed'-ne-go be bound and cast into the BURNING FURNACE. The King's Guards then put the three into the FURNACE fully clothed.

After following the King's instructions, the FURNACE became so hot, the guards putting the three into it were scorched by the heat of it and died, and the King watched as the three men sat in the FURNACE amidst the FLAMES. But after a few minutes, the King noticed there appeared to be FOUR men in the FURNACE and not just the three, and neither their clothes nor the hair on their heads were aflame from the great heat. So the King asked one of the guards, were there not three that were put into the FURNACE? And the Guards answered him, saying; there were only three, O King.

> ***Daniel 3:25*** *He answered and said, Lo, I see FOUR MEN loose, walking in the midst of the FIRE, and they have no hurt; and the FORM of the FOURTH is like the SON of* ***GOD.***

The King then called out to the three saying, Sha'-drach, Me'-shach, and A-bed'-ne-go, YOU SERVANTS OF THE MOST HIGH ***GOD,*** come out of the BURNING FURNACE; and the three men came out of the furnace. When the King and the others gathered with him saw that none of the three had been burned and neither was their hair or their clothes burned; and they didn't even smell like smoke, he and those with him stood in AWE!

> ***Daniel 3:28*** *Then Neb-u-chad-nez'-zar spake, and said, BLESSED BE THE* ***GOD*** *of Sha'-drach, Me'-shach, and A-bed'-ne-go, who hath sent his ANGEL, and DELIVERED* ***HIS*** *SERVANTS that TRUSTED in* ***HIM,*** *and have CHANGED the King's word, and yielded their bodies, that they might not serve nor worship any god, except their OWN* ***GOD.***

After SEEING the POWER of ***GOD,*** the King makes a DECREE that ALL of his Kingdom were to honor the ***GOD*** of Sha'-drach, Me'-shach, and A-bed'-ne-go, for the King said; no other god could do what their ***GOD*** had done. The King further decreed; if anyone were to be caught not HONORING their ***GOD,*** both they and their families would be put to death. Then on that day the King PROMOTED Sha'-drach, Me'-shach, and A-bed'-ne-go to leadership positions in the province of Du'-ra.

NOTE: The FOURTH PERSON seen by Neb-u-chad-nez'-zar in the BURNING FURNACE was the ANGEL GABRIEL and not JESUS CHRIST, as the church so often teaches. ***GOD*** had sent GABRIEL to LOOK after the Children of ISRAEL during the time of their CAPTIVITY. Neb-u-chad-nez'-zar and his Wise Men were well aware of the ANGELS of ***GOD,*** and referred to the ANGELS as both "WATCHERS" and the SONS of ***GOD.*** In nearly every mentioning in the Scriptures of an ANGEL, who either SPEAKS to the Children of ISRAEL or makes a direct contact with them, the ANGEL is always GABRIEL.

Although other ANGELS are mentioned as being seen in the Scriptures, it is always GABRIEL who SPEAKS to them. GABRIEL is the ANGEL of CHRIST, and it is HE whom ***GOD*** sends to either PROTECT or DELIVER a MESSAGE from HEAVEN.

The King's 2nd DREAM

Chapter 4 of the Book of Daniel opens with King Neb-u-chad-nez'-zar honoring ***GOD,*** but doing so out of his FEAR of ***GOD*** rather than for his LOVE of ***GOD.*** As with most men in a position of POWER, Neb-u-chad-nez'-zar believed his POWER had been achieved as a result of his accomplishments. This is contrary to the TRUTH, for it is ***GOD*** who EMPOWERS or DEBASES as ***HE*** chooses.

NOTE: GOD is not like a man, being limited in how many things he may accomplish at one time. ***GOD*** is OMNIPOTENT ***(ALMIGHTY)*** and is UNLIMITED in what ***HE*** can do. ***HE*** is involved in ALL MATTERS on EARTH, throughout the UNIVERSE, and in HEAVEN, and in a single moment can change anything. A SINGLE blade of GRASS cannot grow without ***GOD'S*** EXPLICIT BLESSING, and although the Church teaches that man acts on his own FREE WILL, he does not! ***GOD*** has PREDETERMINED ALL things, and man simply plays a character role of that PREDETERMINATION. Anyone believing they are in control of either their own destiny or the World's DESTINY is but a FOOL, for the CHARACTER ROLE they play on EARTH had been SCRIPTED in DETAIL long before they or the WORLD EVER WAS! When a person glorifies him or herself and does not give the GLORY to ***GOD*** for their accomplishments, SKILLS, or their enterprises, they are following after the order of Lucifer; for he believes what he does, he does on his own. Unbeknown to him, the Devil is but a PAWN, and so also is MAN but a PAWN in THE ***HAND of GOD,*** and ***GOD*** makes ALL the MOVES! This vain belief of being in control of things was a trait that King Neb-u-chad-nez'-zar continually exhibited by his self-glorification, so ***GOD*** decided to show the King who it was that was in ***POWER!***

One evening, ***GOD*** gave the King a 2nd DREAM and the DREAM was meant to be a WARNING. However, the King didn't UNDERSTAND the DREAM so he called for his Magicians, Astrologers, and Advisors and told them of it, but none of them could give the King the INTERPRETATION of the DREAM. The King then once again called upon Daniel, whom had been renamed Bel-te-shaz'-zar, according to name of his FALSE god. And the King said:

> ***Daniel 4:9*** *O Bel-te-shaz'-zar, Master of the Magicians, because I know that the spirit of the holy gods is in thee, and no SECRET troubleth thee, tell me the VISIONS of my DREAM that I have seen, and the INTERPRETATION thereof.*

The King explained how in his DREAM he had seen a great TREE growing out of the earth, whose branches were magnificent and full of fruit and foliage. The TREE provided shade for all of the animals of the earth and the birds dwelt in its branches, and the TREE was so great in stature, it appeared to reach up to HEAVEN. He further explained how he had seen an ANGEL (a WATCHER) in the DREAM that had come down from HEAVEN making a PROCLAMATION and a DECREE; that the TREE should be hewn down and its limbs stripped from it, leaving only the STUMP and its ROOTS in the ground. The ANGEL further PROCLAIMED by DECREE; the TREE should be made to live like a BEAST in the FIELD for SEVEN YEARS, so the tree may come to KNOW it is the ***ALMIGHTY GOD*** who can either EMPOWER or DEBASE; ANYONE ***HE*** so CHOOSES.

> ***Daniel 4:17*** *This matter is by the DECREE of the WATCHERS, and the demand by the WORD of* **THE HOLY ONES***: to the intent that the living may know that THE* **MOST HIGH** *RULETH in the Kingdom of men, and giveth it to whomsoever* **HE** *will, and setteh up over it the basest of men.*

After hearing about the DREAM from the King, Daniel pondered its INTERPRETATION for one hour and was reluctant to give it, and the King saw that its INTERPRETATION was bothersome to Daniel. However the King told Daniel to give him the INTERPRETATION even if it had a NEGATIVE outcome, so Daniel told the King the meaning of the DREAM.

Daniel said, the TREE represented both the King and his power over the Kingdom, and due to the King's behavior, ***GOD*** was going to REMOVE him from being King for SEVEN YEARS. During that SEVEN-YEAR period of time, the King was going to go crazy and act like a mad man and be put into the wilderness to live like a wild animal. While in the wilderness, he would eat grass like the oxen and live among the animals until he has come to REALIZE that it was ***GOD*** who had EMPOWERED him!

Daniel further explains that even though the TREE had been hewn down to a STUMP, its ROOTS remaining in the earth indicated that the King would be given a second chance; providing the King glorified ***GOD*** rather than himself for his EMPOWERING. Then after the King has GLORIFIED the ***ALMIGHTY GOD,*** the Kingdom would be given back to him.

Daniel then recommends to the King that he change his behavior and become a HUMBLE man and GLORIFY ***GOD.*** Daniel says, the King should start tending to the needs of the people rather than to himself, and if he were to do this, his days could be prolonged before the DREAM would COME to PASS. The King then followed Daniel's recommendation for one year and at the end of the year, the King again began to glorify himself.

> ***Daniel 4:30*** *The King spake, and said, Is it not this great Babylon, that I have built for the house of the kingdom by the might of my power, and for the honour of my majesty?*

> ***Daniel 4:31*** *While the WORD was yet in the King's mouth, there fell a VOICE from HEAVEN saying, O King Neb-u-chad-nez'-zar, to thee it is spoken; THE KINGDOM IS DEPARTED FROM THEE.*

In the same hour the VOICE from HEAVEN had spoken out to him, the King went insane and could no longer talk and had to be shackled and bound like a wild animal. The King was then removed from the Palace and taken to the wilderness and released, and there he lived for SEVEN YEARS. While in the wilderness and in a fit of rage, the King ripped off all of his clothing, then over a period of time he grew hair over his entire body and his finger and toenails grew out like claws on a bird. During that period of time, King Neb-u-chad-nez'-zar could no longer speak or think like a man, and hadn't any human intellectual properties remaining in him.

At the CONCLUSION of the SEVEN YEARS, the King's sanity returned to him and he then raised his eyes up to HEAVEN and GLORIFIED ***GOD,*** and PRAISED and HONORED the ***ALMIGHTY.*** Then once Neb-u-chad-nez'-zar had HUMBLED himself before ***GOD; GOD*** then gave him back the Kingdom.

> ***Daniel 4:37*** *Now I Neb-u-chad-nez'-zar PRAISE and EXTOL, and HONOUR the **KING of HEAVEN,** all whose works are TRUTH, and **HIS** ways JUDGMENT: and those that walk in pride **HE** is able to ABASE.*

The WRITING on the wall

After the reign of Neb-u-chad-nez'-zar in Babylon, Bel-shaz'-zar, his grandson reigned in his stead. Bel-shaz'-zar was an irresponsible King who would have feasts and ceremonies that went on for days at a time. During one of his feasts, the King decided to bring out of his treasuries some of the HOLY ARTICLES that had been taken by his grandfather, Neb-u-chad-nez'-zar from the TEMPLE in JERUSALEM.

GOLDEN GOBLETS from the TEMPLE of ***GOD*** were then brought to the King and he and those in attendance drank their wine from them. Then while drinking from the HOLY VESSELS, they praised and worshipped IDOLS made of gold, silver, brass, iron, wood, and stone, proclaiming the IDOLS to be gods. Then, while worshipping the IDOLS, a HAND appeared from out of nowhere, and the HAND WROTE WORDS in the plaster of the Palace wall.

Once the King had seen this, he immediately became frightened and ceased the ceremony and called for his Soothsayers and Astrologers to come and translate the WORDS that the HAND had WRITTEN in the plaster. After several hours were spent trying to INTERPRET the WORDS to no avail, for the WORDS were in an unknown language, the Queen recommended that the Prophet Daniel be called to INTERPRET the WORDS.

King Bel-shaz'-zar had never met Daniel, nor the Queen, however she had heard of him. The Queen had heard how Daniel was used by Bel-shaz'-zar's grandfather, King Neb-u-chad-nez'-zar to INTERPRET DREAMS and also provide SPIRITUAL COUNSELING on supernatural matters. So by the Queen's recommendation Daniel the Prophet was summoned.

When Daniel arrived at the palace the King tells Daniel about his taking the GOLDEN GOBLETS from the TEMPLE in JERUSALEM out of his treasury, and how they had drank from them during their feast. He further tells Daniel how the HAND had mysteriously appeared and WROTE the unknown WORDS into the plaster of the King's Palace WALL. The King then asks Daniel if he could INTERPRET the WORDS for he believed there was a MESSAGE in them.

Daniel tells the King about his grandfather, Neb-u-chad-nez'-zar, and how he had failed to recognize that he had been put into power by ***GOD,*** nor did he realize he needed to FEAR the POWER of the ***ALMIGHTY GOD.*** Daniel explained how ***GOD*** took the King out of power until he had acknowledged and GLORIFIED the ***GOD*** who had put him in power. Daniel further tells Bel-shaz'-zar how Neb-u-chad-nez'-zar his grandfather was made to go mad and put out into the wilderness for SEVEN YEARS to live like an animal, for glorifying himself instead of ***GOD.*** He then tells Bel-shaz'-zar that he had now done something much worse than his grandfather had done, for he had taken the HOLY VESSELS that had been HALLOWED unto ***GOD*** and DEFILED them in a celebration of false gods.

After telling Bel-shaz'-zar this, Daniel gives the King the INTERPRETATION of the WRITING on the WALL. He says, THE LORD has NUMBERED the DAYS of the Babylonian Kingdom and those days have come to an END. He further says, the King's irresponsible behavior has ANGERED ***GOD***, and now ***GOD*** has decided to give his Kingdom to the Medes and the Persians.

After hearing the INTERPRETATION of the WORDS WRITTEN on the wall, the King tries to honor Daniel. He puts a scarlet robe on Daniel and a gold chain around his neck, and further decrees; Daniel be given charge over one-third of the Kingdom of Babylon.

But it wasn't Daniel who the King had DISHONORED that evening, it was ***GOD***; and on that very night the King was slain by the invading Medes soldiers, and DARIUS then reigned as King over the Babylonian Empire.

King DARIUS is DECEIVED

DARIUS, being forewarned by his mother Esther (who was a HEBREW), that he should listen and take heed to what the Prophets of ISRAEL were to say; appoints Daniel to be one of three Presidents. These Presidents oversaw the provinces and the one hundred and twenty Princes who governed the provinces.

DARIUS had great respect for Daniel and it was rummored that the King had elevated Daniel's status, making Daniel second to DARIUS over the Kingdom. However, these rumors of Daniel's promotion troubled the other two Presidents and also the Princes of the provinces, for they despised Daniel because he was a HEBREW. The two Presidents and the Princes were continually plotting against Daniel and tried to find fault with his actions, but it appeared that all that Daniel had done was in accordance with the King's commandments.[2]

After the other two Presidents and the Princes had determined that no fault could be found in Daniel's actions, they decided to devise a plan against him. Whereas, Daniel always PRAYED and WORSHIPPED ***GOD,*** their plan was to in some way make it illegal for him to do so.

So the Presidents went to King DARIUS and told him they wanted to make a STATUE in honor of him, and wanted the King to make a DECREE regarding the matter. The DECREE would say if anyone worshipped any god other than the King or his IMAGE during the thirty-day dedication period of the STATUE, they would then be in violation of the law and cast into the LIONS DEN. Being unaware that the two Presidents and the Princes specifically devised the plan against Daniel, DARIUS agreed and the DECREE was written into law and signified by the King.

After the DECREE was made by DARIUS, the two Presidents and the Princes then went off to spy on Daniel, and through the window of his house they see Daniel on his KNEES facing towards JERUSALEM and PRAYING to ***GOD.*** They then went back to DARIUS to tell him about Daniel, but first remind the King how the law that had been written must stand. They cleverly ask DARIUS, if everyone must obey the law? DARIUS then tells them; once the law has been written it must be OBEYED by all. After hearing the King say this, they then tell DARIUS how Daniel had violated the law by him PRAYING to his ***GOD*** three times a day; whereas the law says he must only worship the King or his image during the thirty-day dedication. They say, therefor the King must order that Daniel to be put into the LIONS DEN for breaking the law.

The King realizing now that the Presidents had DECEIVED him, and tricked him into making a law for the purpose of the entrapment of Daniel, appears then to waiver on his decision. But the men again remind him that once the law had been written and signified by the King it was unchangeable; and the King must ENFORCE it.

> ***Daniel 6:16*** *Then the King commanded, and they brought Daniel, and cast him into the DEN of LIONS. Now the King spake and said unto Daniel, Thy* ***GOD*** *whom thou servest continually,* ***HE*** *will DELIVER thee.*

---

[2] As covered in the PREVIOUS BOOK, DARIUS is a SEVENTH LEVEL ANGEL, although his angelic status was unbeknown to him during his time on EARTH. He and the two succeeding Kings, (CYRUS and ARTAXERXES) were sent to EARTH by ***GOD*** to reign in Babylon over the children of ISRAEL during their time of CAPTIVITY. Even though all three are ANGELS, none of the three OPENLY SERVED ***GOD*** during their time on EARTH, although they did ACKNOWLEDGE ***GOD'S EXISTENCE.*** These THREE Kings could do this and get away with it, because they HAVE a DIVINE RIGHT to HEAVEN. Whereas anyone other than the ANGEL would surely be cast into HELL for not SERVING ***GOD,*** while on EARTH. THE LORD has had ME place this footnote in the BOOK to DEMONSTRATE why ONE should not JUDGE another, before they know SPIRITUALLY who they may be JUDGING; for the SEVENTH LEVEL ANGEL is quite POWERFUL and well above man in HEAVEN. As King, DARIUS did many ruthless things, and history depicts him as being an egotist. However, regardless of his behavior on EARTH, DARIUS' place in HEAVEN is SET.

> ***Daniel 6:17*** *And a stone was brought, and laid upon the mouth of the DEN; and the King sealed it with his own signet, and with the signet of his lords; that the purpose might not be changed concerning Daniel.*

The King then returned to his Palace being very upset over his being tricked by the Presidents into putting Daniel to death. That night DARIUS refused to eat and went immediately to his bedchambers; however he couldn't sleep the entire night. Then on the following morning at the crack of dawn, DARIUS rushed back to the LIONS DEN to check on Daniel's status.

> ***Daniel 6:20*** *And when he came to the DEN, he cried with a lamentable voice unto Daniel: and the King spake and said to Daniel, O Daniel, servant of the living* ***GOD,*** *is thy* ***GOD,*** *whom thou servest continually, able to DELIVER thee from the LIONS?*

> ***Daniel 6:21*** *Then said Daniel unto the King, O King, live for ever.*

> ***Daniel 6:22*** *My* ***GOD*** *hath sent* ***HIS*** *ANGEL, and hath shut the LIONS' mouths, that they have not hurt me: forasmuch as before* ***HIM*** *innocency was found in me; and also before thee, O King, have I done no hurt.*

After hearing Daniel's voice, DARIUS became very happy, for the ***GOD*** of Daniel had DELIVERED him from the LIONS, and he was not harmed in any way. DARIUS then ordered them who had DECEIVED him be put into the LIONS DEN, along with their wives and their children; and the LIONS DEVOURED them all.

To HONOR the ***GOD*** of Daniel, DARIUS makes a new DECREE: that ALL in his Kingdom were to HONOR and REVERE the ***ALMIGHTY GOD*** of Daniel; for Daniel's ***GOD*** is the only TRUE ***GOD*** who RULES the WORLD, and could DELIVER Daniel from the LIONS.

> ***Daniel 6:28*** *So this Daniel prospered in the reign of DA-RI'-US, and in the reign of CYRUS the Persian.*

Daniel's VISION of the FOUR BEASTS

In the first year of King Bel-shaz'-zar's reign, Daniel had a DREAM, and in the

VISION of his DREAM, Daniel sees FOUR GREAT BEASTS rise up out of the EARTH. Daniel sees that each of the BEASTS has a unique appearance; and these are the descriptions of the FOUR GREAT BEASTS:

The 1st BEAST Daniel saw had the appearance of a LION, who had wings on it likening to an eagle. Then Daniel sees that the LION had its wings plucked off, and was made to stand upright like a man, and the LION was given a human heart.

The 2nd BEAST in Daniel's VISION had the appearance of a BEAR, and the BEAR had THREE ribs in its mouth; and the THREE ribs spoke to it and said, rise up and CONQUER!

The 3rd BEAST in the VISION had the appearance of a LEOPARD, and the LEOPARD had FOUR HEADS, and on the LEOPARD'S back it had FOUR wings like bird's wings, and dominion was given to the FOUR HEADS.

The 4th BEAST in Daniel's VISION was the most POWERFUL of the FOUR, and this BEAST had teeth that were made of IRON, and the 4th BEAST DEVOURED all the other BEASTS before him. Then Daniel noticed that the 4th BEAST sprouted TEN HORNS, and ONE LITTLE HORN sprouted out of the TEN. It was also noticed that the LITTLE HORN became more POWERFUL than the THREE most powerful HORNS before it; and ONE MAN controlled the LITTLE HORN, and he made war with the SAINTS or anyone else who came up against him.

Finally Daniel sees in his VISION that ALL of the Kingdoms of the EARTH had been thrown down and nearly destroyed by the 4th BEAST, but the ***ANCIENT of DAYS*** came to the EARTH and took CONTROL of it, and JUDGED it for its SINS. And the 4th BEAST, who had spoken many great words and boasted about itself, was REMOVED from the EARTH by the ***ANCIENT of DAYS*** and CAST DOWN into the LAKE of FIRE. Daniel then saw how the other Kingdoms of the EARTH had their dominions stripped from them by the ***ANCIENT of DAYS***, but were allowed to continue on the EARTH for a period of time.

After the BEASTS were REMOVED from power by the ***ANCIENT of DAYS,*** Daniel then SEES the MESSIAH come down in the CLOUDS from HEAVEN, and the MESSIAH was brought before the ***ANCIENT of DAYS.*** The EARTH was then given to the MESSIAH to be HIS KINGDOM, and THE KINGDOM was to be an EVERLASTING KINGDOM, ONE that could never be DESTROYED.

EXPLANATION of the VISION

What Daniel was being shown in the VISION was the CHANGING of WORLD POWERS up to the SECOND COMING of JESUS CHRIST. The 1st BEAST Daniel saw having the appearance of a LION with wings like an eagle represented the Babylonian Empire. By having its wings CLIPPED and made to stand upright like a man, represented King Neb-u-chad-nez'-zar's having his kingdom taken from him. The 1st BEAST'S receipt of a HUMAN HEART, represented the HUMBLING of King Neb-u-chad-nez'-zar and his GLORIFICATION of the ***GOD*** who had EMPOWERED him.

The 2nd BEAST having the appearance of a BEAR with THREE ribs in its mouth represented the Kingdoms of the Medes and the Persians. The THREE ribs REPRESENTED the THREE KINGS of the Medes and Persians, DARIUS, CYRUS, and ARTAXERXES.

The 3rd BEAST having the appearance of a LEOPARD with FOUR wings like a bird represented the Greeks and their conquering of the known world, led by Alexander the Great. The FOUR wings and FOUR HEADS represented Alexander's FOUR Generals, who took control over Alexander's conquests after his death and made them into FOUR Kingdoms.

The 4th BEAST who had TEETH made of IRON and TEN HORNS represents the ROMAN EMPIRE and EUROPE. The THREE HORNS that were (plucked up) and OVER POWERED by the LITTLE HORN represent the THREE major European nations, France, Great Britain, and Germany. The LITTLE HORN sprouting out of the THREE HORNS is the United States of America, who broke away from Great Britain, and came forth from EUROPE.

> ***Daniel 7:8*** *I considered the HORNS, and, behold, there came up among them another LITTLE HORN, before whom there were THREE of the FIRST HORNS PLUCKED up by the roots: and, behold, in this HORN were eyes like the eyes of man, and a mouth speaking GREAT THINGS.*

The MAN (the LITTLE HORN) spoken of here in the Scripture is the Antichrist; who will seize CONTROL over the United States of America and the world, as it was described in the PREVIOUS BOOK. He will form an alliance with Europe who are represented by the TEN HORNS (Ten Nations) and will control the world up until the COMING of the ***ANCIENT of DAYS (THE DELIVERER, 182 PERSON).*** At that time the ***182 PERSON*** will JUDGE the

EARTH and take it BACK from them who had DESTROYED it; and ***HE*** will CAST DOWN the Antichrist, and turn the WORLD over to ***HIS*** SON, JESUS CHRIST, to RULE OVER IT.

The other nations of the world who will be allowed to live for a season and a time after the Antichrist has been cast down, refer to the 104,000,000 people who will continue to live and repopulate the EARTH during the MILLENNIUM. These are the people who will live outside of the CAMP of the SAINTS, during the MILLENNIUM, as it was explained in the 4th Chapter of the PREVIOUS BOOK.

> ***Daniel 7:12*** *As concerning the rest of the BEASTS, they had their dominion taken away: yet their lives were prolonged for a season and a time.*

The Scriptures in Chapter 7 of the Book of Daniel further go on to tell how Daniel sees JESUS CHRIST (the MESSIAH) come down from HEAVEN in the CLOUDS, and the EARTH is given to HIM and the SAINTS. After seeing all this occur in his DREAM, Daniel asks one of the ANGELS in the VISION the meaning of the DREAM, and the ANGEL tells Daniel that which WE have TOLD YOU!

READ THE 7th CHAPTER of THE BOOK of DANIEL, FOR NOW YOU HAVE AN UNDERSTANDING OF THE SCRIPTURES!

The RAM and the HE GOAT

> ***Daniel 8:1*** *In the third year of the reign of King Bel-shaz'-zar a VISION appeared unto me, even unto me Daniel, after that which appeared unto me at the FIRST.*

NOTE: What Daniel is saying in the opening Scripture of Chapter 8, is that three years after he had received his FIRST VISION regarding the changing of world power, he was given a SECOND VISION on the same subject matter. The SECOND VISION however contained more detail about who would be GIVEN the POWER over the world, and in what order the POWER would be RECEIVED. You will see as WE PROGRESS through the Book of Daniel that all of Daniel's VISIONS pertain to the same subject matter, the changing over time of WORLD DOMINANCE!

In his VISION Daniel sees a RAM having TWO HORNS sprouting out of his head, and the SECOND HORN was HIGHER than the FIRST HORN.

Daniel notices that the RAM is pushing towards several different directions, towards the west, the north and the south, and it appears that no other BEAST was able to stop him.

Daniel also sees in his VISION a HE GOAT appear, and the HE GOAT came by way of the west and was moving at an incredible speed. He saw that the HE GOAT had a GREAT HORN between its two eyes, and with its incredible speed, the HE GOAT ran into the RAM and knocked him down to the ground and the RAM was unable to get up. Once the HE GOAT had knocked down the RAM, the GREAT HORN between the eyes of the HE GOAT broke off, and in its place grew out FOUR smaller horns. And, out of one of the smaller HORNS came forth yet another LITTLE HORN, and this LITTLE HORN grew into a GREAT HORN who eventually took control over the entire EARTH. The GREAT HORN became so powerful it took with it one-third of the Angels in HEAVEN, and brought them down to the EARTH.

> ***Daniel 8:11*** *Yea, he magnified himself even to the PRINCE of the HOST, and by him the DAILY SACRIFICE was taken away, and the place of his sanctuary was cast down.*

> ***Daniel 8:12*** *And an host was given him against the daily sacrifice by reason of transgression, and it cast down TRUTH to the ground; and it practised, and prospered.*

While in the VISION, Daniel hears two SAINTS talking to one another. One asks the other how long would this GREAT HORN have control over the world, and the other SAINT replies, “SIX YEARS and THREE MONTHS”!

The ANGEL GABRIEL, also in the VISION, was then told by a VOICE from HEAVEN to tell Daniel what the VISION meant, and GABRIEL tells Daniel how the changes in WORLD DOMINANCE depicted by the HE GOAT and the RAM would continue on through to the END TIME. GABRIEL says, for at the TIME APPOINTED the END SHALL BE, and continues on to explain the meaning of the VISION:

GABRIEL says, the RAM with the TWO HORNS represents the nations of Media and Persia, with the LARGER of the two HORNS being the nation of Persia, because it will be the GREATER of the two nations. The HE GOAT represents the nation of Greece, and its GREAT NOTABLE HORN that had been broken off, represents Alexander the Great; who will die after conquering the known world and leave his holdings to be under the control of his four Generals. The FOUR Generals are represented by the FOUR smaller horns growing out of the GREAT HORN that had been broken off, and the Generals will divide Alexander's conquests by four and into four nations. GABRIEL then says, out of one of those four nations will come forth a LITTLE HORN, who will become a GREAT NATION (the United States of America).

Then after some period of time, Lucifer will take possession of the Leadership of that GREAT NATION (Daniel 8:12 "*and an HOST was given him*"). They together will then deny PRAYER and the READING of the *WORD of **GOD,*** and set up the ABOMINATION that makes DESOLATE in the TEMPLE in JERUSALEM; and there the possessed one (the Antichrist) will proclaim himself to be god. The Antichrist (the possessed one), being under the control of Lucifer will also CHALLENGE the AUTHORITY of JESUS CHRIST, who is called by the Scripture, the "PRINCE of princes" (Daniel 8:25). However his efforts will FAIL, and he will be REMOVED from power, not by hand, but rather by the *WORD of **GOD!***

NOTE: Daniel is being told by GABRIEL the same thing the Apostle John was told in the Book of Revelation.

> ***Revelation 19:21*** *And the remnant were slain with the SWORD of HIM that sat upon the horse, which SWORD proceeded out of HIS MOUTH: and all the fowls were filled with their flesh.*

NOTE: The previous Scripture refers to JESUS CHRIST'S SECOND COMING, when HE defeats the DEVIL, not by HAND, but rather by the *WORD of **GOD;*** PROCEEDING FROM HIS MOUTH!

The SEVENTY WEEKS

In the 1st verse of Chapter 9 in the Book of Daniel it is REVEALED by Scripture that King DARIUS is the SON of King A-has-u-e'-rus and Queen Esther of the Medes (as explained in the PREVIOUS BOOK). During the first year of King DARIUS' reign, THE LORD brought to the attention of Daniel; that which was WRITTEN by the Prophet Jeremiah, in regard to the SEVENTY YEARS of DESOLATION for JERUSALEM.

By Daniel knowing the DESOLATION of JERUSALEM had been brought to bear on ISRAEL for its SINNING against ***GOD,*** he decides to fast and PRAY to THE LORD for their FORGIVENESS. Daniel also seeks to find out from THE LORD how long it would be before the Children of ISRAEL could return to JERUSALEM. Daniel recalled from the prophecy of Jeremiah how there would be SEVENTY YEARS of DESOLATION (Jeremiah 25:11), and he believed that their time of DESOLATION had nearly been completed. However, Daniel did not UNDERSTAND the PROPHECY given by Jeremiah applied to not only the SEVENTY YEARS of DESOLATION they were now experiencing, but it also applied to the SEVENTY WEEKS of YEARS that must pass before the 2nd COMING of JESUS CHRIST. This SEVENTY WEEKS of YEARS would be the required time for ***GOD*** to put an END to ALL SIN.

> ***Daniel 9:20*** *And whiles I was speaking, and PRAYING, and CONFESSING my SIN and the SIN of my people ISRAEL, and presenting my SUPPLICATION before THE LORD my* ***GOD*** *for the HOLY MOUNTAIN of my* ***GOD;***

> ***Daniel 9:21*** *Yea, whiles I was speaking in PRAYER, even the man GABRIEL, whom I had seen in the VISION at the beginning, being caused to FLY swiftly, TOUCHED ME about the time of the evening OBLATION.*

GABRIEL tells Daniel that he had been sent by ***GOD*** to further his UNDERSTANDING of the PROPHECY given to Jeremiah; for Daniel had not fully understood its meaning. GABRIEL explains that there would be SEVENTY WEEKS of YEARS for SIN to CONTINUE, and at the CONCLUSION of those SEVENTY WEEKS of YEARS, an END would be put to ALL SIN.

NOTE: If you read the cited Scripture in Jeremiah, you will see that Jeremiah refers to SEVENTY YEARS of DESOLATION, whereas in the Scriptures of Daniel, GABRIEL speaks of SEVENTY WEEKS. Then by putting the Scriptures of Jeremiah and Daniel together, the SEVENTY YEARS and SEVENTY WEEKS, become SEVENTY WEEKS of YEARS, thus meaning FOUR HUNDRED and NINETY YEARS. This would be the elapsed time from the initial captivity of JERUSALEM until the COMING of JESUS CHRIST, the FINAL SACRIFICE for SIN! However, the SEVENTY WEEKS of YEARS also applies to HIS 2nd COMING; for the FINAL WEEK of YEARS (SEVEN YEARS) represents the SEVEN YEARS of TRIBULATION that is NOW upon the EARTH.

> ***Daniel 9:24*** *SEVENTY WEEKS are determined upon thy people and upon thy HOLY CITY, to finish the TRANSGRESSION, and to make an END of SINS, and to make reconciliation for INIQUITY, and to bring in EVERLASTING RIGHTEOUSNESS, and to seal up the VISION and PROPHECY, and to ANOINT the* ***MOST HOLY.***

NOTE: The ANOINTING of THE ***MOST HOLY*** refers to both JESUS CHRIST, and THE ***182 PERSON,*** for it applies to the *TWO ANOINTED ONES, BEAUTY and* ***BANDS*** *(Zechariah 11:10 through 11:17).*

GABRIEL then breaks down the SEVENTY WEEKS of YEARS as FOLLOWS: he says that there will be SIXTY-NINE WEEKS of YEARS to pass after they are allowed to rebuild JERUSALEM and until the COMING of JESUS CHRIST (the MESSIAH). GABRIEL states the TIME allotment PURPOSELY in two increments, SEVEN WEEKS, and THREE SCORE and TWO WEEKS (being SIXTY-NINE WEEKS in ALL). He does this, because after the SEVEN WEEKS of YEARS has passed, ISRAEL would be allowed to start rebuilding JERUSALEM and its TEMPLE, and then SIXTY-TWO WEEKS of YEARS later, JESUS CHRIST (the MESSIAH) WILL COME to the EARTH (JESUS' 1st COMING).

GABRIEL says that at the CONCLUSION of the SIXTY-TWO WEEKS of YEARS (after the rebuilding of JERUSALEM), JESUS CHRIST (the MESSIAH) will be cutoff; thus referring to JESUS' CRUCIFIXION, and it also applies to JERUSALEM'S being DESTROYED the 2nd TIME by the Romans, shortly thereafter!

> ***Daniel 9:26*** *And after three score and two weeks shall MES-SI'-AH be cut off, but not for HIMSELF: and the people of the Prince that shall come shall DESTROY the CITY and the SANCTUARY; and the end thereof shall be with a flood, and unto the end of the war DESOLATIONS are DETERMINED.*

NOTE 1: By Scripture, GABRIEL refers to the THREE times the TEMPLE in JERUSALEM is DESTROYED. The FIRST time it was DESTROYED by Neb-u-chad-nez'-zar and the Chaldeans, and that had already occurred at the time of the PROPHECY. The SECOND time JERUSALEM and its TEMPLE are DESTROYED is by Titus and the Romans, leaving only the WESTERN WALL standing. The THIRD TIME of the DESTRUCTION of JERUSALEM and its TEMPLE is yet to COME, and that will be at the END TIMES! The WAR that GABRIEL speaks of in the Scripture refers to THREE major wars that will take place after he had given Daniel this PROPHECY (WORLD WAR I, WORLD WAR II, and WORLD WAR III, THE END).

NOTE 2: There has been a TWO THOUSAND-YEAR GAP in TIME from the COMPLETION of the SIXTY-NINE WEEKS of YEARS until NOW, and now the FINAL WEEK of YEARS BEGINS. The Final WEEK of YEARS is the SEVEN-YEAR period of TRIBULATION (a TIME of TROUBLE for the

EARTH). In the MIDST of the SEVEN YEAR TRIBULATION begins the GREAT TRIBULATION, the TIME for the "Mark of the BEAST", and the DENOUNCING of ***GOD*** by the DAMNED. However, during this SEVEN-YEAR PERIOD of TIME many will be CONVERTED and SAVED, due to the TRIBULATION, ***SAITH THE LORD!***

> ***Daniel 9:27*** *And* ***HE*** *shall CONFIRM the COVENANT with many for ONE WEEK: and in the MIDST of the WEEK* ***HE*** *shall cause the SACRIFICE and the OBLATION to CEASE, and for the overspreading of ABOMINATIONS* ***HE*** *shall make it DESOLATE, even until the CONSUMMATION, and that DETERMINED shall be poured upon the DESOLATE.*

NOTE: This Scripture is saying that during the TRIBULATION PERIOD many will be CONVERTED and SAVED. It also says, once the GREAT TRIBULATION BEGINS, (which is in the middle of that SEVEN-YEAR PERIOD of TIME), except for ***GOD'S*** ANOINTED, ***GOD*** will REFUSE to HEAR or ANSWER the peoples PRAYERS. ***GOD*** does this because the SINS of the WORLD have come up like SMOKE into ***HIS NOSTRILS,*** and ***HE*** CAN NO LONGER BEAR TO LOOK UPON ***HIS CREATION; AND HE SHALL POUR HIS FURY OUT UPON THE EARTH!***

Daniel's FINAL VISION

Chapter 10 of the Book of Daniel opens with Daniel saying; in the third year of King CYRUS he was given a VISION of the CHANGES in WORLD POWER; from his TIME continuing through to the END TIMES. Daniel also opens by saying; he had been given the UNDERSTANDING of the changes in POWER, and knew they would take place over a very long SPAN of TIME.

NOTE: Although Daniel opens the Chapter by saying he knows the meaning of his VISION; he thought he did, but he did not! At the end of Chapter 12, Daniel retracts what he had said in his opening statement of the chapter and says, although he was given the answer to the VISION he did not UNDERSTAND it. ***Daniel 12:8*** *And I heard, but I UNDERSTOOD NOT: then said I, O my LORD, what shall be the END of these things?*

Daniel in the Scripture recalls the various events that had taken place after he had first received his FINAL VISION. He recalls how he had fasted for three full weeks, eating nothing and drinking only water, and how on the 24th day of April during PRAYER at the river Hid'-de-kel, the ANGEL GABRIEL once again came to him.

Even though Daniel had others with him at the time of his VISION, once GABRIEL had came to him, the ground started shaking (quaking) and the other men with him ran and hid themselves out of fear. Only Daniel saw the ANGEL GABRIEL and the other ANGELS. Daniel says he was very weak from not eating for three full weeks and hadn't any strength when he heard the VOICE of GABRIEL. After hearing his VOICE, Daniel recalls falling fast to sleep and laying with his face to the ground, and says; GABRIEL came over to him and TOUCHED him, and sat him up on his hands and knees.

GABRIEL then told Daniel that from the very first day he had PRAYED for an UNDERSTANDING of the VISION, ***GOD*** had sent him to GIVE Daniel the UNDERSTANDING; but the Devil (the Prince of Persia) had restrained him for twenty-one days. GABRIEL said he had to SUMMON help from the ANGEL MICHAEL, so he could get by the Devil and that is what had detained him. And now, he could GIVE Daniel the UNDERSTANDING of the VISION, but wanted him to know that the VISION pertained in part, to the VERY DISTANT FUTURE!

After hearing GABRIEL speak to him, Daniel found that he was so weak he could not speak; another one of the ANGELS then came over to Daniel and TOUCHED his lips, and he could then speak. Daniel tells GABRIEL how the VISION had troubled him and how he had fasted for twenty-one days seeking an answer from ***GOD,*** and was very weak and didn't even have the strength now to speak to him.

> ***Daniel 10:18*** *Then there came again and TOUCHED me ONE like the appearance of a MAN, and HE strengthened me.*
>
> ***Daniel 10:19*** *And said, O man greatly BELOVED, fear not: PEACE be unto thee, be STRONG, yea, be STRONG. And when he had spoken unto me, I was STRENGTHENED, and said, Let my lord speak; for thou hast STRENGTHENED me.*

GABRIEL tells him, shortly after he leaves he must return to continue the fight with the Devil, so the ANGEL MICHAEL could then return to HEAVEN. However, while he and the Devil are fighting, Alexander the Great of Greece will come into Babylon and take control over it. He further tells Daniel that he will now explain that which has been WRITTEN in the Scriptures, and how it applies to Daniel's VISION, and that only he and MICHAEL have KNOWLEDGE of the FUTURE EVENTS.

GABRIEL tells Daniel about how he had come to support King DARIUS during his reign, and how there would be three more Persian Kings reigning after him, and the fourth reigning King after DARIUS would threaten the Greeks and go to war against them. The Greeks being led by Alexander will win the war and he will then take control of the land. But shortly thereafter, Alexander will die and leave the control of the land to his four Generals; who would then divide Alexander's conquered lands into four nations. Those four nations at a latter time will be overthrown by the Romans, and other European nations will rule over them as well over a course of many years.

He tells Daniel about the formation of Russia, and how it will come forth from Eastern Europe, and he says the Russians will at the END TIMES align themselves with the Western World. GABRIEL also speaks about the breaking up of the Soviet Union, and how the Eastern European countries will break away from Mother Russia during the END TIMES.

> ***Daniel 11:6*** *And in the END of YEARS they shall join themselves together; for the king's daughter of the south shall come to the king of the north to make an agreement: but she shall not retain the power of the arm; neither shall he stand, nor his arm: but she shall be given up, and they that brought her, and he that begat her, and he that strengthened her in these times.*

NOTE: The Scripture speaks about how both Eastern and Western Europe will come together at the END TIMES. It also speaks about the breaking up of the Soviet Union and the coming together of East and West Germany. The Scripture also says that even though they are combined by an agreement, none of the countries taking part in the agreement retain the power they once had independently. It may also be noted that when the Scripture relates to the King of the North and to the King of the South, it relates to the TWO WORLD POWERS at the TIME of the EVENT. Therefor with these POWERS continually changing throughout time, the Scriptures refer to different nations having world power at that time, with there eventually being only ONE WORLD POWER in existence at the END TIME!

> ***Daniel 11:7*** *But out of the branch of her roots shall one stand up in his estate, which shall come with an army, and shall enter into the fortress of the King of the North, and shall deal against them, and shall prevail:*

> ***Daniel 11:8*** *And shall also carry captives into Egypt their gods, with their princes, and with their precious vessels of silver and gold; and he shall continue more years than the King of the North.*

NOTE: These Scriptures refer to the rise of Germany in World War I and how it defeated Russia after combining forces with Austria, taking back Poland and the Russian Fortresses protecting Russia's southern frontier. The Scripture also states that the Kaiser of Germany would outlive Lenin of Russia. Lenin died in 1924 and the Kaiser of Germany (Friedrich Wilheim Viktor Albert) died in 1941. It also speaks about Germany under Adolph Hitler and how Germany would attack Russia a second time and initially prevail. The Scripture further tells of how the war will carry over into Africa.

> ***Daniel 11:10*** *But his sons shall be stirred up, and shall assemble a multitude of great forces: and one shall certainly come, and overflow, and pass through: then shall he return, and be stirred up even to his FORTRESS.*

> ***Daniel 11:11*** *And the King of the South shall be moved with choler, and shall come forth and fight with him, even with the King of the North: and he shall set forth a great multitude, but the multitude shall be given into his hand.*

NOTE: These Scriptures refer to World War II, when Hitler and Nazi Germany attack Russia. In this case the King of the South is Nazi Germany, and the King of the North is Russia. It says that initially Germany prevails with Russia taking on many casualties, similar to those it had taken on in World War I.

> ***Daniel 11:12*** *And when he hath taken away the multitude, his heart shall be lifted up; and he shall cast down many ten thousands: but he shall not be strengthened by it.*

> ***Daniel 11:13*** *For the King of the North shall return, and shall set forth a multitude greater than the former, and shall certainly come after several years with a great army and with much riches.*

NOTE: This refers to Russia (the King of the North) reassembling its army making it now much stronger than its former army, and how after several years of fighting, Russia marches into Berlin Germany, taking control over many countries in Eastern Europe on its way into Berlin.

The following Scripture talks about how other European nations and the United States of America join in the fight against the King of the South (Hitler, Nazi Germany and its Allies).

> ***Daniel 11:14*** *And in those times there shall many stand up AGAINST the King of the South: also the ROBBERS of thy people shall exalt themselves to establish the VISION; but they shall fall.*

NOTE: The "ROBBERS of thy people" refer to the Palestinians who shortly after the war lost their status as a nation when ISRAEL took back control of its land. The reason the Palestinians are referred to as "ROBBERS", is because they are the remnant of the Philistines who had ROBBED ISRAEL of their possessions throughout the years.

> ***Daniel 11:15*** *So the King of the North shall come, and cast up a mount, and take the most fenced cities: and the arms of the South shall not withstand, neither his chosen people, neither shall there be any strength to withstand.*

NOTE: The King of the North in the Scripture still pertains to Russia; who forms the Soviet Union and builds up the Red Army (*"cast up a mount"*). The Soviet Union then claims most of Eastern Europe for itself, and Western Europe cannot do anything on its own to stop them because they are so weakened by the war. This also refers to the Allies of Germany (Italy and Japan) being defeated by their not being able to withstand the USA and its Allied forces.

> ***Daniel 11:16*** *But he that cometh against him shall do according to his own will, and none shall stand before him: and he shall stand in the Glorious Land, which by his hand shall be consumed.*

NOTE: This Scripture refers to the United States of America as being both the one who defeats Germany and its Allies and also the one who stands up to Russia and defends Western Europe from the Soviet Union. The Scripture also says that it is the United States of America who will support ISRAEL in its effort to reclaim its land (*"the Glorious Land"*) and once again become a nation. However the Scripture WARNS how this relationship between the USA and ISRAEL will eventually cause the land to be consumed (DESTROYED).

Daniel 11:17 *He shall also set his face to enter with the strength of his whole Kingdom, and upright ones with him; thus shall he do: and* ***HE*** *shall give him the DAUGHTER of WOMEN, corrupting HER: but SHE shall not stand on his side, neither be for him.*

NOTE: The Scripture says the United States of America and its Allies will use their military strength and political clout to support ISRAEL'S EXISTENCE as a nation. It also says that the CHRISTIAN CHURCH and the BRIDE of CHRIST (*the DAUGHTER of WOMEN*) will spring forth abundantly from the United States of America. However, the government and its leaders will eventually corrupt the CHURCH, causing the CHURCH to turn against them.

Daniel 11:18 *After this shall he turn his face unto the isles, and shall take many: but a prince for his own behalf shall cause the reproach offered by him to cease; without his own reproach he shall cause it to turn upon him.*

NOTE: The Scripture is once again speaking about the Soviet Union, and how it reacts to being stymied in Europe. It says that the USSR then starts to look elsewhere other than Europe for its OCCUPATION of land. But eventually one of its own (*"prince for his own behalf"*) (East Germany) will defect, and this will cause internal problems within its governing body.

Daniel 11:19 *Then he shall turn his face toward the fort of his own land: but he shall stumble and fall, and not be found.*

NOTE: In the Scripture GABRIEL tells Daniel, that the King of the North (the Soviet Union) stops its aggression and looks to its own internal problems. But the problems are insurmountable and this causes the fall of the Soviet Union (*but he shall stumble and fall, and not be found*).

Daniel 11:20 *Then shall stand up in his estate a raiser of taxes in the glory of the Kingdom: but within a few days he shall be destroyed, neither in anger, nor in battle.*

NOTE: The Scripture says, sometime after the fall of the Soviet Union there will be a change in the nation bearing the TITLE of the King of the North. This nation will now be the power in the world that becomes the aggressor nation; assuming the role that Russia once had. This nation's Leader will be one who will raise taxes, and this person will serve for only a short period of time until he is defeated in an election (*destroyed, neither in anger, nor in battle*).

> ***Daniel 11:21*** *And in his estate shall stand up a vile person, to whom they shall not give the honour of the Kingdom: but he shall come in peaceably, and obtain the kingdom by flatteries.*

NOTE: This Scripture says that sometime after the switching of nations bearing the title of the King of the North, an EVIL PERSON will take control of that same nation. This PERSON'S legitimacy for the leadership role will be somewhat in question by the people (*to whom they shall not give the honour of the Kingdom*). But the Scripture says that he will soon win over the people's confidence by BRIBERY (*flatteries),* and by him saying and doing what will appear to be all the right things.

> ***Daniel 11:22*** *And with the arms of a flood shall they be overflown from before him, and shall be broken; yea, also the PRINCE of the COVENANT.*

NOTE: The Scripture states that once this person establishes himself in office, the people will be overwhelmed by his ability to take control. This CONTROL will be gradual and grow to a point where the people have lost all of their rights, even their right to practice their FAITH in ***GOD*** and JESUS CHRIST; for he will also CONTROL the CHURCH!

Summary: Let US summarize as to where WE are now at in the Scriptures of Daniel. GABRIEL has explained thus far to Daniel; how there would be continual changes in world domination and its LEADERSHIP. In all cases the changes occurred as result of the military strength of the WORLD POWER changing from one nation to another over a course of time. The AGGRESSOR NATION at first was called the King of the South, and this represented the Nations of Europe starting with Alexander the Great and then the Romans and so forth up through World War II and Nazi Germany. Then at the conclusion of World War II, the King of the North took on the role of the AGGRESSOR, with Russia initially assuming that role. Then after the fall of the Soviet Union, the United States of America continues on in the role of the AGGRESSOR (or the King of the North) up until the time of the ANTICHRIST, and this is the point in the Scriptures where WE are at now. From this point forward in the Scriptures, the King of the North will represent the Antichrist, the United States of America and its Allies. However those Allies will eventually dwindle to be only the USA and ISRAEL (being CONTROLLED by the Antichrist) at the very END. Furthermore, from this point forward, the balance of the WORLD POWERS (those who are OPPOSED to the United States of America and its Allies), will be referred to in the Scriptures as the King of the South.

Back to Daniel's VISION

The Scriptures continue on to say that once the new World Leader (the King of the North) establishes a coalition of forces and control over the people, he will become very close to the Nation of ISRAEL, who is referred to in the Scriptures as a small people. He will then work deceitfully against all them who are under his control, including ISRAEL, and do so by giving tax relief and BRIBES to those within the USA, and foreign aid and arms to those outside of the USA who support his coalition.

> ***Daniel 11:23*** *And after the League made with him he shall work deceitfully: for he shall come up, and shall become strong with a small people.*

> ***Daniel 11:24*** *He shall enter peaceably even upon the fattest places of the province; and he shall do that which his fathers have not done, nor his fathers' fathers; he shall scatter among them the prey, and spoil, and riches: yea, and he shall forecast his devices against the strong holds, even for a time.*

The Scriptures continue on to say that the King of the South (those in opposition to the Antichrist, the USA and its Allies) will put together their own coalition of forces to try to stop the King of the North's aggression. But this effort will fail miserably and the King of the South's coalition will fall apart once they CONFRONT the FIGHTING POWER of the King of the North, and they will take many casualties.

Then the leaders of both coalitions (North and South) will meet and make a truce, but the truce won't last; for THE END shall be at the time appointed. The Antichrist (the King of the North) will also see that the TRUE CHRISTIANS are in OPPOSITION to him, and he will devise a plan to take control of the CHURCH. He will also plan a surprise attack against the opposing coalition of nations; but some of the TRUE CHRISTIANS within his administration will inform the other side of the attack, causing his effort to fail. He will then be infuriated over his betrayal by the CHRISTIANS, and will use the Muslim Terrorists like pawns and covertly support them in their killing of CHRISTIANS.

> ***Daniel 11:31*** *And arms shall stand on his part, and they shall pollute the SANCTUARY of STRENGTH, and shall take away the daily SACRIFICE, and they shall place the ABOMINATION that maketh DESOLATE.*

> ***Daniel 11:32*** *And such as do wickedly against the COVENANT shall he corrupt by flatteries: but the PEOPLE that do know their* ***GOD*** *Shall be STRONG, and do EXPLOITS.*

NOTE: The Scriptures say that the Antichrist will abolish any form of PRAYER or the WORSHIPPING of ***GOD,*** and by his POWER, he will take control over the TEMPLE in JERUSALEM. The Antichrist will then have a STATUE made in the IMAGE of HIMSELF and place it within the TEMPLE (This is the ABOMINATION that makes DESOLATE). The Antichrist will reward the Terrorists with payoffs for their killing of the CHRISTIANS and also implement the “Mark of the Beast”, once the ABOMINATION has been placed in the TEMPLE. He will offer a BOUNTY for the capture of CHRISTIANS and many of them will be TORTURED and KILLED by the Terrorists who are acting on behalf of the Antichrist. Even those called Christians, who are not, will take BRIBES (*but many shall cleave to them with flatteries*) for their betrayal of the TRUE CHRISTIANS. Then anyone who is caught trying to SERVE ***GOD*** will be tortured and killed. However, them who die trying to SERVE ***GOD*** will not suffer the SECOND DEATH even though they are not SAVED. They will ALL be ADMITTED into the MILLENNIUM through Resurrection, to reign with CHRIST for the ONE-THOUSAND YEAR MILLENNIUM PERIOD.

> ***Daniel 11:35*** *And some of them with UNDERSTANDING shall fall, to TRY them, and to PURGE, and to make them WHITE, even to the TIME of THE END: because it is yet for a TIME APPOINTED.*

> ***Daniel 11:36*** *And the King shall do according to his will; and he shall exalt himself, and magnify himself above every god, and shall speak marvellous things against the* ***GOD*** *of gods, and shall prosper till the INDIGNATION be accomplished: for that that is DETERMINED shall be DONE.*

> ***Daniel 11:37*** *Neither shall he regard the* ***GOD*** *of his fathers, NOR*

THE DESIRE of WOMEN, nor regard any god: for he shall magnify himself above all.

Daniel 11:38 *And in his estate shall he honour the God of Forces: and a god whom his fathers knew not shall he honour with gold, and silver, and precious stones, and pleasant things.*

NOTE: At the time the "ABOMINATION that makes DESOLATE" is set up in the TEMPLE and the "Mark of the Beast" implemented, Lucifer, the Devil, will enter into the one called the Antichrist (the King of the North). He will then have many of the CHRISTIANS KILLED, and will proclaim himself to be god. After entering into the Antichrist, he will cast away the woman who had been married to the Antichrist, proclaiming her to be unholy and unworthy to be with god, and further offer her as a sacrifice on his altar. He will also honor a god whom he will name the "God of Forces", and demand that all should worship both him and the "God of Forces" (The two are called in the Book of Revelation, the 1st and 2nd BEAST). The Antichrist will demand that TRIBUTE money be paid to the "God of Forces", and force many of the people to sell their properties to accommodate his demands. Lucifer will give those who are closest to him and are serving him temporary power over the people, and they will do horrific things to them. Many of them will be used for human sacrifices to his god; and this will be done at the altar in the TEMPLE at Jerusalem.

Daniel 11:40 *And at the TIME of THE END shall the King of the South push at him: and the King of the North shall come against him like a whirlwind, with chariots, and with horsemen, and with many ships; and he shall enter into the countries, and shall overflow and pass over.*

Daniel 11:41 *He shall also enter into the GLORIOUS LAND, and many countries shall be overthrown: but these shall escape out of his hand, even E'-dom, and Moab, and the chief of the children of Ammon.*

Daniel 11:42 *He shall stretch forth his hand also upon the countries: and the land of Egypt shall not escape.*

NOTE: The Scriptures say that the King of the South and its coalition that will consist of nations mostly out of Western Europe will attack the Antichrist, but they will fail in their efforts and retreat. The Antichrist will overwhelm them with his army and weaponry, and after they retreat, the Antichrist will seize power over nearly every Middle Eastern Country leaving only the King in Jordan in power. He will then take control of Egypt, and shortly thereafter take control of Africa (*Lib'-y-ans and the E-thi-o'-pi-ans shall be at his steps*).

> ***Daniel 11:44*** *But tidings out of the EAST and out of the NORTH shall trouble him: therefore he shall go forth with great fury to destroy, and utterly to make away many.*

NOTE: Once the Antichrist takes control over the Middle East and its oil, China and Russia will join forces against him, and nuclear attacks on one another will take place causing many people to die and the DESTRUCTION of many cities.

> ***Daniel 11:45*** *And he shall plant the tabernacles of his palace between the seas in the GLORIOUS HOLY MOUNTAIN; yet he shall come to his END, and none shall help him.*

NOTE: Once Washington DC is DESTROYED in one of the many nuclear attacks against the United States of America, the Antichrist will then make Jerusalem his Capitol City. It is there at Jerusalem where the physical bodies of the Antichrist (the Devil, the Beast, and the False Prophet) will TERMINATE.

Reference:

> ***Revelation 16:13*** *And I saw three unclean spirits like frogs come out of the mouth of the DRAGON, and out of the mouth of the BEAST, and out of the mouth of the FALSE PROPHET.*

> ***Revelation 16:14*** *For they are the spirits of DEVILS, working miracles, which go forth unto the Kings of the EARTH and of the whole WORLD, to gather them to BATTLE of that GREAT DAY of **GOD ALMIGHTY.***

GABRIEL Concludes Daniel's VISION

> ***Daniel 12:1*** *AND at that TIME shall MI'-CHA-EL stand up, the GREAT PRINCE which standeth for the CHILDREN of thy*

PEOPLE: and there shall be a TIME of TROUBLE, such as never was since there was a nation even to that same time: and at that TIME thy PEOPLE shall be ***DELIVERED,*** *every one that shall be found WRITTEN in the BOOK.*

Daniel 12:2 *And many of them that SLEEP in the DUST of the EARTH shall AWAKE, some to EVERLASTING LIFE, and some to SHAME and EVERLASTING CONTEMPT.*

NOTE 1: GABRIEL explains to Daniel how MICHAEL, the PRINCE of the THRONE, will cast Lucifer and those who follow him down to the EARTH. He says that once this EVENT takes place there will be a TIME of TROUBLE that the likes of which have never been experienced in the world before (THE GREAT TRIBULATION). THIS IS THE SOUNDING OF THE FIRST TRUMPET! GABRIEL tells Daniel about the ***DELIVERANCE;*** this refers to both them who are of the BRIDE of CHRIST, and those who are to be GUESTS of the WEDDING SUPPER. He further explains how at the CONCLUSION of the WORLD, many will be RAISED from the DEAD and ***JUDGED.*** Some who are RAISED will go to HEAVEN (these are those who served ***GOD*** before JESUS' RESURRECTION and now SLEEP in the EARTH) and how some will go to HELL!

NOTE 2: GABRIEL tells Daniel that he shouldn't worry himself about this matter for it will take place many years after his death, and both carnal knowledge and SPIRITUAL KNOWLEDGE will increase over the years to follow. Then, one of the Angels in Daniel's VISION asks GABRIEL, how long will these atrocities continue? And yet another ANGEL replies, " for a time, times, and a half", thus meaning for FORTY-THREE MONTHS. GABRIEL says it shall continue on until all the SAVED SOULS have been taken out of the world, and there is only EVIL remaining. And, then ***GOD*** will END THE GREAT TRIBULATION! He says, once the "ABOMINATION that makes DESOLATE" is set up in the TEMPLE in Jerusalem, there will be ONE THOUSAND TWO HUNDRED and NINETY DAYS of TROUBLE. He further says, those who are left alive and survive the GREAT TRIBULATION (survived FORTY-FOUR and ONE-HALF MONTHS) are BLESSED, for they are part of the 104,000,000 people who will be left alive to repopulate the EARTH, during the MILLENNIUM.

This concludes Daniel's VISION! If you have read the PREVIOUS BOOK, it should be apparent to you that Daniel's VISION is quite similar to the VISION of Apostle John, that is DESCRIBED in the Book of the Revelation of

JESUS CHRIST. You should also be AWARE that the only difference between Daniel's VISION and John's VISION, is that Daniel's VISION was one LOOKING FORWARD in TIME, while John's VISION is one LOOKING BACK in TIME.

Chapter 25
RELATIONSHIPS

The WORD "RELATIONSHIP" is defined as "The STATE of being RELATED or INTERRELATED". The topic of discussion for this Chapter will be how people relate or interrelate to one another and what are the necessary ingredients insuring a GOOD RELATIONSHIP.

FRIENDSHIPS and PARTNERSHIPS

Relationships between two people are generally initiated by their having some similarity in BELIEFS and also the ability to share in each other's INTERESTS. In general, when there are DIFFERENCES in BELIEFS and INTERESTS amongst individuals, the relationship between them will be one having CONFLICTS, thus causing the RELATIONSHIP to eventually fail. The failure in the RELATIONSHIP will be primarily due to the lack of INTEREST by either party in the other's desires, achievements, and goals in life, making it difficult for the two to agree on matters. Also, by having extreme differences in points of view and beliefs, the two can never agree to accept the others opinions, making them incompatible for a FRIEND or PARTNER RELATIONSHIP.

In a GOOD RELATIONSHIP there can be some diversity between the two in their points of view on any particular subject, and at times this can even be a positive attribute in the relationship, because their INTERESTS become the PRIORITY and not their OPINIONS of them. By the two enjoying the same or similar things in life, even though they may differ in opinion on the specifics of them, both are willing to accept the other one's opinions even though they may not subscribe to them.

For instance, if two people in a relationship were watching a baseball game together and the question arises between the two as to whether a left-handed pitcher or a right handed pitcher is better suited to pitch against a particular batter? Even though the two may differ in their opinions, they both still share a COMMON INTEREST in baseball. Therefor, the COMMON INTEREST of the two is the GAME and not the details of it. And, although their opinions may differ in regard to the particulars of the game, they can still ENJOY watching it together without CONFLICT. This is because the two are COMPATIBLE by MUTUAL INTERESTS. Whereas if they were INCOMPATIBLE, and one of the persons wanted to watch something other than the baseball game, the one of the two not wanting to watch the game would feel they were DEPRIVED of their INTERESTS.

As you can see from the previous example, one of the BINDING FACTORS of a RELATIONSHIP is the ability of the two to SHARE in a COMMON INTEREST. And, although there may be varying points of view of those INTERESTS, this will rarely cause CONFLICTS to occur within the RELATIONSHIP.

Conflicting PERSONALITY FACTORS within the RELATIONSHIP can have a NEGATIVE effect on it, even when both of the people share in COMMON INTERESTS. PERSONALITIES are driven by BELIEFS, and even though the two might share in COMMON INTERESTS, if their variances in BELIEFS are so divergent they collide, this will also cause CONFLICT to occur. This can also be illustrated by referring to the last example of the baseball game, only this time the two in the RELATIONSHIP have conflicting PERSONALITIES as well as opposing opinions.

In this case the details of the game are relevant due to PERSONALITY clashes, and the two can NEVER come to an agreement on any matter because they have opposing BELIEFS driving their PERSONALITIES. And, although they share in a common interest, neither of the PERSONALITIES will allow themselves to set aside their BELIEFS or even slightly modify them to the other's satisfaction, thus causing ongoing turmoil within the RELATIONSHIP. When PERSONALITIES conflict like this, there isn't any middle ground for mutual agreement, and the two will continually argue even over subjects that neither of them care about; just to show the other their disapproval of their particular point of view.

Throughout this Chapter WE will discuss matters regarding RELATIONSHIPS and how one can either SHARE IN or DISPUTE another person's points of view and INTERESTS. RELATIONSHIPS cannot be one-sided, because the success of a RELATIONSHIP depends on both persons benefiting by it. The basic factor in determining the OUTCOME of a RELATIONSHIP is in how ONE person RELATES to the BELIEFS and INTERESTS of the OTHER, even though they may differ in OPINIONS.

Family RELATIONSHIPS

You will find in most families on certain subject matters there is an extreme diversity in opinions amongst the family members. You will also find that these varying opinions rarely affect the FAMILY UNIT'S RELATIONSHIP! There is a reason as to WHY this can exist within a family unit and not detract from the family's ability to live peacefully together; while the same differences in opinions can cause CONFLICT between non-family members.

The COMMON BOND keeping an entire family INTACT, is the family's ability to LOVE one another regardless of differences in opinions, and respect each of its members INDIVIDUALITY. The Mother and the Father of the family RELATE to one another SOLELY by LOVE, whereas it is different for the siblings. The siblings further share in GENE STRUCTURE, and this provides a genetic connection between brothers and sisters allowing even a greater diversity to exist between them without CONFLICT, as compared to their parents. When the siblings are of a different GENE STRUCTURE (having different parents), only LOVE can keep the family unit intact when CONFLICT arises. Therefor the KEY to having a successful family RELATIONSHIP lies with the family's having a LOVING BOND, which will supersede any CONFLICT arising from parental or sibling differences.

GOD made each and every one of YOU DIFFERENT, because DIVERSITY is the spice of LIFE! Furthermore, the DIVERSITY of the family can even add to the DEPTH of the FAMILY UNIT'S STRUCTURE, and also strengthen it, if the LOVE of the parents and the LOVE of each family member BOND the family together as a UNIT.

As mentioned before, when the siblings share in the same parents they also share in a combination of their genetic structures. This gives the family unit a higher probability of blending the various PERSONALITIES in it, because the children are able to genetically relate to one another, thus minimizing CONFLICT. This is why members of a family are called "RELATIVES", because they RELATE to one another through their gene structure.

Siblings sharing in the same genetic structure can workout their differences in opinions, rarely having conflict, because the siblings genetically RELATE to one another. The genetic similarities among brothers and sisters, provides a geophysical connection of them to each other, and it is this GENETIC RELATIONSHIP that allows them to be cohabitants, while not having to capitulate on their BELIEFS, self INTERESTS and POINTS of VIEW.

However, even with the genetic connection between siblings, without the LOVING BOND of the family being initiated and held intact by the parents, the family unit over time will deteriorate. This is because the SIBLING RELATIONSHIP by GENE STRUCTURE deteriorates over time, and as the siblings age the tolerance of the differences between them degrades. Therefor LOVE is the KEY in a FAMILY or PARTNER RELATIONSHIP, whereas the sharing in COMMON INTERESTS and BELIEFS are KEY in FRIENDLY relationships.

You will see as WE proceed on into this Chapter regarding RELATIONSHIPS that LOVE is the determining factor for a LASTING ONE, even in a RELATIONSHIP among FRIENDS, whereas it is the LACK of LOVE that will cause its DEMISE. So what INGREDIENTS are necessary for a LOVING and LASTING RELATIONSHIP?

I'M sure you have heard the expression; ***"GOD is LOVE"***, and if you have not heard this before, you should remember it, for it is the TRUTH! If you were to see the people of the world as being your brothers and sisters (siblings) and not as strangers, and see ***GOD*** as your ***FATHER,*** and not as a FIGUREHEAD, ***GOD*** would provide the LOVING BOND between you and them.

Furthermore, by ***GOD'S*** CHILDREN sharing in the SAME PARENT, ***GOD,*** you can say you and your siblings share in ***GOD'S*** GENETIC MAKE UP; or more correctly say, you share in ***HIS*** SPIRITUAL MAKE UP. This SPIRITUAL MAKE UP can be RELATED to a sibling's genetic makeup by the siblings sharing in the same PARENTS. THEREFOR, with ALL the SIBLINGS having a similar MAKE UP given to them by their PARENTS, it can be said that ALL ***GOD'S*** CHILDREN ARE INTERRELATED THROUGH THEIR SPIRITUAL MAKE UP.

It can also be said, you CANNOT LOVE without the LOVE OF ***GOD*** within you, for your LOVE comes from ***GOD.*** JESUS CHRIST told the Scribes and the Pharisees that they were HOPELESS, because they didn't have the LOVE of ***GOD*** within them, and were incapable of LOVING. This is also why the Pharisees and Scribes REFUSED to BELIEVE in JESUS CHRIST, FOR JESUS IS THE LOVE OF ***GOD, AND INSEPARABLE FROM HIM!***

> ***John 5:42 BUT I KNOW YOU, THAT YE HAVE NOT THE LOVE OF GOD IN YOU.***

SOLOMON, in the Book of Ecclesiastes stresses the importance of Family and other LOVING RELATIONSHIPS, and how ***GOD*** intends to BOND together those RELATIONSHIPS by ***HIS*** PRESENCE in them. It is ***GOD*** who both STRENGTHENS and PROVIDES the CONNECTION needed for a LOVING RELATIONSHIP, and it is ***GOD*** who provides BOTH a PRIME COMMON BELIEF and a PRIME COMMON INTEREST for the TWO to SHARE IN.

> ***Ecclesiastes 4:9*** *TWO are better than ONE; because they have*

GOOD REWARD for their labour.

Ecclesiastes 4:10 *For if they fall, the ONE will lift up his FELLOW: but woe to him that is ALONE when he falleth; for he hath not another to help him up.*

Ecclesiastes 4:11 *Again, if TWO lie together, then they have heat: but how can ONE be warm alone?*

Ecclesiastes 4:12 *And if ONE prevail against him, TWO shall withstand him; and a THREEFOLD cord is not quickly broken.*

NOTE: The THREEFOLD CORD mentioned in the Scriptures represents TWO CORDS being wound around a THIRD, with TWO CORDS representing the TWO PERSONS in the RELATIONSHIP and the THIRD CORD representing ***GOD.*** The MESSAGE in the Scriptures is, ***GOD*** wants you to have RELATIONSHIPS with OTHERS thus enabling you to HELP one another, but it must be ***GOD*** who is the CENTER CORD; BINDING the TWO TOGETHER. In the EYES of ***GOD*** there isn't any such thing as a MULTI-PARTY RELATIONSHIP; for a relationship consisting of more than TWO PEOPLE is an ORGANIZATION and not a RELATIONSHIP. THEREFOR, any LOVING RELATIONSHIP must be CONSISTENT with this UNDERSTANDING. ALL LOVING RELATIONSHIPS MUST CONSIST of THREE, the TWO PARTNERS and ***GOD,*** for ***GOD is*** the ***LOVE*** that BINDS the RELATIONSHIP together.

Within a FAMILY UNIT, it is the INDIVIDUAL LOVING RELATIONSHIPS of its members that make it COMPLETE, with each LOVING RELATIONSHIP consisting of TWO PERSONS and ***GOD***. These RELATIONSHIPS cannot be commingled with the others nor should they be characterized, for they are ALL DIFFERENT, with the only COMMONALITY in them, being ***GOD***.

Marital RELATIONSHIPS

Marital RELATIONSHIPS are TWO PERSONS UNIFIED by MARRIAGE making them ONE COMPLETE PERSON in the EYES of ***GOD.*** This means that the BOND between the THREE (the two partners and ***GOD***) is so tightly WOUND that they are INSEPARABLE. On EARTH there is a MANDATE by ***GOD*** requiring a MARRIAGE to CONSIST of BOTH GENDERS, one MALE and one FEMALE, whereas the MANDATE in HEAVEN is somewhat DIF-

FERENT. This is why ***GOD*** frowns upon homosexuality, for it does not serve any PURPOSE in ***GOD*** and therefor ***HE*** WILL NOT participate in this type of RELATIONSHIP.

By the homosexual relationship being VOID of ***GOD,*** it is also VOID of LOVE. In the EYES of ***GOD*** this type of relationship is merely a sexual encounter and not a marriage; because UNITY in the homosexual relationship cannot be achieved ***SAITH THE LORD!*** This doesn't mean a MAN cannot LOVE another MAN or a WOMAN a WOMAN, for this type LOVE occurs amongst SIBLINGS and FRIENDS. MARRIAGE on the other hand extends well beyond the LOVE that is expressed between SIBLINGS and FRIENDS. MARRIAGE is the GREATEST expression of LOVE; for this is the BEGINNING and the FOUNDATION of a FAMILY UNIT being built on LOVE, and same-sex partners CANNOT create a family unit!

You cannot take a MALE pipe fitting and mate it to another MALE pipe fitting, nor a FEMALE to a FEMALE, and this same interrelationship holds TRUE for homosexual marriages. Marriage is the UNITING (CONNECTION) of a MALE to a FEMALE, and on EARTH this must be done both in FLESH and in SPIRIT. Therefor MARRIAGE MANDATES the RELATIONSHIP consist of a MALE and FEMALE GENDER, so the TWO may PROPERLY MATE (come together), thus providing the necessary OFFSPRING for the BEGINNING of a FAMILY UNIT.

By EVE being taken out of ADAM, ADAM can only be COMPLETE when HE and EVE come together again as ONE. Even though two people of the same gender may sexually enjoy an encounter with one another, they cannot provide the GENDER differences required for a MARITAL RELATIONSHIP. This is because both parties of the homosexual relationship remain in an INCOMPLETE STATE, by lacking in the opposite GENDER. As explained in the PREVIOUS BOOK, Lucifer, the Devil, is an INCOMPLETE ANGEL by him being a MALE and lacking in his FEMALE counterpart. It is his desire that all of mankind follows after this order of being in an INCOMPLETE STATE, as he is; and he PROMOTES homosexuality, instead of MARRIAGE.

Selecting a MARITAL MATE

Where most people fall short in their obtaining a mate for a LASTING MARITAL RELATIONSHIP is in the methodology used for their CHOOSING the MATE. People have a tendency to base their choice of MATES solely on the EXTERIOR of the PERSON, rather than on the INTERIOR of the PERSON. Whereas the EXTERIOR can fulfill the FLESH connection for the marriage, it cannot fulfill the SPIRITUAL CONNECTION, and ***GOD*** will not participate in a MARRIAGE lacking in SPIRITUAL substance. Furthermore, by ***GOD*** providing the SPIRITUAL and LOVE CONNECTION needed for the MARRIAGE BOND, without ***HIM*** the MARRIAGE is INCOMPLETE. Although appearances should not be the sole basis in MATE SELECTION, the APPEARANCES of MATES to each other is still of IMPORTANCE.

If you are either of the Angel, or a Child of ***GOD,*** in HEAVEN you have a counterpart called your SOUL MATE. This is the other half that is missing from you on earth, and the SPIRITUAL IMAGE of your MATE in HEAVEN is deeply ingrained within you. It is this IMAGE of your MATE that drives your SEXUAL and SPIRITUAL DESIRES; and INFLUENCES your decisions in MATE SELECTION. This causes you to look for an earthly mate who is similar in appearance and behavioral traits to that of your SOUL MATE in HEAVEN. This is not done consciously but rather SPIRITUALLY, and neither the HUSBAND nor the WIFE are AWARE of the SPIRITUAL INFLUENCES drawing the two together.

If ALL ***GOD'S*** CHILDREN would LOOK to THE LORD for help in selecting a mate, and let ***HIM*** send one to you rather than your looking on your own behalf, there wouldn't be a need for DIVORCE! As told to you previously, it is the ***FATHER*** who CHOOSES the BRIDE for the SON and it is also ***HE*** who GIVES the DAUGHTER in MARRIAGE; and if ONE would be patient and WAIT for ***GOD*** to FULFILL that OBLIGATION, FAILURE in MARRIAGE would not occur. At the RIGHT TIME and the RIGHT PLACE, ***GOD*** would SEND the PERFECT MATE to you, and there wouldn't be any DOUBT by either of the two regarding the RELATIONSHIP. The APPEARANCES of BOTH PARTIES would be pleasing to each other, but more IMPORTANTLY there would be a SPIRITUAL CONNECTION between the TWO, making it a MARRIAGE MADE BY ***GOD.***

However, the PERSON ***GOD*** would send **would not** be an ETERNAL MATE, for your ETERNAL MATE awaits you in HEAVEN. This is why the EARTHLY MARRIAGE VOWS taken, state; "TILL DEATH DO WE PART"; for an earthly marriage is not a PERMANENT one and terminates at the death of either party. However, even though it is not a PERMANENT MARRIAGE, your ***GOD*** given MARITAL RELATIONSHIP on EARTH will be a VERY GOOD ONE, and either PARTY would embrace the thought of SHARING their ETERNITY with the other in HEAVEN.

RELATIONSHIPS with SOUL MATES

For those of you who have COME DOWN from HEAVEN, while on earth, ***GOD*** erases all MEMORY of your LIFE in HEAVEN. However, because your SOUL MATE is the other half of you, you still SPIRITUALLY remember them. This causes you to continually search for that missing half of yourself while on earth. You will find that those of the OPPOSITE SEX, who even remotely resemble your MATE, will appear to be most ATTRACTIVE to you. The search on EARTH for a PERFECT MATE is a futile search, because the ONE you seek is in HEAVEN. This is why it is so CRITICAL that THE LORD SELECTS your mate for you, for ***HE*** will find the one BEST SUITED for you.

There are only SEVEN TIMES during every cycle of the EARTH that SOUL MATES come together on earth; with the FIRST time being with ADAM and EVE. Each and every time the SOUL MATES have come together on the earth, they SERVED a PURPOSE for ***GOD***. All SEVEN TIMES that this EVENT has happened is RECORDED in the Scriptures of the HOLY BIBLE.

When JESUS CHRIST was on earth, HE was allowed to RETAIN a GREAT DEAL of HIS MEMORY about HEAVEN. ***GOD*** allowed this to aid JESUS in HIS MINISTRY of TEACHING about the KINGDOM of HEAVEN. By HIS retaining much of HIS MEMORY, JESUS vividly REMEMBERED HIS SOUL MATE, ASAPH, and this is why HE hadn't any desire whatsoever to be with a WOMAN, albeit HE LOVED female FELLOWSHIPS. JESUS' lack of interest in having a wife caused HIS Disciples to believe HE was a EUNUCH and had sworn himself to celibacy, so they asked HIM in the Scriptures if they should also be EUNUCHS.

NOTE: The WORD "EUNUCH" as used in the HOLY BIBLE, does not always refer to one who has been castrated. This WORD is often used in the Scriptures to IDENTIFY a PERSON who has DEDICATED themselves to ***GOD*** and have set aside their desires for marriage or sexual activity by SWEARING themselves to CELIBACY. They have done this so no one can interfere with their work for ***THE LORD***. The EUNUCHS that were castrated were them who JESUS refers to in the Scriptures as being made EUNUCHS by men.

> ***Matthew 19:10*** *HIS Disciples say unto HIM, If the case of the MAN be so with his wife, it is not good to marry.*

> ***Matthew 19:11*** *But HE said unto them,* ***ALL MEN CANNOT RE-***

CEIVE THIS SAYING, SAVE THEY TO WHOM IT IS GIVEN.

Matthew 19:12 FOR THERE ARE SOME EUNUCHS, WHICH WERE BORN FROM THEIR MOTHER'S WOMB: AND THERE ARE SOME EUNUCHS, WHICH WERE MADE EUNUCHS OF MEN: AND THERE BE EUNUCHS, WHICH HAVE MADE THEMSELVES EUNUCHS FOR THE KINGDOM OF HEAVEN'S SAKE. HE THAT IS ABLE TO RECEIVE IT, LET HIM RECEIVE IT.

JESUS' being a EUNUCH falls into the THIRD CATEGORY of the last Scripture, for HE had made HIMSELF CELIBATE for the sake of HIS MATE in HEAVEN. JESUS quite clearly remembered HIS MATE, ASAPH, and simply was not interested in a mate on earth. JESUS also was not meant to have any OFFSPRING on EARTH, for JESUS is the HEIR to the EARTH and if HE had OFFSPRING the OFFSPRING would be HEIR to HIS INHERITANCE.

SEXUAL INTERCOURSE

Although many of the Church's Clergy believe and teach that SEXUAL INTERCOURSE is a SINFUL ACT, it is NOT, ***SAITH THE LORD!*** Most who BELIEVE it to be a sin do so because of their inability to UNDERSTAND Scripture. They BELIEVE that by the HOLY BIBLE saying man is BORN of SIN, it refers to the SEXUAL ACT that caused the man to be born. However, the Scriptures referring to man being BORN of SIN refers to the child being BORN into a PLACE of SIN (the WORLD); for the child cannot commit a SIN, until they have come forth from the WOMB and into this WORLD.

This is why one MUST RECEIVE SPIRITUAL REBIRTH by BAPTISM to be freed from the SIN of the WORLD. This REBIRTH of the SPIRIT is a SPIRITUAL BIRTH IN HEAVEN, making the REBORN-PERSON of the EARTH, a NEWBORN PERSON IN HEAVEN. Then by being REBORN in HEAVEN, the PERSON is no longer BORN of SIN out of the EARTH, but rather BORN of THE ***HOLY SPIRIT,*** JUST LIKE JESUS!

Another point of discussion is that of PHYSICAL FORNICATION, versus SPIRITUAL FORNICATION. Physical fornication refers to the physical act of SEXUAL INTERCOURSE by unmarried couples, and this by itself is NOT a SIN ***SAITH THE LORD***. However, THE LORD does frown upon this type of behavior and if CONCEPTION occurs as a result of the ACT, it is the RESPONSIBILITY of BOTH partakers in the FORNICATION to be a PARENT to the CHILD created by the ACT!

On the other hand, when the BIBLE refers to FORNICATORS, these are SINNERS in SPIRIT, for this refers to SPIRITUAL FORNICATION and not physical fornication. SPIRITUAL FORNICATION occurs when one goes outside of their HOLY MARRIAGE to ***GOD*** to fulfill their desires, and this is the SINFUL act of ADULTERY ***SAITH THE LORD.*** SPIRITUAL FORNICATION also refers to someone worshipping someone or something other than ***GOD.***

ADULTERY

JESUS explains in the Scriptures about ADULTERY and how neither the man or the woman should commit the act of ADULTERY for they are BREAKING ***GOD'S 7th COMMANDMENT.*** However even this is misunderstood by the CHURCH, for it refers to one's seeking a REPLACEMENT of their SPOUSE, and not to one's desire to have sex outside of the MARRIAGE. Although ***GOD*** FROWNS upon this type of behavior by the man, ***HE*** FORBIDS IT for the woman, for she has in some way DEPRIVED the man of his sexual desires, and in Genesis 3:16 ***GOD*** says a woman's desires are to be to her husband! JESUS EXPLAINS in the Scriptures that when a MAN goes outside of the marriage for only SEX (FORNICATION), he has NOT committed ADULTERY.

> ***Matthew 19:9 AND I SAY UNTO YOU, WHOSOEVER SHALL PUT AWAY HIS WIFE, EXCEPT IT BE FOR FORNICATION, AND SHALL MARRY ANOTHER, COMMITTETH ADULTERY: AND WHOSO MARRIETH HER WHICH IS PUT AWAY DOTH COMMIT ADULTERY.***

NOTE: The Scriptures are saying, if a man puts away his wife to marry another he has committed ADULTERY. However, if a man goes outside of the marriage to fulfill his sexual desires only, then the man has not committed ADULTERY. The Scripture also states that if a woman is put out of the marriage for any REASON, and she remarries, both she and the one she marries have committed ADULTERY. This may seem to be POLITICALLY INCORRECT and unfair to the woman and so be it, HOWEVER IT IS THE LAW! In the EYES of ***GOD,*** when a man puts a woman out of the MARRIAGE for any reason whatsoever, she has failed in her OBLIGATION of MARRIAGE to him, and is unfit to have another! Marriage should be taken more SERIOUSLY for BOTH PERSONS, for in the EYES of ***GOD,*** BOTH PARTNERS are required to fulfill their OBLIGATION to MARRIAGE until their time of DEATH.

RELATIONSHIPS with *GOD*

The only COMMONALITY in RELATIONSHIPS with ***GOD*** is the INDIVIDUALITY of the RELATIONSHIP, for there aren't any two of them the SAME. Some people ***GOD*** will allow to get very close to ***HIM,*** and others ***GOD*** will NEVER allow to be close to ***HIM.*** As ONE'S ANOINTING is INCREASED so is their NEARNESS to ***GOD*** INCREASED.

A RELATIONSHIP with ***GOD*** is either a 24/7 RELATIONSHIP or none at all, because you cannot have a part time RELATIONSHIP with ***GOD***. This is to say, if you have a RELATIONSHIP with ***GOD*** it is to be an hourly, daily, weekly, monthly, annually, and ETERNALLY ***GOD FILLED*** RELATIONSHIP, without BREAK or DIVISION in it. There are many people BELIEVING they SERVE ***GOD*** by the various things they do for charity and the Church. But these people are serving themselves, for they neither KNOW ***GOD*** nor do they INCLUDE ***HIM*** in their daily lives. It is ALL or NONE ***SAITH THE LORD***.

People find it very easy to call on ***GOD*** in a TIME of TROUBLE, but yet they don't bother to thank ***HIM*** or even ACKNOWLEDGE ***HIS*** existence when things appear to be going well. They will pat themselves on the back for their accomplishments, rather than GLORIFYING and THANKING ***GOD*** for ***HIS*** BLESSINGS. This is the VANITY of MANKIND, thinking they only need ***GOD*** when they are enduring hardships or grieving. The problem with this kind of thinking is that ***GOD*** will eventually REFUSE to hear your PRAYERS because you have TURNED your back to ***HIM*** one too many times, thus causing ***HIM*** to turn ***HIS BACK*** to YOU!

Once you have drawn your FINAL BREATH in this WORLD and have not established a RELATIONSHIP with ***GOD*** before that LAST BREATH, you will stand BEFORE ***HIM*** in JUDGMENT. At the TIME of JUDGMENT there will be MANY who will beg THE LORD for just ONE MORE CHANCE, but they will be DENIED! This is why JESUS CHRIST said at the TIME of JUDGMENT, "THERE SHALL BE WEEPING AND GNASHING OF TEETH"!

> ***Matthew 24:50 THE LORD OF THAT SERVANT SHALL COME IN A DAY WHEN HE LOOKETH NOT FOR HIM, AND IN AN HOUR THAT HE IS NOT AWARE OF,***

> ***Matthew 24:51 AND SHALL CUT HIM ASUNDER, AND APPOINT HIM HIS PORTION WITH THE HYPOCRITES:***

THERE SHALL BE WEEPING AND GNASHING OF TEETH.

Having a RELATIONSHIP with ***GOD*** is not an OPTION but rather a MANDATE, for your RELATIONSHIP with ***GOD*** will determine the outcome of YOUR ETERNITY. If it is a GOOD ONE, so shall your ETERNITY BE a GOOD ONE. If it was LACKING, so shall your ETERNITY BE LACKING, and if it is NON-EXISTENT, so shall you BE DAMNED for ETERNITY!

> ***Ecclesiastes 6:3*** *If a man beget an hundred children, and live many years, so that the days of his years be many, and his SOUL not be filled with GOOD, and also that he have no burial; I say, that an untimely birth is better than he.*

> ***Mark 8:36 FOR WHAT SHALL IT PROFIT A MAN, IF HE SHALL GAIN THE WHOLE WORLD, AND LOSE HIS OWN SOUL?***

> ***Mark 8:37 OR WHAT SHALL A MAN GIVE IN EXCHANGE FOR HIS SOUL?***

A RELATIONSHIP with ***GOD*** begins by YOUR READING THE *WORD of* ***GOD.*** This is MORE IMPORTANT than either PRAYER or WORSHIP ***SAITH THE LORD.*** For it is the *WORD of* ***GOD*** that will bring about your CONVERSION by way of ***HOLY SPIRIT*** BAPTISM, and neither PRAYER nor WORSHIP alone can accomplish that.

JESUS told HIS Disciples to go into the world and PREACH the GOSPELS (Mark 16:15), therefor, if you haven't READ them how can you PREACH them? JESUS also said that the PREACHING of the GOSPELS in every nation throughout the WORLD must be accomplished prior to its END, and that PREACHING has nearly been COMPLETED.

> ***Matthew 24:14 AND THIS GOSPEL OF THE KINGDOM SHALL BE PREACHED IN ALL THE WORLD FOR A WITNESS UNTO ALL NATIONS; AND THEN SHALL THE END COME.***

JESUS CHRIST is your ONLY CONNECTION to ***GOD,*** for HE IS THE *WORD of* ***GOD.*** Furthermore you CANNOT start your RELATIONSHIP with ***GOD*** until you start READING THE HOLY BIBLE. Then ONCE you BEGIN to READ, ASK AND YOU WILL RECEIVE, SEEK AND YOU WILL FIND, KNOCK AND THE DOOR SHALL BE OPENED UNTO YOU!

Chapter 26

PROMISES

Contained within the Scriptures of the FORTY-FOUR Books of THE HOLY BIBLE are ***SEVEN THOUSAND PROMISES***. It would take an entire book to list and simply explain each one; therefor in this Chapter WE will only list the SEVEN most SIGNIFICANT PROMISES and they are the following:

1. The PROMISE of PROTECTION
2. The PROMISE of COUNSELING
3. The PROMISE of PEACE
4. The PROMISE of WELFARE
5. The PROMISE of FORGIVENESS
6. The PROMISE of DELIVERANCE
7. The ***PROMISE of ETERNITY***

> ***Isaiah 64:4*** *For since the BEGINNING of the WORLD men have not heard, nor perceived by the ear, neither hath the eye seen, O* ***GOD,*** *beside thee, what* ***HE*** *hath prepared for him that waiteth for* ***HIM.***

The last Scripture taken from the Book of Isaiah says; for them RECEIVING SAVING GRACE via ***HOLY SPIRIT*** BAPTISM, ***GOD*** has prepared a PLACE in HEAVEN for you that is so WONDERFUL, neither your MIND nor your senses can PERCEIVE or COMPREHEND its MAGNIFICENCE. This is the ***PROMISE of ETERNITY*** in the ***KINGDOM of GOD,*** and will be the LAST PROMISE covered in this Chapter for it is the GREATEST PROMISE of ALL. WE have listed it FIRST in this Chapter, so that the LAST may be FIRST, and the FIRST, LAST!

It MUST be UNDERSTOOD that the SEVEN THOUSAND PROMISES contained within the Scriptures apply only to them having RECEIVED SAVING GRACE, and NOT to ANYONE ELSE; JESUS said:

John 6:44 "NO MAN CAN COME TO ME, EXCEPT THE FATHER WHICH HATH SENT ME DRAW HIM: AND I WILL RAISE HIM UP AT THE LAST DAY."

JESUS CHRIST is that SAVING GRACE! In HEBREWAH (TONGUES), JESUS is CALLED "LAH-RO'-SAH", meaning, SAVIOR; and in HEAVEN HE is also REFERRED TO as, "BRA-KAH-TAH-UNAH", meaning; "HE WHO BRINGS THE LIGHT". In the SPIRITUAL SENSE, the word "LIGHT" means, LIFE and TRUTH, and therefor it can be said; JESUS CHRIST BRINGS LIFE and TRUTH to the WORLD.

JESUS BRINGS the LIGHT to the WORLD by way of HIS GOSPELS and the *WORD of **GOD,*** both of which are INSEPARABLE and found ONLY in the BIBLE. This is why WE have stressed the IMPORTANCE of READING the BIBLE so many times in this BOOK, for SAVING GRACE comes only by way of the SCRIPTURES.

The PROMISE of PROTECTION

GOD PROMISES to PROTECT them who SERVE ***HIM.*** In this PROMISE, ***GOD*** doesn't say YOU will not be exposed to HARM, but rather says ***HE*** will get YOU through HARMS WAY. This PROMISE is best EXPRESSED in the 91st Psalm, so WE will use it to EXPLAIN ***GOD'S*** PROMISE of PROTECTION.

> ***Psalm 91:1*** *HE that dwelleth in the SECRET PLACE of the **MOST HIGH** shall abide under the shadow of the **ALMIGHTY.***

NOTE: As explained in the PREVIOUS BOOK, the ***MOST HIGH*** is THE ***HOLY SPIRIT of GOD*** and the ***FATHER*** of JESUS CHRIST. Therefor what the Psalm is saying in the OPENING SCRIPTURE is; ANYONE, WHO HAS RECEIVED SAVING GRACE BY ***HOLY SPIRIT*** BAPTISM, IS PLACED UNDER THE PROTECTION OF ***GOD!***

> ***Psalm 91:2*** *I will say of THE LORD, **HE** is my REFUGE and my FORTRESS: my **GOD;** in **HIM** will I TRUST.*

NOTE: This Scripture further clarifies that which was said in the 1st Scripture, by the Psalmist saying; ***GOD*** is both his PLACE of PROTECTION, and his PLACE to HIDE in a time of trouble. He also says that he can DEPEND on

GOD and will only place his TRUST, in ***GOD.***

> ***Psalm 91:3*** *Surely **HE** shall **DELIVER** thee from the SNARE of the FOWLER, and from the noisome PESTILENCE.*

NOTE: The Scripture says ***GOD*** will ***DELIVER*** you from whatever clever traps the Devil has set for you (*the SNARE*), and from any raging epidemic of DISEASE (*PESTILENCE*) you may have been exposed to.

> ***Psalm 91:4 HE*** *shall cover thee with **HIS** feathers, and under **HIS** wings shalt thou TRUST: **HIS** TRUTH shall be thy SHIELD and BUCKLER.*

NOTE: The Scripture says, ***GOD*** will put you under ***HIS PROTECTION.*** It also says that the *WORD of* ***GOD*** (***HIS*** *TRUTH*) will act as a SHIELD and ARMOR for YOU against the FORCES of EVIL. This CONFIRMS what WE had TOLD YOU earlier in this BOOK, how ONE, when ARMED with THE ***ROD of IRON*** (*WORD of* ***GOD***), can DEFEAT any form of EVIL!

> ***Psalm 91:5*** *Thou shalt not be afraid for the TERROR by night; nor for the ARROW that flieth by day;*

> ***Psalm 91:6*** *Nor for the PESTILENCE that walketh in darkness; nor for the DESTRUCTION that wasteth at noonday.*

NOTE: These Scriptures say that ***GOD*** will remove any FEAR from YOU, and YOU will be PROTECTED from any type of hazard, even though it may be in YOUR PRESENCE and affecting the people around you.

> ***Psalm 91:7*** *A thousand shall fall at thy side, and ten thousand at thy RIGHT HAND; but it shall not come nigh thee.*

> ***Psalm 91:8*** *Only with thine eyes shalt thou behold and see the reward of the wicked.*

NOTE: The 7th and 8th verses say; YOU will SEE many horrible things happening to the people around you, whom have not been SAVED; and even though you may be in the midst of their TROUBLE, it cannot in anyway harm YOU. The Scripture also says, ***GOD*** wants YOU to SEE ***HIM*** PUNISH them who have refused to SERVE ***HIM,*** and ***GOD*** purposely does this; to let YOU know that it is ***HE*** who either PUNISHES or PROTECTS!

> ***Psalm 91:9*** *Because thou hast made THE LORD, which is my REFUGE, even THE **MOST HIGH,** thy HABITATION;*

> ***Psalm 91:10*** *There shall no EVIL befall thee, neither shall any PLAGUE come nigh thy DWELLING.*

NOTE: This is JESUS CHRIST who is speaking in these SCRIPTURES. HE says, **BECAUSE YOU HAVE PLACED YOUR TRUST IN *GOD,* AND HAVE RECEIVED THE SAME BAPTISM HE WAS BAPTIZED WITH; NO HARM SHALL EVER COME UPON YOU; WHETHER IT BE AN EVIL CURSE, OR A PLAGUE, YOU ARE PROTECTED FROM IT *SAITH THE LORD!***

> ***Psalm 91:11*** *For **HE** shall give **HIS** ANGELS charge over thee, to keep thee in ALL thy WAYS.*

> ***Psalm 91:12*** *They shall BEAR thee up in THEIR HANDS, lest thou dash thy foot against a stone.*

NOTE: To insure your PROTECTION, THE ***HOLY SPIRIT*** assigns ANGELS to LOOK after YOU. The ANGELS will not only see to your PROTECTION, but will also KEEP YOU from SIN and also from falling into trouble. ***GOD*** takes care of ALL them who LOVE and WORSHIP ***HIM,*** and ***HE*** will GUARANTEE THEIR SAFETY by PROVIDING ANGELS to LOOK AFTER THEM.

The 13th verse of the 91st Psalm says, once the ANGELS have come to look after YOU, neither lions nor venomous snakes can harm YOU, and, YOU can TRAMPLE the Devil under YOUR feet.

THE PROMISE of PROTECTION (SALVATION):

> ***Psalm 91:14*** *Because he has set his LOVE upon **ME,** therefore will **I DELIVER** him: **I** will set him on HIGH, because he hath KNOWN **MY NAME.***

> ***Psalm 91:15*** *He shall call upon **ME,** and **I WILL ANSWER** him:*

I will be with him in TROUBLE; ***I WILL DELIVER*** *him, and honour him.*

Psalm 91:16 *With LONG LIFE will* ***I*** *SATISFY him, and SHOW HIM* ***MY SALVATION.***

NOTE: The 91st Psalm PROMISES the "SAVED" PROTECTION. ***GOD*** says ***HE*** will send the ANGELS to LOOK after YOU and keep YOU out of HARMS WAY, and regardless of what the circumstances may be all around YOU, YOU WILL BE PROTECTED!

The PROMISE of COUNSELING

Judges 20:18 *And the CHILDREN of ISRAEL arose, and went up to the HOUSE of* ***GOD,*** *and asked COUNSEL of* ***GOD,*** *and said, Which of us shall go up first to battle against the children of Benjamin? And THE LORD said,* ***JUDAH SHALL GO UP FIRST.***

GOD also PROMISES COUNSELING for the "SAVED" and it comes by way of the SPIRIT of COUNSEL. Unlike the GIFTS GIVEN by THE ***HOLY SPIRIT,*** the SPIRIT of COUNSEL is transferable from one person to another; providing the RECIPIENT has been BAPTIZED and in RECEIPT of the GIFT of ***FAITH***. The SPIRIT of COUNSEL is one of the ***SEVEN SPIRITS of GOD,*** who provides GUIDANCE for the NEWBORN SPIRIT. For a person to make use of the COUNSELING provided, they must first be familiar with the SCRIPTURES in the HOLY BIBLE. The SPIRIT of COUNSEL will DIRECT your SPIRIT by reminding it of a Scripture relating to the matter in need of COUNSELING, and that Scripture will DIRECT YOUR COURSE of ACTIONS.

Isaiah 11:2 *And THE* ***SPIRIT of THE LORD*** *shall rest upon him, the SPIRIT of WISDOM and UNDERSTANDING, the SPIRIT of COUNSEL and MIGHT, the SPIRIT of KNOWLEDGE and the FEAR of* ***THE LORD;***

The PROMISE of COUNSELING in many cases takes place while one is asleep; and this is why the WISE, SLEEP ON THE MATTER prior to their making a decision. Then after RECEIVING the SPIRIT of COUNSEL while they have slept, the WISE awaken with an ANSWER; for the SPIRIT of COUNSEL has vividly placed in their MIND a SOUND SOLUTION to the problem.

> ***Psalm 16:7*** *I will bless THE LORD, who hath given me COUNSEL: my reins also INSTRUCT me in the NIGHT SEASONS.*

NOTE: The WORD "REINS" in the Scripture, refers to one's "MIND", and the WORDS "in the NIGHT SEASONS" means, "WHILE I HAD SLEPT".

As WE had mentioned earlier, the SPIRIT of COUNSEL can be transferred from one SAVED PERSON to another SAVED PERSON, and THE ***HOLY SPIRIT*** does this in a rather UNIQUE WAY. When ADVICE (COUNSELING) from the ANOINTED is given to another SAVED INDIVIDUAL, that ADVICE will be SPIRITUALLY ACCEPTED and PROCESSED by the other INDIVIDUAL without further need of verification. It will be fully UNDERSTOOD and utilized by the RECIPIENT without delay, for the SPIRIT of the RECIPIENT will know that which has been given to it is the TRUTH, for the MESSAGE comes by way of THE ***SPIRIT of TRUTH.***

Earlier in this chapter when WE had explained about the PROMISE of PROTECTION, WE used the 91st Psalm as a reference guide. In the 11th and 12th verses of the 91st Psalm, the Scriptures say how the ANGELS are sent to LOOK AFTER YOU. This is also part of ONE'S PROMISE of COUNSELING, for the ANGELS will also provide COUNSELING and GUIDANCE to those to whom they are sent.

The PROMISE of PEACE

GOD PROMISES PEACE to the SAVED, and this is why JESUS CHRIST couldn't LEAVE HIS PEACE with HIS Disciples until after HE had been RESURRECTED, for before HIS RESURRECTION the Disciples had not yet been SAVED. As with the other PROMISES, PEACE comes by way of THE ***HOLY SPIRIT,*** and is RECEIVED at the TIME of ONE'S BAPTISM.

> ***John 20:19*** *Then the same day at evening, being the first day of the week, when the doors were shut where the Disciples were assembled for fear of the Jews, came JESUS and stood in the MIDST, and saith unto them,* ***PEACE BE UNTO YOU.***

> ***John 20:20*** *And when HE had so said, HE shewed unto them HIS HANDS and HIS SIDE. Then were the Disciples glad, when they saw THE LORD.*

John 20:21 *Then said JESUS to them again,* ***PEACE BE UNTO YOU: AS MY FATHER HATH SENT ME, EVEN SO SEND I YOU.***

John 20:22 *And when HE had said this, HE BREATHED on them, and saith unto them,* ***RECEIVE YE THE HOLY GHOST:***

You should SEE from these Scriptures, PEACE comes by way of ***HOLY SPIRIT*** BAPTISM, and the PROMISE of PEACE will remain within you after YOUR BAPTISM. However, the PEACE you RECEIVE is an INTERNAL PEACE, for the WORLD that you live is one of CHAOS. This INTERNAL PEACE allows you to be at PEACE within YOURSELF by your knowing you are both PROTECTED and COUNSELED to deal with the EVIL around you.

The entire 23rd Psalm is dedicated to the PEACE GIVEN to ***GOD'S*** ANOINTED:

Psalm 23:1 THE LORD *is my SHEPHERD; I SHALL NOT WANT.*

NOTE: The opening STATEMENT in the Psalm says you will RECEIVE PEACE by not wanting anything, for how could one be at PEACE if they are wanting?

Psalm 23:2 HE *maketh me to lie down in green pastures:* ***HE*** *leadeth me beside still waters.*

NOTE: This is the PROMISE of SERENITY given by ***GOD'S*** PEACE. The Scripture says that ***GOD*** has put you in a SERENE STATE of MIND, and this is represented in the Psalm by being put into a place where there are GREEN PASTURES and STILL WATERS.

Psalm 23:3 HE *RESTORETH my SOUL:* ***HE*** *LEADETH me in the paths of RIGHTEOUSNESS for* ***HIS NAME'S*** *sake.*

NOTE: By the Psalmist (DAVID) saying that ***GOD*** has RESTORED HIS SOUL, refers to HIM being SAVED. HE further says HE has RECEIVED the SPIRIT of COUNSEL, who leads HIM down a path of RIGHTEOUSNESS for HE NOW BELONGS TO ***GOD.***

Psalm 23:4 *Yea though I walk through the VALLEY of the*

SHADOW of DEATH, I will fear no EVIL: for thou art with me; thy ROD and thy STAFF they COMFORT ME.

NOTE: This is the expression of PEACE that comes by way of the PROMISE of PROTECTION; even though you remain in a place of CHAOS (the Valley of the SHADOW of DEATH), you KNOW that ***THE LORD*** will get YOU safely through it. The ROD and the STAFF giving you your COMFORT (PEACE), is the *WORD of* ***GOD*** and the ANGELS who are sent to assist you.

> ***Psalm 23:5*** *Thou preparest a table before me in the presence of my enemies: thou ANOINTEST my HEAD with oil; my CUP runneth over.*

NOTE: This Scripture says that you will be at PEACE even in the midst of your enemies, for ***GOD*** has ANOINTED YOU with ***HIS HOLY SPIRIT.*** And, by YOUR BAPTISM, the *WORD of* ***GOD*** is OVERFLOWING IN YOU LIKE A WELL OF *LIVING WATERS.*

> ***Psalm 23:6*** *Surely GOODNESS and MERCY shall follow me ALL the days of my LIFE: and I will dwell in the HOUSE of* ***THE LORD*** *FOR EVER.*

NOTE: With the PROMISE of PEACE comes GOOD things into your LIFE, and ***GOD,*** knowing you are of FLESH and not FREE from mistakes, will have MERCY on YOU and FORGIVE those MISTAKES, as quickly as you make them. The CLOSING statement in the Psalm refers to the 7th PROMISE that WE have saved for the LAST, ***THE PROMISE of ETERNITY!***

The PROMISE of WELFARE (Looking after your NEEDS)

The PROMISE of WELFARE is not to be CONFUSED with ***GOD'S*** fulfilling ALL of your WANTS and DESIRES, for that will not be fulfilled on EARTH ***SAITH THE LORD***. The PROMISE of WELFARE given by ***GOD*** will SIGNIFICANTLY VARY amongst individuals. It can consist of providing only the bare essentials needed for LIFE on EARTH, up to the EXTENT of SOLOMON'S TREASURES of WEALTH. ***GOD*** will PROVIDE that which is NEEDED by YOU to FULFIL YOUR PURPOSE IN ***HIM***, for everything on earth is TEMPORARY. However, what ***GOD*** has set aside for YOU in HEAVEN will be PERMANENT, and there, ***HE*** will fulfil YOUR EVERY DE-

SIRE.

> ***Matthew 6:19 LAY NOT UP FOR YOURSELVES TREASURES UPON EARTH, WHERE MOTH AND RUST DOTH CORRUPT, AND WHERE THIEVES BREAK THROUGH AND STEAL:***

> ***Matthew 6:20 BUT LAY UP YOURSELVES TREASURES IN HEAVEN, WHERE NEITHER MOTH NOR RUST DOTH CORRUPT, AND WHERE THIEVES DO NOT BREAK THROUGH NOR STEAL:***

> ***Matthew 6:21 FOR WHERE YOUR TREASURE IS, THERE WILL YOUR HEART BE ALSO.***

NOTE: Whenever the Scriptures refer to one's HEART, they are referring to ONE'S SPIRIT. Therefor the Scriptures say, the TREASURES YOU DESIRE are awaiting YOUR SPIRIT in HEAVEN, for HEAVEN is a PLACE having ALL YOUR DESIRES.

The Promise of WELFARE that ***GOD*** has made will see that ALL of your NEEDS are PROVIDED, and by this PROMISE so should you TRUST in THE LORD. The GIFT of FAITH will TEACH YOU to DEPEND on ***GOD*** and no one else, for ***GOD*** WILL PROVIDE.

> ***Matthew 6:31 THEREFORE TAKE NO THOUGHT, SAYING, WHAT SHALL WE EAT? OR, WHAT SHALL WE DRINK? OR, WHEREWITHAL SHALL WE BE CLOTHED?***

> ***Matthew 6:32 (FOR AFTER ALL THESE THINGS DO THE GENTILES SEEK:) FOR YOUR HEAVENLY FATHER KNOWETH THAT YE HAVE NEED OF ALL THESE THINGS.***

The PROMISE of FORGIVENESS

In the OLD COVENANT, FORGIVENESS by ***GOD*** for SIN was done by one's remission of SIN to the Priest. The Priest then bore the SIN of that person, and a specific sacrifice was given to ***GOD*** for their ATONEMENT in the name of the SINNER. If ***GOD*** then ACCEPTED the sacrifice in the name of the sinner, then the SIN was FORGIVEN!

In the NEW COVENANT the process has been slightly modified. One MUST now REPENT of their SIN DIRECTLY to ***GOD*** (without the need of a Priest), for JESUS CHRIST is the PRIEST. Then after REPENTANCE of the SIN has been made, ***GOD*** takes the SINNER and the SIN to the "CROSS of CRUCIFIXION", and there, the SACRIFICE is made on behalf of the SINNER. The SACRIFICE is the LAMB of ***GOD,*** JESUS CHRIST, who DIED on the CROSS and has RISEN from the DEAD to ETERNAL LIFE.

> ***Luke 24:45*** *Then OPENED HE their UNDERSTANDING, that they might UNDERSTAND the SCRIPTURES.*
>
> ***Luke 24:46*** *And said unto them,* ***THUS IT IS WRITTEN, AND THUS IT BEHOVED CHRIST TO SUFFER, AND TO RISE FROM THE DEAD THE THIRD DAY:***
>
> ***Luke 24:47 AND THAT REPENTANCE AND REMISSION OF SINS SHOULD BE PREACHED IN HIS NAME AMONG ALL THE NATIONS, BEGINNING AT JERUSALEM.***
>
> ***Luke 24:48 AND YE ARE WITNESSES OF THESE THINGS.***
>
> ***Luke 24:49 AND, BEHOLD, I SEND THE PROMISE OF MY FATHER UPON YOU: BUT TARRY YE IN THE CITY OF JERUSALEM, UNTIL YE BE ENDUED WITH POWER FROM ON HIGH.***

NOTE: This was the FIRST PROMISE of FORGIVENESS; for before JESUS CHRIST had been crucified on the CROSS and RESURRECTED from the DEAD, there was NO such PROMISE of FORGIVENESS. Furthermore, when JESUS TOLD HIS Disciples this they hadn't yet RECEIVED the PROMISE, because they hadn't yet been BAPTIZED in THE ***HOLY SPIRIT.*** This is why they were TOLD to REMAIN in JERUSALEM until they were EMPOWERED from ABOVE, and the EMPOWERMENT they were to RECEIVE was to come by way of BAPTISM, in the NAME of JESUS CHRIST by THE ***HOLY SPIRIT of GOD!***

Thus far WE have covered the first FIVE PROMISES, FOUR of which had come from the OLD COVENANT. However, the 5th, 6th, and 7th SIGNIFICANT PROMISES, FORGIVENESS, DELIVERANCE, and ETERNITY ALL COME BY WAY OF JESUS CHRIST'S CRUCIFIXION and RESURRECTION from the DEAD! For prior to that TIME the LAST THREE PROMISES were NON-EXISTENT. This is why JESUS told the Pharisees to search out the Scriptures for the ETERNAL PROMISE, for prior to HIS COMING there was no such PROMISE MADE by ***GOD.*** There was no PROMISE of FORGIVENESS, no PROMISE of DELIVERANCE, and no PROMISE of ETERNAL LIFE. ***A-MEN'***

> ***John 5:39 SEARCH THE SCRIPTURES; FOR IN THEM YE THINK YE HAVE ETERNAL LIFE: AND THEY ARE THEY WHICH TESTIFY OF ME.***

The PROMISE of *DELIVERANCE*

There are TWO TYPES of DELIVERANCE, the DELIVERANCE from something, and the DELIVERANCE to SOMETHING! For instance; The CHILDREN of ISRAEL were DELIVERED from BONDAGE (slavery in Egypt) by MOSES, and DELIVERED to the point of CROSSING over the JORDAN RIVER and into PROMISE LAND. However MOSES stopped at the brink of the JORDAN, and it was Joshua who took them across the JORDAN and into the PROMISE LAND. Therefor it was MOSES who had DELIVERED them "FROM" BONDAGE, and it was Joshua who had DELIVERED them "TO" the PROMISE LAND, thus taking TWO INDIVIDUALS to PROVIDE complete DELIVERANCE!

The PROMISE of DELIVERANCE by ***GOD,*** after JESUS CHRIST, does not stop short of THE PROMISED LAND (ETERNITY) as it did with MOSES' DELIVERANCE of the CHILDREN of ISRAEL. After JESUS' FIRST COMING, the PROMISE of COMPLETE DELIVERANCE was made for ALL of ***GOD'S*** PEOPLE (ISRAEL).

GOD through the PROMISE of JESUS CHRIST will DELIVER YOU COMPLETELY from EVIL and out of HARM'S WAY, and SEE to your PROTECTION. ***HE*** will also INSURE you REACH YOUR FINAL DESTINATION, and DELIVER YOU INTO THE KINGDOM of HEAVEN. ***GOD*** will not leave YOU on this side of the GAP (the Jordan River) as ***HE*** had done with the CHILDREN of ISRAEL during the time of MOSES, for ***GOD WILL*** FULFIL the PROMISE of JESUS CHRIST.

COMPLETE DELIVERANCE comes by way of ***HOLY SPIRIT*** BAPTISM, for ***HE*** is the CONDUIT between JESUS CHRIST and ***GOD. HE*** is the ***ONE*** who will DELIVER YOU FROM SIN and into ETERNITY. ***HE*** is the ***ONE*** who DELIVERS THE BRIDE to the GROOM and INSURES that those on the GUESTS LIST are ALL IN ATTENDANCE of the WEDDING SUPPER.

> ***John 4:23 BUT THE HOUR COMETH, AND NOW IS, WHEN THE TRUE WORSHIPPERS SHALL WORSHIP THE FATHER IN SPIRIT AND IN TRUTH: FOR THE FATHER SEEKETH SUCH TO WORSHIP HIM.***

> ***John 4:24 GOD IS A SPIRIT: AND THEY THAT WORSHIP HIM MUST WORSHIP HIM IN SPIRIT AND IN TRUTH.***

THE ***HOLY SPIRIT*** is called, the ***SPIRIT of TRUTH,*** and by ***HIS*** BAPTISM so shall you WORSHIP in TRUTH, and by ***HIS SPIRIT*** so shall YOU WORSHIP in SPIRIT; and this is the PROMISE of ***DELIVERANCE.***

> ***John 16:13 HOWBEIT WHEN HE, THE SPIRIT OF TRUTH, IS COME, HE WILL GUIDE YOU INTO ALL TRUTH: FOR HE SHALL NOT SPEAK OF HIMSELF; BUT WHATSOEVER HE SHALL HEAR, THAT SHALL HE SPEAK: AND HE WILL SHOW YOU THINGS TO COME.***

NOTE: SO SHALL HE COME FIRST IN THE SPIRIT, AND THEN IN THE FLESH SAITH THE LORD; FOR AS IT IS WRITTEN, SO SHALL IT BE!

> ***Genesis 6:3*** *And THE LORD said,* ***MY SPIRIT SHALL NOT ALWAYS STRIVE WITH MAN, FOR HE ALSO IS FLESH:*** *yet* ***HIS*** *days shall be an hundred and twenty years.*

THE PROMISE of ETERNITY *(The FINAL PROMISE)*

The PROMISE of ETERNITY is the GREATEST GIFT of ALL! In the PREVIOUS BOOK you were given a GLIMPSE of HEAVEN, but HEAVEN is beyond all imagination for its MAGNIFICENCE and BEAUTY is incomprehensible.

JESUS explains HEAVEN in the GOSPEL of Matthew (13:44), as being a TREASURE found in a field, and the TREASURE is so GLORIOUS the person finding it sells everything he owns to buy the field. What JESUS is trying to express in the GOSPEL, is that HEAVEN is GREATER than anything that can be found on the EARTH, and anyone who may ever experience HEAVEN would willingly give all their earthly belongings in exchange for it.

There isn't any good thing found on EARTH that isn't in abundance in HEAVEN. Everyone entering into HEAVEN BEHOLDS (SEES and FEELS) the MAGNIFICENCE of their every DESIRE being FULFILLED BEYOND MEASUREMENT; and the fulfillment is OVERWHELMING to ALL SENSES. Whatsoever a PERSON had found pleasing on EARTH will be available to them in HEAVEN, and there are MANY more WONDERFUL things as well available to them, without price or limit.

Nothing grows old in HEAVEN, not its INHABITANTS, nor its DWELLINGS, or the FULFILLMENT of it. HEAVEN is vast in its SIZE being many times greater than the size of the UNIVERSE. Throughout the FIRST SIX LEVELS of HEAVEN are SPECTACULAR MANSIONS and VINEYARDS, having GROVES of TREES and TERRACES with FOUNTAINS made of CRYSTAL and other precious stones. There are PATHWAYS made of GOLD and PEARLS lined with low walls on each side of the path that are embedded with all types of PRECIOUS STONES.

There are BENCHES setting all along the paths that are made of IVORY and CORAL of every imaginable color. The pathways wind around throughout HEAVEN and have FLORAL displays in abundance along their ways. The FRAGRANCE of ROSES and CARNATIONS and flowers of ALL SORTS permeate the air like perfume. The weather is always the same in HEAVEN feeling like a BEAUTIFUL SPRING MORNING, and there are MAGNIFICENT SUNSETS to view, although it never grows dark in HEAVEN. In HEAVEN, when one of its SUNS starts to set then another ARISES only allowing its SKY to vary in color from BLUE to PURPLE while its SUNS change from YELLOW to ORANGE in the background of the changing skies.

The ANGELS see to all of HEAVEN'S NEEDS and keep its appearance PRISTINE. They are quite active in their duties but still make themselves available to the HEAVENLY INHABITANTS when assistance by them may be required. HEAVEN is a place with the EXPRESSION of LOVE, JOY and FULFILLMENT RADIATING throughout. From its DÉCOR to its INHABITANTS, HEAVEN exhibits an ENVIRONMENT most suitable for the ***ALMIGHTY GOD*** to DWELL.

The ANGELS are MAGNIFICENT in APPEARANCE and are WONDERFUL HOSTS who make EVERYONE FEEL WELCOME and at HOME in HEAVEN. Being with ***GOD*** from the BEGINNING, the ANGELS will share their experiences and the HISTORY of HEAVEN and ***GOD'S*** CREATION with ANYONE having an INTEREST in it, and they are MARVELOUS STORY-

TELLERS.

There are innumerable GAZEBOS made of IVORY in HEAVEN that are surrounded with SPECTACULAR FOUNTAINS. The people gather at the GAZEBOS and converse with one another, and the setting there is both beautiful and SERENE. From the GAZEBOS you can see off in the distance the MAGNIFICENT WATER FALLS that feed the many rivers and streams in HEAVEN. The MIST rising from the FALLS create a RAINBOW AURA above them INDICATING that the WATER FEEDING THE FALLS PROCEEDS FROM THE ***THRONE of GOD.***

At the SEVENTH LEVEL of HEAVEN there is a MAGNIFICENT THEATER having perfect ACOUSTICS for MUSIC and SINGING, and the SEVENTH LEVEL is also where the TEMPLE of ***GOD*** and the ARK of the COVENANT sit. There are very large PALACES there and the FOUR PRINCES MICHAEL, GABRIEL, RAFAEL, and CE'-PHAS along with the other SEVENTH LEVEL ANGELS reside in those PALACES. The PALACES have great hedges and TERRACES all about, requiring many caretakers, all being Angels, to maintain their facilities. There are also many angelic servants who tend to PRINCES and ARK LEVEL ANGEL'S needs. The CARETAKERS of the SEVENTH LEVEL are all MASTER CRAFTSMEN in all sorts of skills.

By HEAVEN continually growing in POPULATION and in AREA, the need for new DWELLINGS is always underway. It is the CARETAKERS of the SEVENTH LEVEL who oversee any new construction, for they supervise ALL HEAVENLY ARCHITECTURE. They also TEACH anyone having an interest, a skill they may desire to use for either a personal project or a hobby. However other than the Angels, no one works or has a need for a job in HEAVEN; for ALL THINGS are PROVIDED without PRICE or LIMIT.

The FOUR SERAPHIM and the FOUR COVENANT ANGELS along with THEIR many SERVANTS reside at the EIGHT LEVEL of HEAVEN. There are FOUR GREAT PALACES there with each PALACE being similar in AREA to that of NEW YORK CITY. HEAVEN is DIVIDED into FOUR KINGDOMS, a NORTH, a SOUTH, an EAST, and a WEST KINGDOM, with each of the FOUR SERAPHIM being the KING and RULER over ONE of the FOUR KINGDOMS.

Each KINGDOM is in the shape of a PYRAMID with a TRUNCATION at the EIGHTH LEVEL. All FOUR KINGDOMS come together from their prospective DIRECTIONS (NORTH, SOUTH, EAST and WEST) at the NINTH LEVEL, thus FORMING a CUBE within a CUBE and the THRONE of ***GOD,*** where the ***GODHEAD RESIDES.***

John 3:16 FOR GOD SO LOVED THE WORLD, THAT HE GAVE HIS ONLY BEGOTTEN SON, THAT WHOSOEVER BELIEVETH IN HIM SHOULD NOT PERISH, BUT HAVE EVERLASTING LIFE.

THIS IS THE 7th PROMISE, THE PROMISE OF ETERNITY! A-MEN'

Chapter 27
WARNING Signs

In THREE of the FOUR GOSPELS, JESUS speaks about the END TIMES. JESUS tells the Disciples what signs would appear prior to the SEVEN-YEAR TRIBULATION, and how there would be earthquakes in many places throughout the world and both wars and rumors of wars at the TIME nearing the END. As explained in the PREVIOUS BOOK, there are SEVEN SEALS BROKEN over a SEVEN-YEAR period of time, MARKING the TIME of TRIBULATION. In between the BREAKING of the THIRD and FOURTH SEALS the FIRST TRUMPET WILL SOUND, and at its SOUNDING there are SEVEN MAJOR EVENTS that will take place. These EVENTS will MARK the BEGINNING of the GREAT TRIBULATION, which will continue on for FORTY-TWO MONTHS (three and one-half years) after the SOUNDING of the FIRST TRUMPET. The following is a listing of the SEVEN EVENTS:

1. The CHURCH (THE BRIDE of CHRIST) will RECEIVE RAPTURE.
2. THE ***HOLY SPIRIT*** leaves the earth (as the ***182 PERSON***).
3. THE GREAT TRIBULATION BEGINS!
4. The TWO WITNESSES are awakened in the earth and START their MINISTRIES.
5. The TRIBULATION SAINTS are MARKED and SEALED.
6. A meteor shower hits the earth causing one-third of it to be deprived of sunlight.
7. The ANGEL MICHAEL cast Lucifer (the Devil) down to the earth.

As you can SEE from the list, there are SEVEN significant warning signs marking the beginning of THE GREAT TRIBULATION. However this occurs THREE and ONE-HALF YEARS after the beginning of the TRIBULATION, and the signs for its beginning are significantly more subtle than the SEVEN SIGNS listed above. In the GOSPEL of Matthew JESUS gives HIS Disciples some of the WARNING SIGNS leading up to the beginning of the SEVEN-YEAR TRIBULATION.

Matthew 24:4 *And JESUS answered and said unto them,* ***TAKE HEED THAT NO MAN DECEIVE YOU.***

Matthew 24:5 FOR MANY SHALL COME IN MY NAME, SAYING, I AM CHRIST; AND SHALL DECEIVE MANY.

NOTE: JESUS is telling HIS Disciples to be CAUTIOUS of them claiming to be CHRISTIANS who are not CHRISTIANS at all, but are rather FALSE PROPHETS preaching a FALSE word. This WARNING is more so DIRECTED to HIS Disciples of today than to them who had HEARD HIS WARNING personally. A Disciple of JESUS CHRIST is ANYONE BELIEVING IN HIM and SEEKING TO UNDERSTAND THE *WORD of* ***GOD.*** Being a DISCIPLE does not just apply to the ones that had followed after JESUS while HE was on earth, but rather applies to ANYONE following in HIS FOOTSTEPS. JESUS in the Scripture WARNS about how at the END TIMES, there will be many preachers calling themselves CHRISTIANS. Them, who JESUS WARNS about, are currently the heads of many Churches; and many who attend those Churches will be DECEIVED by them, believing they have been SAVED, but they are not SAVED ***SAITH THE LORD!***

Matthew 24:6 AND YE SHALL HEAR OF WARS AND RUMOURS OF WARS: SEE THAT YE BE NOT TROUBLED: FOR ALL THESE THINGS MUST COME TO PASS, BUT THE END IS NOT YET.

Matthew 24:7 FOR NATION SHALL RISE UP AGAINST NATION, AND KINGDOM AGAINST KINGDOM: AND THERE SHALL BE FAMINES, AND PESTILENCES, AND EARTHQUAKES, IN DIVERS PLACES.

Matthew 24:8 ALL THESE THINGS ARE THE BEGINNING OF SORROWS.

NOTE: Let US review what JESUS is TELLING HIS Disciples about the SIGNS of the END TIME, in the Scriptures of Matthew 24:4 through 24:14. (READ the balance of the SCRIPTURES (Matthew 24:9 through 24:14) that are not listed):

1. HE says, there will be a RISE in the NUMBER of FALSE PROPHETS

within the Christian Church!

2. HE says, the world will be in turmoil with ongoing wars, and continuing rumors of more wars about to start!
3. HE says, there will be starvation and food shortages throughout the world.
4. HE says, there will be deadly DISEASES at epidemic proportions throughout the world.
5. HE says, there will be ongoing EARTHQUAKES in different areas of the world.
6. HE says during the time of these EVENTS, them, who are not Christians, will hate ALL CHRISTIANS, and the false Christians in the churches will BETRAY the TRUST of the TRUE CHRISTIANS.
7. HE says, SIN in the world will be so GREAT, the people will stop LOVING one another and will turn against each other.

JESUS continues on to say in the Scriptures of Matthew, during those times, the ones who SURVIVE the first THREE and ONE-HALF YEARS of TRIBULATION will be SAVED, and RECEIVE RAPTURE. This represents "THE BRIDE of CHRIST" who will receive the FIRST RAPTURE at the SOUNDING of the FIRST TRUMPET. These are ***GOD'S*** CHOSEN; many of which do not regularly attend a Church.

HE then tells the Disciples about the BEGINNING of the GREAT TRIBULATION, when the "Mark of the Beast" is implemented and the "Abomination that makes DESOLATE" is set up in the TEMPLE in JERUSALEM.

Matthew 24:15 WHEN YE THEREFORE SHALL SEE THE ABOMINATION OF DESOLATION, SPOKEN OF BY DANIEL THE PROPHET, STAND IN THE HOLY PLACE, *(Whoso readeth, let him UNDERSTAND:)*

Matthew 24:16 THEN LET THEM WHICH BE IN JU-DAE'-A FLEE INTO THE MOUNTAINS:

Matthew 24:17 LET HIM WHICH IS ON THE HOUSETOP NOT COME DOWN TO TAKE ANY THING OUT OF HIS HOUSE:

Matthew 24:18 NEITHER LET HIM WHICH IS IN THE FIELD RETURN BACK TO TAKE HIS CLOTHES.

NOTE: JESUS WARNS in Scriptures, once the "ABOMINATION that makes DESOLATE" is set up in the TEMPLE in JERUSALEM, anyone being in the area of the TEMPLE should FLEE from it IMMEDIATELY. HE gives this WARNING because the temple at that time will have became Satan's Seat, and the "Mark of the Beast" will have been implemented. At that TIME the Devil will start killing CHRISTIANS and he will start FIRST in Jerusalem, thus fulfilling the PROPHECY of Ezekiel (Ezekiel 9:5). The Antichrist will then proclaim himself to be god, and refer to the Devil as the "God of Forces", and force ALL to worship him and his god, allowing no one to either buy or sell anything without the "Mark of the Beast". Those refusing the "Mark" will be decapitated on television, starting with their children first and the parents last. These EVENTS will be so HORRIFIC, JESUS WARNS that once the ABOMINATION is set up in the temple, anyone being near to it should FLEE the area and under no circumstances return to Jerusalem for anything.

Matthew 24:19 AND WOE UNTO THEM THAT ARE WITH CHILD, AND TO THEM THAT GIVE SUCK IN THOSE DAYS!

Matthew 24:20 BUT PRAY YE THAT YOUR FLIGHT BE NOT IN THE WINTER, NEITHER ON THE SABBATH DAY:

Matthew 24:21 FOR THEN SHALL BE GREAT TRIBULATION, SUCH AS WAS NOT SINCE THE BEGINNING OF THE WORLD TO THIS TIME, NO, NOR EVER SHALL BE.

NOTE: JESUS says in the Scriptures, HE pities those who will have little children with them at that time, for everyone will be running in panic for their lives. HE also says those who remain on earth that have been left behind from the FIRST RAPTURE, should PRAY they will not have to endure the EVENT in the winter time, nor on a Saturday when Jerusalem has come to a halt for the SABBATH. The EVENT of the ABOMINATION of DESOLATION, and the "Mark of the Beast" will occur TWENTY-ONE MONTHS after the BEGINNING of the GREAT TRIBULATION. This also MARKS the POURING OUT of the FIRST VIAL of the WRATH of ***GOD.***

Matthew 24:22 AND EXCEPT THOSE DAYS SHOULD BE SHORTENED, THERE SHOULD NO FLESH BE SAVED: BUT FOR THE ELECTS SAKE THOSE DAYS SHALL BE

SHORTENED.

NOTE: In the Scripture JESUS speaks about the RAPTURE of the TRIBULATION SAINTS and the GUESTS of the WEDDING SUPPER, who are referred to in the Scripture as the "ELECTS". THIS RAPTURE will occur just prior to the POURING OUT of the FIRST VIAL of the WRATH of ***GOD.*** The following Scriptures taken from the Book of Revelation also speak of this EVENT:

> ***Revelation 14:1*** *And I looked, and, lo, a LAMB stood on the mount Si'-on, and with HIM an hundred and forty and four thousand, having* ***HIS FATHER'S NAME*** *WRITTEN in their FOREHEADS.*
>
> ***Revelation 14:2*** *And I heard a VOICE from HEAVEN, as the VOICE of many WATERS, and as the VOICE of a GREAT THUNDER: and I heard the VOICE of HARPERS harping with their harps:*
>
> ***Revelation 14:3*** *And they sung as it were a NEW SONG before the THRONE, and before the FOUR BEASTS, and the ELDERS: and no man could learn that SONG but the hundred and forty and four thousand, which were redeemed from the earth.*

NOTE: The VOICE spoken of in the Scriptures is the "VOICE of RAPTURE", speaking the WORDS "***COME UP HITHER***" through the OPEN PORTAL in HEAVEN! The HUNDRED and FORTY-FOUR THOUSAND TRIBULATION SAINTS are ALL JEWS, and at the time of their RAPTURE the GUESTS of the WEDDING SUPPER numbering two billion people will also RECEIVE RAPTURE! Only these two GROUPS will hear the "VOICE of RAPTURE"!

The ABOMINATION that makes DESOLATE

> ***Daniel 9:27*** *And* ***HE*** *shall CONFIRM the COVENANT for ONE WEEK: and in the MIDST of the WEEK* ***HE*** *shall cause the SACRIFICE and the OBLATION to CEASE, and for the overspreading of ABOMINATIONS* ***HE*** *shall make it DESOLATE, even until the CONSUMMATION, and that DETERMINED shall be* ***POURED*** *upon the DESOLATE.*

NOTE: The ONE WEEK spoken about in the Scripture taken from the Book of Daniel, is ONE WEEK of YEARS (the SEVEN-YEAR TRIBULATION PERIOD). References made to the "MIDST of the WEEK", refer to the time being THREE and ONE-HALF YEARS into the TRIBULATION; thus marking the BEGINNING of the GREAT TRIBULATION and the denial of PRAYER and the WORSHIPPING of ***GOD.*** The Scripture also says, at the TIME the ABOMINATION that makes DESOLATE is set up in the TEMPLE, the FIRST VIAL of the WRATH of ***GOD*** will be POURED OUT UPON THE EARTH (the DESOLATE)! The DESOLATE RECEIVING the WRATH of ***GOD*** are them who are DAMNED and PREDESTINED for HELL, however there are yet a few good people still left on earth and ***GOD*** PLEADS for their REPENTANCE.

> ***Revelation 18:4*** *And I heard another VOICE from HEAVEN, saying,* ***COME OUT OF HER MY PEOPLE, THAT YE BE NOT PARTAKERS OF HER SINS, AND THAT YE RECEIVE NOT OF HER PLAGUES.***

The EVENT of the setting up the "ABOMINATION that makes DESOLATE" is a very KEY EVENT for it marks the POURING OUT of the VIALS of the WRATH of ***GOD.*** The POURING OUT of the VIALS occur over the LAST TWENTY-ONE MONTHS of the GREAT TRIBULATION, and during that time nearly everyone on the earth are DESTROYED!

The Prophet Ezekiel is shown this EVENT in a VISION and it is WRITTEN into the 8th and 9th Chapters of the Book of Ezekiel. WE will describe Ezekiel's VISION to YOU, however, you SHOULD at this time READ BOTH the 8th and 9th CHAPTERS of Ezekiel.

The 8th and 9th Chapters of Ezekiel

Chapter 8 opens with Ezekiel saying that he was at home and speaking with the Elders of Judah, when the ***HAND of GOD*** fell upon him. (This means Ezekiel was taken up in the SPIRIT.) Ezekiel then describes the appearance of the ANGEL who was sent to get him, and how a HAND reached out and took hold of him by a lock of his hair, and he was taken UP into the GAP (called in the Scripture a place between HEAVEN and the EARTH).

Ezekiel was then taken in the VISION to JERUSALEM, and while there he again WITNESSED the ***THRONE of GOD*** come down from HEAVEN, for this was similar to what he had PREVIOUSLY WITNESSED in his FIRST VISION

(Ezekiel Chapter 1).

> ***Ezekiel 8:4*** *And, BEHOLD, the GLORY of the* ***GOD*** *of ISRAEL was there, according to the VISION that I saw in the PLAIN.*

> ***Ezekiel 8:5*** *Then said* ***HE*** *unto me, Son of man, lift up thine EYES now the way toward the NORTH. So I lifted up mine EYES the way toward the NORTH, and BEHOLD northward at the GATE of the ALTAR this IMAGE of JEALOUSY in the ENTRY.*

NOTE: Once in JERUSALEM (in SPIRIT only), the THRONE of ***GOD*** came down to Ezekiel, and he is told then to look towards the NORTH at the GATE where the ALTAR sat in the TEMPLE of ***GOD.*** When Ezekiel looks, he sees sitting before the ALTAR the ABOMINATION that makes DESOLATE, called in the Scripture, "the IMAGE of JEALOUSY".

After seeing the "IMAGE of JEALOUSY", ***GOD*** tells Ezekiel ***HE*** will show him further ABOMINATIONS being committed in the TEMPLE, so Ezekiel is brought to the wall of the court. Once there, Ezekiel sees a HOLE in the WALL and is TOLD to dig through the WALL and SEE what is being done inside the TEMPLE. After digging through the wall, Ezekiel SEES IMAGERY all over the WALLS within the TEMPLE, and Devil worship and Witchcraft being practised by the Priests. He then overhears them speaking in the TEMPLE saying, we need not worry because ***GOD*** cannot SEE what we are doing, and ***HE*** has FORSAKEN the EARTH.

Ezekiel then tells in the Scriptures, the details on what he had SEEN going on inside the TEMPLE. How there were women weeping for Tam'-muz, who is the god of the flocks, and how homosexual activity between men was going on throughout the TEMPLE, while they worshipped the sun and other FALSE IMAGERY.

NOTE: The ABOMINATIONS being carried out within the TEMPLE by the people represent the DEFILING of ***GOD'S NAME*** in revenge for their being left behind. They feel that ***GOD*** has forsaken them and the earth and now they are free to do as they please!

> ***Ezekiel 8:17*** *Then* ***HE*** *said unto me, HAST THOU SEEN THIS, O SON OF MAN? IS IT A LIGHT THING TO THE HOUSE OF JUDAH THAT THEY COMMIT THE ABOMINATIONS WHICH THEY COMMIT HERE? FOR THEY HAVE FILLED THE LAND WITH VIOLENCE, AND HAVE RETURNED TO PROVOKE ME*

> *TO ANGER: AND, LO, THEY PUT THE BRANCH TO THEIR NOSE.*

NOTE: THE LORD tells Ezekiel that what he has witnessed in the TEMPLE has provoked ***HIM*** to ANGER, and the references made of "putting the branch to the nose", refers to the men in the Temple having oral sex with one another.

> ***Ezekiel 8:18*** *THEREFORE WILL* ***I*** *ALSO DEAL IN FURY:* ***MINE EYE*** *SHALL NOT SPARE, NEITHER WILL* ***I*** *HAVE PITY: AND THOUGH THEY CRY IN* ***MINE EARS*** *WITH A LOUD VOICE, YET WILL* ***I*** *NOT HEAR THEM.*

NOTE: This last Scripture WARNS of the POURING OUT of the FIRST VIAL of the WRATH of ***GOD*** that OCCURS after the SETTING UP of the "ABOMINATION that makes DESOLATE" in the TEMPLE of ***GOD*** in Jerusalem.

Chapter 9, begins with Ezekiel seeing SIX ANGELS come down from HEAVEN, being referred to in the Scripture as the HIGHER GATE, and with the SIX ANGELS is a MAN having a WRITER'S INKHORN on HIS side, and the MAN with the INKHORN is SUMMONED to ***GOD. GOD*** then tells the MAN with the INKHORN to go through Jerusalem and put a MARK on the WORTHY (the WEDDING GUESTS) who are left in Jerusalem. (The ones being MARKED are receiving the same MARK as the TRIBULATION SAINTS have RECEIVED (Revelation 7:3), the SEAL of PROTECTION from ***GOD***).

NOTE: The MAN with the WRITER'S INKHORN on HIS side is the ***DELIVERER,*** THE ***182 PERSON,*** whom WE have DESCRIBED both in this BOOK and in the PREVIOUS BOOK. The ***DELIVERER*** is the FOURTH SERAPHIM, the FIRST DESCENDANT of ***GOD, CALLED SHILOH and BANDS.*** Although ***HE*** had left the EARTH in the FIRST RAPTURE with the BRIDE of CHRIST, ***HE*** RETURNS with the SEAL of ***GOD*** for the WEDDING GUESTS; for ONLY ***HE*** can AUTHORIZE the giving of the MARK and SEAL, ***SAITH THE LORD***!

After those MARKED RECEIVE RAPTURE; THE WRATH of ***GOD*** (the SEVEN VIALS) are POURED OUT on the EARTH, and the ANGELS go through the WORLD DESTROYING the WICKED! Ezekiel then PLEADS with THE LORD to not kill everyone, but ***GOD*** says ***HE*** hasn't any PITY for those who are left on the EARTH.

Ezekiel 9:11 *And, BEHOLD, the MAN clothed with linen, which had the INKHORN by HIS side, reported the matter, saying, I HAVE DONE AS THOU HAST COMMANDED ME.*

Relating the WARNING Signs to THE END TIMES!

Matthew 24:32 NOW LEARN A PARABLE OF THE FIG TREE; WHEN HIS BRANCH IS YET TENDER, AND PUTTETH FORTH LEAVES, YE KNOW THAT SUMMER IS NIGH:

Matthew 24:33 SO LIKEWISE YE, WHEN YE SHALL SEE ALL THESE THINGS, KNOW THAT IT IS NEAR, EVEN AT THE DOORS.

It is IMPORTANT that this GENERATION KNOW that the TIME of the END is NOW, ***SAITH THE LORD.***

Revelation 3:22 HE THAT HATH AN EAR, LET HIM HEAR WHAT THE SPIRIT SAITH UNTO THE CHURCHES.

Chapter 28
EMPOWERMENT

Earlier WE had discussed ANOINTING, and how it was a form of EMPOWERMENT rather than an ORDAINING, as many believe it to be. ORDAINING or being CHOSEN for MINISTRY happens after ONE has been ANOINTED and EMPOWERED by ***GOD*** to do so, and NOT BEFORE. A man cannot ORDAIN another for MINISTRY, even if they themselves have been BAPTIZED in THE ***HOLY SPIRIT*** and have RECEIVED the THREE or more GIFTS GIVEN by THE ***HOLY SPIRIT,*** NECESSARY for MINISTRY.

This is a MISUNDERSTANDING by the Church and is the PRIMARY REASON why there are so many FALSE PROPHETS at the PULPIT today! In the EYES of ***GOD*** there is no such a place where ONE can go to LEARN the HOLY BIBLE, for the MESSAGE within it cannot be TAUGHT by one man to another, and ONLY BY ANOINTING can it be LEARNED.

With ANOINTING comes EMPOWERMENT and with EMPOWERMENT comes MINISTRY, ***SAITH THE LORD.*** When the Church feels they can EMPOWER a person for MINISTRY they are MISTAKEN, and have been caught up in the SNARE of the FOWLER, and have DEFILED themselves and their ministry. MINISTRY is not a man made choice it is ***GOD'S*** CHOICE, and ***HE*** determines who will MINISTER for ***HIM.***

NOTE: THE LORD has shown ME on several occasions where a Father was a minister and his son became a minister after him, and the Church he then ministered at became lacking in ANOINTING. Whereas the Father was called to MINISTRY by THE LORD, the son was called to ministry by his Father, and NOT by ***GOD.*** YOU will not find a single case in the BIBLE, where the Father's ANOINTING could be passed down from him to his son. Even in the case of AARON, when he died, it was ***GOD*** who TOLD MOSES to put AARON'S priestly garments on his son, E-le-a'-zar. It was also made quite clear by the ANGEL GABRIEL to Zacharias, the Father of John the Baptist, that his son John's ORDAINING came from ***GOD,*** and not from him!

In this Chapter WE want to talk about the VARIOUS LEVELS of EMPOWERMENT, and how the EMPOWERMENT can vary from an EMPOWER-

MENT of FAITH to a LEVEL of OMNIPOTENCE, the ***ALMIGHTY POWER of GOD!*** As WE had discussed earlier, there are NINE GIFTS GIVEN by THE ***HOLY SPIRIT,*** and MAN can only RECEIVE up to SIX of those GIFTS. The ANGEL of the ARK LEVEL can however RECEIVE up to SEVEN of the GIFTS, the METATRON EIGHT, and the SERAPHIM and the COVENANT ANGEL (through MARRIAGE) can RECEIVE ALL NINE!

Once ALL NINE GIFTS have been RECEIVED, then there are FOUR GREAT LEVELS of EMPOWERMENT above them. The FIRST SERAPHIM, DAVID, has RECEIVED the 1st LEVEL of EMPOWERMENT which is an EMPOWERMENT over ALL the ANGELS and GUESTS in HEAVEN. SOLOMON, the SECOND SERAPHIM, has RECEIVED both the 1st and the 2nd LEVELS of EMPOWERMENT, thus giving HIM that which DAVID has as well as the EMPOWERMENT over the TEMPLE of ***GOD*** in HEAVEN. JESUS CHRIST, the THIRD SERAPHIM has RECEIVED ALL that DAVID and SOLOMON have and also the 3rd LEVEL of EMPOWERMENT, which is OMNI-PRESENCE. THE ***DELIVERER*** who is the FOURTH SERAPHIM, and the 1st DESCENDANT of ***GOD,*** has RECEIVED ALL that the first THREE have RECEIVED and the 4th LEVEL of EMPOWERMENT, which is OMNIPOTENCE, the ***ALMIGHTY POWER of GOD!*** This is the ONLY PERSON in the FORM of a MAN outside of the ***TRINITY (GODHEAD)*** having this POWER, and ***HE,*** being the ***FATHER*** of JESUS CHRIST, is GREATER than ALL BEFORE ***HIM.*** This is WHY JESUS CHRIST said MY ***FATHER*** is GREATER than I.

The *GOD* GIVEN GIFTS to the FOUR SONS

Along with the GIFTS of GREAT EMPOWERMENT, come FOUR ADDITIONAL PAIRS of GIFTS that COMPOUND, as do the LEVELS of GREAT EMPOWERMENT through the HIERARCHY of the SERAPHIM. The FIRST SERAPHIM RECEIVES the GIFTS of LEADERSHIP and COURAGE. The SECOND SERAPHIM RECEIVES that of the FIRST SERAPHIM and the GIFTS of WISDOM and WEALTH. The THIRD SERAPHIM RECEIVES that of the first TWO SERAPHIM and the GIFTS of LOVE and UNDERSTANDING. The FOURTH SERAPHIM, THE ***DELIVERER,*** RECEIVES that of the first THREE SERAPHIM, and also the GIFTS of CREATION and DELIVERANCE.

WE would like to further your UNDERSTANDING on what these GIFTS GIVEN by ***GOD*** to the FOUR SERAPHIM entail, so WE shall list them in the ORDER they are GIVEN.

1. The GIFTS of LEADERSHIP and COURAGE
2. The GIFTS of WISDOM and WEALTH
3. The GIFTS of LOVE and UNDERSTANDING
4. The GIFTS of CREATION and DELIVERANCE

The GIFTS of LEADERSHIP and COURAGE are the GIFTS needed to be a KING, for a KING must LEAD the PEOPLE in a TIME of PEACE and in a TIME of TROUBLE. And, this is why COURAGE is also GIVEN to the LEADER, so HE can LEAD the PEOPLE even in a TIME of TROUBLE.

The GIFTS of WISDOM and WEALTH are GIVEN together, for WISDOM is NEEDED to CONTROL WEALTH and SHARE IT with OTHERS. The WEALTH entails ALL TYPES of WEALTH, including the WEALTH of KNOWLEDGE, which needs WISDOM to GOVERN and PROPERLY use that KNOWLEDGE.

The GIFTS of LOVE and UNDERSTANDING are GIVEN together, for LOVE is being able to UNDERSTAND ONE'S FEELINGS and the ABILITY to EXPRESS those FEELINGS through LOVE to ANOTHER.

The GIFTS of CREATION and DELIVERANCE are GIVEN together; for what GOOD is a CREATION if it cannot be UTILIZED? This can be further EXPRESSED as the CREATION being a PRODUCT, and the DELIVERANCE being the USE of the PRODUCT; for what GOOD would a PRODUCT be if there weren't a NEED for it? ALL CREATION must SERVE a PURPOSE somewhere, and the DELIVERANCE is the MEANS in which the CREATION ARRIVES at its INTENDED DESTINATION. There is both a TIME and a PLACE for ALL THINGS ***SAITH THE LORD.***

LEVELS of EMPOWERMENT

Earlier in this BOOK and also in the PREVIOUS BOOK WE had spoken about the FOUR QUADRANTS in HEAVEN that make up FOUR KINGDOMS, one of the NORTH, one of the SOUTH, one of the EAST, and one of the WEST. You were also TOLD that EACH KINGDOM was in the shape of a PYRAMID, and when the FOUR KINGDOMS COME TOGETHER they form a CUBE, and this CUBE is called the ***KINGDOM of GOD.***

To UNDERSTAND the HIERARCHY in HEAVEN, one must UNDERSTAND the UNITY in HEAVEN first. In HEAVEN, NOTHING is INDEPENDENT of ***GOD***, and ALL THAT IS IN HEAVEN DEPENDS ON ***GOD*** for its EXISTENCE. ***GOD*** is the SOURCE of ALL that EXISTS, and NOTHING can EXIST without ***HIM,*** for ALL have come FORTH FROM ***HIM.***

Earlier WE talked briefly about the DESCENDING NATURE of ***GOD*** and how ***HE DESCENDS*** within the ***GODHEAD (TRINITY)*** into the FOURTH SERAPHIM and then into the THIRD SERAPHIM, and so forth DOWN into MAN. This can be viewed as a string of LIGHTS that require a SOURCE of ENERGY to be LIT. If the string of LIGHTS were UNPLUGGED from the ENERGY SOURCE, all of the LIGHTS would go out. And if the LIGHTS were all wired in SERIES, such as it is with the DESCENDING NATURE of ***GOD,*** if ONE LIGHT were to go out so would the others go OUT as well. As with the LIGHTS in the STRING DEPEND on the ENERGY SOURCE, and the OTHER LIGHTS as well to be LIT, so does LIFE also DEPEND on ***GOD*** and those who have DESCENDED through ***HIM***!

WE can take this scenario even a bit further! If each of the LIGHTS on the string of LIGHTS were BRIGHTER as they got closer to the ENERGY SOURCE, you could see how the BRIGHTER LIGHTS would REQUIRE MORE ENERGY (POWER) than those who were LESS BRIGHT. Therefor the POWER CONSUMPTION of the LIGHT BEING the CLOSEST to the ENERGY SOURCE would be the GREATEST and require the MOST POWER to remain LIT. Thus, SO IS THE EMPOWERMENT of ***GOD*** to ***HIM*** WHO is CLOSEST TO ***HIM!*** LET US now list the FOUR LEVELS of GREAT EMPOWERMENT and DESCRIBE them to YOU:

The 1st LEVEL of EMPOWERMENT gives the FIRST SERAPHIM RULE over ALL the ANGELS in HEAVEN except THREE of the FOUR COVENANT ANGELS, and THREE of the FOUR METATRON (however, the METATRON are not ANGELS, but rather DESCENDANTS of the SERAPHIM). HE also RULES over ALL of the GUESTS of the WEDDING SUPPER, those who are of CHRIST, but not in CHRIST.

The 2nd LEVEL of EMPOWERMENT gives the SECOND SERAPHIM RULE over the TEMPLE of ***GOD*** in HEAVEN, and also the same EMPOWERMENT of the FIRST SERAPHIM. However HE RULES over TWO COVENANT ANGELS rather than only ONE, but as with the FIRST SERAPHIM, HE RULES over only ONE of the FOUR METATRON, the METATRON of the SOUTH QUADRANT. HE also RULES over ALL the HEAVENLY HOSTS including those who are in CHRIST.

The 3rd LEVEL of EMPOWERMENT GIVEN to the THIRD SERAPHIM, JESUS CHRIST, GIVES HIM RULE OVER ALL THE HEAVENLY HOSTS, the BRIDE and the WEDDING GUESTS, THREE of the FOUR COVENANT ANGELS and the METATRON of the EAST QUADRANT. HE ALSO RULES OVER THE ENTRY to the THRONE of ***GOD,*** and ALL WISHING TO ENTER IN, CAN ONLY ACCESS ***GOD*** THROUGH JESUS CHRIST. HE HAS

ALSO OMNI-PRESENCE, THUS ALLOWING HIM TO BE IN ALL PLACES AT ALL TIMES!

The 4th LEVEL of EMPOWERMENT GIVEN TO THE FOURTH SERAPHIM, THE ***DELIVERER,*** IS THAT of the first THREE, also the RULE OVER ALL FOUR OF THE COVENANT ANGELS, and WHEN HANDED DOWN, RULE OVER ALL FOUR METATRON as well. HOWEVER, even ***HE*** MUST ENTER INTO the THRONE of ***GOD*** through JESUS CHRIST, for JESUS is the ONLY ACCESS to the THRONE. ***HE,*** as with JESUS, has OMNI-PRESENCE and has ALSO OMNIPOTENCE, enabling ONLY ***HIM*** OUTSIDE of the ***GODHEAD*** THAT LEVEL OF GREAT POWER!

NOTE: THE LORD has told ME that ONCE THE ***DELIVERER*** lets ***HIS PRESENCE*** be known on the EARTH, if ***HE*** so CHOOSES, ***HE*** could LITERALLY SPEAK a PERSON OUT of EXISTENCE! This is to say, if ***HE*** were to SAY, "GO AND BE NO MORE" to a PERSON, that PERSON'S EXISTENCE would have NEVER BEEN and not even their own Mother or Father would have any memory whatsoever of them. Nor would there be even a TRACE of EVIDENCE that they ever had EXISTED!

> ***Revelation 19:15*** *And OUT of* ***HIS MOUTH*** *goeth a SHARP SWORD, that with it* ***HE*** *should SMITE the NATIONS: and* ***HE*** *SHALL RULE THEM with a* ***ROD of IRON:*** *and* ***HE*** *TREADETH the WINEPRESS of the FIERCENESS and* ***WRATH of ALMIGHTY GOD.***

Reference Guide